Sylvester Rosa Koehler

The United States Art Directory and Year-Book

A Chronicle of Events in the Art World, and a Guide for all interested in the

Progress of Art in America

Sylvester Rosa Koehler

The United States Art Directory and Year-Book
A Chronicle of Events in the Art World, and a Guide for all interested in the Progress of Art in America

ISBN/EAN: 9783337208950

Printed in Europe, USA, Canada, Australia, Japan

Cover: Foto ©Andreas Hilbeck / pixelio.de

More available books at **www.hansebooks.com**

THE

UNITED STATES ART DIRECTORY

AND YEAR-BOOK.

(SECOND YEAR.)

A CHRONICLE OF EVENTS IN THE ART WORLD, AND A GUIDE FOR ALL INTERESTED IN THE
PROGRESS OF ART IN AMERICA.

COMPILED

BY

S. R. KOEHLER.

CASSELL & COMPANY, LIMITED,

NEW YORK, LONDON AND PARIS.

1884.

CORRECTIONS AND ADDITIONS, FOR USE IN FUTURE EDITIONS, ARE
EARNESTLY SOLICITED. Please address all communications to

S. R. KOEHLER,
BEECH GLEN AVENUE, ROXBURY (BOSTON), MASS.

PREFACE.

THE fact that a second edition of the U. S. ART DIRECTORY AND YEAR BOOK is presented to the public is evidence sufficient that its usefulness has been acknowledged. To those familiar with the first edition no explanation need be offered of the aim and scope of the book. The following remarks, chiefly extracts from the preface to the previous issue, are more especially addressed, therefore, to new readers.

The purpose of the book is fully explained by its title :—it aspires to be a practical guide for all interested in the progress of art—art patrons, students of art and of its history, artists, and travellers of an artistic turn of mind—by pointing out to them the facilities existing in the United States for the enjoyment, the study, and the commerce of art.

Concerning the policy followed, the reader will please notice that facts only have been given, and that in the selection of these facts no judgment has been exercised or criticism applied. In the case of the educational institutions especially, it has been the constant aim to let them speak for themselves by quoting either the printed documents issued by them, or the written reports received from persons connected with them. The facts thus obtained and the claims thus put forward are simply offered as material from which those interested can draw their own conclusions. It will be well also to state that the length of the notices has nothing whatever to do with the importance of the institutions to which they are devoted. There is apparently a curious discrepancy in this particular. But a moment's reflection will show that it is much easier to compress into a short paragraph the well-defined activity of so prominent an association as "The Society of American Artists" than the multifarious efforts of an amateur club in some out-of-the-way village.

One glaring instance of incompleteness will be found in the list of colleges and universities included. It would have been interesting to show the extent to which the study of art, either theoretically or practically, is carried in all these institutions, but, for the present at least, this almost Herculean task could not be undertaken. Even so, however, the few statements of college courses given will convey some idea as to the place assigned to art in our higher institutions of learning, although it was impossible to give these courses with that completeness which might have been desirable. In view of the economy elsewhere practised, it may seem strange that so much space has been devoted to the purely technical course pursued in the Military Academy at West Point. But many persons will no doubt be interested to know to what extent art is made tributary to war in this celebrated national school. As an additional excuse, it may be stated that the information here given is nowhere else to be found in print.

The list of educational institutions has been furthermore limited by excluding instruction in drawing as incorporated into the public-school system on the one hand, and purely private schools on the other. The line has been drawn, rather arbitrarily perhaps, at incorporated institutions, and associations which do not look for profit.

Some persons may possibly think that the only result of the enumeration of the Archæological Collections admitted into these lists has been an unnecessary increase in the number of pages. Archæology is, however, an indispensable aid in the study of the development of art, and as the students in this department of science are fast increasing, their interests had to be considered as well as those of others. For this reason mention has also been made of the small collections, so far as known, brought together by the Historical Societies. Many of these collections contain specimens illustrating the art of the aborigines, and occasionally a few good old portraits are hidden away in them, of the existence of which the lovers of art would be glad to be informed.

A comparison of the present issue with the first edition will show that the work may justly claim to have been considerably augmented and improved, not only— thanks to the publishers—in size and outward appearance, but also in the matter it contains. It is hoped, moreover, that the information conveyed in its pages will be found as correct as may reasonably be expected. Every single item which appeared in the last issue was submitted to the officers of the associations, etc., concerned, and in nearly all cases the slips sent out came back with the necessary corrections and additions. The compiler is under great obligations to the ladies and gentlemen whose kind assistance alone made it possible to give to the book whatever of completeness and reliability it may possess. Wherever such assistance was not obtainable, the fact has been carefully noted.

The new features of the book—the Chronicle, the Illustrations, and the Classified Index—must endeavor to speak for themselves. The change in the date of publication, from fall to spring, may need a few words of explanation. A moment's consideration will show that it must be an advantage. All addresses, etc., gathered during the summer are more or less unreliable, and in many cases indicate only the place of temporary or previous residence. On the contrary, the information brought together at this season of the year is based upon existing facts, and will be quite as useful in the fall as now.

Corrections and additions for use in future issues are earnestly solicited.

                                                        THE COMPILER.

TABLE OF CONTENTS.

LIST OF ILLUSTRATIONS.

SOUVENIRS OF THE EXHIBITION.

PENNSYLVANIA ACADEMY. 53D ANNUAL EXHIBITION, Oct. 23–Dec. 9, 1883.
    1. Evening on the Market Place at San Antonio, Texas. (Fragment.) Thos. Allen.
    2. A Sailor's Story. Henry Bacon.
    3. Battery en Route. W. T. Trego.
    4. Market Day at Pont Aven. C. P. Grayson.
    5. Venice. Walter L. Palmer.
SALMAGUNDI SKETCH CLUB, 5TH BLACK AND WHITE, Dec. 1–21, 1882.
    6. Marines. Harry Chase.
    7. Autumn Walk. Fred. W. Freer.
PHILADELPHIA SOCIETY OF ARTISTS. 4TH ANNUAL EXHIBITION. Dec. 30, 1882–Jan. 27. 1883.
    8. Summer Time in the Land of Weirs. Prosper L. Senat.
BOSTON ART CLUB. 27TH EXHIBITION. Jan. 25–Feb. 17, 1883.
    9. Landscape and Cattle. Chas. F. Pierce.
    10. Waiting for the Tide. Walter F. Lansil.

SOUVENIRS OF THE EXHIBITIONS—*Continued.*

AMERICAN WATER COLOR SOCIETY. 16TH ANNUAL EXHIBITION. Jan. 29–Feb. 25, 1883.

    11. A Voice from the Cliff. (Fragment.) Winslow Homer.

    12. Fishermen in Port, Coast of Maine. A. F. Bellows.

    13. Crumbs. Walter Shirlaw.

    14. The Cliffs of Green River, Wyoming. Thos. Moran.

    15. Old Time Favorites. (Fragments.) Frederick Dielman.

    16. Rough Weather at Scheveningen. R. Swain Gifford.

    17. Swamp Willows, Newburyport. Geo. H. Smillie.

    18. The Closing Hymn. Alfred Kappes.

SOCIETY OF AMERICAN ARTISTS. 6TH ANNUAL EXHIBITION. Mch. 26–Apr. 28, 1883.

    19. Portrait of a Lady. John S. Sargent.

NATIONAL ACADEMY. 58TH ANNUAL EXHIBITION. Apr. 2–May 12, 1883.

    20. The Glass Blowers. (Fragment.) Chas. F. Ulrich.

    21. My Great Grandmother and I. J. G. Brown, N.A.

    22. A Summer Morning. George Inness, N.A.

    23. Silenced. Gilbert Gaul, N.A.

    24. A Monastery Library. F. L. Kirkpatrick.

    25. La Cigale. F. A. Bridgman, N.A.

    26. Moonlight, New England Coast. M. F. H. de Haas, N.A.

    27. Her Only Support. Robert Koehler.

    28. The Collar Shop. Edgar M. Ward.

    29. Near Zaandam, Holland. R. Swain Gifford, N.A.

FOREIGN EXHIBITION, BOSTON. Sept. 3, 1882–Jan. 12, 1884.

    30. Visiting the Sick. P. Joris.

EXHIBITION OF THE N. E. MANUFACTURERS' AND MECHANICS' INSTITUTE. BOSTON. Sept. 5–Nov. 3, 1883.

    31. Place St. Germain-des-Près, Paris. F. M. Boggs.

INTER-STATE INDUSTRIAL EXPOSITION, CHICAGO. 11TH. Sept. 5–Oct. 20, 1883.

    32. Les Amateur. T. Alexander Harrison.

PENNSYLVANIA ACADEMY. 54TH EXHIBITION. Oct. 29–Dec. 8, 1883.

    33. A Little Slave. T. Alexander Harrison.

    34. A Long Island Ship-yard. Arthur Quartley.

    35. Fantaisie. Chas. Sprague Pearce.

    36. Field Flowers. Daniel Strain.

SALMAGUNDI SKETCH CLUB. 6TH BLACK AND WHITE. Dec. 1–21, 1883.

    37. The Morning Task. Frank M. Gregory.

    38. The Ford. Robert C. Minor.

    39. By the Brook. Chas. Harry Eaton.

    40. Vestal Virgin. Napoleon Sarony.

PEDESTAL FUND ART LOAN. Dec. 3, 1883–Jan. 1, 1884.

    41. Among the Vines. F. S. Church and L. C. Tiffany & Co.

    42. Woman Bathing. J. F. Millet.

    43. Mending Sacks. A. Neuyhuys.

SPECIAL EXHIBITIONS.

    44. El Jaléo. John S. Sargent.

MONUMENTS:—

    45. Indian Group. J. J. Boyle.

    46. Monmouth Battle Monument. Jas. E. Kelly, E. T. Little, and D. Smyth.

    47. Liberty Enlightening the World. Aug. Bartholdi.

AMERICAN ART IN EUROPE:—

GROSVENOR GALLERY. LONDON, 1883.

    48. With the Birds. W. J. Hennessy.

EXHIBITION OF AMERICAN WATER COLORS. LONDON, 1883.

    49. Autumn. Henry Farrer.

LIST OF ARTISTS

REPRESENTED IN THE ILLUSTRATIONS.

ix

AMERICAN ART CHRONICLE.

OCTOBER, 1882, TO DECEMBER 31, 1883.

—— — · ——— ———

THE following review of art matters in the United States covers the period from October, 1882, that is to say from the date of issue of the first volume of the *Directory and Year Book*, to the close of the year 1883 :

I. EXHIBITIONS.

The most obvious manifestations of the artistic spirit are to be found in the exhibitions, of which the past year was more prolific than any of its predecessors. The statistical table given elsewhere in this volume enumerates no less than 84, without pretending to include all those held in the smaller cities, and without including any of the numerous special exhibitions devoted to the works of single artists. Of the number specified, 19 belong to the fall of 1882, while 65 opened in the year 1883. They were held in 26 cities, as follows : New York, 19 ; Boston, 10 : Chicago, 8 ; Philadelphia, 7 ; Brooklyn, N. Y., 7 ; Providence. R. I., 4 ; Springfield, Mass., 3 ; Denver, Col., Louisville, Cincinnati. Milwaukee, Portland, Me.. and Atlanta, Ga., 2 each ; Rochester, N. Y., Buffalo, N. Y., Saratoga Springs, N. Y., Syracuse, N. Y., Malden, Mass., Salem, Mass.. Newark, N. J., Indianapolis, Minneapolis, Detroit, Jacksonville, Ill., Charleston, S. C., San Francisco, Cal., 1 each. In the spring or summer of 1882, exhibitions were also held in St. Louis, Mo., Richmond, Va., and New Orleans, La., but no later reports from these cities could be obtained up to the time of writing. According to States, the distribution is as follows : Maine, 2 ; Massachusetts, 15 ; Rhode Island, 4 ; New York, 30 ; New Jersey, 1 ; Pennsylvania, 7 ; Ohio, 2 ; Illinois, 9 ; Indiana, 1 ; Wisconsin, 2 ; Michigan, 1 ; Minnesota, 1 ; Kentucky, 2 ; South Carolina, 1 ; Georgia, 2 ; Colorado, 2 ; California, 1. It is quite impossible to give a detailed report of these exhibitions here. All that can be done will be to recall some of the more salient features of the leading exhibitions.

The principal activity of the Western States, in the matter of exhibitions, is developed in the autumn, when the great industrial expositions, with their attendant art departments, are held in Louisville, Milwaukee, Cincinnati, and Chicago. Boston also has its exhibition of the New England Manufacturers' and Mechanics' Institute at the same time, so that over 2,000 works of art were on exhibition simultaneously in September and October, 1882, in the five cities named. A new policy was inaugurated by the National Academy of Design, New York, by the opening of a Special Autumn Exhibition on October 23, in obedience to the demand, on the part of some of the artists, for increased facilities for selling. The result, namely a rather small exhibition, in which the works of quite a number of representative artists were wanting, seemed to show that the demand was not felt universally. The exhibition was nevertheless acknowledged to be of good quality, and presented some pictures of special excellence, as, for instance, Mr. F. A. Bridgman's " Planting Rape in Normandy," and Mr. Leon Moran's

I

"Milkmaid;" and among the landscapes, Mr. Chas. T. Phelan's "Environs of Brooklyn." The Pennsylvania Academy, of Philadelphia, opened its doors on the same day
of the month. Its exhibitions have for some years received a special interest from the
contributions of American painters studying or residing in Europe. These contributions are secured through a committee of artists on the other side, acting for the Academy, and it is greatly to the credit of the institution that it was the first to adopt this
admirable policy. First and foremost among the works thus secured stood Mr. T. Alexander Harrison's " Chateaux en Espagne," representing a country lad, lying on his back
upon the sands of the sea-shore, looking dreamily into nothing. Mr. Bridgman's
"Roumanian Lady," Mr. Bacon's "A Sailor's Story," Mr. E. L. Weeks's "Soudan
Caravan," and the landscapes of Messrs. Donoho, Chas. H. Davis, and H. Winthrop
Peirce were also prominent among the pictures coming from the other side. Very
naturally, these works bore a decidedly foreign character, and this was true also, as a
matter of course, of Mr. Palmer's delicate "Venice." Of the home contributions, one
of the most remarked was the "Battery en Route," a scene from the late civil war, by
Mr. W. T. Trego, a young artist of Philadelphia. A new experiment was tried in the
month of November, not very successfully, however, in exhibitions of studies and
sketches by the Philadelphia Society of Artists and the American Art Association of
New York. The Winter Loan Exhibition of the Metropolitan Museum, New York,
which also opened in the month of November, offered as a special feature, a series of
fine old tapestries, principally Italian and French. Among the December exhibitions,
the Fifth Black and White of the Salmagundi Sketch Club, New York, the Forty-fifth
of the Brooklyn, N. Y., Art Association, that of the Philadelphia Society of Etchers,
held at the Pennsylvania Academy, and the Fourth Exhibition of the Philadelphia
Society of Artists, were the most prominent. The first of these was about the most
successful ever held by the Club, among the many noticeable things being a number
of very fine charcoal drawings by Mr. Walter Shirlaw, and a series of impressionist
sketches in the same medium by Mr. Frank Currier. The Brooklyn Exhibition was
remarkable not only for its good quality, but also as the first exhibition ever held by
the Association of oil paintings by American artists only. Two thoroughly American
pictures by Mr. C. Y. Turner, "Dorothy Fox" and "The Morning Lesson," were
counted among the chief attractions. The Exhibition of the Philadelphia Society of
Etchers gave a most admirable idea of the achievements of the etchers of America,
and was very full also in the representation of the best European work, but it did not
receive the attention which it deserved. The collection shown by the Philadelphia
Society of Artists was pronounced to be unusually good, although mostly made up of
pictures already seen elsewhere. Of new contributions prominently mentioned may
be named Mr. Prosper L. Senat's "Summer Time in the Land of Weirs," and Mr. J.
G. Brown's "The Confab." A Loan Exhibition arranged by the St. Botolph Club, of
Boston, was remarkable for the high quality of the pictures—mostly modern French—
of which it was composed.

The year 1883 opened with the First Annual Exhibition of the Art Institute (formerly Academy of Fine Arts) of Chicago, consisting of foreign and American pictures
loaned by the owners. In New York the first exhibition was that of Boston artists,
which opened at the gallery of the American Art Association on January 15. As it
was somewhat circumscribed in its scope, its success was not what might have been
expected, from the fact that it comprised the work of many of the best-known painters
of Boston, such as F. P. Vinton, Mrs. Whitman, Geo. Fuller, J. Appleton Brown, J.

Foxcroft Cole, J. J. Enneking, Jno. B. Johnston, Emil Carlsen, etc. The Loan Exhibition held in Brooklyn, N. Y., under the auspices of the Rembrandt Club, for the benefit of the Sheltering Arms Nursery, was especially rich in modern French paintings, thus forming a valuable complement of the St. Botolph Club exhibition in Boston of the previous month. Engravings, etchings, Japanese art objects, etc., served to heighten its interest. In Boston the Twenty-seventh Exhibition of the Art Club took place ; but the principal event of the month was the opening, at the National Academy in New York, of the exhibition of the American Water-Color Society, the sixteenth of the series, and of the New York Etching Club. The water-color exhibition was unanimously acknowledged to be the best of its kind ever held in America, and the first place in it was by common consent assigned to Mr. Winslow Homer's contributions, "Tynemouth," "A Voice from the Cliff," "Inside the Bar," and "The Incoming Tide," all of them subjects which the artist had found among the fisher folk of England, where he spent several years. Among the other noted pictures were an English landscape by Mr. Parsons, with the figures of two young ladies by Mr. Abbey, and the contributions of Messrs. Geo. H. Smilie, R. Swain Gifford, Henry Farrer, Dielman, Shirlaw, Wm. M. Chase, Blashfield, Smedley, Thos. Moran, Gibson, Turner, F. S. Church, Freer, Wood, etc. Impressionism was again largely represented in the work of Messrs. Currier and Muhrman. The exhibition of the Etching Club did not develop any new features, but amply upheld the enviable reputation which the etchers of America have made for themselves. The exhibition of the Artists' Fund Society, the New York Art Club (the first held by it), the Brooklyn Art Association (Forty-sixth, Water Colors and Etchings), and a number of minor shows in various parts of the country, must be passed by to make room for the Sixth Exhibition of the Society of American Artists (March 26–April 28), and the Fifty-Eighth Annual Exhibition of the National Academy (April 2–May 12), as these are undoubtedly the principal occurrences of the year. The impression made by the exhibition of the Society was of a more popular and cheerful kind than in former years ; and this fact was generally recorded with pleasure, as it was not accompanied by any deterioration in the quality of the work. The following were a few of the most noted pictures : "The Prelude," by Mr. T. W. Dewing, specially admired for its delicacy ; a portrait of a lady in white, by Mr. Thayer ; another portrait of a young lady in black, holding a rose, sent from Europe by Mr. Sargent, one of the most complete pieces of painting yet executed by an American artist ; portraits by Messrs. Irwin, J. Alden Weir, Wyatt Eaton, R. B. Brandegee, etc. ; Mr. Dannat's Spanish scene, "After Mass," also sent from the other side ; Mr. George Fuller's "Nydia," showing all the peculiarities of style for which the artist is noted ; a "Hackensack Landscape," by Mr. Wm. M. Chase ; Mr. Gifford's "Evening in Autumn," Mr. Blashfield's "Minute Men," and an exquisite flowerpiece by Mr. J. Alden Weir. At the close of the exhibition the whole collection was transferred to the Museum of Fine Arts, at Boston, where it was likewise greatly admired. The Academy exhibition was accorded the praise of unusual evenness in quality, with only a few very prominent or specially novel contributions. Mr. C. F. Ulrich's "Glassblowers," the most important picture yet shown by that talented young artist, proved to be the chief attraction. "The Queen's Birthday in New York Harbor," by Mr. Quartley, commanded attention by quality as well as size. Mr. Miller's "Potter," Mr. Weldon's "Dreamland," Mr. Turner's "Preparing for Yearly Meeting," Mr. Dielman's "Mora Players," Mr. Van Schaick's "Turkish Idlers," Mr. Robert Koehler's "Her Only Support," Mr. Gaul's "Silenced," and the contributions of Messrs. J. G. Brown, Henry, Loop, Bridgman, Ward, etc., represent only a small part of the figure pictures. Mr. Hinckley's "Alexander at Persepolis," an academic performance painted in Paris, had before been exhibited in Boston. Portraiture was represented in its most varied tendencies by the works of Messrs. Beckwith, Alexander, C. L. Brandt, Irwin, J. F. Weir, Eastman Johnson, Wm. Page, Chartres Williamson, Mrs. Merritt, and others. Nearly all the well-known landscape and marine painters were also among the contributors. The Summer Loan Exhibition of the Metropolitan Museum in New York, which opened in May, was characterized by the excellent quality and large number of works by American artists.

Spring is not only the blossoming time for the trees ; art-life also opens its buds at this time all over the country. In the year 1883 it broke out in April and May in exhibitions held in Chicago, Philadelphia (Society of Artists, Water-Colors), Boston (Art Club, Water-Colors), San Francisco, Denver, Col., Charleston, S. C., Salem, Mass., Rochester, N. Y., and possibly in many other places, from which reports were not obtainable. The closing act of the season in New York city was the exhibition at the gallery of the American Art Association, of pictures, etc., gathered by a committee of artists as the contribution of America to the International Exhibition at Munich. (See the paragraph on American Art in Europe.)

The summer months are usually a quiet period, but the year 1883 knew little rest. On June 1, the newly established American Art Union made its début with an exhibition at the Buffalo Fine Arts Academy, a Summer Exhibition of works of American artists was maintained at the American Art Gallery in New York, and August 1 saw the opening, with great ceremony, by the President of the United States, of the grand Southern Exposition at Louisville, to the art department of which contributions were sent, as an offering of good will to the South, from all sections. The American Art Union made its second exhibition at Louisville, and out of its collection a number of pictures were bought by citizens of the place as a nucleus for a permanent gallery.

The art activity of the West was greater in the autumn of 1883 than in any preceding year. In addition to the regular Industrial Expositions at Louisville (previously mentioned), Denver, Cincinnati, Chicago, and Milwaukee, extensive art loan exhibitions were organized at Detroit, Indianapolis, and Minneapolis, which excited great attention, and will probably lead to the establishment of permanent art institutions at these places. The most important of these exhibitions, in so far as paintings and other works of American art not purely decorative are concerned, was that at Chicago, which contained contributions from many leading artists of the East, and also a number of canvases sent by American painters residing abroad, among them Mr. T. Alexander Harrison's "Les Amateurs," which was bought for the Chicago Art Institute by a number of gentlemen. Next to the Pennsylvania Academy, the Exposition Association of Chicago has thus far been the most active in bringing to the notice of the home public the work of Americans studying abroad. The Art Department of the New England Institute, Boston (September 5 to November 3), was exceptionally full and exceptionally good, especially in pictures by foreign artists, in spite of the curious policy of the Institute, according to which everything sent is admitted. One of the features of this exhibition was the *édition de luxe* of the catalogue, a stately quarto volume, illustrated with seventeen original etchings, and a large number of heliotypes and phototypes—altogether the most ambitious effort yet seen in catalogue making. It will be necessary again to pass over the minor exhibitions in the smaller cities, such as Atlanta, Ga., Newark, N. J., Portland, Me., Providence, R. I., etc., and even such more important ones as the Sketch Exhibitions, repeated this year with better success, artistically considered, in New York and Philadelphia, or the Forty-seventh of the Brooklyn Art Association, which showed a decided falling-off compared with the corresponding exhibition of 1882, and to devote the remaining space to the leading exhibitions held in New York, Philadelphia, and Boston. First, in the order of time, came the Foreign Exhibition in Boston, which opened in September. It created some dissatisfaction, as it was measured by the standard of a world's fair, which it was not. Looked upon as a large bazaar, it was amusing and interesting enough, and its Art Department, although not of the highest class, offered an opportunity to inspect the works of some of the artists, not often seen here, who count among the most outspoken advocates of so-called "impressionism." There was some good work, also, among the water colors. The antiquities and specimens attributed to the old masters were generally looked upon with feelings of doubt, but among these also there were a number of good things, notably two Etruscan sarcophagi of great antiquity and value. The exhibition of Contemporaneous American Art at the Museum of Fine Arts, Boston (October 16–November 27), gave further evidence of the tendency, which had already made itself felt elsewhere, to raise the standard of admission. It was eminently small and select, but of a high quality, and thoroughly local in its principal elements. Some of the pictures had been seen before, as, for instance, Mr. Pearce's "Prelude," which came from the Salon, Mr. Picknell's "Route de Concarneau," from a previous Salon, Mr. Thayer's "Portrait of a Lady" (with horse), etc. Among the new contributions were a number of fine portraits by Mr. F. P. Vinton, Mr. George Fuller, Mrs. Whitman, Mr. Lafarge, Mr. Sargent, Mr. Crowninshield, etc., an excellent genre, a "Breton Girl," by Mr. Walter Gay, a brilliant "Still Life," by Mr. Carlsen, a careful study of an Italian Boy, by Miss E. D. Hale, and good landscapes by H. Bolton Jones, Chas. E. L. Green, J. Foxcroft Cole, Chas. H. Davis, etc. Sculpture was better represented than it usually is in the American exhibitions of to-day, the most important piece being a strong bust of Mr. Jno. I. Blair, by Mr. Olin L. Warner, which was well supported by a number of busts, reliefs, etc., by Miss Gates and Miss Bartol, and Messrs. T. H. Bartlett, Ball, French, etc. The Special Autumn Exhibition of the National Academy (October 22–November 17) repeated, and rather emphasized the experience of the year before, that is to say, it was still smaller, so that three of the rooms had to be closed, as it was impossible to fill them. This was due in part, however, to the action of the jury, which had raised the average of the exhibition by vigorous rejections. Mr. Smedley's "Embarrassment," portraits by Miss Emmett, Mr. Vinton and Mr. Alexander, Mr. J. G. Brown's "As Good as New," Mr. Guy's "A Spare Minute," Mr. Maynard's "Voyage of Discovery," Mr. Mowbray's "Aladdin's Lamp," Mr. Leon Moran's "Eel Fishing" and "Waiting for the Ferry," Mr. F. S. Church's "The King's Flamingoes;" the marines of Messrs. Harry Chase, Dana, De Haas, Quartley, Edward Moran, and Rehn; the landscapes by Messrs. H. Bolton Jones, Geo. H. Smillie, R. Bruce Crane, J. F. Murphy, Thos. Moran, Kost, and Wm. Bliss Baker, and the flower pieces and still-life pictures of Miss K. H. Greatorex, Mr. J. Louis Webb, Mr. J. Decker, and Mr. C. B. Snyder may be named as among those which found most favor with the public. The Fifty-fourth Exhibition of the Pennsylvania Academy, Philadelphia (October 29–December 8), again showed a preponderance of French-American work, although special efforts had been made to attract the artists of New York and Boston. The most prominent place among the French-American contributions was held by Mr. Harrison's "Les Amateurs," which had been sent on from Chicago, and the same artist's "Un Esclave." Other attractions were (not mentioning some that have already been spoken of in connection with previous exhibitions), Mr. Pearce's "Fantaisie" and "Meditation," Mr. Mos'er's "Rainy Day," Mr. Daniel Strain's "Fleurs des Champs," Miss Klumpke's "In the XVI. Century," Miss Dodson's "Bacidæ," two East Indian subjects by Mr. Weeks, and the landscapes of Messrs. Kenyon Cox, Charles H. Davis, R. H. Monks, W. H. How, G. F. Munn, and G. R. Donohoe. Many of the contributions from Boston and New York having passed through exhibitions elsewhere in the earlier part of the year, it will suffice to mention here a few of those which were fresh, such as Mr. Shirlaw's contributions, one of them a magnificent outdoor study, "The Brook," and Mr. Charles H. Miller's "Millpond at Sunset." In this exhibition, also, there was a somewhat better representation of sculpture than is usually found. The pictures sent in under the terms of the Temple Competition will be alluded to in a later paragraph. The Winter Loan Exhibition, at the Metropolitan Museum in New York, which opened in November, was chiefly noticeable for its collection of copies from pictures by the old masters, executed by American artists, and for a small but admirable collection of splendid original portraits, by Rembrandt, Hals, Velasquez, Reynolds, Jurian Ovens, and an unknown artist, loaned by Mr. Marquand. Of the Sixth Black and White Exhibition of the Salmagundi Sketch Club, held at the American Art Gallery, New York (December 1–21), it must be chronicled that it was not a success, although it contained some good work. The exhibition suffered somewhat from the fact that the club had given up its lease of the National Academy to the Pedestal Fund Loan Exhibition, occupying the American Art Gallery instead. The consequence was that it found itself cramped for room, and the competition of the Loan Exhibition helped to diminish the number of visitors. One of the good points to be noted was the greater variety of methods used and consequently less of a predominance of black and white oils. The Loan Exhibition just alluded to, held at the National Academy, New York (December 3–January 1), for the benefit of the fund for building the pedestal of Bartholdi's great statue of Liberty, which is to be set up in New York harbor, as the gift of France to the United States, was an unqualified success. It comprised everything in the way of art, from paintings to fans, laces, etc., or in other words, art pure and art applied in all its forms. The paintings were all foreign, and the somewhat limited scope which they covered, as they had been selected from the painter's point of view exclusively, with a very decided tendency towards a certain point even within this narrow limit, gave rise to some criticism. But this point of view allowed, the exhibition was most excellent, with few exceptions. It will be many a day before such a fine collection of works by Millet, Mettling, the brothers Maris, Neuhuys, Ribot, Roybet, Stevens, Corot, Daubigny, Vollon, Manet, Cazin, etc., can be brought together again. To speak in detail here of the various other departments, the miniatures, the stained glass, the embroideries, ivories, arms, metal work, silverware, jewelry, Japanese art, engravings, manuscripts, musical instruments, etc., would be impossible. It will be well, however, to dwell for a moment upon the department of aboriginal art, as it helped to call attention to the artistic motives to be found in our Western country, and especially among the Indians. The exhibition netted $13,792.51 for the pedestal fund. The year was brought to a close most auspiciously by the exhibition, for the benefit of the Academy Prize Fund, of the private collection of Mr. Thomas B. Clark, composed exclusively of paintings by American artists. This well selected collection of 140 pictures by 116 artists, comprising nearly all American painters of reputation, was a revelation to many of the numerous visitors, who had heretofore been compelled to judge of American art by the miscellaneous collections generally shown. Its exhibition has no doubt done much to give an impetus to native art, and it is to be hoped that it may prove lasting.

Of the many special exhibitions of the year, one only can be mentioned, that of Mr. Whistler's etchings, held at the rooms of Messrs. Wunderlich & Co., New York, in October. The "arrangement in yellow and white," which caused such a stir in London some time ago, was repeated here with much the same result. Of single pictures by American artists, brought over from Europe, and publicly exhibited during the period embraced by this report, Mr. Sargent's "El Jaléo," deserves to be noticed for its daring execution, as well as for the varied comment which it called forth.

A rapid survey of a large number of exhibitions, such as that just given, can do no more than convey some idea of the activity noticeable all over the country. Nor is there much else to be said. That the character of these exhibitions was rather higher, on the average, than in previous years, has been noted. The surprise which seized the public when the latest generation of American students began to return from Paris and Munich some years ago has worn off, and it is hardly time as yet to look for further developments. The only new tendency noticeable within the year is found in the work of the skilful and careful detail painters, such as Messrs. Ulrich, Miller, and Moeller, which was so well represented in Mr. Clarke's exhibition. The European-American students, including those who are still on the other side, as well as those who have returned, might be said to have abated something of their ambition, in the sense that they are less prone to paint large exhibition pictures. That, however, is simply the result of circumstances—the impossibility of finding purchasers for such works—and it would be incorrect to interpret the fact as a retrogression, so long as the quality of the work is upheld.

2. MONUMENTS.

On the evidence of the public exhibitions, a foreigner would be likely to adjudge the people of the United States to be possessed of but small love for sculpture. On the evidence of a record of the monuments planned and erected here, he would come to the conclusion that sculpture was the leading art, and enjoyed an extraordinary development. A careful list, made up from all attainable sources, yet, as a matter of course, incomplete, gives a total of about eighty monuments and statues either finished, in progress, or projected during the period embraced by this review.

Most important, perhaps, of all the monuments set up during the year is the colossal bronze statue of Washington, by Mr. J. Q. A. Ward, the pedestal designed by Mr. R. M. Hunt, on the steps of the sub-treasury, Wall Street, New York, unveiled on Evacuation Day. Opinions as to the artistic value of this work seem to be somewhat divided. Much praise was given to an Indian group, also in bronze, modelled by Mr. J. J. Boyle, of Philadelphia, on an order from Mr. Ryerson, for erection in Lincoln Park, Chicago. Of other statues, etc., the erection or unveiling of which was reported, may be named Mr. W. W. Story's bronze statue of Prof. Henry, near the Smithsonian Institution, Washington; Mr. Howard Roberts's Fulton, in marble, for the National Capitol, Washington; Miss Anne Whitney's Harriet Martineau, a seated statue in marble, temporarily placed in the Old South Meeting House, Boston; a memorial tablet, with bas-relief portrait, to the memory of the late President Rogers, in the Technological Institute, Boston, by Mr. T. H. Bartlett; a statue of John Bridge, one of

the earliest settlers of Cambridge, Mass., executed on the order of one of his descend-
ants, by the late Thos. R. Gould, the finishing touches by his son, Marshall J. Gould ;
a statue to Gen. Zach. Taylor, near Louisville, sculptor not named ; and a monument
to the Confederate Dead, sculptor or architect not given, in Magnolia Cemetery,
Charleston, S. C.

The queer custom of ignoring the artist in the newspaper notices of monuments,
etc., prevents the giving of a full list, with artists' names, of such works, completed,
taken in hand, or ordered, within the period stated. That following is, therefore,
necessarily incomplete : Bissell, of Poughkeepsie, bronze statue of liberty, on a column
fifty feet high, to be erected at Waterbury, Conn. : Alexander Doyle, of New Orleans,
colossal bronze statue of General Lee ; D. C. French, statue of Emerson, for the
Public Library Yard at Concord, and Harvard statue, for Harvard University ; Harnish,
of Philadelphia, statue of Calhoun, for Charleston ; Jas. E. Kelly, New York, sculptor,
E. T. Littell and D. Smyth, New York, architects, Monmouth Battle Field Monument,
statue of Liberty, on granite column ; Henry Manger, of Philadelphia, bronze fountain, surmounted by a statue of the late Francis M. Drexel, for erection on Drexel
Boulevard, Chicago : Julius J. Melchers, Detroit, statue of Lasalle, for the façade of the
City Hall, Detroit : Niehaus, of Cincinnati, marble statue of Garfield, to be placed in
the Capitol, Washington ; John Rogers, bronze equestrian statue of General Reynolds,
to be erected in Philadelphia ; Augustus St. Gaudens, bronze statue of Capt. Randall,
the founder of Sailors' Snug Harbor, Staten Island, and memorial of Colonel Shaw, to
be erected in Boston as part of the street wall in front of the State House ; Franklin
Simmons, bronze statue of Senator Morton, for Indianapolis ; W. W. Story, statue of
Chief-Justice Marshall, for Washington ; Launt Thompson, equestrian statue of General
Burnside, for Providence, and statue of Admiral Dupont, for Dupont Square, Washington ; J. Q. A. Ward, bronze statue of Lafayette, to be placed in the grounds of the
University of Vermont, Burlington.   It is reported, also, that Mr. Ward has been
selected by a committee of the Society of the Army of the Cumberland as the sculptor
of a Garfield monument to be erected at Washington, for the benefit of which a bazaar
was held in the Capitol, December, 1882, which netted $7,593.39.   Olin L. Warner,
bronze statue of the late Governor Buckingham, seated, for the State Capitol at Hartford, and statue of William Lloyd Garrison, for Boston.   Woods, of Hartford, statue
of Nathan Hale.

Several Garfield monuments are in contemplation for Cincinnati (competition
alluded to in another paragraph), Chicago, and San Francisco, besides the one for
Washington above mentioned.   Monuments to President Lincoln are also spoken of
for Washington and for Chicago.   The obelisk at the National Capital, in memory of
Washington, is slowly nearing its completion.   Of several Washington monument
projects now in hand, one of the most important is that looking towards the erection
of a memorial at Washington's Headquarters, at Newburgh.   For this monument Congress appropriated $35,000, and the State of New York $10,000.   Other important
projects are a monument to De Kalb, at Annapolis ; an equestrian statue of General
Howard, of revolutionary fame, for Druid Hill Park, Baltimore ; a monument over
the grave of Thomas Jefferson ; statues to Peter Cooper, to Wm. C. Bryant, and to
Wm. E. Dodge, in New York ; a Longfellow statue for Portland, Me., and a Longfellow memorial for Cambridge, Mass. ; a monument to Commodore Perry, for Newport ; an equestrian statue of Paul Revere, for Boston ; and a statue of Daniel
Webster, which the Webster Historical Society proposes to erect.   Soldiers' and Sailors'

Monuments are to be reared at Brooklyn, N. Y., Portland, Me., Buffalo, N. Y., and Germantown, Pa.

It remains to say a few words about the monuments in progress, or to be erected, on the battle grounds of the Revolution. Of these, the Monmouth Battle Field Monument has already been noted. All these projects have the assistance of the United States. The Bennington Battle Monument, which is in charge of the Bennington Battle Monument Association, is to cost from $100,000 to $120.000, to which amount the United States have contributed $40,000. A number of designs have been submitted, but, so far as known, none of them has as yet been accepted. The shaft of the Oriskany Monument, about ten miles west of Utica, N. Y., is completed, and awaits only the placing of the memorial tablets. At latest accounts two of these were provided for, but $1,500 were wanting to pay for the others. The Saratoga Monument, J. C. Markham, sculptor, in charge of the Saratoga Monument Association, has thus far cost $55,000, and is still far from completed. At a late meeting of the Association, estimates of $25.000 were approved, to be expended on bas reliefs at the base of the monument, and of $15.000 for the interior bronze stairway.

The centre of interest during the year was the colossal statue of Liberty, by Bartholdi, presented as a gift to the United States by citizens of France, and to be set up on Bedloe's Island, in New York harbor. The statue itself is 150 feet high : the pedestal, which has been in course of construction for some time, will be 114 feet, and 52½ feet for the foundation. The cost of the pedestal, to be provided by citizens of the United States, will be about $250,000. Unfortunately, and not to the credit of the country, the response to the appeal for funds has been anything but hearty. In spite of mass meetings, committees of all sorts, amateur theatrical performances, and the splendid and very successful Pedestal Fund Loan Exhibition held in New York, only about one-half the amount needed had been subscribed up to the time of writing. It is very much to be wished that the new year may speedily see the completion of the fund. The general committee which has the matter in hand is constituted as follows : William M. Evarts, chairman ; Henry F. Spaulding, treasurer (Pres. Central Trust Co., N. W. cor. Nassau and Pine streets, New York, to whom subscriptions may be sent) ; Richard Butler, secretary ; Executive Committee, J. W. Drexel, Parke Godwin, J. W. Pinchot, V. Mumford Moore, and F. A. Potts.

3. ARCHITECTURE.—DECORATIVE ART.

The enormous activity in building is apparent from the statement that in the one city of New York alone 2,623 buildings were erected in 1883, at a cost of $44,304,638. Nevertheless, no account can be given here of the artistic features developed, beyond the general remark that the tendency towards picturesqueness continues. Some idea of recent doings may be gathered by those especially interested from an article by Mr. M. Schuyler in *Harper's Monthly* for September, 1883. An account of government architecture can be found in the illustrated reports of the Supervising Architect.

Quite as much is it to be regretted that nothing more than a simple allusion can be devoted to decorative and industrial art. The progress made in these departments has been astonishing, especially in glass work for windows, embroidery, and wall decoration. This progress is due in great measure to the fact that several leading artists have interested themselves in decorative work, so that it is no longer left, at least in its most sumptuous forms, to the professional decorator. The great decorators of past ages were also great artists in other departments, who had studied something more than

geometrical ornament and conventionalized plant-forms. The advances made in decoration since Messrs. La Farge, Tiffany, Colman, etc., and Mrs. Candace Wheeler
began to interest themselves in it, again show the necessity of more than technical
training in the decorator. The painting of walls and ceilings, or of pictures and decorations to be fixed to them permanently, has also been taken up within a few years
by artists properly so-called, as is shown by the work of Messrs. Walter Shirlaw, E. H.
Blashfield, Robert Blum, Frank Hill Smith, A. A. Anderson, etc.
Another year, it may be feasible to go into details.

4. THE REPRODUCTIVE ARTS.

New developments are hardly to be chronicled in the department of reproductive
arts, which is rather an inadequate term, as it includes original etching.
Further progress would appear almost impossible in wood-engraving, after the
rapid advances made within the past ten years. As to the tasks set the engravers, they
seem to have been somewhat less ambitious than in former years. This is to be
regretted. In the light of the capacities which wood-engraving has shown, it might be
wished that some one would give it a chance to exercise its powers in still more dignified undertakings. An opportunity such as that enjoyed by Mr. T. Cole, who is at
present engaged in engraving pictures by the old masters directly from the originals in
the Louvre, at Paris, would be highly valued by many of the ambitious men in the
profession. It is hardly necessary to say that the record of the year's doings is to be
found chiefly in *The Century Magazine, Harper's Monthly*, and *Harper's Weekly*. The
portfolio promised by the Society of American Wood-Engravers is still unpublished. An
attempt has been made to raise wood-engraving to the dignity of an original art. Mr.
Closson has published a block from one of his own studies, and Mr. Elbridge Kingsley
has contributed several " original engravings " to the *Century Magazine*. But it is difficult to see in how far they are more "original" than the plates executed by some of the
old French portrait engravers after their own drawings.
Among the original etchers the older men have held their ground, and the younger
have evidently improved. No accession to the ranks, of special importance, is, however,
to be noted. The growing favor with which the public looks upon etching is seen in the
increasing use of the art as a means of book illustration, and in the welcome given the
volume of "Original Etchings by American Artists," published by Messrs. Cassell &
Company. As a reproductive art, strictly so-called, etching is as yet but little employed
in the United States. The most important production of the year is the fine plate
executed by Mr. Shirlaw for the Art Union. The reader who desires to get an idea of
the year's productions is referred to the catalogue of the New York Etching Club.
Line-engraving is neglected everywhere, and it is not to be wondered at, therefore,
that little of importance in this specialty is produced in the United States. There is,
nevertheless, a very excellent achievement to be chronicled : Mr. Schoff's plate after
Hunt's " Bathers."
It is difficult to give a list of prints produced in this country. Such as have
been announced will be found grouped together in another part of this volume.
The standing which the American etchers and engravers have gained in Europe is
sufficiently shown by the statements in the paragraph on American Art in Europe.

5. SALES AT EXHIBITIONS.—AUCTION SALES.

In spite of the fact that the exhibitions of the year 1883 were generally allowed to be above the usual average, the sales were not satisfactory, and in some cases fell considerably below those of the year before. The figures, so far as attainable, are given in the "Statistical Table of Exhibitions." A comparative statement of some of the leading exhibitions is subjoined :—

	1881.		1882.		1883.
N. A. of Design, Annual.......	$42,838.00	....	$40,800.00	....	$41,039.00
do do Autumn......	....	....	18,850.00	....	12,078.00
Am. W. C. Society............	28,068.00	....	27,000.00	....	19,248.00
Society of American Artists.....	2,000.00	....	4,000.00	....	3,400.00
Brooklyn Art Association...42d	3,200.00	44th	4,806.00	46th	5,690.00
do do 43d	3,590.00	45th	14,550.00	47th	4,000.00
Black and White	5,900.00	....	5,965.00	....	1,500.00
Pennsylvania Acad., Spring.....	5,958.00	....	....	....	....
do do Autumn.....	9,858.00	....	6,836.50	....	3,815.00
Philadelphia Soc. of Artists. 3d	15,010.00	W. C.	3,250.00	W. C.	1,870.00
do do do	....	4th	7,790.00	Sketch	800.00
Cincinnati Exposition..........	2,275.00	....	5,000.00	....	4,141.50
Chicago Exposition............	30,075.00	....	19,296.60	....	17,835.00
Milwaukee Exposition.........	3,510.00	....	10,885.00	....	14,394.25
Boston Art Club..........23d	....	25th	3,335.00	27th	3,380.00
do do 24d	2,500.00	26th	1,438.75	28th	1,727.00

It will be seen that, generally speaking, the West did better than the East. Of the old-established exhibitions in the latter section, the annual exhibition of the National Academy of Design was the only one which did not lose ground, as regards sales.

The same general statement, of unsatisfactory results, holds good of auction sales. Of these, it is impossible, however, to give reliable details, as in many cases the figures named cannot be depended upon, owing to the custom of "bidding in," which is quite as prevalent here as elsewhere.

One of the most important sales was that of the American Art Gallery collections, New York, November, 1882, which contained excellent examples of the work of leading American artists. The total result was given at about $14,000 for 140 works. The highest bid was $2,300 for Mr. Bridgman's "Royal Pastimes in Nineveh." The picture was withdrawn, however, as it was limited. Some of the better prices quoted were as follows : Wyant, "Landscape," $200 ; McEntee, "The Wings of Morning," $230 ; Inness, "St. Peter's, Rome," $200 ; Wm. M. Chase, "Still Life," $240 ; Quartley, "Calm Morning, Chesapeake Bay," $200 ; W. Thompson, "Noonday in the Olden Time," $250 ; Smith, "Storm on the English Coast," $205 ; Inness, " Landscape and Cattle," $255 ; De Haas, "Steaming Up the Bay," $345 ; Kensett, "Scene on the Hudson," $340 : De Haas, "Moonlight Marine," $340 ; S. R. Gifford, "Villa Malta," $340 : Wm. Hart, "Near Napanock," $410 ; Guy, "One for Mamma, One for You, One for Me," $640 ; F. A. Bridgman, "Cottage in Normandy," $745 ; Wyant, "In the Adirondacks," $720 ; Guy, "The Mother's Supplication," $790 ; J. G. Brown, "The Lost Child," $1,550. The Artists' Fund Sale, February, 1883, was characterized as a perfect slaughter, 109 pictures realizing $12,815, without frames. Prices ranged from $5 for a picture in a $22 frame, to $585 for Mr. Guy's "Hush!" and $660 for Mr. J. G. Brown's "Lost and Won." One picture had to be passed for want of a bid. At the sale of the Brush and Palette Club, Brooklyn, N. Y., in October, 1882, the prices ranged from $6 to $175. The pictures offered were mostly by local painters. Several other sales by this club and by the Art Club, of the same city, gave similar results. The totals will be found in the "List of Exhibitions." Reports of a like nature came from other parts of the country. At an artists' sale of paintings and sketches, in San Francisco, the bids amounted to $6,500 for 245 pictures, or an average of $26 each, $400 being the highest bid. At another, some of the works had to be withdrawn, as $19 was the highest bid obtainable for a picture characterized as one of the gems of the collection. These special sales of the works of one or more artists, which were quite frequent in former years, have almost gone out of fashion. It may be said, also, that pictures by leading American artists are seldom seen at auction sales, except in such special cases as those mentioned at the beginning of this paragraph.

The leading sales of foreign pictures held in the period embraced by this review were those of the Truax Collection, December, 1882; the Runkle Collection, March, 1883, and the Hurlbert Collection, May, 1883. Some of the prices were reported as follows :

Truax Collection: Rosa Bonheur, "A Lamb" (water color). $350 ; Brissot de Warville, "Feeding the Flock," $225 ; Clays, "A Harbor," $1,050 ; Corot, "House at Barbizon," $120, "A Pastoral," $300, "The Path Through the Woods," $525 ; Courbet, "Among the Mountains," $300, "A Rill in the Mountains," $250 ; Diaz, "Flowers," $550, "Interior of the Forest of Fontainebleau," $1,250, "Clump of Trees near Barbizon," $920, "A Wood Nymph and Cupids," $200, "The Setting Sun," $1,150 ; Delort, "Bric-à-Brac Shop, 1780," $200 ; De Neuville, "On Guard," $300 ; C. F. Daubigny, "Landscape, Upper Seine," $1,050, "Landscape," $275 ; Domingo, "Inamovible," $400 ; Jules Dupré. "Marine," $850, "Evening," $850 ; Ed. Frère, "Domestic Life," $290 ; Fromentin, "The Ravine," $300 ; Henner, "A Head," $550 ; Imer, "View in Egypt," $750 ; Jacque, "Landscape and Sheep." $425 ; Kæmmerer, "Teasing the Parrot," $675; Munthe, "Winter Twilight," $560 ; Munier, "Washing Day on the Banks of the Marne," $300 ; Merle, "The Harem," $230, "The Gleaners, $1,600 ; Michel, "Landscape," $100, "The Old Château," $400 ; Palmaroli, "Waiting," $900 ; Rousseau, "Landscape, After the Storm," $2,600 ; Roybet, "A Soldier of the XVI. Cent.," $400 ; Schreyer, "The Advance Guard," $700 ; Tamburini, "A Pinch of Snuff," $275 ; Troyon, "Goat and Landscape," $200, "A Milkmaid and Cows," $325 ; Van Marcke, "Landscape and Cattle," $350 ; Verboeckhoven, "Sheep and Fowls," $750 ; Vely, "The Forbidden Book," $1,680 : Paul Vernon, "Turkish Children at Play," $265 ; Vibert, "Embarrassed for a Choice." $550 ; Zamacois, "An Awful Story," $600, "Waiting and Watching," $250 ; Ziem, "Venice," $300. Whole amount of sale, 83 pictures, $32,620.

Runkle Collection: Aubert, "Winter," $600 ; Bouguereau, "The Oranges," $700 ; Braith, "Bavarian Sheep," $1,100 ; Boldini, "In the Hammock," $775 ; Cederström, "The Comic Paper," $550 ; Corot, "River Scene," $1,550, "Italian Landscape," $600 ; C. F. Daubigny, "Evening," $3,150, "Early Spring," $1,250, "Twilight on the River," $1,000 ; Defregger, "Tyrolese Girl," $1,000 ; Detaille, "Incroyables," $1,525 ; Diaz, "Gathering Faggots," $2,000, "Opening in the Forest," $1,425, "Cupid's Flight," $2,250, "Study of Trees," $925, "Flowers," $530 ; Domingo, "Spanish Muleteer," $1,000 ; Jules Dupré, "Oak by the River," $1,700, "After the

Shower," $1,500, " The Cottage," $735 ; Fromentin, " On the Nile," $1,050; Goubie,
" Waiting at the Gate," $825 ; Gérôme, " Pifferari," $2,500 ; Henner, " Nymph at the
Fountain," $1,500 ; E. Isabey, " French Coast," $600 ; Jacque, " Shepherdess and
Sheep," $1,225, " Coming Storm," $1,050, " Moonlight," $906 ; Jacquet, " Falling
Leaves," $1,600, " The Duchess," $1,225 ; Knaus, " Ready for Bed," $1,600, " First
Love-letter," $1,525 ; Millet, " Water Carrier," $3,850, " Drying Clothes," $3,100 ;
Mettling, " Boy's Head," $210 ; Munkacsy, " The Font," $880 ; A. Pasini, " Cross-
ing the Desert," $770 ; Piot, " Far from Home," $1,000 ; Rousseau, " The Hamlet,"
$2,525 ; Roybet, " Death of Roxana," $250 ; Schreyer, " Arab Sentinel," $1,210 ;
Troyon, " Sheep in Pasture," $1,050, " Landscape," $400 ; Van Marcke, " Coming
Home," $2,050. Whole amount of sale, 66 pictures, $66,195. Most of the pictures
were medium sized. An *édition de luxe* of the catalogue was published, illustrated by
fifteen etchings. Price, $3.

Hurlbert Collection (old and modern pictures, and bric-à-brac) : Turner, " Venice,"
$15,000 ; Ruysdael, " Hunters Resting," $2,275 ; Boucher, " Leda," $2,800 ; Canaletti,
" The Grand Canal," $2,600. The prices obtained for the pictures were considered
unsatisfactory. The tapestries, furniture. etc., gave a better result. A descriptive
pamphlet, " The Art Collection of Mr. Wm. Henry Hurlbert," was published by
Mrs. M. G. Van Rensselaer.

Reports might be added of a number of dealers' sales, but they give no definite
criterion of the market value of pictures.

6. ART EDUCATION.

The Art schools of various grades, all over the country, so far as reports have been
obtainable, are in a flourishing condition. Most of them show an increase in the
number of pupils, and several new ones have been organized, or are about to be organized, especially in Western cities.

The schools of the National Academy, New York, are full (capacity about 200).
Newly established classes in painting and modelling have considerably enlarged their
scope. The Art Students' League reports a prosperous year, with 410 students, an increase of 96 over last year. The facilities for teaching and the number of classes have
also been increased. As the classes are open to both sexes on equal terms, it is
claimed that the facilities now offered by the League to women studying art professionally are greater than those afforded by any other school, either here or abroad. The
Ladies' Art Association, the benefits of which are intended more especially for ladies
and children, announces new classes and several new series of lectures. A unique
feature, lately added, is a collection of paintings, etc., which are loaned to schools and
private students, at a nominal rent, for use as copies. A curious change in numbers
is noticeable in the Free Art School for Women, maintained by the Cooper Union.
The report issued in 1882, gave the number of applications at 1,397 ; students admitted,
711; remaining at close of term, 680. The figures for 1883 are as follows : Applications, 1,450 ; admitted, 275 ; remaining, 202. The number of pupils in the wood-
engraving class also decreased from 35 to 28. The Free Night Art School for Men,
on the other hand, shows a considerable increase. Total admitted, 1882, 1,227 ; remaining at close of term. 729. Figures for 1883, 1,797 and 903, respectively. The
Technical Art Schools of the Metropolitan Museum, with about 100 pupils (against
163 last year), but room for 1,000, have been reorganized under the directorship of
Mr. John Ward Stimson, and rather more of the art element than heretofore has been

infused into them. A new feature at these schools is the introduction of the Chautauqua or correspondence system of teaching in the carriage drafting classes, for the benefit of young men in other cities. At the New York Trade Schools, education of a more technical kind is imparted to about 160 pupils, all of them artisans. In Brooklyn, the Art Students' Guild has consolidated with the Art Association, which latter body announces that it intends to provide every possible advantage for students, has doubled the accommodations of the school, and has added several new classes. The Rochester, N. Y., Art Club reports 50 students in its classes. The College of Fine Arts, of Syracuse University, reports 48 students, an increase of 15. The College of Fine Arts, of Ingham University, Le Roy, N. Y., has enlarged its building, so as to afford greater facilities. Present number of pupils not given.

At the Art School connected with Yale College, New Haven, the number of pupils has remained about stationary. The School of Drawing and Painting of the Museum of Fine Arts, at Boston, reports a successful year, with 112 pupils, against 121 the year before. A Life School has been started at the Boston Art Club, for members, and for such outsiders as may be recommended, in case of vacancies. At the Rhode Island School of Design, Providence, the attendance has been about the same as last year. The Portland, Me., Art League is one of the new organizations started during the year.

At Newark, N. J., the Essex Art Association has established an art school, under Prof. John W. Bolles. The College of New Jersey, at Princeton (Princeton College), has received $60,000 from the residuary legatees of Mr. Frederick Marquand, to endow a school and professorship of art. The Pennsylvania Academy of the Fine Arts, at Philadelphia, reports a falling off in attendance, owing, no doubt, to the change from free to paid tuition, carried out at the beginning of the year. At the Philadelphia School of Design for Women, and at the Pennsylvania Museum and School of Industrial Art, the number of pupils remained about the same. The drawing classes of the Franklin Institute were attended by 194 pupils during the spring term, against 123 the year before. In the classes of the Spring Garden Institute the increase was from 458 to 800. The report for 1883, of the School of Design for Women, at Pittsburgh, Pa., shows 132 pupils against 107 in 1881 (Report for 1882 not received). The Maryland Institute, Baltimore, under its new director, Prof. Otto Fuchs, reports gratifying improvement, with an attendance of 177 in the day school, and 497 in the night school, against 190 and 337, respectively, last year. At Charleston, S. C., the Carolina Art Association opened an art school in November, 1882, in a building bought specially for the purpose, which has at present an attendance of 140 pupils. The Southern Art Union and Woman's Industrial Association, of New Orleans, reports 36 students in its classes, against 150 the year before. Nashville, Tenn., is to have an art school, under the management of its newly-formed Art Association, but no steps in that direction have as yet been taken. The Polytechnic Society of Kentucky, at Louisville, maintains classes for drawing from life, etc., which will be developed in connection with the permanent art gallery about to be formed. The Richmond, Va., Art Association reports an average attendance of 25 in the classes which it maintains. According to a newspaper item, some of the more advanced pupils in these classes have been induced to turn their attention from picture-making to industrial designing.

The Cleveland (O.), Academy of Art organized its classes during the year, with a full corps of teachers (record of attendance, etc., not obtainable), and in the same city the Western Reserve School of Design for Women was established in November, 1882.

This school has now 60 pupils. At the School of Design connected with the University of Cincinnati, the attendance remains about the same. Mr. Jos. Longworth, lately deceased, offered, some time ago, to add a considerable sum to the foundation previously given by him to the University School of Design, provided the school be transferred to the control of the Museum Association. As this offer was rejected, Mr. Longworth settled an endowment of $15,000 annually on the association just named, for the formation of an art school.* No report has been received from the Ohio Mechanics' Institute, of the same city. The Art School at Columbus, O., maintained by the Columbus Art Association, has increased during the year from 220 to 244 pupils. The Art Institute of Chicago (formerly known as the Chicago Academy of the Fine Arts), effected the removal to its new building in December, 1882. Its schools are rapidly growing, and show an attendance of 359 against 300 last year. The Academy of Design, of the same city, an older organization, is making vigorous efforts to secure a substantial basis, so as to be able to make its schools free to pupils. Attendance not given. Detroit, Mich., as an outcome of the Loan Exhibition lately held there, is trying to raise the funds for an art school and museum. There are several art classes in the city, and the interest manifested in them showed itself about a year ago in quite a lively discussion concerning the propriety of studying from the nude, in which the advocates of such study seem to have carried the day. At Milwaukee, Wis., the Museum established an art school, which was opened in January, 1884. Art schools are also to be organized at Indianapolis, Ind., and Minneapolis, Minn. The St. Louis School of Fine Arts reports that it is making progress, with 301 workers enrolled during the year, against 200 according to previous report. It is stated that the object of this school, despite its name, is not so much to train students to become professional artists, as it is to help practical workers of various kinds, and to increase their proficiency in their special calling.

The average number of students in the California School of Design, maintained by the San Francisco Art Association, has risen from 78 to 86. The finances of the school are in satisfactory condition. It is now clear of debt, and the prospects are improving. A school has lately been established by the San Francisco Chapter of the American Institute of Architects for the benefit of students working in the offices of its members. The Colorado Fine Arts Academy, at Denver, had to be discontinued, owing to want of support. The College of Fine Arts connected with the University of Denver, reports 75 students, against 60 in 1882.

Mr. Albert Jay Jones, of Providence, has offered to provide a lot of land and a building on Monte Baldino, in Rome, Italy, for the establishment there of an American art academy. Whether anything will come of the project, it is impossible to say at the present moment.

7. PRIZES AND COMPETITIONS.

The year 1883 was marked by the establishment of several prize funds, a fact which may be looked upon as one of the most hopeful signs of a sincere and intelligent desire to encourage American art.

Mr. Thomas B. Clarke, of New York, established a prize of $300 for the best American figure composition to be awarded at each annual exhibition of the National

* Since the above was written, it has been announced that the University School is to be transferred to the Museum, so that there will be only one school in Cincinnati.

Academy of Design, the payment of which he guarantees during his lifetime, until the interest on a fund started by him shall be sufficient to provide the sum.

Mr. Julius Hallgarten, since deceased, by a deed of trust to the National Academy, endowed prizes of $300, $200 and $100, to be awarded, subject to certain regulations, to the painters of the three best pictures in oil colors at each annual exhibition of the Academy.

The awards of these four prizes will be made by a vote by ballot of all the exhibitors of the season, at a meeting to be held for the purpose during the third or fourth week of the exhibitions.

Mr. Hallgarten also gave a second fund of $5,000 to the National Academy, the interest of which is to be used at the discretion of the Council for school prizes. A third fund, finally, of like sum, was by the same gentleman placed in the hands of Mr. J. Carroll Beckwith, Mr. Augustus St. Gaudens and Prof. Felix Adler, as trustees, the interest to be used for the benefit of pupils of other schools.

A prize for young architects has been established by the children of the late Mr. Benj. S. Rotch, in accordance with his known wishes. From the income of a fund yielding $2,000 a year, two young men are to be constantly maintained as travelling students of architecture in Europe, each studentship to last two years. Candidates must have had at last two years' experience in the office of a practising architect in the State of Massachusetts. The method of awarding the studentships has not yet been announced.

The Art Students' League of Cincinnati, Mr. Matthew Morgan, principal and manager, announces a European scholarship of $1,200, which is to be awarded annually, beginning October 15, 1884, to the painter of the best picture from a given subject, the competitors to be chosen from the pupils of the school. A consolation prize of $200 is to be awarded to the painter of the second best picture.

The medals, etc., annually given to the best pupils at the schools of the National Academy of Design, were awarded as follows on May 11, 1883 : Life School—Suydam medal (silver), August Kreutzberg; Suydam medal (bronze), J. W. Clawson : honorable mention, F. C. Martin and Joseph H. Gies. Antique School—Elliot medal (silver), for full length figure, Ernest C. Rost ; honorable mention, Walter Chippendale ; Elliot medal (bronze), for half-length figure, L. E. Van Gordon ; Elliot medal (bronze), for head, Nora E. Landers ; honorable mention, Lucy T. Fenner and Wm. J. Whittemore. At the exhibition of the Pennsylvania Academy, Philadelphia, the Mary Smith Prize of $100 for the best painting by a resident lady artist was awarded to Miss Emily Sartain, for a " Portrait Study," No. 309 of the catalogue. Of the two Charles Toppan Prizes, of $200 and $100 respectively, for the two best pictures by students of the Academy, the second only was awarded, to Miss Gabrielle D. Clements, for " Boys Picking Berries," No. 64 of the catalogue.

At a competitive exhibition, held in November, 1882, by the Society of Decorative Art, San Francisco, Cal., which attracted contributors from all parts of the United States, the following prizes were awarded for decorative work of various kinds : Miss Hannah Wild, of Jamaica Plain, Mass, $100 ; Miss D. L. Martin, San Francisco, $75 ; Miss Ingalsbe, San Francisco, and Miss Higham, Detroit, each $50 ; Misses E. J. Cavannah, of San Francisco, Lee, of Boston, Allen, of New York, Carter, of Providence, and Dean, of San Francisco, $25 each.

The two most interesting events of the year which come under the heading of this paragraph were the Harper Competition and the Temple Competition, both of which unfortunately failed. Messrs. Harper & Brothers offered $3,000 for the best original drawing to illustrate Alfred Domett's "Christmas Hymn," the drawing to be suitable for publication in *Harper's Monthly*, and to be exclusively the work of an American artist not over twenty-five years of age, the successful competitor to use the money for the prosecution of art study at home and abroad. Over 3,000 aspirants signified their intention to compete, by applying for a copy of the poem ; but of these only about ten per centum finally sent in designs, and of the latter, according to the decision of the judges, Messrs. R. Swain Gifford, F. D. Millet, and Charles Parsons, only a small proportion was found to be of sufficient artistic merit to warrant their selection for engraving, but not one of them adequately illustrated the idea expressed in the poem. The prize, therefore, was not awarded, but the competition was renewed, under about the same terms, which those interested will find in *Harper's Weekly*.

The Temple Competition was for the best four pictures by American artists, subjects to be taken from the revolutionary history of the United States. The prizes, given by Mr. Joseph E. Temple, of Philadelphia, were $3,000 for the first, the picture for which it might be awarded to become the property of the Pennsylvania Academy, and a gold, a silver, and a bronze medal for the second, third, and fourth, respectively. The competition, which was to be decided at the exhibition of the Academy, October, 1883, attracted only four artists, who sent in the following pictures : Wm. Thos. Trego, " The March to Valley Forge " ; Miss Sarah Dodson, " The Signing of the Declaration of Independence " ; Mr. H. T. Cariss, " Taking the Oath of Allegiance at Valley Forge " ; Mr. F. F. English, " The Action between the Bon Homme Richard and the Serapis." The jury, composed of Messrs. Martin Brimmer, of Boston, John Durand, of New York, George B. Coale, of Baltimore, and Wm. L. Baker, Chas. Henry Hart, and Jas. S. Martin, of Philadelphia, awarded only one prize, the third, or silver medal, to Mr. Trego, and gave it as their opinion that none of the pictures permitted the awarding of the other prizes. This decision called forth a protest from some of the artists of Philadelphia, who, in a meeting held December 12, 1883, declared the withholding of the other prizes, for a reason not mentioned in the circular announcing the competition, a breach of contract, and there is some talk of a suit to be brought by Mr. Trego.

Of the many competitions for works of sculpture or architecture announced or decided during the year, it is impossible to give an account here. Suffice it to say, that the terms of most of them were unsatisfactory to the artists, and that several ended in squabbles and threatened lawsuits. As one of the most notable of these may be mentioned the Cincinnati Garfield Monument competition. The *American Architect* has made it its business to call attention to these matters quite frequently, and it is to be hoped that its proposition of a code of laws for affairs of this kind may be carried out at the earliest possible moment. As competitions are at present conducted in the United States, they are, as a rule, anything but an honor to the country.

The competitions for designs for small houses, established by the *American Architect*, also deserve passing mention. A competition for a building for the Institute of American Architects, among its members, resulted in the production of only one design, by Mr. John Moser, of Anniston, Ala., in which the attempt was made to express the cosmopolitan character of American civilization by the superposition of all known styles of architecture in historical order. A reproduction of this curious design is given in the journal above named for January 19, 1884.

2

8. MUSEUMS AND PUBLIC COLLECTIONS.

A full record of the development of the museums and public collections of the United States would form a most interesting chapter, but lack of space forbids. In a general way it may be stated that, in spite of the generosity of our citizens, who have not been backward in providing the means, most of these institutions are still cramped financially, and the universal cry is for permanent endowments, so as to end the unpleasant and precarious hand-to-mouth condition in which they find themselves. Under present circumstances, a logical, systematic enlargement is hardly possible, and acquisitions depend almost entirely upon donations and subscriptions in money, so that the best chances for making valuable purchases must often be allowed to go by.

Some extracts are appended from the reports of the two principal museums of the country, to show that these remarks are not unwarranted. The Trustees of the Metropolitan Museum, in New York, say, in their last (thirteenth) report, p. 7 : "For some years, whatever additions have been made, have been by gift. Our accumulations, in various departments of art, form already a grand gathering, and, there is no reason to doubt, will in the same way continue to increase in educational value and importance. But until the Trustees are supplied with money, which they can devote to careful and judicious purchases, there will always remain more or less unfilled blanks in illustrative series of objects in the several departments. We cannot believe that the public-spirited citizens of New York will long be content to witness the crowds of visitors who throng the Museum on the four free days of each week, and permit the expense of keeping the exhibitions open to the public to rest on its small list of members. Your moneys annually given, should be devoted to making the Museum every year more and more valuable for this and for coming generations; and, if it is to be a free Museum to the whole people, as it is our unanimous desire, a permanent provision for that specific purpose, by endowment, should be made without delay." The Trustees of the Museum of Fine Arts, Boston, in their last (seventh) report, p. 4, speak as follows : "The building, even as now enlarged, is not sufficient to display the collections, or to accommodate the very numerous visitors. Such institutions in other countries have the aid of the state, and are among the most costly of the objects to which public money is applied. This institution relies solely on the munificence of private citizens, and without the continuance of that munificence yearly and monthly, without large and constant drafts on its generous friends, it cannot fulfill public expectation as an ornament to the city and a useful assistant in popular education."

Subjoined is a list of the most important of these institutions, to serve as a sort of short guide to those desirous of visiting them. For details regarding terms of admission, character of collections, etc., see the special accounts given elsewhere in this volume.

Metropolitan Museum of Art, Central Park, Fifth Avenue and 82d Street, New York.

New York Historical Society, 170 Second Avenue, New York. Art gallery and museum.

Lenox Library, 1001 Fifth Avenue, 70th and 71st Streets, New York. Art gallery.

American Museum of Natural History, Manhattan Square, Central Park, 77th Street and Eighth Avenue, New York. Archæological Department.

Powers Art Gallery, Rochester. This is a private gallery, but open to the public.

Buffalo Fine Arts Academy, Austin Building, Buffalo. Permanent collection of Paintings, etc.

Yale School of Fine Arts, Yale College, New Haven. Art Gallery.

Wadsworth Gallery, Wadsworth Athenæum, 206 Main Street, Hartford.

Museum of Fine Arts, Dartmouth Street and St. James Avenue, Boston.

Peabody Museum of American Archæology and Ethnology, Divinity Avenue, Cambridge, Mass.

Pennsylvania Academy of the Fine Arts, N. Broad, cor. Cherry Street, Philadelphia. Permanent collection of paintings, engravings, etc.

Pennsylvania Museum, Memorial Hall, Fairmount Park, Philadelphia. Industrial art.

Peabody Institute, Baltimore. Art Gallery.

Corcoran Gallery of Art, Pennsylvania Avenue, cor. 17th Street, Washington.

United States National Museum, Washington. Archæological Department, costumes, reproductive arts, etc.

Cincinnati Museum, Cincinnati, O. Temporarily located in Music Hall. Ground was broken for the building of the Museum, which is to be one of the finest in the country, in Eden Park on Sept. 21, 1882. It will not be finished before October, 1885.

Art Institute, cor. Michigan Avenue and Van Buren Street, Chicago. The beginning has been made of a permanent collection. For the present the gallery is filled principally with works of art loaned.

Milwaukee Museum of Fine Arts for the State of Wisconsin, Milwaukee. Temporarily located at 423 Milwaukee Street. This is the youngest of the Museums of the United States, having been incorporated July 1, 1882.

Museum of Fine Arts, St. Louis.

A movement towards the establishment of a permanent art gallery has lately been made in Louisville, in connection with the Polytechnic Society of Kentucky. A number of paintings by American artists were bought for this institution at the Southern Exposition held in Louisville last summer.

Detroit is also to have a museum. The Art Loan Exhibition lately held in that city left a surplus, which is to be applied to the purpose. Efforts are now making to raise $40,000 for the purchase of the necessary land, and several gentlemen are reported to have signified their willingness to do more as soon as this first step is accomplished.

The Art Association of Indianapolis and the Minneapolis Society of Fine Arts, lately organized, both declare one of their aims to be the establishment of permanent art galleries.

There has been some talk lately of the establishment of a National Art Gallery at Washington, the works for which are to be bought with funds provided by Congress. It does not appear, however, upon what basis this proposition rests.

9. BEQUESTS.

The bequests made in the interests of art (and archæology) during the period covered by this review have not been many, but several of them are of considerable importance.

Mr. Peter Cooper gave $100,000 to the Cooper Union, of New York, the institution which owed its organization and maintenance to the liberality exercised during his lifetime.

Mr. Levi Hale Willard left the bulk of his estate to the Trustees of the Metropolitan Museum, New York, to be applied, under certain restrictions, to the purchase of a collection of models, casts, photographs, engravings, etc., illustrative of the art and science of architecture. The remainder, if any, of the fund is to be employed in the purchase of pictures of the modern French school, to be added to the galleries of the Museum. The will of the late ex-Gov. Morgan stipulates a contingent bequest in favor of the Metropolitan Museum, according to the terms of which, in case his grandson should be without children, the residuary estate (after all other bequests have been settled), which is said to be enormous, is to be divided into 415 shares, of which 100 are to go to the Museum, to be used in the establishment, maintenance, and enlargement of a gallery of modern paintings.

The College of New Jersey (Princeton College) has received $60,000 from the residuary legatees of Mr. Frederick Marquand, to endow a school and professorship of art.

Mr. Henry Seybert, a wealthy Philadelphian, left $2,000 and such a selection of his paintings, engravings, books, etc., as his executors may choose, to the Pennsylvania Academy, and $2,000 to the Social Art Club for its library. The Academy of Natural Sciences, Philadelphia, has come into possession, by bequest, of the fine collection of antiquities belonging to the late Wm. S. Vaux.

Mr. Joseph Longworth, of Cincinnati, left an endowment of $15,000 annually to the Trustees of the Cincinnati Museum Association, to be used in the establishment of an art school in connection with the Museum. (See note, p. 15.)

The late Mr. Winthrop Hillyer, who founded the Art Gallery of Smith College, Northampton, Mass., left $50,000 for its endowment.

The Museum of Fine Arts, Boston, reports a bequest of $5,000 by the late Mr. Otis Norcross.

10. SOCIETIES AND CLUBS.

No attempt can be made here to relate the history during the year of the thousand and one art societies and clubs which exist in all parts of the United States. What follows is principally a record of associations lately established or reorganized.

The most important society established during the period under review is the American Art Union, with rooms at 44 East 14th Street, New York, where it opened a permanent exhibition on December 19, 1883. Its principal function is to be the providing of better markets for the works of American artists, by arranging exhibitions in various cities. Its other features are those usually found in the organizations known as Art Unions. Further details are given in the List of Local Institutions.

The Art Club, of New York, composed entirely of artists, and for a time allowed to lie dormant, began a new period of activity in December, 1882. It proposes to have exhibitions at stated periods, the first of which was held at the American Art Gallery in February, 1883. A Society of American Embroiderers is to be organized. The present organization, of which Mrs. Candace Wheeler is Acting President, is preliminary only. The exhibition of embroideries at the recent Pedestal Loan Exhibition, was held under the auspices of this society.

The Brooklyn (N. Y.) Art Association has been reorganized. It is reported that the former stockholders, having voluntarily cancelled one-half of their stock, and a large amount of new stock having been subscribed for, the Association is now clear of debt. The Association discontinued its own art classes a year or two ago, but has since undertaken the maintenance and development of the school formerly known as the Brooklyn Art Guild.

An Art Club, for the mutual improvement of its members, was organized by a number of the artists of Buffalo, in February, 1883.

The Essex Art Association was formed at Newark, N. J., April 16, 1883, for the establishment of an industrial art school and of exhibitions, and to offer an opportunity to artists for improvement and such social advantages as the association may afford. Its first exhibition was held in November. The opening of its school has before been alluded to.

An Academy Art Club was formed in March, 1883, by students of the Pennsylvania Academy, of Philadelphia, for the promotion of artistic work and the common artistic interests of its members.

The Portland, Me., Art League, established early in the year, for the improvement of its members in practical art work, held a first exhibition in May, and meets two days each week at the rooms of the Portland Society of Art. The new club-house of the society named, described as a handsome structure in the Queen Anne style, was nearly completed at the end of the year, and its dedication appointed for the latter part of January, 1884.

The Art Guild, of Chicago, incorporated December 7, 1882, is a new society, formed for the mutual assistance and entertainment of persons actively engaged in the pursuit, or known as patrons and critics, of art. The Illinois Art Association, also of Chicago, organized September, 1882, with a capital of $25,000, has for its object the collection, exhibition, and distribution of works of art. It has held several exhibitions, and owns at present fourteen paintings, acquired through purchase and by gift.

The Detroit Water Color Society, for the advancement of the art of water color painting, was organized March 22, 1883. It has thus far had two exhibitions, one at the Detroit Art Loan Exhibition, the other, in December, at the store of Messrs. Sigler & Stratton.

The Art Association of Indianapolis, formed May, 1883, held an exhibition in November, and proposes to establish an art school, courses of lectures, and a permanent gallery.

The Minneapolis Society of Fine Arts was organized in January, 1883. It proposes to hold exhibitions, arrange courses of lectures, establish a museum, and provide means of systematic art education. Its first Public Loan Exhibition was opened November 20, 1883.

The Nashville Art Association, organized in January, 1883, has for its object the cultivation of a taste for the fine arts, and the encouragement of better rewards for artists of merit. To this end meetings, discussions, lectures and exhibitions are to be arranged, and art classes and a collection of works of art to be established.

The Salmagundi Sketch Club, of St. Louis, Mo., for the development of the creative faculty, and the cultivation of sociability among artists, was organized in November, 1883.

The University Art Club, of Denver, Col. (date of organization not given), is connected with the College of Fine Arts of the University of Denver.

Applications have been made to the Board of Trustees of the American Institute of Architects, from the cities of St. Louis, Nashville, and Indianapolis, for the granting of charters to new chapters.

The going out of existence of associations of a private nature is seldom brought to the notice of the public. Among those lately discontinued may be named the Albany Art League, the Albany Chapter of the American Institute of Architects, the Hingham, Mass., Art Cïub, the Salem, Mass., Art Club, and the Social Art Club, of Baltimore.

The Art Union of Central Illinois is not a new association, and an allusion to it may therefore seem out of place here. A few words concerning it will not, however, be amiss. One of the evils which militates against the usefulness of the art associations of the country is their isolation. A general organization has more than once been proposed, but nothing has been done as yet toward the carrying out of the proposition. Such an organization might prove to be of special benefit for the regulation of the exhibitions which at present frequently interfere and compete with one another. The Art Union of Central Illinois is the only organization in the United States which binds together a number of subordinate societies. It is composed of nine such societies, most of them small clubs for reading upon and studying the history of art, which meet together in convention once a year, for the reading of reports and papers, and the general interchange of views and suggestions. The last convention was held at Jacksonville, Ill., in May, 1883, the next is appointed to meet at Decatur, Ill. The president elected for the year is Mr. Charles Ridgely, of the Springfield Art Club. The proceedings of the Union, with a synopsis of the minutes of all the meetings held since its organization, in the year 1880, have been published in pamphlet form. That such a fellowship must be beneficial, there can be no doubt ; and the formation of a similar organization among other associations, with a more extended field of activity, may be well worth while considering.

11. DECORATIVE ART SOCIETIES.

The Decorative Art Societies play a not unimportant part among the art associations of the country, both as dispensers of art education, more especially to young women and children, and as agents for the sale of art needle-work and similar productions, sent to the larger cities by workers living in less frequented localities. The New York Society, for instance, which is the parent of all similar associations in the United States, has done good service in both these directions, as well as by its loan exhibitions and competitions, and by its Lending Library, which is used as a means of instructing distant workers, to whom books, designs, etc., are sent by mail. The Competitive Exhibition of the San Francisco Society has already been spoken of in the paragraph on Prizes and Competitions. No general account of the activity of these societies can be given, as but few of them have sent in reports up to the time of writing. A list of these societies will be found in the index.

12. ARCHÆOLOGY.

The investigations conducted at Assos, in Asia Minor, under the auspices of the Archæological Institute of America were successfully completed, and the members of the expedition have returned. The fruits of the expedition, in architectural and sculptured fragments from the temple of Assos, terra-cotta vases, inscriptions, coins, etc., have been received at the Museum of Fine Arts, Boston. The Institute is now endeavoring to raise the sum of $20,000 to enable Mr. Joseph Thacher Clarke, the chief of the expedition, and Mr. F. H. Bacon, its draughtsman, to prepare and publish an exhaustive illustrated report. To this end, a committee was appointed, at a mass meeting held at Huntington Hall, Boston, Oct. 31, 1883, composed of the following gentlemen : Samuel L. Cobb, Henry Lee, Wm. Endicott, Jr., Oliver W. Peabody, and John C. Phillips. Contributions may be sent to any member of this committee, or to the treasurer of the Institute, Mr. Henry L. Higginson, No. 44 State St., Boston. The sum needed to complete the printing of Mr. A. F. Bandelier's report on his re-searches in Mexico has been secured. No announcement has yet been made of new undertakings by the Institute.

The American School of Classical Studies at Athens, Greece, founded by the Archæological Institute, and supported by a number of the principal colleges in the United States, entered upon its second year, under Professor Lewis R. Packard, of Yale College. That it is not limited to philology, is best shown by a quotation from the report of Prof. Wm. W. Goodwin, its first director : "One class [of students] con-sists of those who have a definite object in view, such as professional study of Greek architecture, or special study of Greek art, or of some department of antiquities which can best be studied at Athens." Among the theses presented by students of the first year are two upon architectural subjects : The Erechtheum, by H. A. Fowler, A.B., of Harvard University, and The Theatre of Dionysus at Athens, by Jas. R. Wheeler, A.B., of the University of Vermont. To secure the permanency of the school, an en-dowment of about $120,000 is needed.

The bearing of American archæology upon the study of the history of primitive art, one of the most interesting factors in the history of mankind, is but little under-stood as yet, and the replies to circulars asking for information about such collections have not been given with the fulness that might have been desired. In one instance the assurance was twice sent in reply to repeated inquiries, that the collection in question had "nothing whatever to do with art." Of the institutions specially devoted to Ameri-can archæology (and ethnology), the Peabody Museum at Cambridge, Mass., connected with Harvard University, takes the lead. In New York, the Metropolitan Museum, the Historical Society, and the American Museum of Natural History are rich in archæ-ological collections, and the similar collections of the Academy of Natural Sciences of Philadelphia, lately enriched by the Vaux bequest, previously alluded to, are also quite extensive. The Pennsylvania Museum, Fairmount Park, Philadelphia, contains a valuable collection of Greco-Italian and ancient American pottery. It goes without saying, that the United States National Museum, at Washington, possesses very impor-tant collections, especially of American antiquities. A late addition is a collection of casts from Palenque and other places in Yucatan, Mexico, etc., procured by Mr. Charnay, and given to the Museum by Mr. Pierre Lorillard.

Mention may also be made here of the set of electrotypes from the finest ancient coins in the British Museum, published by the English authorities, lately bought by a number of gentlemen of New York, and to be placed on exhibition in the rooms of the American Numismatic and Archæological Society, in the University Building, Wash-ington Square, New York. The set is composed of 793 coins, covering the period from B.C. 700 to the beginning of the present era.

A list of the Numismatic societies is given in the general index.

13. "OLD MASTERS" IN THE UNITED STATES.

It is sufficiently well known that most of the art museums and public collections contain specimens of the work of the "old masters," which, although they may not include any works of really first-class importance, are nevertheless well worthy of attention and study. The exhibitions of the year 1883 have, besides, brought to light quite a number of pictures bearing well-known names, in the possession of private owners.

The fine portraits by Rembrandt, Velasquez, etc., exhibited by Mr. Marquand at the Metropolitan Museum, have already been alluded to.

At the exhibition of the Esthetic Society of Syracuse, N. Y., June 25–July 14, 1883, there was shown a collection of 23 paintings by Backhuysen, Jan and Andreas Both, Carlo Dolci, Claude Lorraine, Canaletti, Hobbema, Murillo, Gaspar Poussin, Rembrandt, Rubens, Jacob Ruysdael, David Teniers, David Teniers the Younger, Aart Van der Neer, A. Van de Velde, Van Dyck (attributed to), Velasquez, C. J. Vernet, and Jan Wynants, owned by Miss Elizabeth Hathaway, of Solon, N. Y. Most of these pictures, according to the catalogue, were bought of M. Van Royde, a banker of Antwerp, whose ancestors acquired them from the artists themselves. Mrs. J. V. L. Pruyn, of Albany, contributed to the same exhibition a "Madonna and Child," by Bernardo Luini.

Mr. H. W. A. Nahl, artist, of San Francisco, Cal., about a year ago had sent to him from Europe a large number of old paintings which formed the collection of the late J. W. Nahl, of Cassel, a member of the well-known Nahl family of artists, whose history, as artists, dates back to the seventeenth century. The catalogue names Raphael, Correggio, Tintoretto, Giorgione, Il Sodoma, Paul Veronese, Guido Reni, Guercino, Carlo Cignani, Gaspar Poussin, Titian, Leonardo da Vinci, Domenichino, Cranach, Gonzales Coques, Jan Van Goyen, Van der Helst, A. Van Ostade, Rembrandt, Rubens, Ruysdael, Wouverman, Velasquez, Ribera, etc. The owner states that he has documentary evidence concerning many of these pictures. The collection comprises, besides, about 8,000 sheets of drawings and old engravings, and other antiquities.

In the Southern Exposition at Louisville was shown "The Lesson in Anatomy," by Rembrandt, of which the catalogue spoke as follows : "Supposed to be the original study for the great picture in the Royal Gallery at the Hague. Note the experimental sketches along the right-hand edge of the canvas."

The catalogue of the Detroit Art Loan Exhibition contains the names of Boucher, Pietra da Cortona, Perugino, Gaspar Poussin, Reynolds, Salvator Rosa, Rachel Ruysch, Van Dyck, A. Van Ostade, C. J. Vernet, Leonardo da Vinci, and W. Von Bemmel. As one of the curiosities in which collectors sometimes take delight, may be mentioned a portrait of Luther, as monk, also in this exhibition, attributed to Raphael.

At the Loan Exhibition of the Milwaukee Museum of Fine Arts there were to be seen a Carlo Cignani, "St. Helena Presenting her Son, the Emperor Constantine, to the Throne of Heaven ;" two Carlo Dolcis, "St. John " and "St. Catherine," and a portrait of Rembrandt, attributed to the artist himself. The Cignani was offered for sale at $5,000. The Carlo Dolcis are owned by Mrs. Alexander Mitchell, of Milwaukee ; the Rembrandt is the property of Mr. Jos. Harris, of Sturgeon Bay, Wis.

These notices are, of course, given for what they may be worth, and in the hope that some one of the art institutions may find it feasible to collect as many of these pictures as possible in a Loan Exhibition, even at the risk of disappointment to some of the owners.

14. THE TARIFF QUESTION.

No question has excited a greater interest among artists, the friends of art, and art dealers, than that of duties upon works of art, and none has been more warmly discussed. There are three parties in the field : the free-traders, who desire all duties removed, because they think the introduction of foreign works of art desirable ; the protectionists, who believe that American art cannot compete with the art of Europe, and therefore advocate a high *ad valorem* duty ; and those who are in favor of admitting high-class works on favorable conditions, but keeping out cheap and bad work by the imposition of a specific duty of $25, $50. or $100, which would be a comparatively insignificant tax on expensive works, while it would be prohibitory on those costing only a small sum. As the law stood at the beginning of the year, it exacted a duty of 10 per cent. on all foreign works of art. Under the leadership of the Society of American Artists, many, especially of the younger artists, petitioned Congress to remove the duty, and their petition was seconded by several other art associations, such as the Art Club of New York, the Pennsylvania Academy of the Fine Arts, the Boston Art Club, and the Carolina Art Association of Charleston, S. C. The National Academy, as a body, held aloof from the discussion. A bill, embodying the views of the friends of free trade in art was introduced in the House of Representatives, by the Hon. Perry Belmont, but instead of passing it, Congress preferred to listen to the advocates of protection, and actually raised the duty to 30 per cent., at which rate it remains for the present. Considerable indignation was expressed at this action here as well as in Europe, and the hot heads among the artists of France proposed to retaliate by closing the Salon to American artists and excluding American students from the École des Beaux-Arts. The small favor in which this high rate is held is evident from the fact that most of those who were said to have been instrumental in bringing about its enactment publicly declared their dissent. At the present session of Congress, Mr. Perry Belmont has once more proposed the abolition of all duties on works of art as well as on antiquities ; and these measures, although the bills in which they are embodied have been criticised for their loose wording, have again the indorsement of the Society of American Artists. On the other hand, the protectionists, under the leadership of Mr. Thomas Donaldson, have taken steps to petition Congress for the retention of the law as it stands. The advocates of a specific duty seem to have taken no measures to enforce their views. No intimation as to the result can as yet be given, as no action has as yet been taken by Congress.

15. THE COPYRIGHT LAW.

The copyright law, in so far as it applies to works of art, is generally unsatisfactory to artists, as the formalities to be observed are somewhat involved, and in many cases cannot be complied with. An agitation was begun several years ago for a remodelling of the law, but nothing came of it, nor has anything been done in the matter the past year. The law, therefore, remains as it was. For the information of artists who may desire to protect their works, the full text is given in another part of this volume.

16. MISCELLANEOUS.

The visits to the United States of Dr. Francis Seymour Haden, and of Mr. Hubert Herkomer, were among the interesting events of the year. Dr. Haden lectured repeatedly on his favorite art of etching in New York, Boston, Philadelphia,

Cincinnati, etc., provoking no small amount of criticism by some of his statements, especially in regard to the comparative position of the etcher and the engraver. Mr. Herkomer also delivered several lectures, to students and general audiences, and was quite successful in the number of orders for portraits which he obtained, and executed to the satisfaction of his patrons.

The birthday of Raphael was allowed to pass by almost unnoticed. The only art institution which officially took cognizance of it, or whose action in the matter was publicly reported, was the Philadelphia School of Design for Women. The celebration took the shape of a reception held on the evening of April 6. Later in the year a tribute was paid to the memory of the great artist by the Esthetic Society of Syracuse, N. Y. At the exhibition held by this society from June 25 to July 14 to celebrate the completion of its first decennium, the works of Raphael were represented by a collection of 265 engravings, photographs, etc.

The question of opening art exhibitions, museums, etc., on Sundays, was discussed rather freely, in consequence of the opening on these days of the Pedestal Fund Loan Exhibition. The National Academy of Design, in whose halls the exhibition was held, protested, and the Sunday Closing League threatened to appeal to the law. The managers of the exhibition were not, however, molested. As a demonstration in favor of more liberal ideas, the Thos. B. Clarke exhibition, for the benefit of the Academy Prize Fund, was also opened Sundays. The practice in this matter is far from being uniform throughout the country. While the Museum of Fine Arts, in Boston, and the Pennsylvania Academy and the Pennsylvania Museum, in Philadelphia, have for some time past admitted the public on Sundays, the art institutions of New York, with the exception of the Society of American Artists at its annual exhibitions, have so far refused to follow the same policy.

An event of social as well as of artistic importance was the art reception given to gentlemen by Mr. Wm. H. Vanderbilt, on December 20, 1883, at his residence on the corner of 51st St. and Fifth Ave., New York. The opening of a second picture gallery, lately built by Mr. Vanderbilt, furnished the occasion for this reception. It need hardly be said that Mr. Vanderbilt's collection of over 200 works by the most celebrated modern European artists is one of the finest in the United States.

The month of November, 1882, which is within the limits of this review, was singularly marked by a number of fires destructive of works of Art. On the morning of the 11th, Mr. Albert Bierstadt's summer residence at Irvington on the Hudson, was burned, with all its contents, among them many works by Mr. Bierstadt and other artists. On the night of the 24th, a fire broke out in the studio of Filippo Donnarumma, fresco-painter, of New York, destroying his large and valuable collection of drawings and paintings, chiefly by Italian masters. At two o'clock the following morning fire was discovered in one of the parlors of the Lotos Club, New York, in which a collection of pictures had been hung for a reception to take place in the evening. Mr. Wm. M. Chase's powerful portrait of Mr. Peter Cooper and a landscape by Mr. W. J. Alexander were completely destroyed, and a number of other works badly damaged.

A successful picture-theft must also be chronicled among the events of the year. Four oil paintings, valued at about $15.000, were stolen from the store of Mr. Thos. A. Wilmurt, No. 54 East 13th Street, New York, where they had been sent for reframing. The paintings are described as a "Mother and Child," by Bouguereau; a "Desdemona," by Cabanel; a "Child at Prayer," by Meyer von Bremen; and a "Flower Girl," by Perrault.

The suit of Gaston L. Feuardent *vs.* Louis P. di Cesnola cannot be left without mention, since upon its decision are dependent a number of questions which are of some importance in connection with the Metropolitan Museum of Art, of New York. As the suit is still pending, it would be manifestly improper to say anything as to its probable issue.*

17. AMERICAN ART IN EUROPE.

The tendency of American art students to go to Europe for the purpose of either revising or completing their education continues, and the custom of exhibiting there is rather on the increase.

In the principal London exhibitions, those of the Royal Academy and at the Grosvenor Gallery, the representation is mostly confined to American artists living in England. Of these latter there were pictures at the Academy by Messrs. Geo. H. Boughton, Mark Fisher, and Ernest Parton, and Mrs. A. L. Merritt. Messrs. F. A. Bridgman and G. P. A. Healy were also contributors. At the Grosvenor were to be seen works by Mrs. A. L. Merritt, and Messrs. Eugene Benson, Geo. H. Boughton, Mark Fisher, W. J. Hennessy. Ernest Parton, and J. M. Whistler. An exhibition of American Water Colors, held in London, in May, 1883, elicited much favorable criticism, but the sales were small, owing, it is said, to the high prices asked. Only three drawings were sold, by Messrs. Blum, Volkmar, and Farrer. An exhibition of American etchings, held at the same time, yielded better financial results. The list of sales published shows the names of Messrs. Bellows, Champney, Farrer, Thos. Moran, Nicoll, Parrish, H. W. Robbins, Satterlee, Van Elten, and T. W. Wood. It may be said in a general way that the efforts of the etchers of America are fully appreciated in England. This is clearly shown by the fact that of the 81 members of the Society of Painter-Etchers, established in London under the presidency of Dr. F. Seymour Haden, and including English, French, Dutch and German artists, 15 are Americans, either by birth or adoption. During the months of September and October, 1884, the Society of American Artists is to hold an exhibition of the work of its members at the Grosvenor Gallery, upon invitation of the managers.

At the Paris Salon, American art is always largely represented and well received, and the past year was not an exception to the rule. Something like 60 works were exhibited by about 45 American artists, not counting the wood engravings, etc., sent in. Many of these were seen here after the close of the Salon, a few before they went there. Some of the more important are grouped together in the following list, with the places where they were shown in America : J. C. Beckwith, "Cordelia" (American Art Gallery, New York, 1884) ; F. M. Boggs, "Place de St. Germain-des-Prés" (N. E. Institute, Boston) ; F. A. Bridgman, "La Cigale" (American Art Gallery ; preliminary sketch at the Academy) ; G. W. Chambers, "Shepherdess" (Penns. Academy) ; Wm. M. Chase, "Young Girl Reading" (Society of American Artists) ; C. H. Davis, "The End of the Village" (Penns. Academy) ; Miss Sarah Dodson, "The Bacidæ" (Penns. Academy) ; G. R. Donoho, "Mauvaises Herbes," and "Springtime" (Penns. Academy) ; G. W. Edwards, "Return from Fishing" (N. E. Institute, Boston) ; Miss E. D. Hale, "Beppo" (Museum of Fine Arts, Boston) ; T. A. Harrison, "Les Amateurs" (Chicago Exposition and Penns. Academy), and "Un Esclave" (Penns. Academy); Miss A. Klumpke, "In the XVI. Century" (Penns. Academy); G. J. Melchers, "Pater

---

* It is well-known, as a matter of course, that the suit has since been decided against the plaintiff on two counts, while on the third the jury disagreed.

Noster" (Cincinnati Exposition and Penns. Academy); G. F. Munn, "Brittany" (Penns. Academy); C. S. Pearce, "Prelude" (Museum of Fine Arts, Boston); H. W. Peirce, "October" (Doll & Richards, Boston, 1884); J. R. Rich, "At Grand Menan" (Art Club, Boston, 1884); E. E. Simmons, "A Market Corner" and "The Winnowers" (Doll & Richards, Boston, 1884); R. Vonnoh, "Portrait of Mr. C." (Penns. Academy, and Art Club, Boston, 1884); J. Alden Weir, "Portrait of his Father" and "Flora" (Society of American Artists); J. M. Whistler, "Portrait of the Artist's Mother" (Society of American Artists, Penns. Academy, Museum of Fine Arts, Boston). Others, not shown here, were: Henry Bacon, "Le Pleinairiste"; F. M. Boggs, "Le Port d' Isigny"; W. M. Chase, "Portrait of Miss Dora Wheeler"; W. T. Dannat, "Aragonese Smuggler"; Miss E. J. Gardner, "The Captive"; D. P. Knight, "Without Dowry": Mrs. A. L. Merrrit, "Portrait of Mr. Lowell"; E. H. May, "Milton dictating to his Daughters"; Henry Mosler, "The Morning of the Wedding"; C. S. Pearce, "Watercarrier," and "The Spinner"; J. S. Sargent, "Portraits of Children." As usual, the appreciation of American art was shown by the award of a number of medals, and the purchase of several pictures by the French government. Third-class medals were given to Messrs. Wm. T. Dannat, Charles Sprague Pearce, and James McNeill Whistler, painters, and to Mr. Robert Hoskin, wood-engraver. The pictures bought by the government were, "The Port of Isigny," by Mr. F. M. Boggs, and "Aragonese Smuggler," by Mr. Wm. T. Dannat.

At the Exposition Nationale, which opened in Paris on Sept. 15, 1883, the following works by American artists were shown: F. M. Boggs, "The Place de la Bastille in 1882"; F. A. Bridgman, "A Boy"; W. T. Dannat, "Aragonese Smuggler"; D. R. Knight, "Sorrow"; Henry Mosler, "The Return," "The Wedding Toilet," and "The Morning of the Wedding."

Special efforts were made to secure an adequate representation of American art at the third International Exhibition, which opened at Munich on July 1, 1883. A committee of artists was formed in New York, for the purpose of collecting desirable works and the necessary funds, which was constituted as follows: President, Chas. H. Miller; Secretary, Robert Koehler (formerly secretary of the American Artists' Club, of Munich, who had come over on a special mission of agitation in the interest of American art at the exhibition); Treasurer, J. C. Beckwith: and Walter Shirlaw, Wm. M. Chase, B. F. Reinhart, Geo. H. Yewell, Edw. Moran, Kruseman Van Elten, and F. D. Millet. This committee succeeded in bringing together 68 original works, mostly oil paintings, by 53 artists, and a large collection of black-and-whites, wood-engravings, etchings, etc., all of which were exhibited at the American Art Gallery, New York, from May 18 to 23, 1883, previous to being shipped to Munich. Some dissatisfaction with the character of the collection was expressed in New York, and some of the rejections of the committee aroused ill-feeling, although the works selected represented a wide range of tendency, and were in no way limited to any one school. Moreover, its numbers were largely swelled and its variety increased by contributions sent directly to the exhibition by artists living in Munich, Paris, London, etc. The material advantages accruing from the exhibition to American artists do not seem to have been great, but it brought them some honors, in the shape of second-class medals to Messrs. E. A. Abbey, Wm. M. Chase, and Toby Rosenthal, painters, and Mr. Frederick Juengling, wood-engraver.

At the Amsterdam Exhibition a medal was awarded to Mr. Kruseman Van Elten, for etchings.

The position which the wood-engravers, and next to them the etchers of the United States, have made for themselves, was best shown by the circular announcing the International Special Exhibition of the Graphic Arts, held at Vienna from September 15 to November 1, 1883. According to this circular, the exhibition was to afford a complete survey of the development of the reproductive arts in the second half of the Nineteenth century "in all the artistic States of Europe, and in the United States of North America." Invitations were sent to most of the etchers, wood and other engravers personally, and the result was a tolerably complete representation of these branches at the Austrian capital. The American contributions attracted considerable attention, but the only awards which went to the United States were three diplomas, given respectively to the New York Etching Club, Mr. George Barrie, publisher, of Philadelphia, and Messrs. L. Prang & Co., chromo-lithographers, of Boston. As only fifteen medals were awarded, for which all the artists of France, Germany, and England competed, this result is natural enough. An extensive work, in the nature of a report on the exhibition, is now in preparation, and to this the engravers and etchers of the United States have been earnestly requested to contribute.

18. NECROLOGY.

BACON, GEO. C., painter, died at Malden, Mass., December 27, 1883, aged twenty-eight years. Mr. Bacon was a natural genius, especially in wall decoration, and many of the finest houses in Boston and its vicinity, according to a notice in the Boston *Advertiser*, bear evidence of his skill in this branch of art.

BAILLY, JOSEPH A., sculptor, died at his residence in Philadelphia, June 15, 1883. He was born in France, but the greater part of his life was spent in the United States. Mr. Bailly's best known work is the statue of Washington, in front of Independence Hall, Philadelphia, which was paid for by the contributions of the school children of the city. Among his other works may be named a colossal statue of Witherspoon, for Fairmount Park, Philadelphia, and an equestrian statue of President Blanco, of Venezuela. For some time previous to his death, Mr. Bailly was employed in Washington.

BAKER, JAMES, glass painter, died in New York, October 18, 1883, at the age of sixty years. Mr. Baker was a native of England, and came to the United States in 1868. He was well and favorably known in his specialty, and much of its present development in this country is due to him, as he was one of the first here to improve the manufacture of glass for artistic purposes. A somewhat more extended notice of his career may be found in the *American Architect*, of November 3, 1883.

BELLOWS, ALBERT F., N.A., painter and etcher, died at his family residence at Auburndale, near Boston, on November 24, 1883. Mr. Bellows was born in Milford, Mass., in 1830, of a family, one of whose ancestors sailed from England in 1635, and was among the earliest settlers of what is now the State of Massachusetts. At the age of eighteen he was placed with a lithographer in Boston, but he soon laid aside the crayon for brush and colors, until, guided by the advice of relatives, he entered the office of an architect, with whom he remained for three years. The passion for painting again, however, proving too strong, he went to Paris, after he had spent some time in teaching, and thence to Antwerp, where he became a pupil of the Royal Academy. Upon his return to America he established himself in New York, and devoted his attention to painting subjects combining the figure with landscape. In 1867 he again went to Europe, and spent sixteen months in England, studying principally its picturesque rural scenery, which had a great charm to him. During his stay he made the acquaintance of many of the leading water-color painters, and the study of their methods gave a perceptible English flavor to his works for the rest of his life. From England he extended his travels to Germany and Switzerland, first visiting again Belgium and France, studying diligently wherever he happened to be, and filling his portfolios with large numbers of sketches. Mr. Bellows was a regular exhibitor at the National Academy and at the exhibitions of the American Water Color Society. He also contributed frequently to the Dudley Gallery in London, and to the annual exhibitions of the Société Royale des Aquarellistes, of Belgium, of which he was an honorary member. His forte lay decidedly in landscape, especially in water colors, although he painted also quite a number of figure pieces, some of them the size of life. There is probably no American artist whose works have been so widely disseminated as those of Mr. Bellows, through engravings and etchings. As an etcher he was quite prolific, and as popular as in his paintings. Those who had the pleasure of knowing him will never forget his kindly and urbane manners, and they will think with admiration of the heroic fortitude with which he struggled against the terrible disease, cancer, that gnawed away his life. Mr. Bellows was elected a National Academician in 1861. He was also a member of the American Water Color Society, the New York Etching Club, the Philadelphia Society of Etchers, and the Society of Painter-Etchers of London. The biographical details here given are from memoranda in Mr. Bellows's own handwriting.

BISPHAM, HENRY C., animal painter, died at Rome, Italy, December 22, 1882. He was born in Philadelphia in 1841, studied there under Wm. T. Richards, and later in Paris. Owing to sickness, which for years kept him in constant pain, he was compelled to exile himself, as the climate of his native country did not agree with him. An appreciative, although critical notice of his work, with a mention of some of his most important pictures, from the pen of Mrs. Schuyler Van Rensselaer, appeared in *The Studio* of February 10, 1883.

BOYD, CLARENCE, a young painter of Louisville, Ky., was shot in that city by his brother-in-law, Dr. Barnes, on June 6, and died, June 8, 1883. Mr. Boyd was a man of great promise, and repeatedly exhibited figure pieces, many of them in illustration of Shakespeare, at the National Academy, New York, and the Pennsylvania Academy, Philadelphia. He was for some time in charge of the life class maintained by the Polytechnic Society of Kentucky.

BRISCOE, DANIEL, engraver, died at his residence, 801 East Sixth Street, South Boston, Mass., October 27, 1883, at the age of fifty-seven years.

BURLEIGH, CHARLES C., painter, died in Germany, about the beginning of the year 1883, of heart disease. He was a native of Northampton, Mass., and a son of the late C. C. Burleigh, the well-known anti-slavery advocate. His portraits attracted considerable attention for their beauty of color, more especially at the exhibitions of the Pennsylvania Academy, to which he was a frequent contributor. He was also a good copyist, and reproduced a number of important paintings for Cornell University, Ithaca, N. Y., on an order given to him by President White of that institution.

DITMARS, WILLIAM B., architect, committed suicide by hanging, at his residence, 224 Quincy Street, Brooklyn, on November 1, 1883. He was about fifty years old, and had lived the greater part of his life in Brooklyn.

ELLIOTT, CHARLES WYLLYS, died at Guilford, Conn., August 20, 1883. Some years ago he delivered a course of lectures before the Lowell Institute, Boston, on "Household Art and Life in the Middle Ages." He also published a book entitled "American Interiors," which contained photographs of some of the most elegant libraries of the residences in the Back Bay district of Boston. The article on " Pottery and Porcelain," in the catalogue of the Museum of Fine Arts, Boston, is also signed with the initials of his name.

FERNBACH, HENRY, architect, died suddenly in his office, in New York, on November 12, 1883. Mr. Fernbach was born in Breslau, Germany, in 1828, graduated at the Building Academy in Berlin, and came to the United States in 1855. Among the buildings which he erected are named the Germania Savings Bank, the *Staats Zeitung* building, and the Hebrew Orphan Asylum on 77th Street, New York. He was a member of the American Institute of Architects. For a somewhat more extended notice. the reader is referred to the *American Architect* of November 24, 1883.

GÖRTELMEYER, FREDERICK, painter, a pupil of Gérôme and Carolus Durand, died in New York, December 26, 1882, at the age of thirty-five years.

JUMP, EDWARD, caricaturist, shot himself, in Chicago, in April, 1883. A letter by Mr. Frank Bellew, published in the New York *Tribune* of May 14, 1883, gives many of the details of his roving life.

LE CLEAR, THOMAS, N.A., portrait painter, died at Rutherford Park, N. J., November 26, 1882, after a short illness. He was born in Owego, N. Y., in 1818, and seems to have been entirely without instruction. His artistic career began very early, as he is reported to have sold ideal heads of his own painting to his parents' neighbors when he was only nine years old. Three years later he executed a picture of St. Matthew which pleased people so well that he had to make several copies of it. After roving about the country for some time, he took a studio in New York, and was elected a National Academician in 1863. Although known more exclusively as a portrait painter, Mr. Le Clear nevertheless executed also a few genre pictures, more especially in his younger days. Among his sitters were Edwin Booth (as Hamlet), Sanford R. Gifford and Jervis McEntee, the artists, President Fillmore, Dr. Vinton, Bayard Taylor, Parke Godwin, George Bancroft, and many other people of distinction. Portraits of General Grant and President Arthur were in his studio at the time of his death.

LE FEVRE, W. J., painter and etcher, died at his home in Dover, N. J., September 6th, 1883. after a long illness. Mr. Le Fevre was a member of the Philadelphia Society of Etchers. He occupied a studio in Philadelphia for some time before his death.

MILLS, CLARK, sculptor, died of heart disease, at Washington, D. C., January 12, 1883. He was born in the State of New York, in the year 1815. The story of his life, and of the equestrian statues of Jackson and of Washington. which are his principal works, has been told so often that it is not necessary to repeat it here.

MILMORE, MARTIN, sculptor, died at his residence, No. 113 Hammond street, Boston, July 21, 1883, of congestion of the liver. According to notices published during Mr. Milmore's lifetime, he was born in Boston, in 1845. The obituary notices published in the Boston papers give county Sligo, Ireland, as the place, and September 14, 1844, as the date of birth, and state that the family did not emigrate to Boston until 1851. Young Milmore gave early evidences of artistic talent while he was employed as an office boy, and he advanced rapidly in his profession after he had entered the studio of Thomas Ball, in 1860. At the age of twenty he had already attracted the attention of Mr. Turner Sargent, who commissioned him to execute the granite figures of Ceres, Flora, and Pomona, which decorate the façade of Horticultural Hall, Boston. His most ambitious works are the Soldiers' Monument, in Forest Hills Cemetery,

Boston, and the Soldiers' and Sailors' Monument, on Boston Common, dedicated September 17, 1877. Both these monuments are above the average of the many similar works scattered all over the country, although neither of them has escaped criticism. Perhaps the most satisfactory achievements of Mr. Milmore's chisel are to be found in a series of characteristic portrait busts executed in his earlier years, and including such celebrated subjects as Charles Sumner, Wendell Phillips, George Ticknor (in the Boston Public Library), Ralph Waldo Emerson, etc. Of his ideal works, a bust entitled "Miranda," met with special success. Mr. Milmore visited Italy twice.

NORCOTT, REUBEN H., portrait painter and caricaturist, committed suicide by drowning, at Clifton, Staten Island, N. Y., June 25, 1883. He was thirty years old, and about a year before his death came from Louisville, Ky., to New York, where he lived at No. 127 Charlton Street. He was gifted with a faculty for caricature likenesses, and made sketches also of public gatherings, etc., for the illustrated papers. The probable cause of his suicide was illness.

ORMSBY, WATERMAN L., engraver, died in Brooklyn, N. Y., on November 2, 1883, at the age of seventy-four years. He was chiefly known as a bank note engraver, and one of the founders of the Continental Bank Note Company, of New York. His largest work, done many years ago, was a reproduction of Durand's "Signing of the Declaration of Independence," after Trumbull. The result was obtained by transferring an impression to his plate, and following the lines of the original.

PLATT, JAMES C., portrait, landscape, and still-life painter, died at Brooklyn, N. Y., December 24, 1882.

SEARLE, HENRY ROBINSON, a well-known architect, died at New York, October 22, 1882, at the age of forty-six years.

SLADE, J. MORGAN, a young architect of New York, of growing reputation, died suddenly in the first week of December, 1882.

STEPHENS, HENRY LOUIS, painter and illustrator, died at Bayonne, N. J., December 13, 1882. He was born at Philadelphia, February 11, 1824, and studied at the Academy in his native city. He was best known as an illustrator of humorous books and children's tales, although his water-colors are said also to have shown considerable merit. Many will remember him as the principal caricaturist of *Vanity Fair*, a comic paper published in New York about twenty years ago.

TRAUTWINE, JOHN C., architect and engineer, of Philadelphia, died in September, 1883. For a more extended notice of his life and works, see the *American Architect* of September 29, 1883.

WALTERS, Miss M. JOSEPHINE, landscape painter, of Hohokus, N. J., died at Brooklyn, L. I., in the latter part of the year 1883. She studied under A. B. Durand, and was a contributor to the exhibitions of the National Academy and the American Water Color Society.

WRIGHT, JAMES H., portrait, fruit, and still-life painter, died in Brooklyn, N. Y., in May, 1883, at the age of seventy years. He occupied a studio in New York for many years, and was an exhibitor at the National Academy up to 1871.

STATISTICAL TABLE

OF EXHIBITIONS.

Note.—The List of Exhibitions to come is omitted, as the dates are not yet fixed. The regular exhibitions always recur about the same time, and the following Statistical Table is, therefore, a sufficient guide to intending exhibitors.

	YEAR.	OPENING AND CLOSING DAYS.	CITY.	EXHIBITION.	NO. OF ARTISTS EXHIBITING.	NO. OF WORKS EXHIBITED.
1	1882.	Sept. 5 Oct. 21	Louisville........	Industrial Exposition.............	196	333
2	"	" 5 " 21	Milwaukee......	Industrial Exposition, 2d.........	161	358
3	"	" 6 " 7	Cincinnati........	Industrial Exposition.............	262	465
4	"	" 6 Nov. 18	Boston....	N. E. Mfc's and Mech's Institute...	352	680
5	"	" 18 " 23	Chicago.........	Industrial Exposition, 10th.......	199	329
6	"	Oct. 23 " 18	New York	National Academy................	316	529
7	"	" 23 Dec. 9	Philadelphia.....	Pennsylvania Academy, 53d..... ...	267	475
8	"	" 25 Oct. 31	Brooklyn........	Brush and Palette Club...........	19	50
9	"	Nov. April	New York........	Metropolitan Museum............	...	...
10	"	" ?	Chicago.........	Illinois Art Association	?	?
11	"	Nov. 4 ?	Philadelphia.. ...	Society of Artists................	?	?
12	"	" 9 ?	New York.......	Studies and Sketches, 1st.........	176	300
13	"	" 22 Dec. 16	Atlanta, Ga	Young Men's Library Association...	?	?
14	"	Dec. 1 " 21	New York......	Black-and-White, 5th............	216	494
15	"	" 5 " 16	Brooklyn........	Art Association, 45th.............	202	303
16	"	" 14 " 19	Boston..........	Paint and Clay Club, 2d..........	22	88
17	"	" 27 Feb. 23	Philadelphia.....	Society of Etchers, 1st...........	45	356
18	"	" 30 Jan. 13	Boston..........	St. Botolph Club................	51	95
19	"	" 30 " 27	Philadelphia.....	Society of Artists, 4th..........	184	376
20	1883.	Jan. 13 ?	Chicago........:.	Art Institute....................	...	...
21	"	" 15 ?	New York........	Boston Artists....................	20	95
22	"	" 22 Feb. 3	Brooklyn........	Rembrandt Club..............	...	...
23	"	" 25 " 17	Boston..........	Art Club, 27th.................	120	173
24	"	" 29 " 25	New York.......	American Water Color Society, 16th.	264	605
25	"	" 29 " 25	New York.......	New York Etching Club..........	69	195
26	"	Feb. 3 ?	Springfield, Mass.	Gill's Sixth Annual.............	67	100
27	"	" 5 Feb. 6	New York.......	Artists' Fund, 23d..............	64	110
28	"	" 12 " 23	"	Art Club, 1st....	49	101
29	"	" 19 " 24	Jackson, Ill	Art Association, 9th.............	?	?
30	"	" 23	Providence......	Brooklyn Brush and Palette Club....	16	55
31	"	Mch. 12 April 1	Chicago.........	Chicago Art League........	?	?
32	"	" 14 Mch. 24	Brooklyn........	Art Association, 46th...........	189	405
33	"	" 14 April 14	Providence......	Art Club, 4th Annual...........	65	115
34	"	" 26 " 28	New York........	Society of American Artists, 6th.....	113	148
35	"	" 27	Brooklyn........	Art Club...................	23	45
36	"	" 27 Mch. 31	Malden, Mass....	Middlesex Institute.............		
37	"	April 2 May 12	New York.......	National Academy, 58th..........	450	746
38	"	" 3 April 10	Chicago..... ...	Bohemian Art Club.............	21	162
39	"	" 9 May 12	Philadelphia.....	Society of Artists................	115	300
40	"	" 14 " 12	Boston..........	Art Club, 23th.................	145	247
41	"	" 24 ?	San Francisco....	Art Association, 9th.............	73	145
42	"	" ? ?	Boston..........	Boston Etching Club...........	8	40
43	"	May Oct.	New York.......	Metropolitan Museum............	...	...
44	"	" . ?	Denver, Col......	Academy of Colorado.............	28	76
45	"	" " ?	Charleston, S. C...	Carolina Art Association..........	95	146
46	"	" 3 ?	Chicago.........	Illinois Art Association..........	...	...

34

OF EXHIBITIONS,

given, in most cases, at catalogue prices.)

NO. OF WORKS SOLD.	VALUE OF WORKS SOLD.		EXPLANATORY REMARKS.	
?	?		....	1
54	$10,885	..	Paintings only given; 59 etchings, etc., sold for $987.00..............	2
22	5,000	..	....	3
12	2,020	..	....	4
54	19,296	60	....	5
96	18,850	..	Special Autumn Exhibition	6
26	6,836	50	....	7
48	1,931	..	Auction Sale...	8
..	......	..	Loan Collection..	9
?	5,700	..	First Annual Exhibition of Paintings.......................	10
?	?		First Sketch Exhibition....................................	11
60	4,200		American Art Association...................................	12
5	1,528		Miscellaneous Loan Exhibition..............................	13
97	5,965		Salmagundi Sketch Club....................................	14
58	14,550		American Oil Paintings.....................................	15
?	?		Limited to Members..	16
?	831		American only given. Foreign Etchings also shown..........	17
..	......		Loan Exhibition of Foreign Pictures........................	18
28	7,790		Oil Paintings only, and a few pieces of Sculpture..........	19
..	......		First Annual Loan Exhibition. Foreign and American Pictures.......	20
6	?		Held at American Art Gallery..............................	21
..	......	..	Miscellaneous Loan Exhibition for benefit of Sheltering Arms Nursery.	22
15	3,380	..	Oil Paintings..	23
150	19,248	..	....	24
179	2,202	50	Foreign Etchings included..................................	25
26	10,725	..	American Paintings...	26
109	12,815	..	Auction Sale. Frames not included.........................	27
2	?		Limited to Members	28
?	?		Miscellaneous Exhibition...................................	29
51	1,734	50	Auction Sale...	30
?	?		Catalogue not obtainable...................................	31
43	5,690		Water Colors and Etchings..................................	32
?	?		Oils and Water Colors......................................	33
9	3,400	..	Exhibited later at Museum of Fine Arts, Boston.............	34
45	2,576	..	Auction Sale...	35
..	......		Miscellaneous Loan Exhibition	36
126	41,039	..	....	37
16	667	..	Ladies' work only..	38
28	1,870	..	Second Annual Water Color Exhibition......................	39
34	1,715	..	Water Colors and Black-and-Whites.........................	40
?	?		....	41
..	......		Held at J. Eastman Chase's Gallery........................	42
..	......		Loan Exhibition..	43
?	?		....	44
13	3,500	..	....	45
125	2,200	..	Black-and-White, including engravings, ancient and modern..........	46

35

YEAR.	OPENING AND CLOSING DAYS.	CITY.	EXHIBITION.	NO. OF ARTISTS EXHIBITING.	NO. OF WORKS EXHIBITED.
47	1883. May 7 June 3	Boston	Museum of Fine Arts	113	148
48	" " 18 May 23	New York	Contributions to Munich Exhibition	53	68
49	" " 21 " 26	Rochester	Art Club, 4th	77	211
50	" " 25 ?	Salem, Mass	Essex Institute, 7th	...	...
51	" June 1 ?	Buffalo	American Art Union	97	140
52	" " 15 Sept. 15	Saratoga	Mt. McGregor Art Association	109	155
53	" " 25 July 10	Syracuse, N. Y.	Esthetic Society	...	...
54	" " ? ?	Springfield, Mass.	Gill's Loan Exhibition	41	90
55	" July 17 Sept. 30	Denver	Min. and Industrial Exposition	72	194
56	" Aug. 1 Nov. 10	Louisville	American Art Union	97	144
57	" Sept. 1 Oct. ?	Detroit	Detroit Art Loan	...	...
58	" " 3 Jan. 12.	Boston	Foreign Exhibition	...	...
59	" " 5 Oct. 6	Cincinnati	Industrial Exposition	239	441
60	" " 5 " 20	Chicago	Industrial Exposition, 11th	293	502
61	" " 5 Nov. 3	Boston	N. E. Mfc's and Mech's Institute	432	731
62	" " 6 Oct. 20	Milwaukee	Industrial Exposition	159	290
63	" Oct. 4 " 14	Portland, Me	Society of Art	...	...
64	" " 10 " 25	Providence	Art Club	56	110
65	" " 16 Nov. 27	Boston	Museum of Fine Arts	139	236
66	" " 19 ?	New York	Sketches and Studies, 2d	237	363
67	" " 22 Nov. 17	New York	National Academy	236	357
68	" " 23 " 23	Atlanta, Ga.	Young Men's Library Association	?	?
69	" " 29 Dec. 8	Philadelphia	Pennsylvania Academy, 54th	315	518
70	" Nov. April	New York	Metropolitan Museum	...	...
71	" " 7 Nov. 28	Newark, N. J.	Essex Art Association	...	...
72	" " 7 " 30	Indianapolis	Art Association	...	...
73	" " 8 ?	Chicago	Illinois Art Association	96	135
74	" " 15 Nov. 30	Portland, Me	Society of Art	95	229
75	" " 20 Jan. 2.	Minneapolis, Min.	Society of Fine Arts	...	...
76	" " 27	Brooklyn	Art Club	20	57
77	" " 27 Dec. 8 "	Art Association, 47th	177	250
78	" " ? ?	Philadelphia	Society of Artists	210	519
79	" Dec. 1 Dec. 21	New York	Black-and-White, 6th	155	281
80	" " 3 Jan. 1	New York	Pedestal Fund Art Loan	...	...
81	" " 6 Dec. 21	Providence	Art Club	68	138
82	" " 17 " 29	Springfield, Mass.	Art Association	40	48
83	" " 28 Jan. 13	New York	Thos. B. Clarke Loan	116	140
84	" " ? ?	Boston	St. Botolph Club	22	53

SEPTEMBER, 5, 1882, TO DECEMBER 31, 1883.

given, in most cases, at catalogue prices.)

NO. OF WORKS SOLD.	VALUE OF WORKS SOLD.		EXPLANATORY REMARKS.	
....			Exhibition of Society of American Artists, transferred from New York.	47
....			Paintings only given; included also 77 Black-and-Whites........ ...	48
?	?		....	49
?	$ 224	50	Miscellaneous Exhibition of Local Art...	50
2	525	..	Held as the Annual Exhibition of the Buffalo Fine Arts Academy.....	51
14	9.700		....	52
....		..	Loan Exhibition. Old Paintings. Also Engravings, etc., after Raphael.	53
....		..	American pictures owned in Springfield...........................	54
?	?	..	Oils and Water Colors only given. Studies, bric-à-brac, etc., besides..	55
35	15,400	..	As part of Southern Exposition. Loan Exhibition besides..........	56
203	20,000	..	Sales include 87 paintings, 79 prints, 37 miscellaneous articles.......	57
?	?	..	Foreign industrial products, paintings, statuary, etc.................	58
28	4,141	50	In addition, about $75 worth of etchings were sold...............	59
36	17,835		....	60
12	3,350	..	....	61
54	14,394	25	Oils and Water Colors only given. Black-and-Whites besides........	62
..	......	..	Special exhibition of portrait engravings...........................	63
?	?	..	Work of local artists........................	64
13	1,795	..	Contemporaneous American Art....................................	65
27	1,370	..	American Art Association..	66
55	12,078	..	Second Special Autumn Exhibition	67
2	50	..	Miscellaneous Loan Exhibition, 2d..........................	68
10	3,815	..	....	69
....		..	Loan Exhibition...	70
20	2,000	..	Miscellaneous Loan Exhibition....................	71
8	850	..	Miscellaneous Loan Exhibition....................................	72
?	3,946		Oils and Water Colors, foreign and American.....................	73
?	?	..	Sixth Exhibition of Local Art...................................	74
5	1,050	..	Miscellaneous Loan Exhibition...................................	75
56	1,681	50	Auction sale, frames not included...............................	76
20	4,000	..	American Oil Paintings...	77
25	800	..	Second Exhibition of Sketches and Studies......................	78
30	1,500	..	Salmagundi Sketch Club...	79
. .|......		..	Foreign pictures, decorative art, etc............................	80
?	?		Water Colors	81
?	?		Oil Paintings, mostly American..................................	82
...|......			American Paintings, exhibited for benefit of Academy Prize Fund......	83
?	?		American Paintings..	84

ETCHINGS AND ENGRAVINGS,

Published in the United States from October, 1882, to December 31, 1883.*

American Art Union, 44 East 14th Street, New York.

THE REPRIMAND.—Etched by Walter Shirlaw, after Eastman Johnson. (Issued to subscribers only.)

Cassell and Company, Limited, 739 and 741 Broadway, New York.

ORIGINAL ETCHINGS BY AMERICAN ARTISTS.—Twenty etchings by Henry Farrer ; T. W. Wood, V.P.N. A. ; Stephen Parrish ; Thos. Moran, A.N.A. ; Joseph Pennell ; F. S. Church, A.N.A.; Geo. H. Smillie, N.A.; Mrs. M. Nimmo Moran ; J. Foxcroft Cole ; Chas. A. Platt ; I. M. Gaugengigl ; K. Van Elten, N.A. ; Peter Moran ; Sam'l Colman, N.A.; F. Dielman, N. A.; R. Swain Gifford, N.A.; M. F. H. de Haas, N.A.; Jas. D. Smillie, N.A. ; J. C. Nicoll, N.A. ; and J. A. S. Monks. Introduction and text by S. R. Koehler. Parchment edition, 3 copies, $300 (sold); Edition de Luxe, signed proofs on Japan paper, $125 ; Regular edition, $20.

EVENING BY THE RIVER.—Etched by Henry Farrer, size (of etched surface), 12 x 18, printed on plate paper, 19 x 25 inches. (Issued only to subscribers to the MAGAZINE OF ART for 1884.)

J. Eastman Chase, 7 Hamilton Place, Boston.

GLOUCESTER HARBOR.—Etched by Stephen Parrish, after Wm. M. Hunt, 13 x 19 inches, Remarque proofs, on parchment, $30 ; Artist's proofs, on Japan paper, $15.

SAXON.—Original wood engraving by Wm. B. Closson. Signed proofs, $5.

Houghton, Mifflin and Co., 4 Park Street, Boston.

HAWTHORNE PORTFOLIO.—Containing copies of the etchings made for the *édition de luxe* of Hawthorne's works, including portrait. Boston, 1883. $15.

F. Keppel, 23 East 16th Street, New York.

LOW TIDE, BAY OF FUNDY.—FISHERMEN'S HOUSES, CAPE ANN. —Two original etchings by Stephen Parrish.

PORTRAIT OF LONGFELLOW.—Engraved by Chas. Burt, from a photograph.

---

* The above list, being made up principally from advertisements and other public announcements, must necessarily be quite incomplete. Of the many etchings put upon the market by the artists themselves, it gives no account whatever. A partial list of these etchings is supplied by the catalogues of the exhibitions of the New York Etching Club. Art publishers will confer a great favor upon the editor by sending to his address all announcements of publications of this kind. Only those plates are included which are either by American etchers and engravers, or from originals by American artists. Periodical publications containing etchings will be found in the list of journals.

C. Klackner, 17 East 17th Street, New York.

INLET.—MILLSTREAM.—Two original etchings by A. F. Bellows.

A GLIMPSE OF THE LAKE.—Original etching by Kruseman Van Elten.

UNCLE NED AND I.—Engraved by J. N. J. Wilcox, after T. W. Wood.

DREAMLAND.—Etched by S. J. Ferris, after C. D. Weldon.

INSPIRATION.—Etched by S. J. Ferris, after G. Doyen.

VENICE.—Etched by Stephen Parrish, after W. H. Brown.

FAR AWAY.—Engraved by F. Girsch, after J. G. Brown.

IN CLOVER.—Engraved by H. S. Beckwith, after J. Carleton Wiggins.

ST. OUEN CATHEDRAL PORCH.—ABBEVILLE.—Two etchings by John T. Bentley, after T. C. Dibdin.

John A. Lowell and Co., 70 Kilby Street, Boston.

THE BATHERS.—Engraved by S. A. Schoff, after Wm. M. Hunt.

New York Etching Club, J. C. Nicoll, Sec., 51 West 10th Street, New York.

Catalogue of the New York Etching Club Exhibition. Illustrated with etchings by W. M. Chase, F. S. Church, R. Swain Gifford, Thos. Moran, J. C. Nicoll, Joseph Pennell, C. A. Platt, Walter Shirlaw, T. W. Wood. New York, 1883, 4to, $1.

Philadelphia Society of Etchers, J. Neely, Jr., Sec., 617 Market Street, Philadelphia.

Catalogue of the First Annual Exhibition of the Philadelphia Society of Etchers. Illustrated with etchings by F. S. Church, P. Moran, J. Simpson, H. Farrer, S. J. Ferris, T. Moran, J. Pennell, B. Uhle. Phil., 1882, 4to, $1.

The Studio Company, 59 Cortlandt Street, New York.

ETCHINGS OF THE SAN FRANCISCAN MISSIONS OF CALIFOR-NIA.—Twenty-four etchings by Henry Chapman Ford. Mounted, 17 x 22 inches. With letterpress, in portfolio. 50 copies, etchings on Japan paper, $100 ; 250 copies on fine paper. $75.

H. Wunderlich and Co., 868 Broadway, New York.

AUTUMN.—Original etching by Henry Farrer.

OLD MILL.—ANNAPOLIS RIVER.—A PROVINCIAL FISHING VIL-LAGE.—Three original etchings by Chas. A. Platt.

IN CLOVER.—SOLITUDE.—ON THE EAST RIVER.—SUNSET ON THE MARNE.—Four original dry points by C. A. Vanderhoof.

HIGH TIDE, SHREWSBURY RIVER.—Original etching, with dry pointing. by C. A. Vanderhoof.

BOOKS

On Art and Archæology, Industrial and Decorative Art and Related Subjects, Published in the United States from October, 1882, to December 31, 1883.*

AMERICAN COTTAGES.—New York, W. T. Comstock [1883]. 4 pp. 44 plates, Folio, cloth, $5.

ANNUAL REPORT of the Supervising Architect of the Secretary of the Treasury for the year ending September 30, 1882. Washington, Government Printing Office, 1882. 45 pp. Illustrated, 8vo.—Same for 1883. 55 pp., illustrated, 8vo.

ARCHÆOLOGICAL INSTITUTE OF AMERICA.—Regulations, Officers, and List of Members. Boston, A. Mudge & Son, Printers, 1883. 14 pp. 8vo.

ARCHÆOLOGICAL INSTITUTE OF AMERICA.—Bulletin I., January, 1883. Boston, A. Williams & Co. Illustrated, 40 pp. 8vo.

ARCHÆOLOGICAL INSTITUTE OF AMERICA.—Fourth Annual Repor: of the Executive Committee, and Second Annual Report of the Committee on the American School of Classical Studies at Athens, 1882-3. Presented at the Annual Meeting of the Institute. Boston, May 19, 1883. Cambridge, John Wilson & Son, University Press, 1883. 56 pp. 8vo.

ARCHÆOLOGICAL INSTITUTE OF AMERICA.—Bulletin of the School of Classical Studies at Athens. I. Report of Wm. W. Goodwin, Professor in Harvard College, Director of the School in 1882-1883. Boston, Cupples, Upham & Co., 1883. 29 pp. 8vo.

ARMITAGE, E.—Lectures on Painting delivered to the students of the Royal Academy. New York, G. P. Putnam's Sons, 1883. Illustrated, 8vo, cloth, $1.75.

ASHENHURST, T. R.—Design in Textile Fabrics. New York, Cassell & Co., 1883. 6+248 pp., 10 colored plates and 106 diagrams, 16mo. (Manuals of Technology, edited by Prof. Ayrton and R. Wormell), cloth, $2.

BACON, II.—Parisian Art and Artists. Boston, James R. Osgood & Co., 1883 [1882]. 3+239 pp. illustrated, square 12mo, cloth, $3.

BAKER, Lucas.—The Theory of Design. New York, Ivison, Blakeman, Taylor & Co., 1883. 248 pp. illustrated, 12mo, cloth, $1.25.

BAKER, Lucas.—The Science and Art of Model and Object-Drawing. New York, Ivison, Blakeman, Taylor & Co., 1883. 102 pp., illustrated, 12mo. cloth, 85 cents.

BENJAMIN, S. G. W.—A Group of Etchers ; with text. New York, Dodd, Mead & Co. [1882], no paging, illustrated, folio, cloth, $15.

BENSON, Eugene.—Art and Nature in Italy. Boston, Roberts Bros., 1882. 188 pp. square 16mo, cloth, $1.

---

* Contrary to the policy adopted in last year's issue, this list contains not only the original works and the actual reprints of foreign books issued by American publishers, but also the imported publications with American imprints on the title page, or put upon the market by publishers having branches in the United States.

40

BISHOP, Rev. H. H.—Pictorial Architecture of the British Isles. New York, E. & J. B. Young & Co. [1883]. 3+114 pp. illustrated, oblong 8vo, cloth, $1.20.

BOOT, W. H. J.—Trees and How to Paint Them in Water Colors: with 18 colored plates and numerous wood engravings. New York, Cassell & Co., 1883. 24 pp. and colored plates, oblong 12mo, cloth, $2.50.

BOYD, E. W., *comp.*—English Cathedrals, their Architecture, Symbolism, and History. New York, T. Whittaker. 1884 [1883]. 63 pp. illustrated, square 24mo, boards, 60 cents.

BRYANT, W. M.—Philosophy of Landscape Painting. St. Louis, St. Louis News Co., 1882. 8 +282 pp. 12mo, cloth, $1.50.

BURNHAM, S. M.—History and Uses of Limestones and Marbles ; with 48 chromo-lithograph illustrations of antique and modern marbles. Boston, S. E. Cassino & Co., 1883. 410 pp. 8vo, cloth, $6.

BUXTON, H. J. Wilmot.—English Painters: with a chapter on American Painters by S. R. Koehler. New York, Scribner & Welford, 1883. Illustrated, 12mo. (Illustrated Art Hand-books), cloth, $2.

CAINE, T. Hale.—Recollections of Dante Gabriel Rossetti. Boston, Roberts Bros., 1882. 297 pp. 8vo, cloth, $3.

CALDECOTT, R.—A Sketch-Book of R. Caldecott's ; Reproduced by Edmund Evans, the Engraver and Printer. New York, G. Routledge & Sons [1883]. No paging, illustrated, oblong 16mo, cloth, $1.50.

CAMERON, K.—Plasterer's Manual. *Revised edition.* New York, W. T. Comstock, 1883. 67 pp. illustrated, 16mo, cloth, 75 cents.

CARR, Lucien.—The Mounds of the Mississippi Valley Historically Considered. Cincinnati, Robt. Clarke & Co., 1883. 107 pp. 4to, paper, $1.50.

CARR, Lucien, and Shaler, N. S.—On the Pre-Historic Remains of Kentucky. Cincinnati, Robt. Clarke & Co., 1883. 31 pp. 7 plates, 4to (Geological Survey of Kentucky), paper, $2.50.

CARTER, *Mrs.* Susan N.—Drawing in Black-and-White ; Charcoal, Pencil, Crayon and Pen-and-Ink. New York, G. P. Putnam's Sons, 1882. 5+55 pp. illustrated, 16mo. (Putnam's Art Hand-books, No. 8), boards, 50 cents.

CASSELL'S Doré Gallery ; containing 250 engravings, selected from the Doré Bible, Milton, Dante's Inferno, Dante's Purgatorio and Paradiso, Atala, La Fontaine, Fairy Realm, Don Quixote, etc.; with memoir of Doré, critical essay and descriptive letter press by Edmund Ollier [*Memorial edition.*] In 50 parts, part 1. New York, Cassell & Co. [1883]. 6 pp., 5 plates, 4to, paper, 25 cents.

[**CATALOGUE** of the Boston Etching Club.] Eight leaves ; title page, five illustrations, two pages lists, all etched. Boston, 1883. 8vo, 75 cents.

CATALOGUE of the First Annual Exhibition of the Philadelphia Society of Etchers. Illustrated with etchings by F. S. Church, P. Moran, J. Simpson, H. Farrer, S. J. Ferris, T. Moran, J. Pennell, B. Uhle. Philadelphia, 1882. 4to, $1.

CATALOGUE of the New York Etching Club Exhibition. Illustrated with etchings by W. M. Chase, F. S. Church, R. Swain Gifford, Thos. Moran, J. C. Nicoll, Joseph Pennell, C. A. Platt, Walter Shirlaw, T. W. Wood. New York, 1883. 4to, $1.

CHAMPNEY, Lizzie W.—John Angelo at the Water Color Exhibition; with illustrations by members of the American Water Color Society. Boston, D. Lothrop & Co. [1883]. No paging, 8vo, cloth, $1.

CHATTOCK, R. S.—Practical Notes on Etching; with 8 illustrations, showing different stages and processes of the art. New York, Scribner & Welford. 1883. 8vo, cloth, $3.

CLARK, T. M.—Building Superintendence. Boston, James R. Osgood & Co., 1883. Illustrated, plans and diagrams, 8vo, $3.

CLEMENT, Clara Erskine.—An Outline History of Painting for Young People and Students; with complete indexes. New York, White, Stokes & Allen, 1883. 7+320 pp., illustrated, 8vo, cloth, $2.50.

COAN, Titus Munson, *Editor.*—Art and Literature. New York, G. P. Putnam's Sons, 1883. 3+ 194 pp., 16mo. (Topics of the Time, No. 6), paper, 25 cents.

CONDIT, C. L.—Painting and Painters' Materials; a book of facts for painters and those who use or deal in paint materials. New York, *The Railroad Gazette*, 73 Broadway, 1883. 485 pp., 16mo, cloth, $2.25.

CRANE, Lucy.—Art and the Formation of Taste; six lectures, with illustrations drawn by T. and Walter Crane). New York, Macmillan, 1883. 292 pp., 12mo, cloth, $2.

DECORATION in Painting, Sculpture, Architecture and Art Manufactures. *New Series.* Volume 5. New York, Scribner & Welford, 1883. Illustrated, 4to, cloth, $3.

DE LEON, Nestor Ponce. Diccionario tecnológico, Inglés-Español y Español-Inglés, de los términos y frases usados en las ciencias aplicadas, artes industriales, bellas artes, mecánica, maquinaria, minas, metalurgia, agricultura, comercio, navegacion, manufacturas, arquitectura, ingenieria civil y militar, marina, arte militar, ferro-carriles, telégrafos, etc. Parts 1 and 2. New York, N. Ponce de Leon, 40 and 42 Broadway, 1883. 48 ; 49–96 pp., 4to, paper, each 50 cents.

DRESSER, Christopher.—Japan; its Architecture, Art and Art Manufactures. New York, Scribner & Welford, 1882. 467 pp., 200 illustrations, 8vo, stamped crash binding, $10.

BU BOIS, H. P.—Historical Essay on the Art of Bookbinding. New York, Bradstreet Press [1883]. 42 pp., 12mo, vellum.

DUNLOP, M. A. Wallace.—Glass in the Old World. New York, Scribner & Welford, 1882. 272 pp., colored plates, 8vo, cloth, $5.

EASTLAKE, C. L.—Notes on the Principal Pictures in the Louvre Gallery at Paris, and in the Brera Gallery at Milan. Boston, Houghton, Mifflin & Co., 1883. 10+322 ; 6+121 pp., illustrated, 4to, cloth, $2.

EBERS, G.—Egypt. Descriptive, Historical and Picturesque; from the German, by Clara Bell; with Introduction and Notes by S. Birch. New York, Cassell & Co. 2 vols., 24+314 ; 22+ 388 pp., illustrated, folio, cloth, $25 ; half and full morocco, $37.25 ; 2 vols. in 1, cloth, $33.25.

ELLIS, Tristram J.—Sketching from Nature; Hand-book for Students and Amateurs; with frontispiece and 10 illustrations by H. Stacy Marks, and 27 sketches by the author. New York, Macmillan, 1883. 10+156 pp., 12mo. (Art at Home Series), cloth, 90 cents.

FLETCHER, Robert, M. D.—Human Proportion in Art and Anthropometry; lecture delivered at National Museum, Washington, D. C. Cambridge, Mass., Moses King, 1883. 37 pp., illustrated, 8vo, paper, 50 cents.

FORD, Henry Chapman.—Etchings [twenty-four] of the San Franciscan Missions of California. Mounted, 17 x 22 inches. With letter press, in portfolio. 50 copies, etchings on Japan paper, $100 ; 250 copies on fine paper, $75.

FREEMAN, J. E.—Gatherings from an Artist's Portfolio in Rome. Boston, Roberts Bros., 1883. 8+357 pp., 12mo, cloth, $1.50.

FRENCH, Harry W.—Gems of Genius : Famous Painters and their Pictures. Boston, Lee & Shepard [1883]. 203 pp., illustrated, 8vo, boards, $2.

FROMENTIN, Eugène.—The Old Masters of Belgium and Holland (*Les maîtres d'autrefois*). Translated by Mrs. Mary C. Robbins. Boston, James R. Osgood & Co., 1882. 9+339 pp, illustrated, square 12mo, cloth, $3.

GARDNER, Percy.—Samos and Samian Coins. New York, Macmillan, 1883. 90 pp., illustrations and plates, 8vo, cloth, $3.

GONSE, M. Louis.—Eugène Fromentin, Painter and Writer ; Translated by Mary Caroline Robbins. Boston, James R. Osgood & Co., 1883. 11 + 280 pp., illustrated, square 8vo, cloth, $3.

HAMERTON, Philip Gilbert.—Etching and Etchers. *New Edition.* Boston, Roberts Bros., 1883. 8vo, cloth, $5.

HAMERTON, Philip Gilbert.—Works. *New edition,* Boston, Roberts Bros., 1882. 10 vols., portrait, 16mo, cloth, $12.50 ; half calf or morocco, $15.

HARTLEY, B.—A Guide to Collodion-etching ; illustrated by the author. N. Y. Industrial Pub. Co., 1882. 48 pp., 6 plates, $1.

HATTON, T.—Hints for Sketching in Water-color from Nature; edited by Susan N. Carter ; from 16*th London edition.* New York, G. P. Putnam's Sons, 1882. 69 pp., 16mo. (Putnam's Art Hand-books, No. 7), boards, 50 cents.

HAWTHORNE. Portfolio : containing copies of the etchings made for the *édition de luxe* of Hawthorne's works, including portrait. Boston, Houghton, Mifflin & Co., 1883. $15.

HEAD, Barclay V.—A Guide to the Gold and Silver Coins of the Ancients, exhibited in electrotype by the American Numismatic and Archæological Society. From the English edition. New York, 1884 [1883. Limited edition, for private circulation]. 12+128 pp., 12mo.

HEATON. M. Compton.—Correggio. New York, Scribner & Welford, 1882. 86 pp., illustrated, 16mo. (The Great Artists' series), cloth, $1.

HILL, F. Stanhope.—Porcelain Painting after the Dresden Method : practical hints for amateurs. New York, Judson Printing Co., 1883. 12mo, paper, 35 cents.

HOW to Build a House : co-operative building plans, containing the most approved designs for villages, cottages, farm-houses and suburban residences. New York, Co-Operative Building Plan Association, 1883. 48 pp., illustrated. Folio, paper, 50 cents.

HOWELLS, W. D.—A Little Girl among the Old Masters : with introduction and comment. Boston, J. R. Osgood & Co., 1884 [1883]. 65 pp., illustrated, oblong 24mo, cloth, $2.

HUNT, W. M.—Talks on Art. *Second Series,* edited by Miss H. M. Knowlton. Boston, Houghton, Mifflin & Co., 1883. 8vo, $1.

JANES, Margaret P.—The Artist's Year: original and selected poems of the months ; illustrated by Arthur Quartley, D. Johnson, J. M. Hart, T. Moran, R. Swain Gifford, G. H. Smillie and others. New York, White & Stokes, 1883 [1882]. 55 pp., oblong 8vo, tied with silk cord, cloth, $4.50 ; vellum, $9.

JEWETT, L., *and* Hall, S. C.—The Stately Homes of England. *New edition.* New York, R. Worthington, 1883. 2 vol., 8vo, cloth, $7.50.

KEMBLE, Marion.—Introductory Lessons in Drawing and Painting in Water-colors : self-instructive. *New edition, revised and enlarged.* Boston, S. W. Tilton & Co., 1883. 94 pp., 12mo, paper, 50 cents.

KITTREDGE, A. O.—The Metal-worker's Pattern-book : a Practical Treatise on the Art and Science of Pattern-cutting as Applied to Sheet-metal work. *Second Edition.* New York, D. Williams, 83 Reade St., 1882. 242 pp., 4to, cloth, $5.

KNOWLTON, Helen M.—Hints for Pupils in Drawing and Painting. *Cheaper edition,* with a frontispiece by the late W. M. Hunt. Boston, Houghton, Mifflin & Co., 1882. 16mo, cloth, $1.

KOEHLER, S. R., *comp.*—The United States Art Directory and Year-book ; a guide for artists, art students, travellers, etc. New York, Cassell & Co., 1882. 6+146 pp., 8vo, paper, 50 cents.

KURTZ, Chas. M., *editor.*—Illustrated Art Notes upon the fifty-eighth annual exhibition of the National Academy of Design, New York. Third year. New York, Cassell & Co., 1883. 84 pp., 90 illustrations, 8vo, paper, 35 cents.

[**LAWRENCE,** Richard Hoe].—Catalogue of the Numismatic Books in the Library of the American Numismatic and Archæological Society. With a subject index to the important articles in the *American Journal of Numismatics* and other periodicals, to the end of 1882. New York, 1883. 31 pp. Large 8vo.

LAWRENCE, Richard Hoe.—Medals by Giovanni Cavino, the Paduan. New York, Privately printed, 1883. 31 pp., illustrated, 8vo.

LEWIS, Florence.—China Painting. New York, Cassell & Co., 1883. 52 pp., cloth, $2.50.

LINTON, W. J.—The History of Wood-engraving in America. Boston, Estes & Lauriat, 1882. Illustrated, 4to, cloth, $7.50.

LLOYDS, F.—Practical Guide to Scene-painting and Painting in Distemper. New York, Jesse Haney & Co., 1883. Illustrated, $1.

LOOMIS, Lafayette C.—The Index Guide to Travel and Art Study in Europe ; a compendium of Geographical, Historical, and Artistic information for the use of Americans ; alphabetically arranged ; with plans and catalogues of the chief Art galleries, tables of routes, maps and 160 illustrations. *New edition* for 1883-4. New York, C. Scribner's Sons, 1883. 16+635 pp., 16mo, leatherette, $3.50.

MANSON, G. J.—Work for Women. New York, G. P. Putnam's Sons, 1883. 5+139 pp., 16mo. (Putnam's Handy-Book Series), boards, 60 cents. [Contains papers on industrial designing.]

MERRIAM, A. C.—The Greek and Latin Inscriptions on the Obelisk-crab in the Metropolitan Museum, New York : a monograph. New York, Harpers, 1883. 3+49 pp., 8vo, paper, 50 cents.

MERRILL, Selah.—A Record of Travel and Observation in the Countries of Moab, Gilead and Bashan, during the years 1875-1877. *New edition.* New York, C. Scribner's Sons, 1883. Illustrations and maps. 8vo. *Reduced* to $2.50.

MEYE, H., and Schmidt, Julius.—The Stone Sculptures of Copán and Quiriguá, drawn by H. Meye ; with Historical and Descriptive Text by Dr. Julius Schmidt ; from the German, by A. D. Savage. New York, Dodd, Mead & Co., 1883. No paging, 20 plates, folio, half morocco, $20.

MEYNELL, Wilfrid, *editor.*—Some Modern Artists and their Work. New York, Cassell & Co., 1883. 7+244 pp., illustrated, 4to, cloth, $5 ; full morocco, $10.

MICHAELIS, Adolf.—Ancient Marbles in Great Britain ; from the German, by C. A. M. Fennell. New York, Macmillan, 1882. 26 + 834 pp., illustrated, 4to, cloth, *net*, $12.

MITCHELL, Lucy M.—A History of Ancient Sculpture ; with numerous illustrations and 6 plates in phototype. New York, Dodd, Mead & Co., 1883. 29 + 766 pp., 4to, cloth, $12.50 ; half morocco, $18 : full morocco, $25.

MINGHETTI, Marco.—The Masters of Raffaelo (Raphael Sanzio) ; translated by Louis Fagan. New York, Scribner & Welford, 1882. 77 pp., 8vo, vellum, $6.

MOLLETT, J. W.—An Illustrated Dictionary of Words used in Art and Archæology, explaining terms frequently used in works on architecture, arms, bronzes, Christian art, color, costume, decoration, devices, emblems, heraldry, lace, personal ornaments, pottery, painting, sculpture, etc. Boston, Houghton, Mifflin & Co., 1882. 4 + 350 pp., about 750 illustrations, small 4to, cloth, $5.

MOLLETT, J. W.—Modern Etchings of Celebrated Paintings. New York, R. Worthington, 1883 [1882]. Illustrated, 4to, cloth, $12.50.

MOORE, C. H.—Examples for Elementary Practice in Delineation, designed for the use of schools and isolated beginners. Boston, Houghton, Mifflin & Co., 1884 [1883]. 15 pp., 20 plates, 4to, cloth, $2.

MORRIS Exhibit (The), at the Foreign Fair, Boston, 1883-84. Boston, Roberts Bros., 1883. 30 pp., 8vo, paper, 20 cents.

N. E. MANUFACTURERS' and Mechanics' Institute : The Catalogue of the Art Department of the Manufacturers' and Mechanics' Institute, Boston, Mass., 1883. Boston, Cupples, Upham & Co. [printed at the *Art Age* Press of Arthur B. Turnure], 1883. 300 pp., illustrated, 4to, cloth, $3. [Price since raised to $5.]

ORIGINAL Etchings, by American Artists. [With Introduction and Text by S. R. Koehler.] New York, Cassell & Co., 1883. No paging, 20 plates, folio, cloth, $20 ; *édition de luxe* (limited to 200 copies), $125.

OSBORN, H. S.—Ancient Egypt in the Light of Modern Discoveries. Cincinnati, Rob. Clarke & Co., 1883. 232 pp., illustrations and map, 12mo., cloth, $1.25.

PALLISER'S Full Working Plans and Specifications for Modern Eight-room Cottage, with Tower ; also showing how it can be built without tower and with but six rooms and not affect appearance. Bridgeport, Ct., Palliser, Palliser & Co., 1882. Folded, $5.

PERKINS, C. C.—Historical Hand-Book of Italian Sculpture. New York, C. Scribner's Sons, 1883. 654 + 432 pp., illustrated, 8vo., cloth, $4.

PERROT, Georges *and* Chipiez, C.—The History of Art in Ancient Egypt ; translated and edited by Walter Armstrong. New York, A. C. Armstrong & Son, 1882. 2 volumes, small 8vo, 600 illustrations, cloth, $15 ; turkey morocco, $25 ; tree calf, $27.50 ; full levant, $30.

POOLE, R. S., Richmond, W. B., *and others.*—Lectures on Art ; delivered in support of the Society of Ancient Buildings. New York, Macmillan, 1883. 232 pp., 12mo, cloth, $1.50.

PROCTOR, R. A.—The Great Pyramid ; Observatory, Tomb and Temple. New York, R. Worthington, 1883. 8 + 323 pp., illustrated, 12mo, cloth, $2.25.

RAWLINSON, G.—The Seventh Great Oriental Monarchy ; or, the Geography, History and Antiquities of the Sassanian or New Persian Empire ; collected and illustrated from ancient and modern sources. New York, Dodd, Mead & Co., 1882. 2 vols, 16 + 338 ; 12 + 351 pp., map and illustrations, 8vo, cloth, $6.

REBER, Franz von.—History of Ancient Art ; *revised* by the author ; translated and augmented by Joseph Thacher Clarke. New York, Harper, 1882. 20+482 pp., illustrated, 8vo, cloth, $3.50.

REED, S. B.—Cottage Houses for Village and Country Homes ; with complete plans and specifications. New York. The Orange Judd Co., 1883. 3+136 pp., illustrated, 12mo, cloth, $1.25.

RHEES, W. J.—Visitors' Guide to the Smithsonian Institution and United States National Museum in Washington. Washington, D. C., Judd & Detweiler, 1884 [1883]. 58 pp., portrait and illustrations, 8vo, paper, 25 cents.

RIORDAN, Roger.—A Score of Etchings ; twenty examples by the most celebrated English etchers, with critical and descriptive text by Roger Riordan. New York, Dodd, Mead & Co., 1883. Folio, cloth, $15.

RUSKIN, J.—Modern Painters ; Vol. 2, of Ideas of Beauty, and of the Imaginative Faculty. *Re-arranged and revised* by the author. New York, J. Wiley & Sons, 1883. 12+258 pp., 12mo, cloth, $1, $1.50 and $2 ; 8vo, cloth, *subscription edition*. $3.

RUSKIN, J.—The Art of England : Lectures given in Oxford. New York, J. Wiley & Sons, 1883. 4+33 pp., 12mo, boards, 50 cents.

SANDHURST, P. T.—The Table-book of Art ; a history of art in all countries and ages. *New edition.* New York, R. Worthington, 1883. 248 pp., illustrated, 4to, $5.

SATCHEL Guide for the Vacation Tourist in Europe. *Edition for* 1883, with four maps, including a new and excellent route-map, a traveller's calendar of ecclesiastical and popular festivals, pilgrimages, fairs, etc., and a list of the most famous pictures in the public galleries of Europe, arranged according to the nationality of the artists. Boston, Houghton, Mifflin & Co., 1883. 22+335 pp., 16mo, flexible roan, $2.

SCHRIBER, Fritz.—The Complete Carriage and Wagon Painter. New York, M. T. Richardson, 1883. 4+177 pp., illustrated, 12mo, cloth, $1.

SCOTT, Leader.—Della Robbia and Cellini, and other celebrated sculptors of the 15th and 16th centuries. New York, Scribner & Welford, 1883. Illustrated, 12mo. (Illustrated biographies of great artists.) Cloth, $1.

SCOTT, Leader.—The Renaissance of Art in Italy ; an illustrated history. New York, Scribner & Welford, 1883. 22+384 pp., 4to, cloth, $10.50 ; smooth morocco, $22.50.

SHARP, W.—Dante Gabriel Rossetti : a record and study. New York, Macmillan, 1882. 8+432 +17 pp., 12mo, cloth, $3.

SHEDD, *Mrs.* Julia A.—Raphael : his Madonnas and Holy Families ; illustrated with 22 full-page heliotypes of Raphael's most famous and popular paintings. Boston, James R. Osgood & Co., 1883. 4to, cloth, $7.50.

SHELDON, G. W.—Hours with Art and Artists. New York, Appleton, 1882. 8+184 pp., illustrated. Folio, cloth, $7.50.

SKETCH-BOOK of the Architectural Association of Boston. 30 plates, 4to, in portfolio. First issue, 1883. $7. [For sale by Cupples, Upham & Co., and W. B. Clarke & Carruth, Boston. Only 300 copies printed.]

SYLVESTER, W. A.—The Modern House-carpenters' Companion and Builders' Guide : being a hand-book for workmen, and a manual of reference for contractors and builders. *Third thousand enlarged.* Boston, Cupples, Upham & Co., 1883. 210 pp., 45 plates, 12mo, cloth, $2.

UZANNE, Octave.—The Fan ; with English text ; 50 photogravures, in colors by Paul Avril. Philadelphia, J. B. Lippincott & Co., 1883. 8vo, cloth, $10.

UZANNE, Octave.—The Sunshade, Muff and Glove ; with English text ; 60 photogravures, in colors by Paul Avril. Philadelphia, J. B. Lippincott & Co., 1883. 8vo, cloth, $10.

VOGDES, Frank W.—The Architects' and Builders' Pocket Companion and Price Book. *New revised and enlarged edition.* Philadelphia, H. C. Baird & Co., 1883. 368 pp., 32mo, cloth, $1.50 ; pocket-book form, $2.

WEEKS, Joseph D.—Report on the Manufacture of Glass. New York, David Williams, 1883. 8 + 114 pp., 4to, cloth, $2 ; paper, $1.50.

WELLS, Clara S.—The Amphitheatres of Ancient Rome. Boston, Cupples, Upham & Co., 1883. 80 pp., with photographs, small 4to, paper, $2.50 ; without photographs, $2.

WHEATLEY, H. B. *and* Delamotte, P. H.—Art-work in Gold and Silver ; Greek, Etruscan, Roman Pompeian, Byzantine and the Ecclesiastical Gold-work of the Middle Ages ; illustrated with 40 engravings of many celebrated works of mediæval art of the goldsmiths. New York, Scribner & Welford, 1883. 8vo (Illustrated hand-books of practical art), cloth, $1.

WHEATLEY, H. B. *and* Delamotte, P. H.—Art-work in Porcelain ; Chinese, Japanese, Italian, German, French and English ; illustrated with engravings of fifty of the most celebrated examples of ceramic art. New York, Scribner & Welford, 1883. 8vo (Illustrated hand-books of practical art, No. 3), cloth, $1.

WHITE, G. G.—Light and Shade and Landscape ; four series of lessons selected from White's "Progressive Art Studies." New York, Ivison, Blakeman, Taylor & Co., 1883. 168 pp., illustrated, 4to, cloth, $3.

WILKINSON, *Sir* J. Gardner.—The Manners and Customs of the Ancient Egyptians. *New edition, revised and corrected* by S. Birch. In 3 volumes. Vols. 1 and 2. Boston, S. E. Cassino & Co., 1883. 28 + 510 ; 11 + 515 pp., illustrated, colored plates, cloth, 8vo, each $6 ; half calf, $10.

WOODBERRY, G. E.—A History of Wood Engraving. New York, Harper, 1883 [1882]. 221 pp., illustrated, square 8vo, cloth, $3.50.

YRIARTE, C.—Florence, its History, the Medicis, its Scholars, Architecture, Painting, Sculpture, etc. ; illustrated by over 500 engravings and photogravures. New York, Scribner & Welford, 1882. 350 pp., folio, cloth, $20 ; full morocco, $28.

PERIODICALS

DEVOTED TO ART AND ARCHÆOLOGY, INDUSTRIAL AND DECORATIVE ART, AND RELATED SUBJECTS, PUBLISHED IN THE UNITED STATES.

AMERICAN ANTIQUARIAN AND ORIENTAL JOURNAL.—Edited by Rev. Stephen D. Peet. Chicago, Jameson & Morse. $3 per year in advance.

THE AMERICAN ARCHITECT AND BUILDING NEWS.—Illustrated. Weekly. Boston, James R. Osgood & Co., 211 Tremont Street. $7.50 a year ; $6 when paid in advance; single numbers, 15 cents.

AMERICAN JOURNAL OF NUMISMATICS and Bulletin of American Numismatic and Archæological Societies. Illustrated. Quarterly. Edited by Jeremiah Colburn. Boston, The Boston Numismatic Society, 18 Somerset Street. $2 a year in advance ; single copies, 50 cents.

THE ART AGE.—Monthly. New York, Arthur B. Turnure, 132 Nassau Street. $1 a year in advance ; $2 to foreign addresses ; single numbers, 10 cents. [Devoted to artistic printing.]

THE ART AMATEUR.—Illustrated. Monthly. New York, Montague Marks, Editor and Publisher, 23 Union Square. $4 a year, including postage ; single copies, 35 cents.

THE ART FOLIO.—Illustrated. Monthly. Providence, R. I., J. A. & R. A. Reid. (New York, John Beacham, 7 Barclay Street.) $3 per year, with steel plate premium.

THE ART INTERCHANGE.—Illustrated. Fortnightly. Edited by Mrs. Josephine Redding. New York, Wm. Whitlock, 140 Nassau Street. $3 a year ; single copies, 15 cents. With colored supplements.

THE ARTIST.—Illustrated. Weekly. Boston, I. Burt Kimball, 10 Pemberton Square. $2 a year, in advance ; to Europe, $2.50, including postage ; single copies, 5 cents.

THE ART UNION.—Official journal of the American Art Union. Illustrated. Monthly. Edited by Chas. M. Kurtz. New York, The American Art Union, 44 East 14th Street. $3 a year.

CALIFORNIA ARCHITECT AND BUILDING NEWS.—Monthly. San Francisco, Jas. E. and Geo. H. Wolfe, editors and proprietors, 240 Montgomery Street. $2 a year.

THE DECORATOR AND FURNISHER.—Illustrated. Monthly. Edited by A. Curtis Bond. New York, The Decorator and Furnisher Co., Jas. W. Pratt, President, 231 Broadway, P. O. Box 1543. $4 a year in advance ; single numbers, 35 cents.

THE ETCHERS' FOLIO.—Monthly. Three plates with text. Philadelphia, Janentzky & Co., 1125 Chestnut Street. $15 a year. No subscription for less than a year.

THE MAGAZINE OF ART.—Illustrated. Monthly. New York, Cassell & Company, Limited, 739 and 741 Broadway. $3.50 a year ; single numbers 35 cents. (A London publication, issued in the United States with additional American matter.) Premium etching, "Evening by the River," by Henry Farrer, to all subscribers for 1884.

THE SKETCH BOOK.—Illustrated. Issued monthly by the Cleveland Academy of Art. Cleveland, O., W. H. Eckman, editor, Room 27, City Hall Building. $2.50 a year.

THE STUDIO.—Illustrated. Weekly. Conducted by Frank T. Lent, edited by J. C. Van Dyke. New York, The Studio Company, 59 Cortlandt Street. $3 a year in advance, including postage ; single copies, 10 cents.

48

THE LAW OF COPYRIGHT IN THE UNITED STATES.

1. The Law as at Present in Force.

(Reprinted from the circular officially issued by the U. S. Government, and to be had on application to Mr. A. R. Spofford, Librarian of Congress, Washington, D. C.)

SEC. 4948. All records and other things relating to copyrights and required by law to be preserved shall be under the control of the Librarian of Congress, and kept and preserved in the Library of Congress ; and the Librarian of Congress shall have the immediate care and supervision thereof, and, under the supervision of the Joint Committee of Congress on the Library, shall perform all acts and duties required by law touching copyrights.

SEC. 4949. The seal provided for the office of the Librarian of Congress shall be the seal thereof and by it all records and papers issued from the office, and to be used in evidence, shall be authenticated.

SEC. 4950. The Librarian of Congress shall give a bond, with sureties, to the Treasurer of the United States, in the sum of five thousand dollars, with the condition that he will render to the proper officers of the Treasury a true account of all moneys received by virtue of his office.

SEC. 4951. The Librarian of Congress shall make an annual report to Congress of the number and description of copyright publications for which entries have been made during the year.

SEC. 4952. Any citizen of the United States, or resident therein, who shall be the author, inventor, designer, or proprietor of any book, map, chart, dramatic or musical composition, engraving, cut, print, photograph or negative thereof, or of a painting, drawing, chromo, statue, statuary, and of models or designs intended to be perfected as works of the fine arts, and the executors, administrators, or assigns of any such person, shall, upon complying with the provisions of this chapter, have the sole liberty of printing, reprinting, publishing, completing, copying, executing, finishing, and vending the same ; and in the case of a dramatic composition, of publicly performing or representing it, or causing it to be performed or represented by others. And authors may reserve the right to dramatize or translate their own works.

SEC. 4953. Copyrights shall be granted for the term of twenty-eight years from the time of recording the title thereof, in the manner hereinafter directed.

SEC. 4954. The author, inventor, or designer, if he be still living and a citizen of the United States, or resident therein, or his widow or children if he be dead, shall have the same exclusive right continued for the further term of fourteen years, upon recording the title of the work or the description of the article so secured a second time, and complying with all other regulations in regard to original copyrights, within six months before the expiration of the first term. And such person shall, within two months from the date of said renewal, cause a copy of the record thereof to be published in one or more newspapers, printed in the United States, for the space of four weeks.

SEC. 4955. Copyrights shall be assignable in law by any instrument of writing, and such assignment shall be recorded in the office of the Librarian of Congress within sixty days after its execution ; in default of which it shall be void as against any subsequent purchaser or mortgagee for a valuable consideration without notice.

SEC. 4956. No person shall be entitled to a copyright unless he shall, before publication, deliver at the office of the Librarian of Congress, or deposit in the mail addressed to the Librarian of Congress, at Washington, District of Columbia, a printed copy of the title of the book or other article, or a description of the painting, drawing, chromo, statue, statuary, or model or design for a work of the fine arts, for which he desires a copyright ; nor unless he shall also, within ten days from the publication thereof, deliver at the office of the Librarian of Congress, or deposit in the mail addressed to the Librarian of Congress, at Washington, District of Columbia, two copies of such copyright book or

4

other article, or, in case of a painting, drawing. statue, statuary, model, or design for a work of the fine arts, a photograph of the same.

SEC. 4957. The Librarian of Congress shall record the name of such copyright book or other article, forthwith in a book to be kept for that purpose, in the words following : "Library of Congress, to wit : Be it remembered that on the —— day of ——, ——, A. B., of ——, hath deposited in this office the title of a book (map, chart, or otherwise, as the case may be, or description of the article), the title or description of which is in the following words, to wit : (here insert the title or description), the right whereof he claims as author (originator, or proprietor as the case may be), in conformity with the laws of the United States respecting copyrights. C. D., Librarian of Congress." And he shall give a copy of the title or description, under the seal of the Librarian of Congress, to the proprietor whenever he shall require it.

SEC. 4958. The Librarian of Congress shall receive from the persons to whom the services designated are rendered the following fees : 1. For recording the title or description of any copyright book or other article, fifty cents. 2. For every copy under seal of such record actually given to the person claiming the copyright. or his assigns. fifty cents. 3. For recording and certifying any instrument of writing for the assignment of a copyright, one dollar. 4. For every copy of an assignment, one dollar. All fees so received shall be paid into the treasury of the United States.

SEC. 4959. The proprietor of every copyright book or other article shall deliver at the office of the Librarian of Congress, or deposit in the mail addressed to the Librarian of Congress, at Washington, District of Columbia, within ten days after its publication, two complete printed copies thereof, of the best edition issued, or description or photograph of such article as hereinbefore required, and a copy of every subsequent edition wherein any substantial changes shall be made.

SEC. 4960. For every failure on the part of the proprietor of any copyright to deliver, or deposit in the mail, either of the published copies, or description, or photograph, required by Sections 4956 and 4959. the proprietor of the copyright shall be liable to a penalty of twenty-five dollars, to be recovered by the Librarian of Congress, in the name of the United States in an action in the nature of an action of debt in any district court of the United States within the jurisdiction of which the delinquent may reside or be found.

SEC. 4961. The postmaster to whom such copyright book, title, or other article is delivered, shall, if requested, give a receipt therefor ; and when so delivered he shall mail it to its destination.

SEC. 4962. No person shall maintain an action for the infringement of his copyright unless he shall give notice thereof by inserting in the several copies of every edition published, on the title-page or the page immediately following, if it be a book; or if a map, chart, musical composition, print, cut, engraving, photograph, painting, drawing, chromo, statue, statuary, or model or design intended to be perfected and completed as a work of the fine arts, by inscribing upon some visible portion thereof, or of the substance on which the same shall be mounted, the following words, viz., " Entered according to act of Congress, in the year —— by A. B., in the office of the Librarian of Congress, at Washington ;" or, at his option, the word " Copyright," together with the year the copyright was entered, and the name of the party by whom it was taken out, thus : " Copyright, 18—, by A. B."

SEC. 4963. Every person who shall insert or impress such notice, or words of the same purport, in or upon any book, map, chart, musical composition, print, cut, engraving, or photograph, or other article, for which he has not obtained a copyright, shall be liable to a penalty of one hundred dollars, recoverable one-half for the person who shall sue for such penalty, and one-half to the use of the United States.

SEC. 4964. Every person who, after the recording of the title of any book as provided by this chapter, shall within the term limited, and without the consent of the proprietor of the copyright first obtained in writing, signed in presence of two or more witnesses, print, publish, or import, or, knowing the same to be so printed, published, or imported, shall sell or expose to sale any copy of such book, shall forfeit every copy thereof to such proprietor, and shall also forfeit and pay such damages as may be recovered in a civil action by such proprietor in any court of competent jurisdiction.

SEC. 4965. If any person, after the recording of the title of any map, chart, musical composition, print, cut, engraving, photograph, or chromo, or of the description of any painting, drawing, statue, statuary, or model or design intended to be perfected and executed as a work of the fine arts, as provided by this chapter, shall, within the term limited, and without the consent of the proprietor of the copyright first obtained in writing, signed in presence of two or more witnesses, engrave, etch, work, copy, print, publish, or import, either in whole or in part, or by varying the main design with intent to evade the law, or, knowing the same to be so printed, published, or imported, shall sell or expose to sale any copy of such map or other article, as aforesaid, he shall forfeit to the proprietor all the plates on which the same shall be copied, and every sheet thereof, either copied or printed, and shall further forfeit one dollar for every sheet of the same found in his possession, either printing, printed, copied, published, imported, or exposed for sale; and in case of a painting, statue, or statuary, he shall forfeit ten dollars for every copy of the same in his possession, or by him sold or exposed for sale, one-half thereof to the proprietor and the other half to the use of the United States.

SEC. 4966. Any person publicly performing or representing any dramatic composition for which a copyright has been obtained, without the consent of the proprietor thereof, or his heirs or assigns, shall be liable for damages therefor ; such damages in all cases to be assessed at such sum, not less than one hundred dollars for the first, and fifty dollars for every subsequent performance, as to the court shall appear to be just.

SEC. 4967. Every person who shall print or publish any manuscript whatever, without the consent of the author or proprietor first obtained (if such author or proprietor is a citizen of the United States, or resident therein), shall be liable to the author or proprietor for all damages occasioned by such injury.

SEC. 4968. No action shall be maintained in any case of forfeiture or penalty under the copyright laws, unless the same is commenced within two years after the cause of action has arisen.

SEC. 4969. In all actions arising under the laws respecting copyrights the defendant may plead the general issue, and give the special matter in evidence.

SEC. 4970. The circuit courts, and district courts having the jurisdiction of circuit courts, shall have power, upon bill in equity, filed by any party aggrieved, to grant injunctions to prevent the violation of any right secured by the laws respecting copyrights, according to the course and principles of courts of equity, on such terms as the court may deem reasonable.

SEC. 4971. Nothing in this chapter shall be construed to prohibit the printing, publishing, importation, or sale of any book, map, chart, dramatic or musical composition, print, cut, engraving, or photograph, written, composed, or made by any person not a citizen of the United States nor resident therein.

SEC. —.[Approved June 18, 1874, to take effect August 1, 1874.] That in the construction of this act, the words " engraving," " cut," and " print," shall be applied only to pictorial illustrations or works connected with the fine arts, and no prints or labels designed to be used for any other articles of manufacture shall be entered under the copyright law, but may be registered in the Patent Office. And the Commissioner of Patents is hereby charged with the supervision and control of the entry or registry of such prints or labels, in conformity with the regulations provided by law as to copyright of prints, except that there shall be paid for recording the title of any print or label, not a trade-mark, six dollars, which shall cover the expense of furnishing a copy of the record, under the seal of the Commissioner of Patents, to the party entering the same.

2. Directions for Securing Copyrights.

(Reprinted from the circular officially issued by the U. S. Government, and to be had on application to Mr. A. R. Spofford, Librarian of Congress, Washington, D. C.)   :

1. A *printed* copy of the title (besides the two copies to be deposited after publication) of the book, map, chart, dramatic or musical composition, engraving, cut, print, photograph, or a *description* of the painting, drawing, chromo, statue, statuary, or model or design for a work of the fine arts, for which copyright is desired, must be sent by mail or otherwise, *prepaid*, addressed

LIBRARIAN OF CONGRESS,

WASHINGTON, D. C.

This must be done before publication of the book or other article.

The *printed title* required may be a copy of the title page of such publications as have title pages. In other cases, the title must be printed expressly for copyright entry, with name of claimant of copyright. The style of type is immaterial, and the print of a type-writer will be accepted. But a separate title is required for each entry, and *each* title must be printed on paper as large as commercial note. The title of a *periodical* must include the date and number.

2. A fee of 50 cents, for recording the title of each book or other article, must be inclosed with the title as above, and 50 cents in addition (or one dollar in all) for each certificate of copyright under seal of the Librarian of Congress, which will be transmitted by early mail.

3. Within ten days after publication of each book or other article, two complete copies of the best edition issued must be sent, to perfect the copyright, with the address

LIBRARIAN OF CONGRESS,

WASHINGTON, D. C.

The postage must be prepaid, or else the publications inclosed in parcels covered by printed Penalty Labels, furnished by the Librarian, in which case they will come FREE by mail, according to rulings of the Post Office Department. Without the deposit of copies above required the copyright is void, and a penalty of $25 is incurred. No copy is required to be deposited elsewhere.

4. No copyright is valid unless notice is given by inserting in every copy published, on the title page or the page following, if it be a book ; or, if a map, chart, musical composition, print, cut, engraving, photograph, painting, drawing, chromo, statue, statuary, or model, or design intended to be perfected as a work of the fine arts, by inscribing upon some portion thereof, or on the substance on which the same is mounted, the following words, viz.: "*Entered according to act of Congress, in the year——, by——, in the office of the Librarian of Congress, at Washington,*" or, at the option of the person entering the copyright, the words: "*Copyright, 18—, by——.*"

The law imposes a penalty of $100 upon any person who has not obtained copyright who shall insert the notice "*Entered according to act of Congress,*" or "*Copyright,*" etc., or words of the same import, in or upon any book or other article.

5. Any author may reserve the right to translate or to dramatize his own work. In this case, notice should be given by printing the words "*Right of translation reserved,*" or "*All rights reserved,*" below the notice of copyright entry, and notifying the Librarian of Congress of such reservation, to be entered upon the record.

Since the phrase *all rights reserved* refers exclusively to the author's right to dramatize or to translate, it has no bearing upon any publications except original works, and will not be entered upon the record in other cases.

6. The original term of copyright runs for twenty-eight years. *Within six months before* the end of that time, the author or designer, or his widow or children, may secure a renewal for the further term of fourteen years, making forty-two years in all. Applications for renewal must be accompanied by explicit statement of ownership, in the case of the author, or of relationship, in the case of his heirs, and must state definitely the date and place of entry of the original copyright. Advertisement of renewal is to be made within two months of date of renewal certificate, in some newspaper, for four weeks.

7. The time within which any work entered for copyright may be issued from the press is not limited by any law or regulation, but depends upon the discretion of the proprietor. A copyright may be secured for a projected work as well as for a completed one.

8. A copyright is assignable in law by any instrument of writing, but such assignment must be recorded in the office of the Librarian of Congress within sixty days from its date. The fee for this record and certificate is one dollar, and for a certified copy of any record of assignment one dollar.

9. A copy of the record (or duplicate certificate) of any copyright entry will be furnished, under seal, at the rate of fifty cents each.

10. In the case of books published in more than one volume, or of periodicals published in numbers, or of engravings, photographs, or other articles published with variations, a copyright is to be entered for each volume or part of a book, or number of a periodical, or variety, as to style, title, or inscription, of any other article. But a book published serially in a periodical, under the same general title, requires only one entry. To *complete* the copyright on such a work, two copies of each serial part, as well as of the complete work (if published separately) must be deposited.

11. To secure a copyright for a painting, statue, or model or design intended to be perfected as a work of the fine arts, so as to prevent infringement by copying, engraving, or vending such design, a definite description must accompany the application for copyright, and a photograph of the same,

at least as large as "cabinet size," should be mailed to the Librarian of Congress within ten days from the completion of the work or design.

12. Copyrights cannot be granted upon Trade-marks, nor upon mere names of companies or articles, nor upon prints or labels intended to be used with any article of manufacture. If protection for such names or labels is desired, application must be made to the Patent Office, where they are registered at a fee of $6 for labels and $25 for trade-marks.

13. Citizens or residents of the United States only are entitled to copyright.

14. Every applicant for a copyright should state distinctly the full name and residence of the claimant, and whether the right is claimed as author, designer, or proprietor. No affidavit or formal application is required.

ACADEMIES, ART SCHOOLS, MUSEUMS, COLLECTIONS, EXHIBITIONS, DECORATIVE ART SOCIETIES, ART CLUBS, ETC., IN THE UNITED STATES.*

A. National Institutions.

AMERICAN INSTITUTE OF ARCHITECTS.—Office, Bryant Building, 55 Liberty St., New York.—Organized and incorporated in New York, 1857.—Officers: Pres., Thos U. Walter, Public B'ldg., Philadelphia; V. Ps., the Presidents of the various Chapters of the Institute; Treas., O. P. Hatfield, 31 Pine St., New York; Sec., Geo. C. Mason, Jr., Newport, R. I.; Sec. for Foreign Cor., T. M. Clark, 178 Devonshire St., Boston.—Objects: To unite in fellowship the architects of this continent, and to combine their efforts so as to promote the artistic, scientific, and practical efficiency of the profession. The means of accomplishing this end shall be: regular meetings of the members, for the discussion of subjects of professional importance; the reading of essays; lectures upon topics of general interest; a school for the education of architects; exhibitions of architectural drawings; a library; a collection of designs and models, and any other means calculated to promote the objects of the Institute. — Members: Fellows, Associates, Corresponding, and Honorary Members. Fellows must be practising architects; initiation fee, $10; annual dues, $10. Associates must also be practising artists; no initiation fee; annual dues, $5. Both grades are elected by the Board of Trustees. Fellows and Associates who may relinquish their practice and resign their membership, also foreign architects, civil engineers, and other scientific men, may be elected Corresponding Members. Foreign architects, scientific men, and amateurs may be elected Honorary Members. Corresponding and Honorary Members have all the privileges of the Institute, except that of voting. Number of members according to last report, 271. (Fellows, 73; Associates, 90; Cor. Members, 49; Honorary, 59.)—Any association of architects in which there is one Fellow residing in the place where the association has been formed may organize themselves into a Chapter of the American Institute of Architects, provided that upon application the association is recognized by the Board of Trustees. At the date of the last report there were nine such Chapters, as follows: *Albany Chapter* [See, however, remarks under Albany.—*Editor.*]; *Baltimore Chapter*, Sec., John Murdock, Courtland St.; *Boston Chapter*, Sec., T. M. Clark, 178 Devonshire St.; *Chicago Chapter*, Sec., S. A. Treat, 80 Dearborn St.; *Cincinnati Chapter*, Sec., Chas. Crapsey, 46 Wiggins Block; *New York Chapter*, Sec., A. J. Bloor, 55 Liberty St.; *Philadelphia Chapter*, Sec., Edw. Hazlehurst, 508 Walnut St.; *Rhode Island Chapter*, Sec., Edward J. Nickerson, 45 Westminster St. (P. O. address, Box 1031), Providence; *San Francisco Chapter*, Sec., G. H. Wolfe, 240 Montgomery St. [See a more detailed account of these chapters, under the respective cities.] Applications for new chapters have been received from St. Louis, Nashville, and Indianapolis. Not all the members of these Chapters are necessarily also members of the Institute.—The income of the Institute is confined to initiation fees and membership dues.—Its collections and library, which are mostly housed with the New York Chapter, receive occasional accessions from donations.—The Institute holds Annual Conventions, at which the usual routine business is transacted and papers of interest to architects are read. The seventeenth of these Conventions was held at Providence and Newport, Aug. 29, 30, and 31, 1883. The activity of the association, and the results so far attained by it, are thus summarized in a circular issued some years ago: "The Board of Trustees assume that architects old enough to remember the former drawbacks to practice recognize the fact that it is chiefly the Institute which has been instrumental in raising the profession so far toward its natural influential position. The schedule of charges recommended by it is now generally acknowledged in the Courts, by corporations,

---

* Instruction in drawing as incorporated into the public-school system, and private schools, are not accounted for in the following list.

and by private individuals ; and it was mainly through the exertions of its Committee on Publications that the establishment was secured of a proper organ of communication between the profession and the public, viz.: *The American Architect and Building News.* The Institute publishes every year a pamphlet of the proceedings of its successive Annual Conventions, as well as other matter of technical and general interest to practitioners. These are but the beginnings of what may be secured by intelligent interchange and concerted action among the members of the profession, through the medium of its recognized society." — The Institute, when asked to do so, decides questions at issue between members of the profession, and its opinions are occasionally sought by the public authorities. The Committee on Examinations of the New York Chapter has for many years acted under the law, in various needful capacities, with the Building Authorities of the city named. Official letters of introduction are furnished to members travelling abroad, and these letters are particularly valuable to the younger associates, to whom they serve as passports to the professional circles of Europe. — The time and place of holding the annual meeting is decided by the Board of Trustees.

ARCHÆOLOGICAL INSTITUTE OF AMERICA.—Organized in Boston, May 17,

1879.—Officers : Pres., Charles Eliot Norton, Shady Hill, Cambridge, Mass.; V. P., Martin Brimmer, 47 Beacon St. ; Treas., Henry L. Higginson, 191 Commonwealth Ave. ; Sec., E. H. Greenleaf, Museum of Fine Arts, Boston.—Objects : The Archæological Institute of America is formed for the purpose of promoting and directing archæological investigation and research,—by the sending out of expeditions for special investigation, by aiding the efforts of independent explorers, by publication of reports of the results of the expeditions which the Institute may undertake or promote, and by any other means which may from time to time appear desirable.—Members (both sexes) : Life, contributors of not less than $100 ; Annual, contributors of not less than $10 ; Corresponding ; Honorary. Number of members at date of last report, 329 : 90 life ; 233 annual ; 6 honorary. At the meeting at which the Institute was organized it was voted that, after the number of members shall have increased to 350, no more shall be admitted, except when elected by the Executive Committee. The association has already members in forty-six cities, scattered all over the United States, from New England to North Carolina, New Mexico, Arizona, and California.—The work of the Institute is divisible into two departments, American and Foreign. "The vast work of American Archæology," says the third Report, "is only begun. The time is not ripe for safe and sure deduction. Our present business is to gather facts while to do so is yet possible. Other nations, with more or less success, are trying to do our work on our soil. It is time that Americans bestir themselves in earnest upon a field which it would be a shame to abandon to the foreigner." By arrangement with the Institute, Mr. A. F. Bandelier, a well-known student in American archæology, has carried on investigations among the Pueblo Indians of New Mexico. The same scholar also went to Mexico in the interest of the Institute, in connection with the Lorillard Expedition, where he made a thorough examination of Cholula and its so-called pyramid, and visited Mitla and other places. Some preliminary account of his researches has already been published in the papers of the Institute, and he is now engaged in the preparation of a more exhaustive report. The expedition to Assos, in charge of Messrs. Joseph Thacher Clarke and F. H. Bacon, also sent out by the Institute, has completed its work and the fruits of the expedition, in the shape of architectural and sculptured fragments from the Temple of Assos, terra-cotta vases, coins, inscriptions, etc., have been received at the Museum of Fine Arts, Boston.—In addition to its four Annual Reports, the Institute has published the following papers : I. "A Study of the Houses of the American Aborigines," by Lewis H. Morgan ; " Ancient Walls on Monte Leone," by W. J. Stillman ; "Archæological Notes on Greek Shores," by Jos. Thacher Clarke (the foregoing three papers in one vol., together with the First Annual Report) ; II. " Papers of the Archæological Institute of America.—Classical Series. I. Report on the Investigations at Assos, 1881, by Jos. Thacher Clarke. With an Appendix, containing Inscriptions from Assos and Lesbos, and Papers by W. C. Lawton and J. S. Diller " (1 vol.) ; III. " American Series. I. 1. Historical Introduction to Studies among the Sedentary Indians of New Mexico. 2. Report on the Ruins of the Pueblo of Pecos, by A. F. Bandelier " (1 vol.) ; IV. " Bulletin. I. January, 1883. 1. The work of the Institute in 1882. 2. Report by A. F. Bandelier on his investigations in New Mexico in the spring and summer of 1882. 3. Note on a terra-cotta figurine from Cyprus, of a Centaur with human fore-legs, in the Metropolitan Museum of Art, New York, by Thos. W. Ludlow. With a plate."—The Institute is dependent for its income upon membership dues and donations. The results so far achieved have been due in great measure to the self-sacrificing spirit of the agents of the Institute. To enable it to continue its work, and to publish an adequate and exhaustive illustrated report on the Assos Expedition, it is now making efforts to raise the sum of $20,000 by subscription. It is upon the increase in the number of members that the continued efficiency of the Institute must depend.—The Annual meeting is held in Boston on the third Saturday of May.

AMERICAN SCHOOL OF CLASSICAL STUDIES AT ATHENS (Greece).—

Opened October 2, 1882.—Officers of Committee in charge : Chairman, Prof. John Williams White, Harvard University, Cambridge, Mass. ; Secretary, Thos. W. Ludlow, Yonkers, N. Y. ; Treasurer, Frederic J. de Peyster, 7 East 42d St., New York.—The object of this School is to furnish to graduates of American Colleges an opportunity to study Classical Literature, Art, and Antiquities in Athens, under suitable direction ; to prosecute and to aid original research in these subjects ; and to co-operate with the Archæological Institute of America, as far as it may be able, in conducting the exploration and excavation of classic sites.—The Archæological Institute of America was the prime mover in the establishment of this School, which is, for the present, maintained by the united efforts of the following colleges : Harvard, Yale, Brown, Amherst, Johns Hopkins, College of the City of New York, Columbia College of New Jersey, Wesleyan, Cornell, and the Universities of Virginia, Michigan, and California.—The plan of the School is in the main identical with that of the celebrated French and German Schools established at Athens. The directorship for the first year was intrusted to Prof. W. W. Goodwin, of Harvard, who has been succeeded, for the year 1883-4, by Prof. L. R. Packard, of Yale. Graduates of the co-operating Colleges are admitted upon presenting a certificate of competency. All other persons must make application to the Committee. Members are required to prosecute their studies during the school year, from October 1 to June 1, in Greek lands, under the superintendence of the Director. No fees are paid to the School. On the other hand, no scholarships are offered, as there is, as yet, no endowment fund. The financial resources of the School, at present, are limited to the subscriptions of the co-operating colleges, $3,500 p. a., exclusive of the salary of the Director, which is furnished by the college to which he belongs. The library of the school, in its temporary home in the upper part of a house near the Gate of Hadrian, on the west side of the ὁδὸς Ἁμαλίας, numbers upward of 400 volumes, including the most necessary books of reference in all the departments of advanced study embraced in the scheme of the school. It is desirable that the library be added to largely, and that donations be made for this purpose. — The School proposes to publish an annual volume of papers, and a semi-annual Bulletin. The first of these Bulletins, containing Prof. Goodwin's report, was published in 1883. — The meetings of the Managing Committee are held in Boston on the third Friday in May, and in New York on the third Friday in November.

UNITED STATES NATIONAL MUSEUM, at Washington ; UNITED STATES MILITARY ACADEMY, at West Point, and UNITED STATES NAVAL ACADEMY, at Annapolis, see under the respective places.

B. Local Institutions.

ARRANGED ALPHABETICALLY ACCORDING TO CITIES.

1. Albany, N. Y.

ALBANY ART LEAGUE. [Discontinued. An effort to start a new organization had not been successful up to time of writing.]

ALBANY CHAPTER OF THE AM. INST. OF ARCHITECTS. [Discontinued.]

NEW YORK STATE CAPITOL.—This building, of itself important as a work of architecture, contains, in the Assembly Chamber, the two mural paintings, "The Flight of Night," and "The Discoverer," executed by the late William Morris Hunt, in oil colors, directly upon the stone. Unfortunately, they are already going to ruin.

2. Albuquerque, N. M.

NEW MEXICO EXPOSITION AND DRIVING PARK ASSOCIATION.—Officers: President, M. W. Bremen; Treasurer, A. M. Codington; Secretary, D. B. Emmert; Superintendent of Fine Arts, Charles M. Wheelock, Las Vegas. This association held its Second Annual Fair from September 18 to 23, 1882. In Division F, Class 22, devoted to Painting, Sculpture, Drawing, Engraving, Penmanship, and Photography, twenty-two premiums were awarded (1 bullion medal, 2 silver medals, 19 diplomas). [No reply to requests for later information.]

3. Amherst, Mass.

AMHERST COLLEGE.—Officers: President of the Corporation and of the Faculty, Rev. Julius H. Seelye, D.D., LL.D.; Secretary of the Corporation, Rev. Edward S. Dwight, D.D.; Treasurer, Wm. A. Dickinson; Dean of the Faculty, Edward P. Crowell, D.D.—No instruction in drawing or any other practical branch of art is provided in the college course. A course of thirty lectures upon the History of Sculpture is, however, delivered before the Senior Class by Professor Richard H. Mather, D.D., in the very attractive art-lecture room of the college. These lectures are illustrated by a collection of casts, a large number of magic-lantern views, and an extensive collection of photographs of sculpture and architecture.—*The Gallery of Art* contains a large and choice collection of casts of ancient and modern statuary, consisting in all of 141 pieces, many of these being groups and extensive reliefs, such as the "Parthenon Frieze," and a portion of Thorwaldsen's "Triumph of Alexander." The collection illustrates the art of Nineveh, Egypt, Greece (from the early period represented by the Mycenæ Gate downward, and including some of the latest discoveries, such as the "Victory" of Paionios, and the "Hermes" of Praxiteles from Olympia), Rome, the Renaissance (works of Ghiberti, Luca della Robbia, Michelangelo, etc.), and modern times. The collection, including the photographs mentioned above, cost over $18,000.—Funds donated.—Open free to the public every week day from 9 A. M. to 5 P. M., in May, June, September, and October, and all other times from 10-11 A. M., and 3-4 P. M. No catalogue, as every piece is conspicuously labelled.

4. Annapolis, Md.

U. S. NAVAL ACADEMY.—The instruction given in drawing, etc., is entirely practical and scientific. Head of Department of Mechanical Drawing, Commander C. D. Sigsbee; Assistants: Lieut. W. P. Clason, Prof. M. Oliver, passed Assistant Engineer, A. B. Canaga, Assistant Prof. C. F. Blauvelt. Drawing is taught in the third class only. During the first term the subjects are: Use of Instruments; preliminary construction to scale of rectilinear and curved figures; inking in; drawing section lines; practice in drawing ordnance accessories, and various implements, apparatus, and machinery used in the naval service. Reference book: Thompson's Mahan's Industrial Drawing. Second term: Orthographic projections; sections; intersection of surfaces; isometrical drawing; perspective; drawing of screws, bolts, nuts, spur-gears, bevel-gears, and other details of gun-carriages, engines, and various naval machinery. Reference books: Thompson's Mahan's Industrial Drawing, and Tomkin's Machine Construction and Drawing.—The library contains some old portraits of naval officers and some naval relics, and there are several monuments on the grounds. Accessible to the public at all times.

5. Ann Arbor, Mich.

UNIVERSITY OF MICHIGAN.—Officers: Board of Regents; President, Jas. B. Angell, LL.D.; Secretary, Jas. H. Wade; Treasurer, Harrison Soule. Faculty: President, Jas. B. Angell, LL.D., S. University Ave.; Dean and Curator of the Art Museum, Henry S. Frieze, LL.D., Cornwell Pl.; Chas. S. Denison, M.S., C.E., Acting Asst. Prof. of Mechanical and Free-Hand Drawing, 40 S. Ingalls St.; Joseph B. Steere, Ph.D., Curator of the Museum of Archæology and Ethnography, S. Ypsilanti Road.—The University of Michigan is a part of the public educational system of the State, governed by a Board of Regents elected by popular vote. Through the aid received from the United States and the State, it is enabled to offer its privileges, without charge for tuition, to persons of either sex qualified for admission.—Drawing (Geometrical, Mechanical, Topographical,

Perspective, Free-Hand, Pen and Ink, Architect. Water Color) is a required study in the Engineering Course only. The Classical Course includes lectures on the History of Art by Prof. Frieze.—*The Museum* of the University, in a building erected in 1879-80, by legislative appropriation; besides valuable scientific collections, it contains also special Departments of Archæology and Ethnology, consisting of articles of domestic and warlike use among the North American Indians and the Islanders of the South Pacific; numerous remains of the ancient Peruvians, and many specimens of clothing, art, etc., of the Amazonian Indians, modern Peruvians, Chinese, Formosans, and natives of the East Indies and Alaska. The Library Building, erected in 1882-3, by legislative appropriation, contains spacious galleries for sculpture, paintings, coins, and medallions. *The Fine Arts Collection*, now arranged in these galleries, was begun in 1855, and at present comprises : A gallery of casts from the antique, in full size and in reductions ; over 200 reductions and models in terra-cotta, etc., of works of antique art and industry in the Museums at Naples and elsewhere; the statues of "Nydia" and "Ruth Gleaning," by Randolph Rogers ; copies of statues, busts, and reliefs by Michelangelo, Canova, Thorwaldsen, etc.; a series of engravings and photographs, illustrating the architectural and sculptural remains of ancient Rome, Pompeii, Pæstum, Athens, and Corinth ; a small collection of engravings of modern paintings, beginning with those prior to Raphael ; the Horace White Collection of Historical Medallions (450 casts from antique gems, over 500 illustrating the mediæval period and the Renaissance ; about 400 modern portrait medallions); the Governor Bagley Collection of American Historical Medallions, designed to embrace all the commemorative medals struck by order of Congress or other authorities ; the Richards Collection of Coins, chiefly ancient, now numbering over 800. A catalogue has been prepared with great care by Prof. Frieze, and printed by the University. The collections are accessible, both to students and to visitors.

6. Atlanta, Ga.

YOUNG MEN'S LIBRARY ASSOCIATION.—39½ Decatur St.—Organized August 19, 1867.—Officers, 1883-4 : President, Chas. E. Harman ; V. P., N. P. T. Finch ; Secretary, Jos. T. Orme ; Treasurer, Alex. W. Smith ; Chairman Art Committee, N. P. T. Finch.—Object : Collecting a library, establishing reading rooms, and advancing the cause of good literature.—Supported by dues of members, annual, $4; Life, $50.—The association has a building of its own, and a library of over 10,000 volumes.—The association has lately given considerable attention, also, to art matters. Its *First Art Loan Exhibition*, held November 22-December 16, 1882, was quite successful. It was visited by nearly 10,000 visitors, and five pictures were sold for $1,528. *The Second Art Loan Exhibition* opened October 23, 1883, and closed November 23. It attracted 5,000 visitors ; sales, two pictures, value $50. Both exhibitions, of which illustrated catalogues were published, were in charge of Mr. Horace Bradley.

7. Auburndale, Mass.

LASELL SEMINARY FOR YOUNG WOMEN.—Principal, Chas. C. Bragdon. Miss Belle Webster, of Newton, and Miss Jessie J. Macmillan, resident in the school, in charge of the studio. Miss A. E. Clark, resident in the school, instructor in the history of art. The aim is to do rather more work, and that of a higher class, than the average of boarding-schools.—*Collections :* Nearly five hundred engravings and photographs, illustrating the work of the greatest artists, beginning with sculptures of the time of Phidias, and including the earlier and later Pre-Raphaelites, the masters of the renaissance, and many of the moderns.

8. Austin, Tex.

WOMAN'S EXCHANGE OF TEXAS (formerly the Art Exchange).—Masonic Building. P. O. address, Box 836. Organized and incorporated, April, 1882.—Officers: President, Mrs. C. E. Stanley ; Vice-President, Miss Ella Rust ; Secretary, Mrs. N. A. Bass ; Treasurer, Mrs. T. F. Mitchell. The governing power is vested in a board of nine directors (elected annually on the first Tuesday in October), who elect the officers.—Objects : The promotion of art and industry, the encouragement of native talent, and the amelioration and elevation of womankind.—Members, at present 170, are elected by the Board of Directors. Dues, twenty-five cents per month.—An exhibition is held every three months in the store of the association, which is open to the public. From time to time select entertainments are given under the auspices of the Exchange, for the purpose of keeping it before the public. Paintings, plain and fancy needle-work, preserves, pickles, sauces, bread, cake, etc., are received at the store on sale. Commission 5% to members, 10% to others.— Arrangements are being perfected to open a School of Design in the room occupied by the Exchange. This school will be financially independent of the Exchange, but it is thought that an indirect benefit will ensue through the sale of such materials as will be required.

9. Baltimore, Md.

BALTIMORE CHAPTER OF THE AMERICAN INSTITUTE OF ARCHITECTS.—Spurrier's Court.—Founded December 10, 1870.—Officers: President, John Murdoch, 1 Courtland St.; Secretary, J. Appleton Wilson, 52 Lexington St.; Treasurer, J. B. N. Wyatt, 55 N. Charles St.—Present number of members, 15 (architects 9, engineers 6).—Meetings are held on the fourth Monday of January, February, March, April, May, October, November and December. Annual meeting, fourth Monday of October.

DECORATIVE ART SOCIETY OF BALTIMORE.—69 N. Charles St.—Organized May, 1878.—Officers: President, Mrs. Wm. Reed; Vice-Presidents, Mrs. Alan P. Smith, Mrs. Denis Donohoe, Miss Mary Garrett; Treasurer, Mrs. John Duer; Secretary, Faris C. Pitt; Corresponding Secretary, Mrs. Henry Stockbridge.—Objects: 1. The diffusion of knowledge and promotion of taste in art. 2. To encourage and stimulate industries which are exclusively individual handwork, and to afford an opportunity for the sale of such work.--Membership dues, $5. p. a.—The Society frequently holds exhibitions, sometimes of loaned articles, sometimes of articles owned by it, and occasionally of work sent in to compete for prizes. At some of these exhibitions an exhibition fee is charged; others are free to the public.—The articles placed on sale at the rooms of the Society are of the various kinds accepted by similar associations.—*The Classes* in drawing, design, crayon, water color, oil, and china painting, are in charge of Miss Grace Carter, of South Kensington, and assistants; Miss McDowell, from England, teaches embroidery in all its departments. Tuition fees, $10 per 24 lessons. Members have the right of nominating a certain number of pupils.—Annual meeting, first Thursday in November.

JOHNS HOPKINS UNIVERSITY.—Founded by the late Johns Hopkins of Baltimore; endowment fund, in land and stocks, over $3,000,000.—Incorporated August 24, 1867. Opened for instruction in 1876.—Board of Trustees: President, George W. Dobbin; Treasurer, Francis White; Secretary, Lewis N. Hopkins. President of the University, Daniel C. Gilman, LL.D.. 81 Saratoga St.—*Drawing*, both freehand and mechanical, is one of the required studies in the College Course. Instructor in Drawing: Hugh Newell, 68 Lexington St.—*Lectures:* In order to extend the educational influence of the University, courses of lectures are opened to the public on certain conditions, admission being granted first to members of the University, and then to teachers and special students of the subjects announced. During the year 1882-3, these courses included three lectures On Etchers and Etching, by Dr. F. Seymour Haden, and one, On Michelangelo, by Mr. W. W. Story. For the year 1883-4, Mr. J. Thacher Clarke, of Boston, the chief of the exploring expedition sent to Assos by the Archæological Institute of America, has been announced as lecturer on classical archæology.

MARYLAND HISTORICAL SOCIETY.—Athenæum Building, St. Paul and Saratoga Sts.—Organized 1844.—Officers: President, John H. B. Latrobe; Vice-Presidents, Geo. Wm. Brown, John G. Morris, D.D., Henry Stockbridge; Corresponding Secretary, Mendes Cohen; Treasurer, Chas. L. Oudesluys; Librarian and Curator of Cabinet, John W. M. Lee; Committee on the Gallery, John H. B. Latrobe, Chas. L. Oudesluys, Henry C. Wagner, John W. McCoy, Faris C. Pitt.—*The Art Gallery* of the Society contains a number of casts from the antique; copies from paintings by Raphael, Correggio, Titian, Paul Veronese, Domenichino, and Cignani; a few portraits by Stuart, Polk, and other American artists; a portrait of Christopher Hughes by Sir M. A. Shee; one of Charles Carroll of Carrollton by Sir Joshua Reynolds, etc. For full list, see the Descriptive Catalogue published by the Society in 1883.—Open daily, the year round, except Sundays, from 9 A.M. to 4 P.M. Admission free.

MARYLAND INSTITUTE FOR THE PROMOTION OF THE MECHANIC
ARTS.—Baltimore St., over Centre Market.—Organized 1848 ; incorporated 1849.—Officers :
President, F. C. Latrobe : Vice-President, Jos. M. Cushing, Secretary, Geo. L. McCahan ; Treasurer, Edward W. Robinson ; Actuary and Librarian, Alex. F. Lusby.—Membership, p. a., $3 ;
male life members, $25 ; female life members, $10. Present number of members, 700 annual, 600
life.—The institute receives a yearly appropriation from the city and the State.—*The School of Art
and Design* maintained by the Institute, has for its object : To furnish the best and most thorough
instruction in the various branches of artistic drawing, painting and modelling to all persons desiring
to study art with a view to following it professionally, as designers, decorators, or skilled artisans ;
also to give a liberal art education to those who wish to study art as an accomplishment, and for the
enjoyment of its refining and elevating influences. There are two divisions of the school, a day
school and a night school.—*Day School :* Director, Prof. Otto Fuchs ; Head Assistant, S. Herbert
Adams ; Assistants, Miss Emma J. Gay, Miss Annie C. Volck, Miss Olivia Reinhart. Opens in
October ; three sessions yearly. Annual fee for entire course to regular students, $25. Fees per
term to special students : Elementary drawing, $5 ; Advanced Drawing, $8 ; Water Colors, $10 ;
Oil painting, $15 ; Instrumental Drawing, $5 for elementary instruction, $10 for advanced instruc-
tion in one subject, $15 for advanced instruction in all subjects. The method of study is principally
from the object, including the human figure from life. [Nude or draped, not stated.] Number of
pupils, 177, mostly young ladies, including a Saturday class of teachers engaged in other schools. Of
these students, 50 are regular, entered for the full course of three years. Of the special students, 42
are in the elementary class, 47 in the various advanced classes in oil and water color painting, etc.
The Saturday class, 38, are mostly beginners, with a few in the advanced departments. All the
pupils, of both sexes (taught together), must be members of the Institute.—*Night School :* Opens
about the middle of October, and continues three nights in the week, for five months. Director :
Prof. Otto Fuchs. 1. Freehand Division : S. Herbert Adams, in charge ; First Assistant, Geo. B.
Way ; Assist's, H. D. A. Henning, W. J. Stowell, Miss Emma J. Gay. 2. Mechanical Division :
First Assist., Geo. Beadenkopf; Assist., Henry Adams. 3. Archit. Division : First Assist., A. B.
McLaughlin ; Assist., W. G. Keimig. Fee for the annual session of five months, $3. All the
pupils, male only, must be members of the Institute. Number of pupils, 497, of whom 249 are in
the Free-Hand Department, 146 in the Mechanical, and 102 in the Architectural.—Certificates are
given in both the day and the night school. The liberality of the late Geo. Peabody enables the
managers to offer premiums, in sums of $50 and $100, amounting to $500 annually, to the highest
graduates. The city appoints 30 free pupils annually.—Annual meeting of the Institute, third Wednesday in April.

NUMISMATIC AND ARCHÆOLOGICAL SOCIETY OF BALTIMORE
CITY.—48 St. Paul St.—Organized; October, 1880.—Officers : President, O. H. Berg ; Vice-Pres-
ident, Dr. Geo. W. Massamore, 94 N. Eutaw St.; Secretary, Wm. J. Bechtel, 120 N. Howard St.;
Treasurer and Curator, Lennox Birkhead.—Members : 17 active, 8 corresponding ; dues, $4, p. a—
Annual meeting, third Monday in December.

PEABODY INSTITUTE.—Founded 1857, by the late George Peabody.—Officers : Board
of Trustees : Pres., Chas. J. M. Eaton ; V.P., Geo. Wm. Brown ; Treas., Enoch Pratt ; Sec., Geo. P.
Tiffany ; Com. on Gallery, Wm. T. Walters, Chairman, Samuel W. Smith, Geo. Wm. Brown, Reverdy
Johnson, S. Teackc Wallis. Officers of the Inst.: Provost, Nath. H. Morison, LL.D. ; Libr., P. R.
Uhler ; Asst. Libr. and Clerk, Andrew Troeger.— *The Gallery of Art* was first opened to the public on
May 2, 1881. It contains an excellent collection of about 200 casts from antique and Renaissance
statues, busts, and reliefs, paid for out of a fund of $15,000 donated by Mr. John W. Garrett ; Rhine-
hart's ideal statue of " Clytie," the gift of Mr. John W. McCoy ; a reduced copy in bronze, by F. Barbe-
dienne, of Paris, of the second Ghiberti Gate, also paid for out of the Garrett fund ; a marble copy of
an antique Venus, and a bust, in marble, of Pocahontas, by Jos. Mozier, both presented by Mr.
Geo. S. Brown, and a few paintings. The executors of Wm. H. Rhinehart (b. 1825, d. 1874),
" undoubtedly the most accomplished artist Maryland has produced," have also deposited in the Gallery a collection of 44 casts from the works of the sculptor named. The Garrett Collection of Paintings, consisting of 50 pictures by foreign and American artists, lately loaned by Mr. John W. Garrett, has added considerable interest to the Gallery.—Students are allowed, on application, to draw
from the casts, subject to certain regulations. Only four persons availed themselves of the privilege

during the season of 1882-3, but the casts are much used the present season.—The Gallery is open from 10 A.M. to 4 P.M. every day, except Sundays and holidays, from October 1 to June 1. Admission free. Catalogues, 15 cents. The number of visitors, during the eight months from October 1, 1881, to June 1, 1882, was 10,121; from October 1, 1882, to June 1, 1883, 8,091.—*The Library*, for reference only, open free, day and evening, except during the month of August, is well provided with books on art.—*Lectures.* Due attention is given to art in the lectures provided by the Institute during the winter season. An admission fee is charged at these lectures, 25 cents for a single ticket, $1.50 for the season of 30 lectures.

SOCIAL ART CLUB.—[Discontinued.]

10. Bangor, Me.

BANGOR ART ASSOCIATION.—French St.—Organized Feb. 17, 1875.—Officers: Pres., J. S. Wheelwright; V. P., J. L. Crosby; Sec. and Treas., Clarence L. Dakin; Exec. Com., A. C. Hamlin, G. W. Merrill, A. B. Farnham, Mrs. E. H. Hall, Mrs. J. C. Western, Mrs. F. S. Davenport.—Objects: To promote the interests of art in Bangor and vicinity.—Present number of members, 125.—Collections: 86 photographs framed, a few oil paintings; 25 plaster casts.

11. Berkeley, Cal.

UNIVERSITY OF CALIFORNIA.—Pres., Prof. John Le Conte; Libr., J. C. Rowell.—No instruction in free-hand drawing and painting is at present given at the University; but it is earnestly desired and confidently expected by the authorities of the University that those students who shall wish to do so, may sooner or later have the opportunity of beginning art studies in connection with their other academic employments.—*The Bacon Art Gallery of the University of California* had its origin in the gift, by Mr. Henry D. Bacon, of Oakland, Cal., of his private library, art collections, and $25,000 in money toward the erection of a suitable building, for which purpose the State also contributed $25,000, besides a later appropriation of $10,000 for furnishing. The building is mainly used for library purposes, the portion devoted to the Fine Arts being a large hall, 80 ft. in length, divided into three compartments, and averaging 32 ft. in width.—Collections: Three marble groups, "Ariadne on the Panther," a copy of Dannecker's famous work; "Genius of America, or the Abolition of Slavery," by Johann Halbig, of Munich, originally designed as a gift to President Lincoln; "Bathing Nymphs," by the same artist. Bronzes: Five busts by Barbedienne, of Solon, Socrates, Hippocrates, Homer, Franklin. Paintings: About 70, including Leutze's "Washington at Monmouth"; Bierstadt's "Yosemite Winter Scene"; Gebhard's "Koenig See, Bavaria;" Jacob's "Susannah at the Bath"; and many fine copies of the works of old and modern masters, such as Cimabue, Correggio, Albani, Stella, Guido, Claude, N. Poussin, Dürer, Rembrandt, Paul Bril, Teniers, Rubens, Picornet, Le Sueur, Besson, Grosclaude, Horace Vernet, Murillo, Rugendas, Mannlich, Piloty, and others. Thus a fair beginning of a collection illustrating the history of the art of painting has been made. Two valuable paintings, the joint work of Klombeck and Verboeckhoven, have lately been added, also a plaster bust of Henry D. Bacon, by P. Marion Wells. The Gallery was opened for the first time May 31, 1882, and a very large number of visitors (about 2,500 during the first two and a half months) have examined its contents. Admission free.—*The Library* contains a large number of choice engravings, chromolithographs, and illustrated books on art, also a collection of coins, and fine specimens of the printer's and binder's art.—A catalogue of the contents of the gallery, as well as of a number of portraits in the Assembly Room, North Hall, has been published as Library Bulletin, No. 4, of the University of California.—All the works in the Gallery were donated by Mr. Henry D. Bacon, Mr. Chas. Mayne, Mrs. Mark Hopkins, and Mr. F. L. A. Pioche. The portraits were given by Mr. Frederick Billings, and by subscription among the regents students, professors, and friends of the University.

12. Bloomington, Ill.

HISTORICAL AND ART SOCIETY.—Organized Mch. 20, 1879.—Officers: Pres., Mrs. Sue M. D. Fry; V. P., Mrs. M. F. Scott; Sec. and Treas., Miss M. A. Dodson.—Objects: Social and mental culture.—Members limited to 18; present number, 16.—This society is one of those which together form the Art Union of Central Illinois. At its weekly meetings, at the homes of members, essays are read on subjects selected from general history and the history of art. The topics are selected and assigned at the beginning of the season, and a list of them is published for the information of the members.

THE PALLADEN.—Organized May, 1877.—Officers : Miss M. B. Orme ; V. P., Mrs. Chas. Robinson ; Sec., Miss Ange V. Milner.—Objects : The intellectual development of the members. Subject of study, the history of art, and, in connection with it, general history.—Members limited to 15 (not including honorary, of which there are seven), ladies only. The club is full.—The Palladen also belongs to the Central Art Union, and its methods of work are similar to those of the society described in the previous paragraph.—Annual meeting, second Saturday in June.

13. Boston, Mass.

AMERICAN UNIVERSITY OF BOSTON.—[This institution, incorporated Dec., 1882, Dr. Joseph Rodes Buchanan, 123 West Concord St., principal, is described as a College of Industry, with departments of science, art, literature, etc. No reply to request for detailed information.]

ARCHITECTURAL ASSOCIATION OF BOSTON.—Museum of Fine Arts.—Originally organized in 1879 as the Arch. Ass. of the Mass. Inst. of Tech. ; reorganized 1882.—Officers : Pres., Arthur Rotch, 185 Devonshire St. ; V. P., Wm. P. Richardson 18 P. O. Sq. ; Sec., F. E. Alden, care H. H. Richardson, Brookline, Mass. ; Libr., H. Langford Warren, Hillside, Roxbury, Mass. ; Treas., E. G. Hartwell, care Hook & Hastings.—Objects : To afford facilities for the study of architecture, to increase the knowledge and appreciation of art, to advance the interests of the profession, and to promote friendly and intellectual intercourse among the members.—Any gentleman interested in architecture may be admitted to membership. Present number of members about 65, principally young architects and architectural draughtsmen.—The Sketch Club of the Association meets every third Friday. Two classes are to be established this winter, one in Construction, and one in Drawing from the Life. Arrangements are also being made for a series of lectures by prominent members of the profession and others. [From last year's issue.—The association continues its meetings at the Art Museum, but no reply was made to repeated requests for later information. For description of the "Sketch Book" published by the association in 1883, see list of books.]

BOSTON ART CLUB.—Corner Newbury and Dartmouth Sts.—Organized January, 1855 ; incorporated March 3, 1871.—Officers for 1884 : President, Geo. P. Denny, 132 Federal St.; 1st Vice-President, Edgar Parker, 433 Washington St.; 2d Vice-President, Chas. G. Wood, 16 Sears' Building ; Treasurer, Stephen M. Crosby, 18 P. O. Square ; Secretary, Louis D. Brandeis, 60 Devonshire St.; Librarian, Chas. W. Scudder, 4 P. O. Square.—Objects : To advance the knowledge and love of art, through the exhibition of works of art, the acquisition of books and papers for the purpose of forming an art library, lectures upon subjects pertaining to art, and by other kindred means, and to promote social intercourse among its members.—The membership of the club is limited to 750 members (males only), exclusive of such members as may be professional artists resident in Massachusetts. Honorary members may also be elected. Entrance fee, $20, which professional artists may pay in works of art. Assessments not over $15 p. a. for artists, and $30 for others. Present number of members, 876 (126 artists).—The government consists of the officers and an Executive Committee of twelve members, four of whom at least must be professional artists.—The new Club House [see illustration], inaugurated March 4, 1882, was built from plans by Mr. Wm. R. Emerson, at a cost of about $85,000, including the ground. The necessary funds were secured by the issue of bonds, taken by members. It contains, besides library, reading-room, parlors, billiard-room, etc., a spacious gallery, in which the exhibitions of the Club, two or more yearly, are held. These exhibitions have been for a number of years, and still are, the most important general exhibitions held in Boston. Admission to them is practically free, as tickets can be obtained from any member of the Club. The exhibitions of the year 1883 were, The Twenty-Seventh, Oils, January 25-February 17 (sales, 15 works, $3,380), and the Twenty-Eighth, Water Colors and Black-and-Whites (sales, 34 works, $1,715). Informal exhibitions are held at the monthly meetings of the Club, and lectures and other entertainments are given during the winter.—*School of Drawing.* This school, for members (and others, in case there are vacancies), opened at the club house, December 18, 1883, Tomasso Juglaris, instructor. There are two classes, a cast class and a life class. A yearly appropriation of $1,000 has been made for the support of the school.—Annual meeting, first Saturday in January.

BOSTON ART STUDENTS' ASSOCIATION.—Museum of Fine Arts.—Organized May, 1879, by students of the School of Drawing and Painting at the Art Museum.—Officers : President, H. W. Abbott ; V. P., Miss May Hallowell ; Treasurer, Miss Alice S. Tinkham ; Secretary, Miss Edith M. Howes, 67 Chester Square.—Objects : To supplement the academic training of the School of Drawing and Painting ; to assist members in their artistic career. either by establishing a scholarship, or in other ways ; to encourage a social and fraternal spirit among students.—Members (both sexes) must be, or must have been, students in the school at the Museum. Initiation fee, $1 ; annual membership, $5 ; life membership, $25. Present number of members, 160 ; honorary, 12. The committee in charge of the Museum School and its instructors are honorary members, to which grade other persons may also be elected.—The association has paid $100 to the School toward the foundation of a scholarship, and has held several exhibitions at the rooms of the Art Club. Visitors are admitted to these exhibitions to a limited extent on tickets issued by the members. At the next annual exhibition, November, 1884, three prizes are to be given.—Annual meeting, third Saturday in March.

BOSTON ATHENÆUM.—10½, Beacon St.—Incorporated 1807.—Officers for 1884 : President, Samuel Eliott ; V. P., Chas. Deane ; Treasurer, Chas. P. Bowditch ; Secretary, Chas. H. Williams ; Librarian, Chas. A. Cutler.—The Athenæum is a private association, controlled by shareholders. Its library of about 140,000 volumes, which is very rich in works on art, is, however, easily accessible to students who do not belong to the association. In former years the upper floor of the building was devoted to an art gallery, for a long time the only permanent exhibition of the kind in Boston. In this gallery the collections of the present Museum of Fine Arts were first displayed, and upon the completion of the Museum's building, the Athenæum deposited most of its own art treasures with the new institution. Of the pictures and sculptures which it retained, the casts of Ball Hughes's statue of Dr. Bowditch, and of Houdon's Washington, Greenough's " Boy with Eagle," in bronze, and some casts from the antique, are placed in the vestibule. On the walls of the staircase are hung, Leslie's portrait of Benjamin West, after Lawrence ; Harding's Daniel Webster and Chief Justice Marshall ; Cole's immense " Angel appearing to the Shepherds " ; Sully's portrait of Col. T. H. Perkins ; Neagle's " Patrick Lyon at the Forge " ; R. W. Weir's " Indian Captive " ; a landscape by Allston ; several copies from old masters, etc. Paintings by Allston, Stuart, Inman, Waldo, Sully, etc., and sculptures by Dexter, Gould, Powers, Crawford, Ball Hughes, Frazee, Greenough, Clevenger, etc., are in the Reading Room, and the various other rooms.—Open from 9 A. M. to 6 P. M. in summer, till sunset in winter. The paintings, etc., in the vestibule and on the staircase can be examined by all orderly visitors. Permission to see those in the rooms must be asked of the Librarian at the desk in the Reading Room upstairs. There is no catalogue, but printed lists are posted on the staircase, etc.—Annual meeting in February.

BOSTON CHAPTER OF THE AMERICAN INSTITUTE OF ARCHITECTS.—Secretary, T. M. Clark, 178 Devonshire St.—This society was incorporated as the Boston Society of Architects, and that is still its official name. When the federal system was adopted by the American Institute of Architects, it was invited to become a chapter of the Institute, and complied with the request. It is, however, rather attached to its original name, and all its local affairs are transacted under that title.

BOSTON ETCHING CLUB.—427 Washington St.—Organized February, 1880.—Officers : President, W. F. Halsall, 154 Tremont St.; Secretary and Treasurer, C. F. Pierce, 12 West St.— Objects : To encourage the practice of etching among its members, and to increase facilities for such practice.—The condition of membership is the prompt payment of all assessments (initiation fee, $10 ; annual dues, $6), and the production of at least two etchings p. a. Any failure forfeits membership. Present number of members, 13.—The club held an exhibition in 1883, at the gallery of Mr. J. Eastman Chase, of which it published an etched catalogue.—Annual meeting, second Monday in February.

BOSTON MEMORIAL ASSOCIATION.—Established 1880.—Officers : President, M. P.

Kennard, U. S. Treasury, P. O. Building ; Secretary, Prentiss Cummings, 82 Devonshire St.; Treasurer, H. H. Edes, 87 Milk St.—Objects : The ornamentation of the City of Boston, the care of its Memorials, the preservation and improvement of its Public Grounds, and the erection of Works of Art within the limits of the city.—Membership limited to 150, exclusive of life members. Life membership, $50 ; annual membership, $5.—Annual meeting, first Wednesday in November.

BOSTON MUSEUM.—28 Tremont St.—Established 1841.—This is the oldest existing theatre in Boston. In its early days it was called " The Boston Museum and Gallery of Fine Arts," and the performances were subordinate to the exhibition of paintings, statuary, stuffed animals, wax figures, and other curiosities. At present the stage, which is favorably known to all play-goers, forms the principal attraction, but something of the old character is still retained in the large hall on Tremont St., which may be regarded as the *foyer* of the theatre. Along with the stuffed beasts and birds, a number of casts, engravings, and paintings may still be seen there, including some by artists of good repute in the past periods of American art, such as Rembrandt Peale's " Roman Daughter," painted in 1820 ; " Gen. Washington and his Family," by E. Savage (engraved by the painter himself) ; " The Signers of the Declaration of Independence in Carpenter's Hall, Philadelphia," by the same artist ; Chas. Wilson Peale's " Portrait of David Rittenhouse ; " Winstanly's " Portrait of John Adams" when minister at the Hague, 1782-5 ; R. E. Pine's " Mad Woman in Chains ;" Sully's " Passage of the Delaware," and portraits, etc., by Copley, West, and Stuart. There are also a few good old pictures by European artists.

BOSTON NUMISMATIC SOCIETY.—18 Somerset St.—Founded in 1860. Incorporated 1870.—Officers : President, Jerem. Colburn, 33 E. Newton St.; Treasurer, Saml. A. Green ; Secretary, Wm. S. Appleton, 39 Beacon St.—Objects : The collecting of medals and coins and works on the subject of numismatics ; correcting the fallacies of articles on matters relating to medals and coins written by persons having no correct knowledge on the subject.—Membership unlimited ; resident, honorary, and corresponding.—The collection of the Society is not arranged. It publishes the " American Journal of Numismatics," illustrated, quarterly ; $2 a year in advance ; single copies, 50 cents.—Annual meeting in January.

BOSTON PUBLIC LIBRARY.—Boylston, near Tremont St.—Founded 1852.—Officers : Chairman of Board of Trustees, Wm. W. Greenough ; Librarian and Clerk of the Trustees, Mellen Chamberlain.—The Library was the recipient in 1852 of $100,000 in money and books from Mr. Joshua Bates, of London, after whom the upper or " Bates Hall" was named. Many other liberal donations and bequests were added to this sum, besides the yearly appropriation which the institution receives from the city. The Library (over 435,000 vols.) is very rich in works on art and its history, including many of the celebrated illustrated folios on antiquities, and on the galleries and churches of Europe, the large publications on the Paris Salon, Amand-Durand's reproductions of the old masters of engraving ; Charles Blanc's Rembrandt, etc. It is well supplied also with the best foreign art journals.—There are no funds for the purchase of paintings, statuary, and engravings as such, but the Library has come into possession, by gift, of quite a valuable collection of works of art, the most prominent constituent of which is the *Tosti Collection of Engravings*, next to the Phillips Collection in the Penns. Academy at Philadelphia, the largest public print collection in the United States. It consists of about 6,500 prints, and was presented by Mr. Thos. G. Appleton, who bought it in Rome of the heirs of Cardinal Tosti. About 5,100 of the prints are in bound volumes, and several hundred in portfolios. These can be examined on application at the desk in Bates Hall, from 9 A.M. to 12 M. Over 600 prints are framed, and are displayed in the various parts of the Library. The curator has in charge a catalogue of the collection, and there is also a complete card catalogue. Lists of the framed pictures, arranged numerically, can be had for temporary use on application. In the *Fine Arts Room*, on the lower floor, is to be seen one of the best and largest of Copley's paintings, " Charles I. demanding the Five Members," and a number of busts and other works in marble by Thos. Ball, R. S. Greenough, W. W. Story, Troschel, G. Albertoni, etc. There is also an antique marble portrait bust, a silver vase presented to Daniel Webster in 1835, and a " View of the Old State House," painted by Salmon in 1832. This room is open to both sexes during the day ; after 6 P.M. to ladies only. In the *Trustees' Room* are two original portraits of Franklin, painted by Greuze and Duplessis respectively ; and portraits of Joshua Bates, by Eddis ; Edward Everett, by J. Harvey Young ; and Charles Sumner, by Moses Wight. Access to this room can be gained on application at the desk in Bates Hall. A number of busts, etc., are scattered through the various rooms.—Bates Hall is open daily, Sundays and holidays excepted, from 9 A.M. to 6 P.M. from October to March, inclusive, and until 7 P.M. the rest of the year. The Lower Hall is open from 8½ A.M. to 9 P.M., except in July and August, when it closes at 8 P.M. The Central Reading-Room on the lower floor, in which many large framed engravings are hung, is open from 9 A.M. to 10 P.M., week-days, and on Sundays from 2 to 10 P.M., except in July and August, when it closes at 9 P.M. A new edition of the "Handbook for Readers," a very convenient little guide to the Library, was published in 1883. A complete list of the works of art in the Library, as well as of a few portraits, etc., belonging to its branches in Roxbury, Charlestown, Brighton, and Jamaica Plain, is given in this guide.—Books may be taken out under certain restrictions.

BOSTON SCHOOL OF SCULPTURE.—394 Federal St.—Opened 1879; incorporated 1881.—Board of Trustees: Mellen Chamberlain, Public Library; J. Foxcroft Cole, 433 Washington St.; J. Boyle O'Reilly, 597 Washington St.; E. P. Howe, 14 Pemberton Square; Frank Hill Smith, 171½ Tremont St.; F. P. Vinton, 1 Park Square; Wm. S. Dennett, M.D., Hotel Pelham; R. F. G. Candage, 13 Merchants' Exchange; Arlo Bates, 299 Washington St.; Jas. Taylor; Thos. Robinson. Director: Truman H. Bartlett.—This school was originally started as a private enterprise by its Director, with a view to providing adequate tuition for talented young men and women, who want to study modelling. Tuition, $15 per month to those who can pay; free to those who cannot pay. The amount of tuition fees received has been about one-tenth of the expenses. A few small donations have been made toward the maintenance of the institution, and one talented pupil, a girl, has been enabled, by the generosity of a private individual, to go to Paris, with the intention of fitting herself to teach on her return. Present number of pupils 6 (5 girls, 1 boy). There are applicants almost daily, who cannot be accommodated. Nearly all the work thus far executed by the pupils has been modelled in terra-cotta clay, including vases and decorated fireplaces. The latter were made to order, and about one-third of the former were sold.

BOSTON SOCIETY OF ARCHITECTS.—See *Boston Chapter of the American Institute of Architects.*

BOSTON SOCIETY OF DECORATIVE ART.—8 Park Square.—Organized March, 1878.—Officers: President, Roland C. Lincoln, 82 Devonshire St.; Vice-Presidents, John H. Sturgis, 19 Exchange Place, Mrs. Chas. P. Curtis, Jr., and Mrs. Frederick L. Ames; Secretary, Miss Georgina Lowell Putnam; Treasurer, George H. Homans.—Objects: To raise the standard and increase the production of artistic hand-wrought decoration, to furnish a market and assist art-workers, and to promote improvement of designs in manufactures.—Any person may become a member by an annual payment of $5. Number of members, April 1, 1883, 126.—The income of the Society is derived from membership fees, donations, tuition fees, profits on work executed in its work-room, and a commission of 10% charged on sales made for outside contributors.—*The School of Art Needlework* maintained by the Society is in charge of Miss Helen Smith, of South Kensington. Tuition fees, 6 class lessons, $5; 12 class lessons, $8. Classes are held in the Society's rooms, as well as elsewhere in Boston and the neighboring towns. Number of pupils last season, 130. The classes in china painting and in wood carving have been given up.—This Society, like all other kindred societies, combines benevolence with art. The work-rooms and salesrooms maintained by it are carried on mainly in the artistic and financial interest of the workers and of the contributors, that is, of the needlewomen, etc., who send the produce of their skill on sale. All work so sent must pass an examination, and rejected work is criticised, if the contributor demands it. As a charity the Society is quite as worthy of support as for artistic reasons. It gives work to many people needing the money, in an agreeable way, who otherwise would find it difficult, if not impossible, to earn anything. Its career has been quite successful. Sales last year, $17,153.13.—Annual meeting, first Monday in April.

BOSTON YOUNG MEN'S CHRISTIAN ASSOCIATION.—Corner Boylston and Berkeley Streets.—Officers: President, A. S. Woodworth; General Secretary, M. R. Deming.—This Association maintains an Evening Class in Free-Hand Drawing; Alfred J. Anthony, teacher of Drawing in Boston Evening Schools, instructor. Present number of pupils, both sexes, 27. The class is open

5

to members, who pay $1 for class privilege. Special tickets are issued to ladies at $2 for the whole course of 20 lessons.

DORCHESTER ANTIQUARIAN AND HISTORICAL SOCIETY, 18 Somerset St.—[No reply to repeated requests for information.]

FANEUIL HALL.—Over the platform in this "Cradle of Liberty" hangs an immense picture, measuring 16 × 30 feet. "Webster replying to Hayne in the U. S. Senate, Jan. 26 and 27, 1830," painted by Geo. P. A. Healy. A key to the picture, price 10 cents, can be bought at the Superintendent's office. Numerous portraits of celebrated Americans, especially of such as are famed in the history of Massachusetts, are hung upon the walls, and a few busts stand upon the platform. There is no list, however, of these works, the superintendent does not know anything about them, beyond the names of the subjects, which are attached to the frames, and it is impossible to examine them near by. The most interesting among the older pictures, such as Copley's John Hancock and Sam'l Adams, and Stuart's full length of Washington, have been removed to the Old State House and to the Museum of Fine Arts, and replaced by copies.—Open free every day, Sundays and holidays excepted, from 10 A.M. to 5 P.M. from Apr. 1 to Oct. 1 ; from 10 A.M. to 4 P.M. the rest of the year.

INDUSTRIAL ART TEACHERS' ASSOCIATION OF MASSACHUSETTS.—Organized December 28, 1882. (The date given last year, December 29, 1881, was that of a convention of teachers at which the desirability of an organization was first discussed.)—Officers : President, Walter S. Perry, Worcester, Mass.; V. P.. E. C. Colby, Lawrence, Mass.; Secretary and Treasurer, Albert H. Munsell, State Normal Art School, Boston, Mass.; Executive Committee : Geo. H. Bartlett, Miss R. L. Hoyt, E. C. Colby, E. C. Bowler, Eben Rose.—The Association meets once a year, at such time and place as may be appointed by the Executive Committee, for the purpose of comparing notes as to plans and methods of instruction, by the reading of short essays, explanations, and illustrations of personal experience, and discussions.—Members, both sexes, must be teachers of industrial drawing. Initiation fee, $1 ; annual dues, $1. Present number of members, 38.—The meeting is generally held in Boston, on a Thursday of the Christmas vacation. The meeting for 1883 was held December 27, at the rooms of the Art Club, Boston. The Association proposes to publish a paper read by Miss Hoyt, on "The Industrial Arts : Their Relation to the Fine Arts."

MASSACHUSETTS ART TEACHERS' ASSOCIATION.—Should be *Industrial Art Teachers' Association of Massachusetts,* Boston, which see above.

MASSACHUSETTS CHARITABLE MECHANIC ASSOCIATION.—Huntington Ave. and W. Newton St.—Organized 1795 ; incorporated 1806.—Officers for 1884 : President, Chas. R. McLean ; V. P., Thos. J. Whidden ; Secretary, Jos. L. Bates, 13½ Bromfield St.; Treasurer, Frederick W. Lincoln, 126 Commercial St.—This Society is one of the oldest and wealthiest of its kind in the United States. Among its founders were a number of men whose names are well known in American history, notably Paul Revere, silversmith, engraver, and patriot, and the hero of Longfellow's celebrated poem. Although originally conceived as a protective and benevolent Society, the Association early turned its attention to other means of benefiting the mechanic arts and their professors, and out of this desire grew the Industrial Exhibitions, the Fourteenth of which occurred in 1881. As a rule these "Fairs" are held triennially, and the Fifteenth will occur in October, 1884. At all of them, from the very beginning, more or less space was devoted to art, and many of the artists of renown of the present day were here early encouraged and rewarded. As an example may be cited Thomas Ball, whose model of the statue of Webster, from which he afterwards executed the statue ordered by Mr. Gordon F. Burnham for the Central Park, New York, was awarded a gold medal in 1856. The Association moreover claims that it was the first in the United States to add the fine arts to an Industrial Exposition as a separate and distinct department, controlled by connoisseurs and artists, and bestowing medals. This was first done, at the suggestion of Mr. Chas. W. Slack, at the Twelfth Exhibition held in 1874. The experiment was repeated in 1878, and the successes of these two years established the Art Department as a permanent feature of the exhibitions of the Association. The last exhibition was held in the spacious building erected by the Society for its purposes, at a total cost of about $500,000. This building contains, besides two vast halls for the industrial shows, offices, etc., two large picture galleries with skylights, and seven smaller cabinets, with excellent northern exposure, all of which are given up to the various branches of art at the exhibitions. [See illustration.] The awards consist of medals in gold, silver, and bronze, and in diplomas.— Annual meeting in January.

MASSACHUSETTS HISTORICAL SOCIETY.—30 Tremont St.—Founded 1791.— Officers: President, Robert C. Winthrop; Treasurer, Chas. C. Smith; Secretary, Edward J. Young; Librarian, Samuel A. Green, M.D.; Keeper of the Cabinet, F. E. Oliver, M.D.—Membership limited to 100.—The library, which contains over 28,000 books and 50,000 pamphlets, may be used for reference by any person introduced by a member.—The Society possesses many valuable relics and a number of interesting portraits, among which are those of Govs. Endicott, Pownall (a copy by Henry C. Pratt from the original by Francis Cotes), Dudley, Belcher, Winthrop, Hutchinson, Strong (by Chester Harding), Gore, etc. There is also a portrait of John Adams, by Gilbert Stuart Newton; a copy of a portrait of Sir Richard Saltonstall, by Rembrandt; a copy of an excellent portrait of Sebastian Cabot from an original said to be by Holbein; portraits by Stuart of Jeremiah Allen, Edward Everett (unfinished), and Lieut.-Gov. Cobb; and others by Henly, Osgood, Sargent, Marston, Wight, etc. A catalogue of the works of art owned by the Society is in preparation.

MASSACHUSETTS INSTITUTE OF TECHNOLOGY.—Boylston St., between Berkeley and Clarendon Sts.—Incorporated 1861.—Officers of the Corporation: President, Francis A. Walker; Secretary, Lewis Wm. Tappan, Jr.; Treasurer, John Cummings. President of the Faculty, Francis A. Walker, Ph.D., LL.D.—Objects: Instituting and maintaining a Society of Arts, a Museum of Arts, and a School of Industrial Science, and aiding generally, by suitable means, the advancement, development, and practical application of sciences in connection with arts, agriculture, manufactures, and commerce.—The Institute receives annually from the State one-third part of the interest from the fund created under the act of Congress giving public lands to the States in aid of instruction in agriculture, etc. Otherwise it is dependent for its maintenance upon tuition fees and the munificence of private patrons.—There are nine regular *Courses of Instruction*, extending over four years, but provision has also been made for those who desire to pursue special or partial courses. During the first year, which is the same to all regular students, a large amount of time is devoted to practice in drawing. Instructors: Henry K. Burrison, S.B.; A. E. Burton, S.B.; Dwight Porter, Ph.B. In subsequent years, drawing is continued with professional studies as follows:—Civil Engineering: 2d year, Descriptive Geometry and Plans and Profiles; 3d, Engineering Drawing; 4th, Practice in Design. Mechanical Engineering: 2d year, Machine Drawing and Descriptive Geometry; 3d, Machine Drawing and Perspective; 4th, Machine Drawing. Mining Engineering: Drawing in the first terms of 2d and 4th years only. Chemistry: Drawing in second term of 3d year only. Metallurgy: Drawing in first term of 3d and both terms of 4th year. Natural History: Drawing during 2d year; Drawing with the Microscope, first term of 4th year. Physics: No Drawing. General Courses (for such as may not intend to adopt a distinctly scientific profession, yet desire to obtain an education through studies of a predominantly scientific character): Course A, Physics predominating, no drawing; Course B, Chemistry, Botany, and Zoölogy predominating, Drawing of Crystals, first term of second year; Course C, Geology, with Botany and Zoölogy predominating, Drawing of Crystals (1st term, 2d year), Topographical Drawing (2d term, 2d year), Map Drawing (2d term, 3d year, and 2d term, 4th year), and Drawing with the Microscope (1st term, 4th year).—*Course in Architecture.* Instructors: Theodore M. Clark, A.B., Prof. of Architecture; Eugene Letang, Asst. Prof. of Architecture; Edward F. Ely, Instructor in Architecture; Ross Turner, Instructor in Water Color. Lectures on special subjects are occasionally delivered by architects not connected with the Institute. It is the object of this department to give to its students the instruction and discipline that cannot be obtained in architects' offices. The course is, however, practical as well as theoretical, and, besides the scientific study of construction and materials, it comprises the study of building processes, and of professional practice and procedure, as well as that of composition and design, and of the history of the art. The students are also given an opportunity to practice carpentry in the shops of the School of Mechanic Arts (see below), and by their studies in the modern languages, literature, and history, are provided with that general culture which is needed by every person of intelligence. Drawing, including Free-Hand, Perspective, Original Design, Sketching in Water Color, etc., plays an important part throughout the whole of this course. Besides the regular course, designed for students who wish to pursue the study of architecture in the most thorough manner, with all the appliances which literature and science may afford, there is also a special course of two years, which embraces only the architectural, without the scientific, mathematical, mechanical, and engineering studies, for those who desire to fit themselves simply as draughtsmen, or to complement the practical education received in the office.—The conditions of admission to the regular course are, in general, the training of the high school or academy, with a good grounding in mathematics : applicants must have attained the age of sixteen.—Fees for either course, $200 a year; two terms, beginning respectively on the last Monday in Sept., and the first Tuesday after Jan. 28. There are three scholarships, open to students in all the courses, and the Boston Society of Architects has established two special prizes in the department of architecture, of the value of $50 each, which are given in books.—The Degree of Bachelor of Science is awarded to those who pass the requisite examination at the completion of the regular course. Number of students in the Dep't of Architecture : Regular, 5 ; special, 29 (all males).—*The Architectural Museum* of the school contains several thousand photographs, prints, drawings, and casts, bought with funds specially raised for the purpose. To these have been added photographs, lithographs, original drawings, etc., presented to the Institute by French, English, and American architects and architectural societies; together with specimens of metal-work, tile-work, glass-work, wood-work, etc., partly purchased, partly deposited by manufacturers, the whole forming a museum of sanitary and building appliances. A chief part of the collection of casts has been deposited in the Museum of Fine Arts, along with the architectural collections of the Museum, access to which is free to the students.—*The Architectural Library* contains nearly 400 vols. The students are besides given every facility in the use of the Boston Public Library.—*The School of Mechanic Arts* connected with the Institute affords such students as have completed the ordinary grammar-school course an opportunity to continue elementary, scientific and literary studies and drawing, while receiving instruction in the use of the typical tools for working iron and wood. The shop work is conducted on the plan of the Imperial Technical School at Moscow, Russia. Peter Schwaab, S.B., Director of the Workshops; Chas. L. Adams, Instructor in Drawing.—The full course extends over two years. In the first year Mechanical and Free-Hand Drawing is taught ; in the second, Mechanical Drawing only.—Tuition, $150 a year ; special charges for special students. The student is entitled to the products of his work. Two scholarships have been founded by the Mass. Charitable Mech. Assoc. for sons of its members.—Number of students 54 (males).—*The Lowell School of Practical Design* was founded in 1872, by the late John Amory Lowell and other manufacturers, and is maintained by the Trustee of the Lowell Institute. Instructor: Charles Kastner. Students are taught practically as well as theoretically, the art of making patterns for prints, ginghams, delaines, silks, laces, paper hangings, carpets, oilcloths, etc. The school is constantly provided with samples of novelties, and the weaving department connected with the school, in charge of a special assistant, is provided with a great variety of looms. There is also a camera obscura with all the appliances necessary for transferring designs to rollers. All of these have been given by manufacturers, who also supply most of the materials used in the weaving department. During the year the pupils visit print works, carpet mills, etc.—Applicants must have attained proficiency in free-hand drawing and in the use of instruments. Tuition free, but students supply their own materials, etc., Number of students, 60, of both sexes. Of the graduates of the school, according to last published report, 58 are employed in carpet mills, etc., as designers and draughtsmen. Of these 34 are males and 24 females.--*Free Courses of Instruction*, open to both sexes, are given in the evening in a variety of subjects, including drawing and architecture. These courses vary and are announced specially each year.

MUSEUM OF FINE ARTS.—Dartmouth St. and St. James Ave.—Incorporated 1870. —Officers : Pres., Martin Brimmer, 47 Beacon St. ; Treas., Henry P. Kidder, 2 Newbury St. ; Honorary Director, Charles C. Perkins, 2 Walnut St. ; Curator, Chas. G. Loring ; Sec., Edw. H. Greenleaf.—Objects : Erecting a museum for the preservation and exhibition of works of art, making, maintaining, and exhibiting collections of such works, and affording instruction in the fine arts. —Governed by a Board of Trustees, not to exceed thirty, consisting of the original Incorporators, three persons to be appointed annually by Harvard College, three by the Athenæum, and three by the Mass. Inst. of Technology, and *ex officio*, the Mayor of the City, the Pres'd of Trustees of the Public Library, the Supt. of the Public Schools of Boston, the Secretary of the B'd of Education, and the Trustee of the Lowell Institute. Vacancies occurring among the Trustees whose annual appointment is not provided for, are filled by the whole Board.—The income of the Museum is derived from subscriptions, legacies, and donations, from entrance fees, from the interest on several endow-ment funds (Everett Fund, $7,500 ; N. C. Nash Fund, $10,000 ; B. P. Cheney Fund, $5,000 ; John L. Gardner Fund, $20,000 ; Otis Norcross Fund, $5,000). The cash receipts from subscrip-tions, etc., up to the date of the last report, Jan. 18, 1883, amounted to $448,412.32. The popular character of the subscriptions from which the greater part of this sum resulted, the individual amounts ranging from 35 cents to $25,000, is a special and interesting feature in the history of the institution. The Museum began its existence in the galleries of the Athenæum. The present build-ing, erected from plans by Messrs. Sturgis & Brigham, on land given by the city, was first partially opened to the public on July 4, 1876, and represents only about one-fourth of the structure as it is to be in future. [See illustration.] Its cost, exclusive of interior fittings, is $320,944.11. For pur-chases of works of art, only $26,812.02 have thus far been expended. By far the greater part of the collections was acquired by donations and bequests, supplemented by loans and deposits.—This Museum is very systematic and thoroughly educational in its arrangement. Its collections of Egyptian antiquities, the gift of Mr. C. Granville Way and of the Lowell family, and of casts from Assyrian, Greek, and Roman sculptures, partly deposited by the Athenæum, partly purchased with funds obtained from a bequest by Chas. Sumner, illustrate almost every phase of the rise and decline of ancient sculpture. The sculptures, architectural fragments, etc., brought from Assos by the expedition sent out by the Archæological Institute of America, are the most important addition lately made in this department. A number of Tanagra figurines, given by Mr. Thos. G. Appleton, vessels of earthen and glass ware, presented by Mr. J. J. Dixwell, Mr. Thos. G. Appleton, Mr. Henry P. Kidder, and others, a complete set of the electrotypes from ancient coins published by the British Museum, bronzes, and other objects, serve to give a good idea of the minor arts of the ancients. The collec-tion of architectural casts is very rich, including a full-size cast of the Portico of the Caryatides, from Athens. The sculpture of the Renaissance, and its industrial arts, and the industrial arts of the East and of mediæval Europe, in ceramics, enamels, textiles, carvings, metal work, etc., are well represented, and a small beginning has also been made toward a collection illustrating the art of the aborigines of America. The collection of paintings, old as well as modern, is steadily growing. Many of the paintings permanently exhibited have been deposited by the Athenæum and a few have been given, but the greater part are temporary loans. Among those which are destined to remain are excellent specimens by Copley, West, Stuart (including the famous Athenæum heads of General and Mrs. Washington), Allston, Newton, Hunt, and other American artists ; a few good old paint-ings, and several by celebrated modern European artists, especially of the French School. A collec-tion of ten pictures by old Dutch masters, bought at the San Donato sale, by Mr. Stanton Blake, and at present hung in the Museum, will probably be bought for the institution. A number of fine old Italian pictures have been loaned by Prof. T. C. Felton. American sculpture is represented by the work of such artists as Crawford, Horatio and Richard S. Greenough, Harriet Hosmer, Dengler, Rimmer, Aug. St. Gaudens, and Olin L. Warner. The Museum is also the depository of the *Gray Collection of Engravings*, consisting of about 6,000 choice impressions, illustrating the history of the art from its very beginnings, and including some rarities, as, for example, a copy of the " Monte Sancto di Dio." This collection was bequeathed to Harvard College by the late Francis C. Gray, who also left a fund of $15,000 for its maintenance and increase. It has been deposited only tem-porarily, but the Museum has already begun to form the nucleus of a print collection of its own, towards which some bequests and donations have been made, one of the most important being that of the collection of engraved portraits by the late Charles Sumner. A distinctive feature of this col-lection is its American department. The great interest shown by the Museum in the works of the etchers, wood engravers, etc., of the country, has induced many of them to present proofs of their works, and in this they have been followed by some of the publishers. Two of the rooms on the upper floor are devoted to an exhibition of prints, which are changed from time to time. The speci-mens in portfolios can only be examined upon application to the Secretary of the Museum, Mr. E. H. Greenleaf, who is also the curator of the Gray Collection.—*The Library* is as yet small, but is con-stantly growing. It can also be consulted upon application to Mr. Greenleaf.—An important feature in the management of the Museum is found in its *Special Exhibitions*, most of which have been of great interest. (Spanish pictures, loaned by the Duc de Montpensier, in 1874 ; Works of Wm. M. Hunt, 1879-80; Works of Gilbert Stuart, of Dr. Wm. Rimmer, of Wm. Blake, 1880 ; Works of Washington Allston, American Etchings, American Wood Engravings, 1881, etc.). An exhibition of Works by Living American Artists is held annually.—The great need of the Museum—besides the enlargement of the building, which is already too small for the proper display of the collections—is an adequate endowment fund. "The Museum," says one of the reports, "has the ill-deserved reputation of being a wealthy corporation." The truth is, that the current receipts are considerably below the current expenses, and that for purchases, it is compelled to rely almost entirely upon the generosity of its friends.—The Museum publishes a catalogue in two parts, "Part 1, Sculpture and Antiquities." "Part 2, Paintings, Drawings, Engravings, and Decorative Art." Price, 25 cents each part. Revised editions are frequently issued. Special catalogues of the special exhibitions are also issued.—Open on Mondays from 12 M., on other week days from 9 A.M. to 5 P.M.; Sundays from 1 to 5 P.M. Admission free on Saturdays and Sundays; 25 cents on other days. From Jan. 1, 1877, to Dec. 31. 1881, the Museum was visited by 779,270 persons, of whom 89,302 paid an admission fee. Number of visitors, 1882, 183,155. of whom 17,515 paid an admission fee; 1883, 152,551, of whom 16,720 paid an admission fee.—*The School of Drawing and Painting* connected with the Museum, established Dec., 1876, is under the care of a permanent committee. Officers of Comm.: Chairm., Edw. C. Cabot, 60 Devonshire St.; Sec., Wm. P. P. Longfellow, at the Museum ; Treas., Edw. W. Hooper, 40 State St.—Instructors : Otto Grundmann, Freder. Crowninshield, and assistants.—Classes : First Drawing Class: elementary work (ornament, still-life, drapery, antique, living model ; elements of shades, shadows, and perspective ; architectural and decorative form), such as is needed not only by painters, but also by engravers, lithographers, designers, and teachers of drawing. Second Drawing Class (antique, still-life, life, lectures in anatomy); intended as a preparation for the painting class, and mainly for those who wish to become professional artists. Painting Class; candidates must satisfy the instructors that they have sufficiently mastered the preparatory work; the instructors visit this class only often enough to make sure that the students are working in the right direction. Lectures are given on the History of Painting, Sculpture and Architecture, Mythological, Legendary and Sacred Art, Theory and History of Ornamentation, and Costume. Some of the pupils also sketch from nature, and practise composition under the direction of the instructors. The Evening Class in Elementary Drawing has been discontinued, as the City Schools amply supply this instruction; but there is an Evening Class for drawing from the nude, for advanced students, without instruction, the members of which are assessed simply for the expenses incurred.—Tuition fees : Admission fee for new students, $10; fees, $45 a term, or $90 per year ; to artists already practising, $25 a term, or $50 a year. A small sum is also charged for some of the lectures. A number of free scholarships have been established, which are assigned, on application, and after probation, to students who have been six months in the school.—Students are required to work not less than three hours a day, for four days in a week. Three terms of twelve weeks each yearly, beginning for the present season (eighth year), Oct. 2, 1883, and Jan. 1, and Apr. 1, 1884.— Number of students last year, 112 (30 men, 82 women).—The last year of the school has been as successful as its predecessors. The income from tuition fees has covered the cost of maintenance.

NEW ENGLAND CONSERVATORY OF MUSIC.—Franklin Square.—Organized

1857; incorporated 1870 : Art School added, 1882.—Officers : Pres., Hon. Rufus S. Frost ; V.P., Hon. Alex. H. Rice ; Sec., L. A. Chase ; Treas., Hon. Wm. P. Ellison ; Auditor, Wm. O. Grover ; Director, E. Tourjée.—*The Conservatory School of Fine Arts.*—The general aim of the school is to supply as thorough and complete a training in fine art as the professional schools give to the lawyer, physician, or theologian. Industrial drawing merely, or normal instruction only, is not the aim of the school.—There are three departments, the School of Drawing, the School of Painting, the School of Modelling. Certificates are given in each department to those who pass an examination, which is optional, and the Diploma of the Conservatory, to those who pass examinations in all three departments. There are, besides, classes in Wood Carving, Art Embroidery, Special Classes in special subjects, and Saturday Classes for Teachers.—Instructors : Wm. Briggs, Mary E. Carter, F. M. Lamb, T. H. Bartlett, Wm. Willard, F. M. Huntington.—The school year is divided into four terms. Tuition fees, $20 per term of 10 weeks ; variable for special and other classes.—Number of pupils, school year 1882-3, 197. Both sexes taught together.

NEW ENGLAND HISTORIC GENEALOGICAL SOCIETY.—18 Somerset St.

—[No reply to repeated requests for information.]

NEW ENGLAND MANUFACTURERS' AND MECHANICS' INSTITUTE.—

Huntington Ave. Organized 1881.—Officers: Pres., Jas. L. Little ; Treas., John F. Wood, 38

Hawley St ; Sec., F. W. Griffin.—This association holds yearly fairs, combined with exhibitions of works of art, in a building erected specially for the purpose. The second of these Art Exhibitions opened September 5. and closed November 3, 1883. There is no jury of admission.—Com. on Conduct of Exposition : John M. Little. Ch'man ; Jas. L. Little, John F. Wood, Fred. W. Griffin. Director of Art Dept.: Frank T. Robinson, Hotel Pelham.

OLD SOUTH MEETING-HOUSE.—Washington St., cor Milk.

—Visitors to Boston will be attracted to this building by the historical associations connected with it, and the interest is still further enhanced by the Museum of colonial, revolutionary, and other relics which has been established within its walls. Students who take a special interest in the history of art in America will find a few rare specimens of the rude work of the early engravers of the country, such as Peter Pelham's Portrait of Cotton Mather, engraved by him 1727, from his own painting ; the Rev. Wm. Cooper, after J. Smibert, 1743, by the same engraver ; the Rev. Wm. Wellsteed, painted and engraved by Copley, 1753 ; John Adams, engraved by Geo. Graham ; Paul Revere's " Bloody Massacre," etc. There are also a few paintings, among them a full-length of Edward Everett. executed in 1838 by Henry C. Pratt, an artist, who died November 27, 1880. The statue of Harriet Martineau, lately executed by Miss Anne Whitney, has been temporarily placed in the meeting-house.—Open on week days from 9 A.M. to 6 P.M. Admission, 25 cents. The proceeds go to the fund for the preservation of the building.

OLD STATE HOUSE.—Washington and State Sts.

—This building, known until the adoption of the State Constitution in 1780, as Boston Town-House, was erected in 1713, and the brick walls, together with the tower, date from that period. The interior, which was nearly destroyed by the fire of 1747, but restored in 1750, has sustained many changes in its details since the revolutionary period. The floors, walls, and roof are, however, substantially as they existed at that time, all the original timbers remaining in the building. The restoration made by order of the City of Boston, in 1881, follows the original architectural outlines, and all of the structure embraced in the interior above the first story is believed to be an accurate restoration in every respect of the structure of the Revolution. The exterior is entirely that of the latter period, the building occupying the same area which in 1634 was set apart by vote of the inhabitants of Boston as a market-place. The first Town-House was built thereon in 1657, and burned in 1711 ; the walls of the present structure were erected 1711-13, and the building was occupied the beginning of 1713. It is probable that the ground upon which this edifice stands is the only piece of real estate in Boston which has never been bought or sold. It is closely identified with the eventful annals of the provincial and revolutionary periods, and it is also worthy of recollection that, until the occupation of the present State House on Beacon Hill, it was the official seat of the government of the Province and the State, and that the visitor to the Council Chamber looks from the same east window, from the balcony under which three kings of England were proclaimed in provincial days. The City of Boston, desirous that the historic building should be free of access to all citizens in the community, like Faneuil Hall, has placed the upper portion, embracing the ancient Council Chamber and Representatives' Hall, in the custody of a society of citizens known as the Bostonian Society, with the understanding that it shall keep the halls open to the public, and advance the plan of the city by the establishment of a collection of objects connected with, and descriptive of, the historical past of Boston and its vicinity — Among the relics, etc.. already gathered are Copley's portraits of Samuel Adams and John Hancock, formerly in Faneuil Hall ; a Washington, painted by Stuart for Josiah Quincy in 1810 ; Josiah Quincy, Jr., painted by Stuart from an engraving and from recollections ; a view of the Tremont House in 1832, by R. Salmon ; an interesting picture by Moses Wight, " The Laying of the Corner-Stone of Beacon Hill Reservoir, November 22, 1847 ;" portraits of Chief-Justices Sewall and Addington, of the colonial period ; of different members of the Boston clergy of that time, and a number of early views in and around Boston. Here may be seen, also, the table used by the Honorable Council of the Province before the Revolution, occupying its original position in the old Council Chamber ; the old hall clock of the Rev. Mather Byles, the noted loyalist, and first pastor of the Hollis Street Church, and many other objects of interest.—Open week days, free, from 9.30 A.M. to 5 P.M. [The historical account of the building, kindly supplied by Mr. James Rindge Stanwood, of the Bostonian Society, is, perhaps, rather foreign to the aim of this volume. But its very interesting character will readily explain the willingness with which it has been admitted.]

PAINT AND CLAY CLUB.—419 Washington St.—Organized June, 1880.—Officers : Chairm., J. Ph. Rinn ; Sec., J. B. Millet, 4 Park St.; Treas., E. H. Garrett.—Objects: The production of works of art, literature, and music ; and the promotion of social intercourse among the members.—No person admitted who is not a member of the professions of architecture, painting, music, engraving, or literature, or of some profession connected with the practice of art ; no honorary members ; membership unlimited (since reorganization, Dec., 1883). Present number of members, about 40. Entrance fee, $15 ; annual assessment, $15. Special assessments may be made by a two-thirds vote.—The Club gives musical entertainments, and holds receptions and exhibitions. The third exhibition took place at the rooms of the Boston Art Club, in February, 1884. Non-members are admitted to these various entertainments to a limited extent.—The members of the Club have illustrated T. B. Aldrich's poems for Messrs. Houghton, Mifflin & Co., and a similar undertaking is now under consideration.—Annual meeting, second Wednesday in May.

PERMANENT EXHIBITIONS of foreign and American works of art will be found at the galleries of the dealers, of whom the following are the leading ones : *J. Eastman Chase*, 7 Hamilton Pl.; *Doll & Richards*, 2 Park St.; *Thos. Inglis*, 145 Tremont St.; *J. A. Lowell & Co.*, 70 Kilby St.; *Noyes & Blakeslee*, 127 Tremont St.; *Williams & Everett*, 508 Washington St. As a rule these galleries are open free, but the two firms last named occasionally hold special exhibitions, at which an admission fee, usually of 25 cents, is charged.

ROXBURY CRAYON CLUB.—Cox Building, No. 1 Dudley St., Rooms 25 and 26.— Organized Jan. 11, 1879.—Objects: Drawing and painting from life (nude and draped model), and from cast.—The affairs of the Club are managed ,by a Business Committee of three, who are elected annually, and organize themselves. Committee for 1884 : P. Prymatchempko, No. 2 Malbone Pl., Ch'man ; W. F. Brown, 33 Glenwood St., Sec.; D. Fausel, 286 Roxbury St., Treas. The Club has no permanent presiding officer, every meeting electing its own chairman.—Membership limited to 35 (until the Club has better accommodations) ; present number of members, 30.—Small collection of photographs, engravings, educational works, etc.—Besides the meetings for practice, there are two lectures each week, Monday and Thursday evenings. Lecturer, Theo. Chominsky, artist.—Annual meeting, first Monday in January.

SOUTH BOSTON SCHOOL OF ART.—East Fourth, near Dorchester St.—This school was organized under the provisions of the John Hawes fund, left by will in 1829, for religious and educational purposes. The fund is managed by five Trustees. Trustee in charge of school : Chas. T. Gallagher, 26 Thomas Park, So. Boston, or Rogers B'ldg., 209 Washington St.—Objects of the School : To furnish instruction in mechanical and free-hand drawing to residents of South Boston.— Pupils must be at least 16 years of age. Rules generally the same as those of city drawing schools. Instruction free. Implements furnished by school, materials by pupils. - Number of pupils, 67 free-hand, 94 mechanical, in two classes. Both sexes taught together.—Instructors : Mechanical drawing, Thos. S. Brown and H. E. Spiller ; Free-hand, Geo. H. Bartlett, assisted by Miss Lamb. —The work of the school is exhibited at the annual exhibition of the City Evening Drawing Schools.

ST. BOTOLPH CLUB.—85 Bolyston St.—Organized Jan. 10, 1880.—Officers : Pres., Francis Parkman, 50 Chestnut St.; V. Ps., Samuel A. Green, George Fuller ; Treas., Francis A. Osborn ; Sec., Arthur B. Ellis, 209 Washington St.—Object : The promotion of social intercourse among authors and artists, and other gentlemen connected with or interested in literature and art.— Members (males only) must be twenty-one years of age ; entrance fee, $20 ; annual assessments, $30. Membership limited to 350. The Club is full.—The Club holds two exhibitions of works by its members each year, to which non-members are admitted by tickets. Exhibitions of works by non-members are also held occasionally.—Annual meeting, last Saturday in December.

STATE HOUSE.—Cor. Beacon and Mt. Vernon Sts.—A number of portraits of historical interest, of whose authors little definite is known, are hung in the Senate Chamber, including the portraits of governors John Winthrop, John Endicott, Simon Bradstreet, Wm. Burnet, Increase Sumner, and Wm. Eustis. In the Library is a crayon head of Gen. Thos. Gage, which is of special interest as it is supposed to be the only authentic portrait in existence, and came into the possession of the State directly from the family. In the entrance hall, known as Doric Hall, is Sir

Francis Chantrey's statue of Washington and Thos. Ball's statue of Gov. Andrew; also busts of Samuel Adams, Abr. Lincoln, Chas. Sumner, and Henry Wilson. Before the State House stand the statues of Horace Mann, by Emma Stebbins, and Daniel Webster, by Hiram Powers.—The Senate Chamber is accessible during the sessions of the Senate, which begin the first Wednesday in January. The Library is open on week days from 9 A.M. to 5 P.M., except on Saturdays, when it closes at 2 P.M.

STATE NORMAL ART SCHOOL OF MASSACHUSETTS.—1679 Washington St.—This School was established by the State in 1873, and is controlled by the State B'd of Education. Officers of the B'd : Sec., John W. Dickinson, A.M., State House ; Asst. Sec. and Treas., C. B. Tillinghast, State House.—Objects : The School is intended as a training school for the teachers and masters required for the industrial drawing schools of the State, who must also be able to direct and superintend instruction in industrial drawing in the public schools.—Faculty : G. H. Bartlett, Princ., and Instructor in Free-Hand and Light and Shade Drawing ; W. F. Brackett, Architecture and Perspective ; C. M. Carter, A.M., Normal Instruction ; A. H. Munsell, A.M., Sculpture and advanced Perspective ; Miss R. L. Hoyt, Painting in Water Color ; Miss M. A. Bailey, Painting in Oil ; A. K. Cross, Topographical and Ship Draughting ; W. F. Merrill, Machine Construction.—Course of Instruction : Industrial Drawing, including both Instrumental and Free-Hand Drawing, is taught by lectures and by individual instruction ; the artistic work in the studios, comprising Free-Hand Drawing and Designing, is also under the immediate direction of the Instructors. The work of the four classes, representing a four-years' course, is arranged as follows : Class A, Elementary Drawing ; Class B, Form, Color, and Industrial Design ; Class C, Constructive Arts ; Class D, Sculpture and Design in the Round. Students, as a rule, will not be allowed to remain in any class longer than two years. Graduates may review the course of study for one year (without fee) on condition that they will devote some time to teaching in the School. Qualified students of Classes B, C, and D may be selected to act as Assistants in Class A, and from the monthly reports on their conduct and efficiency, recommendations for appointments as teachers will be made. The School does not, however, undertake any responsibility with regard to securing appointments. Special students are also admitted.—Candidates must be above sixteen years of age. An examination in free-hand drawing of ornament from copy, and object-drawing from the solid, is held at the beginning of each term for admission to the regular course. There is no examination for special students.—Tuition is free to residents of the State intending to teach drawing, but $5 per term is charged for incidentals ; to students from without the State, $50 per term. Special students from Massachusetts, $25 per term ; from other States, $50 per term. There are two terms, running, for the present season, from Sept. 3, 1883, to Jan. 18, 1884, and from Feb. 4 to June 28, 1884.—Certificates of four grades are given. The diploma of the School is given to those students who have completed the subjects of study, and passed the examinations of the fourth grade in all the classes.— Number of students, up to June 30, 1883, the end of last school year : 143 (102 females, 41 males). Number of certificates given, examination of 1883 : 1st class, 24 (18 females, 6 males) ; 2d class, 14 (10 females, 4 males) ; 3d class, 5 (1 female, 4 males) ; 4th class, 6 (1 female, 5 males) : total, 49 (30 females, 19 males). Diplomas as art masters, 6 ; art mistresses, 1 : total, 7.

ZEPHO CLUB.—427 Washington St.—Organized Dec., 1879.—Officers 1883-4 : Pres., A. Buhler, 3 Park St.; Treas., C. Storer, 181 Devonshire St.; Sec., A. S. Kilburn, 433 Washington St. —Object : To provide a place where drawing from the life can be practised.—Membership limited to 35. Present number of members, 26. Candidates, previous to election, must submit a sketch.— Entrance fee, $5 ; monthly assessments not to exceed $2.50.—The Club meets twice a week for drawing ; F. P. Vinton, critic.—Annual meeting, first Tuesday in November.

14. Brooklyn, N. Y.

ADELPHI ACADEMY.—Lafayette Ave., cor. St. James Pl.—Incorporated 1869.—Officers : Pres., Chas. Pratt, 232 Clinton Ave.; Treas., Harold Dollner, 259 Washington Ave.; Sec., Edw. F. de Selding, 9 Lefferts Pl.; Principal, Stephen G. Taylor, A.M., Ph.D., 316 Lafayette Ave.— Objects : To afford the very best facilities to both sexes (taught together) for a thorough and complete education. Departments : Preparatory, Academic, Collegiate (with Classical, Literary,

Scientific, and Commercial Courses) and Art.—*Art Department:* Drawing, as a general study, is taught in all the classes, with the exception of those of the Classical Course. The more advanced scholars and special students of art receive instruction in the Studio, which is abundantly furnished with casts from statuary, and models from nature. Unusual facilities are offered to classes for drawing and painting in oil and water-colors from life.—Tuition fees: Drawing, $10 per session of 10 weeks, or $15 for two sessions; Painting, $15 per session.—John B. Whittaker, 745 Lafayette Ave., Prof. of Painting and Drawing; M. Elizabeth Greely, 39 Schermerhorn St., Free-Hand Drawing; Mechanical Drawing, W. C. Peckham.—Special Students in Art Dept., 92 (10 male, 82 female). [From last year's issue. No reply to repeated requests for later information. In June, 1883, the Art Department held an exhibition of students' work, of which an illustrated catalogue was published. The number of students under Prof. Whittaker was at the same time reported to be 175 regular, and 116 from outside.]

ADELPHI ART ASSOCIATION.—Adelphi Academy, cor. St. James Pl. and Lafayette Avenue.—Organized May 22, 1883, by pupils of the Adelphi Academy Art Dept.—Officers: Pres., Miss Eleanor C. Bannister, 191 Montague St.; V. P., Mrs. A. M. Pinkham, 266 Throop Ave.; Sec., Miss N. E. Sawyer, 46 New York Ave.; Treas., Miss L. E. Semonite, 908 Greene Ave.—Objects: Instruction in the art of drawing and painting, such instruction to be gained by a course of study or reading on art topics, by sketching from nature, by original composition, and by lectures.—Conditions of membership: Membership, past or present, in one or more of the art classes of the Adelphi Academy, sufficient knowledge of art, and payment of $1 annually. Present number of members, 54.—Sketching class once a week: meetings once a month for original composition, discussion of art topics, and transaction of business. Prof. J. B. Whittaker, instructor of the Adelphi Academy Art Dept., is identified with the association, and has a general supervision of the work done by members.

BROOKLYN ART ASSOCIATION.—Montague, n. Clinton St.—Instituted 1861; incorporated June 29, 1864.—Officers: Pres., Frederic Cromwell; V. P., Wm. H. Husted; Treas., Gordon L. Ford; Sec., Theod. E. Smith.—Objects: To promote the cultivation of Fine Arts; to establish a Gallery, a Library, and a School of Design.—Real and personal property of the Association exempted from taxation by special act of Legislature, Apr. 23, 1867, so long as the same shall be devoted exclusively to the advancement of the Fine Arts, or be used as a free school of design. Authorized to issue certificates of stock to amount of $100,000, by special act of Legislature, Apr. 30, 1881. Besides the stockholders, there are life-members, upon payment of $100, and annual subscribers, who pay $10 annually, if laymen, or $5 if professional artists.—*Exhibitions:* The Association holds frequent exhibitions, among which the Twenty-fourth, or "Chronological Exhibition of American Art," Mch. 12 to Apr. 6, 1872, deserves special mention. It contained 120 numbers, and illustrated the history of art in America, from John Watson, the first professional artist at work here of whom there is a definite record (1715), down to our own time. Up to the end of the year 1883, forty-seven exhibitions had been held altogether.—The Association owns a spacious and handsome building [see illustration], specially put up for its purposes, and completed in 1872. It is connected with the adjoining Academy of Music, which is utilized at the receptions given during the winter season.—Annual meeting, second Monday in April.—*Students' Guild of the Brooklyn Art Association:* The Free-School of Design, formerly maintained by the Association, was given up some time ago, but with the beginning of the fall season of 1883, it assumed charge of the classes heretofore known as "The Brooklyn Art Guild." The objects of this school are, to furnish in Brooklyn a thorough course of instruction in Drawing, Painting and Modelling, at the lowest rates consistent with the support of the school. It is managed by a Board of Control, consisting of members from the Art Association and the Art Guild, under an agreement which insures that the school shall be conducted in the interest of the students. The school retains its old rooms at 201 Montague St., and, in addition occupies the top floor of the adjoining building, which has been remodelled for the purpose.—Instructor: Thomas Eakins.—Classes: Life Classes, drawing, painting, and modelling, for gentlemen; Portrait Classes, drawing, painting, and modelling, for ladies and gentlemen; Still Life Class, for ladies and gentlemen; Antique Classes, for ladies and gentlemen; Sketch Class, for ladies and gentlemen; Composition Class, Lectures on Perspective and Anatomy.—Terms: Life Classes, drawing, painting and modelling, $65 for the season; Portrait Classes, drawing and modelling, $80 for the season ; One Life and One Portrait Class, $70 for the season ; Still Life Class, painting, $42 for the season ; Day Antique Class, drawing, or painting, $25 for the season ; Evening Antique Class, free ; Sketch and Composition Classes and Lectures, free to members of other classes and $2 per month for each class to others. Students admitted also per month, or for special classes, at fixed rates.—Attendance not given.—The school is open daily, for study from life and the antique, during seven months, from Oct 1. Application for admission should be made at the office of the school, 201 Montague St., on Mondays or Wednesdays during the season, between 9 and 10 A.M., 1 and 2 and 7 and 8 P.M., or at any other time to the Secretary of the Art Association at the Association Building, Montague St., who may also be addressed for further information.

BROOKLYN ART CLUB.—Organized 1879.—Officers : Pres., J. B. Stearns, N. A., 349 Fulton St.; V. P., Geo. L. Clough ; Sec., J. H. Littlefield, Phœnix Bldg.; Treas., Frank Squier, 310 Lafayette Ave.—Objects: To advance sociability and the interest in art among its members (active, professionals only, honorary, and associate) ; to have two exhibitions each year, spring and fall, followed by auction sales.—So far only three sales have been held, the last of which took place Mch. 9, 1882, at Sherk's Gallery, 435 Fulton St., and realized $3,413, for 62 pictures. Monthly meetings are held at the studios of the members. The "Artists' Fund," virtually a life insurance, formerly connected with this Club, has been given up.—Present number of members, about 30. [From last issue. No reply to repeated requests for later information. The Club held two sales in 1883, on March 27 and Dec. 27. For results, see Statistical Table of Exhibitions.]

BROOKLYN ART GUILD.—201 Montague St.—Organized Dec. 23, 1880.—This association, although still continuing, has, to a certain extent, been merged in the Art Association, under the title of *The Students' Guild of the Brooklyn Art Association*. For details, see *Brooklyn Art Association*.

BROOKLYN BRANCH OF THE LADIES' ART ASSOCIATION OF NEW YORK.—167 Taylor St.—Organized by Mrs. S. J. Rafter and Mrs. E. J. Sterling, March, 1879.— Officers : Same as those of the New York Association. Director: Mrs. S. J. Rafter. Pres. Council of Reference : Mrs. E. J. Sterling.—Objects : Same as those of the New York Association.—Instruction given in drawing and painting from objects and casts, continuing to finished paintings from still life ; also in household decoration.—Teachers : Mrs. S. J. Rafter and Miss Annie Morgan.— Terms from $5 to $10 per course of 10 lessons.—Pupils taught during the year 1883, 124. Small boys are instructed in elementary drawing, and admitted to the general studio.

BROOKLYN INSTITUTE.—Washington, cor. Concord St.—Founded by Augustus Graham.—Pres., Jesse C. Smith ; V. P., Dr. Andrew Otterson ; Treas., Duncan Littlejohn ; Sec., Alfred T. Baxter.—This is an Evening Drawing Class limited to 50 pupils. Two sessions a week, Monday and Thursday.—Open six months, from Oct. to April. There are several prizes, the highest of which is the Graham Medal. Tuition fee, $5 for six months. Teacher : Prof. Ferd. T. L. Boyle, A. N. A. (11 East 14th St., New York). The class is full.

BRUSH AND PALETTE CLUB.—Officers : Pres., G. L. Clough ; Sec., E. A. Rorke ; Treas., James Northcote. [No reply to repeated requests for detailed information. This seems to be an association of artists, clubbed together principally for the purpose of holding auction sales of their works. The Club held several sales, on Oct. 31, 1882, in Brooklyn, and on Feb. 23, 1883, in Providence, the result of which is given in the Statistical Table of Exhibitions.]

COLLEGIATE AND POLYTECHNIC INSTITUTE.—Livingston St., betw. Court St. and Boerum Pl.—Incorporated 1854.—Officers : Pres. of B'd of Trustees, Isaac H. Frothingham, 134 Remsen St.; Sec., Benj. T. Frothingham, 45 Remsen St.; Treas., Tasker H. Marvin, 50 First Pl.; Registrar and Clerk, Robert L. Massoneau, Jr., 244 Clinton St.; Pres. of the Fac., David H. Cochran, Ph. D., LL.D., 196 Livingston St.—The Institute provides a course of preparatory study in its Academic Department, and four special courses, namely : Classical or Preparatory Collegiate Course, which diverges from the Academic Course in the second year ; Scientific Course, Liberal Course (Collegiate without classics), and Commercial Course, which begin after the four years of the Academic Course have been finished. Drawing is a required study in some part of every course. In the Classical Course it is taught in the first year after its divergence from the Academic Course (descriptive geometry in the third year.). To the three other courses it is common in the third and fourth years of the Academic Course. In the Scientific Course it is continued throughout its four years ; in the Liberal Course in one term each of the sub-junior and sub-senior year ; in the Commercial Course, in the first term. Students are allowed, also, to take drawing as an additional study at any time when their standing in other studies permits. The Course in Free-hand, which is to some extent required of all, includes in order : 1. Exercises in copying from the flat ; 2. Block drawing and copying raised work and a variety of wooden models ; 3. Drawing from the antique ; 4. Drawing from life, and landscape work in the field. The Mechanical Drawing includes copying of geometrical figures, architectural drawing, machine drawing from models to different scales, and an extended course in application of descriptive geometry and the higher perspective.—Instructor in Drawing : C. Hertzberg, 140 Duffield St.

DÜRER ART CLUB.—14 Red Hook Lane. [No reply to repeated requests for later information. Seems to have been discontinued.]

LONG ISLAND HISTORICAL SOCIETY.—Pierrepont St., cor. Clinton.—Incorporated 1863.—Officers : Pres., Rev. Richd. S. Storrs, D.D.. LL.D.; Home Cor. Sec., Rev. Chas. H. Hall, D.D.; Treas., A. W. Humphreys; Libr., George Hannah; Curator of the Museum, Elias Lewis, Jr.—One of the objects of the Society is the formation of a *Museum of Works of Art, Relics, and Curiosities*, particularly such as are of historical interest in relation to this country. The Museum, which is located on the upper floor of the building occupied and owned by the Society, contains, besides curiosities and specimens illustrative of natural history, the beginnings of an archæological collection. A small number of portraits and other paintings are hung in the Library and the rooms adjoining, among them a large landscape, " The Old Roadway," by George Inness, presented by Mr. Geo. I. Seney, and an old portrait of Jeanne d'Arc, presented by Mr. Wm. Dodsworth.—*The Library*, for reference only, which contains over 35,000 volumes, is quite rich in costly illustrated works on art and its history, many of which have also been given by Mr. Seney, and a number of other friends of the Society. It is open to members from 8.30 A.M. to 9.30 P.M. Non-residents may be introduced by members to the privileges of the Library and Reading-Rooms for the period of one Month. Transient visitors admitted on application to the Librarian.—The terms of membership, payable in advance, are, for Annual Members, $10 the first year, and thereafter $5 a year ; or, for Life Membership, $100 in full for all fees and dues.—Annual Meeting, second Tuesday in May.

PACKER COLLEGIATE INSTITUTE.—Joralemon St., near Clinton.—Incorporated 1846.—Officers : Pres. of B'd of Trustees, A. A. Low ; Treas., Richd. P. Buck ; Sec., Henry P. Morgan ; Pres. of the Fac., A. Crittenden, A.M., Ph.D.—Objects : To furnish to young ladies all the advantages for thorough and complete education enjoyed in the best appointed Colleges.—Drawing, as a general study, is taught in the Preparatory Dept., and in the Second (or lower) Division of the Academic Dept. In the Collegiate Dept., architecture and perspective are taught in the third quarter of the Senior (third) year only. In a Post-Graduate Course, opportunity is offered advanced pupils to pursue the study of art. The Trustees have provided instruction of the highest order in every branch of Drawing and Painting, and have fitted up apartments expressly for the accommodation of pupils in these highly useful and beautiful arts. The students are taught to draw and paint from familiar objects, the design being to cultivate the eye as well as the hand. Lectures on the history of art were given during the past winter, by Miss M. A. Hastings, to an advanced class of ladies. They will be resumed in October, 1882, and are commended to ladies who are planning a tour in Europe, or who desire to revise and systematize their recollections of its art treasures, as well as to graduates of the institution. Peculiar facilities for the study of art are afforded by an extensive series of photographs, illustrating the various schools of architecture and of painting. Casts of antique and modern statues serve not only for the use of students of art and for models in drawing, but as a means of culture to all the pupils, who are, by the daily sight of these works of art, familiarized with the purest types of beauty in form and expression.—Pencil and crayon drawing, $15 per quarter ; oil, water-color, and pastel painting, painting on slate and marble, decorating china, tiles, pottery, etc., and photograph painting, each $20 per quarter.—Miss Virginia Granbery, teacher of drawing, oil painting, etc.; Miss Mary M. Platt, teacher of elementary drawing.—During the last term 68 students were engaged in the study of the higher branches of drawing and painting. [From last year's issue. No reply to repeated requests for later information. From a newspaper item, it appears that Mr. Percival de Luce is engaged as a teacher of painting in the Institute.]

REMBRANDT CLUB.—Organized 1880.—Officers for 1884 : Pres., Geo. M. Olcott, 38 Grace Court; V. P., John H. Hull, 211 Prospect Pl.; Sec., John B. Ladd, 246 Henry St.; Treas., J. W. Stearns, 64 First Pl.—Object : The cultivation and encouragement of art.—Present membership, 65.—Initiation fee, $15 ; annual dues, $10. Honorary members may also be elected.—The Club has no rooms. The meetings, lectures, etc., are held in the drawing-rooms and picture galleries of its members. Papers are read before the Club, as a rule, once a month during the winter, and some of these have been published. A fine loan exhibition was held under the auspices of the Club, in January, 1883, at the rooms of the Brooklyn Art Association, for the benefit of the Sheltering Arms Nursery. In May of the same year the Club publicly protested against the increase in the rate of duty on works of art, and expressed itself in favor of the removal of all duties.—Annual meeting, first Monday in December.

SCRATCHERS' CLUB.—Organized Jan. 25, 1882.—Officers : Pres., G. W. H. Ritchie, 109 Liberty St., New York : V. P., Carleton Wiggins ; Sec., Benj. Lander, 1354 Bergen St., Brooklyn, or 14 John St., New York ; Treas., J. C. Williamson.—Object : The practical study of the art of etching among its members.—Membership confined to professional artists.—The Club meets weekly, from first Wednesday in October to fourth Wednesday of April, inclusive.

U. S. NAVAL LYCEUM.—Navy Yard. (The Yard is in Brooklyn, but the official address is Navy Yard, New York).—Officers : Pres., Commodore J. H. Upshur, U. S. N.; Treas., Chief Engineer, G. W. Magee, U. S. N.; Sec. and Acting Librarian Lieut. Aaron Ward, U. S. N. —The association has established a reading room for members, and maintains a collection of curiosities, models, etc., contributed from different sources, which is open to the public, free, on weekdays, from 10 A. M. to 4 P. M.

WINTER ART ASSOCIATION.—Organized, 1880.—Officers : Pres., Dr. Cruikshank ; Treas., M. J. Gates.—Object : To provide practical instruction, free of charge, in drawing, perspective, anatomy, composition, etc., to young people who need such knowledge in their calling, but cannot afford to visit costly institutions. Instructor, Prof. Peter Winter, 107 Fort Green Pl., who gives his services free of charge.—The association has had to suspend work for the present, as it cannot afford to hire a room. It has repeatedly petitioned the Board of Education for the use of a room, but without success so far.

15. Brunswick, Me.

BOWDOIN COLLEGE.—Officers: Acting Pres., Alpheus S. Packard, D.D.; Sec. of B'd of Tr., Franklin M. Drew, A.M.; Sec. of the Fac., Geo. T. Little, A.M.; Treas., Stephen J. Young, A.M.; Curator of the Art Collections, Prof. Henry Johnson, A.M.—No art instruction of any kind is given in the regular college course.—*The Gallery of Art.* By the will of the Hon. Jas. Bowdoin, the College in 1811 came into possession of his entire collection of paintings, about 100 in number, procured by him during a residence of three years in Paris, after the closing of his services as Minister of the U. S. at the Court of Madrid in Dec., 1805. It is claimed that many of these pictures are genuine works by the old masters ; and when it is remembered that the beginning of the century was a period of great disturbance in Europe, the possibility of obtaining such works at that time is readily seen. For years the College had no room in which the pictures could be properly exhibited, and many of them were so dingy that it was difficult to tell what they were. At the suggestion of Hon. R. C. Winthrop and others, they were, in 1850, put into the hands of D. Chase and G. Howorth, of Boston, for restoration, and when they were replaced, the College first became aware of the value of its possession. Important paintings presented by other donors, including the entire collection of the late Col. Geo. W. Boyd, have since been added, and similar donations are continually being made. A recent report of the College acknowledges the receipt of eight paintings, and quite a number of busts, casts from the antique, etc., within the year. The Gallery of

Paintings occupies the room over the Library, in the east end of the Chapel, and is called the Walker Gallery, in memory of Mrs. Sophia Walker. The statuary is placed in a room in the north wing of the Chapel. The Bowdoin bequest includes also 138 drawings by old masters, marked with the names of Titian, Andrea del Sarto, Correggio, Tintoretto, etc. Two friends of the college have lately made provision for the care and exhibition of these valuable works. A new and complete cat-alogue of the gallery has lately been prepared, and will soon be published. The present catalogue, printed in 1870, contains only a list of the Bowdoin paintings and the Boyd collection. Attached to the former (some of which were sold by the board years ago as "nudities") are such names as Raphael, Titian, N. Poussin, Berghem, Hondekoeter, Van Dyck, Rubens, Vouet, Hogarth, etc. Of works by American artists there are the portraits of Madison and Jefferson by Stuart, and the full-length portraits of Gov. Bowdoin and lady (1748) by Robert Feke, one of the earliest native painters who has left any record. In the Boyd collection there are also several old masters, and a portrait of Thos. Fluker by Copley.—The Art Collections will for the present be open to visitors daily, Sundays excepted, from 1 to 3 P. M.

MAINE HISTORICAL SOCIETY.—[See *Portland, Me.*, to which place the Society has recently removed.]

16. Buffalo, N. Y.

BUFFALO ART CLUB.—Meets at No. 6 Austin B'ldg.—Organized Feb., 1883.— Officers : Pres., Amos W. Sangster; V. P., W. H. Arthur; Sec., Mark M. Maycock, M.P. (teacher of drawing, etc., in State Normal School); Treas., Jno. C. Rother.—Objects: The cultivation and advancement of art in all its branches, and the promotion of social intercourse among its members and all interested in art.—Members : Resident (artists of Buffalo and vicinity), Non-Resident (non-resident artists), Associate (amateurs and connoisseurs), Honorary (persons who have done eminent services to the cause of art). Present number of members : 6 Resident, 6 Non-Resident, 4 Asso-ciate, 1 Honorary.—Initiation fee, $2 ; annual dues, $5. Non-Resident and Honorary members ex-empt.—The Club meets on Tuesday afternoons and Saturday evenings for practice, twice a month for essays, lectures, criticism, etc., and once a month for business.—Annual meeting, first Thursday in April.

BUFFALO FINE ARTS ACADEMY.—Austin Fire Proof Building.—Instituted Nov. 11, 1862 ; incorporated December 4, 1862 ; gallery opened Dec. 23, 1862.—Officers : Pres., Thos. F. Rochester, M.D.; V. Ps., Geo. L. Williams, Geo. B. Hayes, Geo. S. Hazard ; Cor. Sec., L. G. Sellstedt; Rec. Sec., Alb. T. Chester, D.D. ; Treas., Richd. K. Noye ; Fund Commissioners: John Allen, Jr., Wm. P. Letchworth, Josiah Jewett.—Object : To encourage and cultivate the Fine Arts, and to establish and maintain a permanent gallery in the city of Buffalo, for the exhibition of paintings, sculptures, and other works of art, and to use such other means as shall be desirable and efficient for the promotion and advancement of the same.—Members : Annual $5 ; Life $100 (139 in 1883).—The Academy has purchased and acquired by gift a number of paintings by American artists (A. Bierstadt, Wm. Hart, R. Gignoux, J. A. Oertel, A. D. Shattuck, W. Whittredge, W. S. Haseltine, J. Humphrey, E. D. Howard, L. G. Sellstedt, C. C. Coleman, E. Moran, E. H. Rem-ington, Burr H. Nicholls, Hamilton Hamilton, E. K. Baker, F. Penfold, R. Swain Gifford, Thos. Le Clear, W. H. Beard, Wordsworth Thompson, Jervis McEntee, E. Wood Perry, Wm. Graham, Walter Shirlaw, Thos. Moran, A. M. Farnham, F. G. Melby), Phillipoteaux's " French Revolution of 1848," a series of copies from paintings by old masters, some casts from the antique, and a small col-lection of photographs. It also holds transient exhibitions. At the last of these, held in June, 1883, a collection was shown which had been sent on from New York by the American Art Union.—Ad-mission free to members and their families, artists, and resident art students ; others, 25 cents. Number of visitors, 1882, 3,944 (incl. 256 free) ; from Jan. 1 to Dec. 1, 1883, 3,624 (incl. 601 free).— The Academy publishes catalogues of its permanent collection and transient exhibitions. Price 25 cents.—No school is maintained for want of sufficient accommodation, but eventually free schools are contemplated.—When the Buffalo Fine Arts Academy was instituted, thirteen gentlemen sub-scribed $500 each toward the expenses and the purchase of a nucleus for a gallery. After ten years' experience it was found necessary to raise a fund, from the interest on which the deficiencies might be paid, as, however 'economically carried on, the Academy could not be made self-sustaining. The sum named was $10,000, about one-half of which was immediately subscribed. The whole scheme seemed likely to fall through, however, as it proved to be quite difficult to procure the rest, and no subscription was binding until the whole amount had been pledged. At this juncture, Mr. S. S. Jewett changed his figures from $1,000 to $10,000, which, of course, settled the question. . It was then resolved to make strong endeavors to raise the sum originally named for contingent expenses, and to set aside Mr. Jewett's $10,000 as a separate fund, to be called the Jewett Fund, the interest from which was to be devoted to the purchase of pictures. The fund is managed by three commissioners, and from it have been bought most of the best works owned by the Academy. It now amounts to nearly $30,000.—Annual meeting, first Wednesday after first Tuesday in January.

DECORATIVE ART SOCIETY.—51 West Genesee St.—Established Jan., 1879; incorporated Nov., 1881.—Officers: Pres., Mrs. E. Carlton Sprague; V. P's., Mrs. Thos. F. Rochester, Mrs. A. P. Nichols, Mrs. Geo. Truscott, Mrs. F. H. Rosseel, Mrs. H. M. Kent; Sec. and Treas., Mrs. E. B. Seymour; Cor. Sec., Mrs. S. F. Mixer; For. Cor. Sec., Miss M. M. Love.—Objects identical with those of similar associations.—Subscribing members, $2.00, p. a. Present number of members, 227 and 18 honorary.—The Society announces that it "re-opened its *Drawing Classes* on Sept. 18, 1883, with a regular scholastic year, believing that this departure from the old methods would best further the objects and aims of the Department of Instruction. A thorough knowledge of Drawing lies at the foundation of all art, whether it be industrial, mechanical, decorative, or pictorial, and it is the aim of this department to establish a practical working Art School, where all possible influence for the fostering of art knowledge, and criticism, and taste shall centre."—There are three terms: Sept. 18 to Dec. 21, 1883, 13 weeks; Jan. 8 to Apr. 11, 1884, 13 weeks; Apr. 15 to July 1, 1884, 11 weeks. Classes and fees: Each of First two terms, 6 lessons per week, $20; Designing, 1 lesson per week, $4; Oil Painting, 2 lessons, $13. Third term, Drawing, $16.50; Designing, $3.50; Oil Painting, $11. Tuition for Children's Class, each of first two terms, $2.50, third term, $3. Single lessons in Drawing, 30 cents; Oil Painting, 60 cents. Tuition for Summer Sketching, tour of four weeks, $8; for less than full time, at rate of $3.50 per week. A Students' Club, for Sketching from life, meets at the rooms every Wednesday afternoon. Those working in other classes are admitted to the Club. Lessons in Landscape and Flower Painting, oil and water colors, 75 cents; Crayon Portraiture, $1; China Painting, $1; Art Needle Work, $3 for six lessons and $1 for a single lesson. The Society maintains also the following Evening Classes : Free-hand Drawing, at 51 West Genesee St., Monday and Thursday, and at Fitch Institute, cor. Michigan and Swan Streets, Tuesday and Friday; Mechanical Drawing, at Fitch Institute, Monday, Tuesday, Wednesday, and Saturday; terms 10 cents per lesson; Free-hand Classes open to both sexes. Other classes are to be formed as required. Number of pupils 1883, 225.—Students wishing to enter the Class in Designing must submit an outline drawing and a carefully shaded drawing of a plant. For the best pair of these drawings the Society offers as a prize a set of mathematical instruments, and tuition in both the Drawing and Designing Classes free from Jan. 8 to Apr. 11; for the second best pair, tuition in both classes for the same length of time. Those desiring to enter the Oil Painting Class, must present a finished head, life-size, charcoal or crayon, from cast or life, and a small sketch, in pen-and-ink, of a full length figure from life. For the best pair the Society offers a box of oil-colors, brushes, palette, etc., and tuition in Drawing and Oil Painting, from Jan. 8 to Apr. 11; for the second best, tuition in both classes, for the same length of time.—Teachers : Edward L. Chichester, Oil Painting and Free-hand Drawing; Eugene Cramer, Free-hand Drawing; John G. Balsam, Mechanical Drawing; Miss Sarah Chesnutwood, Landscape and Flower Painting; Mrs. G. W. Chandler, Crayon Portraiture; Mrs. F. L. Dole, Art Needle Work.—The financial resources of the Society consist of membership dues, donations, and commissions on orders, and on sales of articles sent to the salerooms by contributors, subject to the usual rules of similar associations.—Annual meeting, Wednesday after first Monday in January.

17. Burlington, Vt.

UNIVERSITY OF VERMONT AND STATE AGRICULTURAL COLLEGE.
—In the Department of Arts of this institution, art is one of the subjects of study assigned to the fourth year. "The instruction in this topic," says the Catalogue, "is philosophical, in distinction from practical. The text-book used is the published lectures upon the Theory of Fine Art by the late

Prof. Joseph Torrey. Important aids to an historical and critical knowledge of art are furnished in the well-selected lists of works on Art in the College and Fletcher libraries, as also in the choice collection of casts, models, etc., in the Park Gallery." Mechanical Drawing is taught throughout the four years of the Department of Applied Science.— *The Park Gallery of Art.*—Trustees: M. H. Buckham, Pres., *ex-officio;* Prof. H. A. P. Torrey, Sec.; Hon. F. C. Kennedy, Treas.; Hon. E. J. Phelps, Hon. G. G. Benedict, Rev. L. G. Ware, Col. Le Grand B. Cannon.—The history and aims of this gallery are best given in the words of a circular issued by the University in Sept., 1873: " It has for some years been a favorite project of a few art-loving friends of this University to establish, as one of its means of instruction and culture, a gallery of the fine arts. To those who know what the institution has long been doing in the way of art culture, this will be no surprise. It is a matter of just pride to the graduates of the University, and it deserves more public recognition than it has hitherto received, that this institution was the first in the country to introduce into its course of study, systematic instruction by lectures on the theory and principle of the fine arts. The lectures by Prof. Torrey, beginning as far back as 1830, anticipated by many years not only what, under the name of Æsthetics or High Art, has now become a recognized department of liberal education in all higher institutions of learning, but also those principles of art criticism which have since been made familiar by European and American writers on the fine arts. The results of this instruction are manifest in the high-toned art-spirit manifest in those upon whom the culture of the University has had its best effect. This may explain and justify the conception of an enterprise which might otherwise appear somewhat ambitious for an institution of such limited resources. By the liberality of Trenor W. Park, Esq., of Bennington, that which has long been a dream, or at most a hope, is soon to be an accomplished fact. Mr. Park has assumed the expense of adding to the Library building a third story, which greatly increases the architectural beauty of the building itself, and gives us a gallery fifty-one feet long by thirty-one feet wide and fifteen feet high, lighted from the roof, easily accessible, and every way admirably adapted to its purpose. It is the wish of Mr. Park, and indeed of all interested, that the gallery should at all proper times be open to the public as well as to the College community. We have also promises from gentlemen of wealth and taste, that they will make contributions of paintings and other works of art to be the nucleus of a collection. We are well aware that for the present the gallery must be a very moderate one in point of size, but who can compute the value to the University and the public, of even a small gallery, provided the works are of a high order of merit ? For two things are to be borne in mind—first, that the educating power of a gallery is in no degree dependent on size. There are so-called art-galleries containing hundreds of pictures whose total value for purposes of art-culture is not equal to that of one first-rate picture. Our enterprise will not, therefore, be a failure, if we succeed in contributing to the University's resources for culture, only two or three masterpieces of native or foreign art, *provided* there be no second or third-rate pieces admitted to degrade the standard and confuse the effect. And, secondly, it is to be remembered that a collection for purposes of art-culture in a University ought to be founded on a totally different plan from that of a miscellaneous art-gallery. The object here is not to gratify the sight-seeing and picture-gazing propensity which it is well enough to encourage elsewhere, but to gather such works of art as will illustrate the great art-ideas that liberal study aims to inculcate. It follows, therefore, that many works of merit might have no appropriate place in such a collection, and might be declined, if offered, without any imputation upon either the merit of the work or the kindness of the giver. To forget this and to yield to the temptation to fill the gallery with even meritorious work foreign to the intent of the collection, would be to sacrifice the unity of plan on which the real success of the whole enterprise depends. Another reason why such a gallery should be kept up to the very highest standard, even at the risk of its remaining small for many years to come, is that artists of the first rank might find it to be for their own interest to contribute to its collection. There are few galleries in the United States in which an Allston or a Kensett does not run the risk of being degraded by being grouped with some anonymous daub. It is not, we venture to say, at all presumptuous to hope that we may gather a small and choice collection in Painting and Sculpture, in which it would be an honor to the works of the best artists to have a place." The gallery at present contains about twenty casts from the antique and from Michelangelo ; three marbles by the late Thos. R. Gould ("The Ghost in Hamlet," and ideal heads, "Rose" and "Lily,"); paintings by A. H. Wyant, David Johnson, K. Ehrenberg (of Dresden), and, J. F. Kensett ; photographs from Raphael's cartoons, and a few engravings and etchings, etc. There is no fund, and the gallery is dependent upon donations, and the proceeds of lectures and exhibitions. There is an Annual Exhibition of the gallery at Commencement in June. Artists' Loan Exhibitions of Paintings, at Commencement and for several weeks thereafter, were held in 1877, 1878 and 1881. Two courses of lectures on art subjects were given by members of the Board of Trustees and others in the winter of 1875–6 and of 1876–7, the proceeds from which were contributed to the gallery. The gallery is open free to the public. At the Loan Exhibitions a small fee is charged. At each of them the attendance was estimated at between three and four thousand.—*The Museum* of the University, on the ground floor of the Library Building, contains, among other things, an archæological collection of several hundred specimens. Permission to visit it may be obtained by applying to the Curator.

18. Cambridge, Mass.

HARVARD ART CLUB.—Gray's Hall.—Composed of students of Harvard College. The Club has arranged several public exhibitions of etchings and of studies, etc., belonging to the Fine Arts Department of the College. It has also published Mr. J. S. Clarke's paper on the Hypæthral Question, and a series of six mezzotints executed by Mr. Chas. H. Moore, from his own drawings ; and has shared in the cost of printing the preliminary Assos Report of the Archæological Institute. [No reply to repeated requests for later and more detailed information.]

HARVARD UNIVERSITY.—Founded 1636.—Pres., Chas. Wm. Eliot, LL. D., 17 Quincy St.; Treas., Edw. Wm. Hooper, Reservoir St.; Bursar, Allen Danforth, 7 Wadsworth House.—The University comprehends the following departments : Harvard College, the Divinity School, the Law School, the Medical School, the Dental School, the Lawrence Scientific School, the Museum of Comparative Zoölogy, the Bussey Institution (a School of Agriculture), the College Library, and the Astronomical Observatory. The Peabody Museum (see below) is a constituent part of the University ; but its relations to it are affected by peculiar provisions.—*Harvard College :* The prescribed studies in the College do not include drawing ; it may, however, be taken as an elective study, and is recommended to those students who intend to study engineering. No Honors are given for proficiency in the Fine Arts, but they are included in the subjects for Honorable Mention. The marks obtained in drawing and principles of design, if taken as one of the prescribed number of elective studies, are counted the same as those for any other study, in the recommendation for a degree.— *Lawrence Scientific School :* In the Engineering Courses, mechanical drawing, perspective, etc., are practised throughout the four years, besides free-hand and water-color drawing, four hours a week, in the third year. The course in Chemistry includes mechanical drawing, four hours a week, in the fourth year ; the courses in Natural History, free-hand and water-color drawing, four hours a week, in the second and third years ; those in Mathematics, Physics, and Astronomy, mechanical drawing, four hours a week, in the third year. Instructors : Chas. H. Moore, 19 Follen St., Drawing and Principles of Design ; Henry L. Eustis, A.M., 29 Kirkland St., Perspective ; Francis W. Dean, S. B., 40 Matthews Hall, Mechanical Drawing.—*The Department of Fine Arts :* The studies in this department are open as electives to all regular students ; special students are also admitted. It includes the following courses : 1. Principles of Delineation, Color, and Chiaroscuro (Ruskin, Viollet-le-Duc, Pyne's Perspective); 2. Principles of Design in Painting, Sculpture, and Architecture (Viollet-le-Duc's "Dictionnaire raisonné de l'architecture française," Ruskin, Sir Joshua Reynolds, Woltmann's "History of Painting"); 3. Ancient Art (Von Reber's "History of Ancient Art," translated by Clarke) ; 4. Art in Italy from the Conquest of Greece by the Romans to the year 1600 ; 5. Greek Art; 6. Romanesque and Gothic Art from the year 1000 to 1350. Ability to read German is required of students taking courses 3 to 6. No preparation is required for admission. The instruction begins with elementary exercises from the flat, and progresses to working from natural objects and casts, in pencil, chalk, and water-colors. The study of the nude and of oil painting is not attempted, as, for the present at least, the school is not of the nature of a professional school. The instruction given is simply disciplinary, and an auxiliary to general culture.—Instructors : Chas. Eliot Norton, A.M., Kirkland St., Prof. of the History of Art ; Chas. H. Moore, 19 Follen St., Drawing and Principles of Design.—Mr. Moore's classes are at present attended by 30 students (27 regular, 3 special ; all males) ; Prof. Norton's lectures on the history of art are much more numerously attended, mostly by regular students.—The tuition fee for regular students is $150, p. a. Special students pay at the rate of $15 for one hour a week of instruction during the academic year, up to $150, but in no case shall the fee be less than $30 a year.—*Art Collections :* The Fine Arts

6

Department is forming a collection to illustrate the leading characteristics of the great schools of painting, sculpture, and architecture, consisting of casts, photographs, autotypes, prints (etchings, plates from Turner's "Liber Studiorum," etc.), and copies in oil and water-colors (many of the latter made by Mr. Chas. H. Moore during a visit to Europe). The collection, which grows but slowly, as the appropriation is very small, has been placed in room B, Sever Hall, and is open to the public during term time, on application by letter to Mr. Moore. — *The Library* of the College in Gore Hall contains a good proportion of books on art and its history, and is being carefully completed as rapidly as the means will permit. There is also a collection of coins in the Library. The Gray Collection of Engravings, formerly kept there, has been temporarily deposited with the Museum of Fine Arts in Boston. The privilege of borrowing books is granted under special regulations, to persons not connected with the University.—Open free every week day, except holidays, from 9 A.M. till 5 P.M., or till sunset when that is before 5; in vacation and recess the hour of closing is 2 P.M. On Sundays, during term time, open to readers only, after 1 P.M.

MEMORIAL HALL.—Cambridge and Quincy Sts.—The Dining Hall in this building (erected in commemoration of students of Harvard University who fell in the service of their country) contains a large and valuable collection of about 80 portaits and portrait busts, mostly of persons connected with the College as officers, benefactors, etc. As a record of the history of portrait painting in the U. S., this collection is quite important. Besides a number of old pictures (most of them of indifferent quality), whose authors are not known, there are specimens of the work of the following painters : Smybert, Copley (quite a number, including the fine portrait of Mrs. Thos. Boylston) Savage (portrait of Washington), Stuart, Stuart and Sully, Frothingham, Trumbull, Newton, Alexander, Alvan Fisher, Bass Otis, Chester Harding, Page, Healey, Hunt, Hayward, Jos. Ames, Mooney, and Cobb; Sculptors : Houdon (bust of Washington), Lander, Hiram Powers, R. S. Greenough, H. Greenough, Carew, Story. Crawford, Clevenger, and Dexter. There is no catalogue, but all the pictures and busts are plainly labelled. The beautiful glass mosaic windows in the same hall are by John La Farge.—Open free to the public on week days, meal hours excepted.

PEABODY MUSEUM OF AMERICAN ARCHÆOLOGY AND ETHNOL-OGY.—Divinity Ave.—Founded by George Peabody, Oct. 8, 1866, as a department of Harvard University.—Officers B'd of Trustees : Chairm., Robert C. Winthrop, 90 Marlborough St., Boston ; Treas., John C. Phillips, Marlborough St., Boston. Officers of the Museum : Curator, F. W. Putnam ; Asst. Curator, Lucien Carr, and three assistants.—Of the fund of $150,000 given by Mr. Peabody, $60,000 have been set apart for building purposes, and the balance has been invested as an endowment fund. The building at present occupied by the Museum, and opened in 1878, is only one-fifth of the structure contemplated. It cost about $70,000 with the cases, and has been paid for entirely from the income of the building fund. The land was given by Harvard College.— This Museum, founded especially for the study of American Archæology and Ethnology, and for the preservation of collections relating thereto, is the only one of its character in the country. To it students may come for special investigations, with the assurance that, so far as American archæology is concerned, they have access to the most important collections that have been brought together, while the material for comparison with that of other parts of the world is not wanting. The large collections from North, Central, and South America, which are extraordinarily rich in everything pertaining to the civilization of the extinct as well as the present native races of these countries, including their architecture, pottery, sculpture, etc., and the smaller collections from Egypt, Southern Africa, Asia, Australia, and the Pacific Islands, have already been placed on exhibition in a series of rooms, while the collections from Europe, particularly rich in objects illustrating the stone age of Denmark and Italy, and in interesting remains from the Swiss Lakes, are now in course of arrangement. The Museum also sends out exploring expeditions, and the investigations carried on during the past few years in Nicaragua, among the mounds and ancient burial-places of the Ohio and Cumberland Valleys, and the shell-heaps on the Atlantic coast, have been very fruitful of important results. Especial interest attaches to a number of remarkable fragments of small-sized sculptures from the Ohio Valley, which place the so-called mound-builders much higher up in the scale of civilization than previous knowledge seemed to warrant. Among the later important additions to the Museum is a collection of small sculptures in gypsum from Yucatan and Mexico, presented by

Mr. Alex. Agassiz.—The Museum publishes Annual Reports, which are offered for sale, and which, besides the account of the growth of the institution, contain papers of interest on subjects pertaining to American archæology and ethnology. The 16th Report has been delayed, owing to the absence of the Curator in the field, and will be published, together with the 17th, in Feb., 1884. During the winter months the curator delivers lectures in the Museum, which are announced in advance in the Harvard Bulletin and in the Weekly Calendar published by the University.—*The Library* of the Museum, as yet small, but constantly growing, is open to students for reference.— The endowment fund being insufficient, the Museum must depend to a great extent upon donations. Its explorations are entirely carried on by funds given by patrons for the purpose.—Open free on week days, holidays excepted, from 9 A.M. to 5 P.M.

19. Champaign, Ill.

ART CLUB OF CHAMPAIGN.—Officers: Pres., Miss M. A. Finley; V. P., Mrs. Prof. Taft; Sec., Mrs. W. S. Maxwell.—This Club was organized five years ago, and consists of about twenty ladies, who meet every two weeks in the afternoon at the homes of the members. It has never had a constitution or by-laws. Money was raised by it for the first time this year, for the purpose of fitting up a nook in the Public Library, and it is to give an Artists' Exhibition in February, 1884, for the benefit of the young artists of the community. The Art Club proper does no practical work. Its object is to study the history of the fine arts, its different schools, and, as far as possible, the principles of art. It has the use of the Art Gallery of the Illinois University.—The Club is a member of the Central Illinois Art Union.

ILLINOIS INDUSTRIAL UNIVERSITY.—See *Urbana, Ill.*

20. Charleston, S. C.

CAROLINA ART ASSOCIATION.—Washington Square.—Organized and Incorporated, 1857.—Officers: Pres., Dr. G. E. Manigault; V. P's., S. Y. Tupper, S. R. Ravenel, Hon. Jas. Simons; Treas., G. W. Dingle; Cor. Sec., Jas. S. Murdoch; Rec. Sec., Jos. W. Barnwell.—Objects: The promotion of the Fine Arts, by means of public exhibitions, by opening a school and a library of art, or by any other modes that may be deemed expedient.—Membership: Life, on payment of $100; annual, $5 initiation fee, and $5 p. a. Present number of members, 150.—This Association was inaugurated in the early part of the year 1857. The list of its members amounted then to over 130, at $10 p. a. each. Its first exhibition of paintings was held in the same year, and consisted of a loan collection, furnished by those residents of the city who were owners of valuable paintings. Most of these were returned at the end of the first year, and over 300 new members having then been enrolled, the Association, with other means that were contributed, was able to order an historical painting of the artist Leutze, the subject being "Sergeant Jasper rescuing the Flag during the Attack of the British Fleet upon Sullivan's Island, June 28, 1776." Arrangements were at the same time made with a picture dealer in Germany by which paintings by German artists were sent to the Association, at their expense, for exhibition and sale. Several of these were purchased, and there seemed in 1861, at the expiration of four years, every prospect of the future of the Association being assured. The great fire of Dec., 1861, however, destroyed the gallery and all of its contents, except one painting by the late J. Beaufain Irving, the subject being the execution of Sir Thomas More. There being a small invested fund that was still owned by the Association, it was revived in Feb., 1879, and in June of that year it defrayed the expenses of the inaugural of the bust of Wm. Gilmore Simms. In Dec., 1880, an exhibition of paintings was held in Market Hall, which was composed of works loaned by citizens, and over 50 oil paintings and water-colors sent on by New York artists, all of which were for sale. The Association purchased three of the best of these, and distributed them by lot among its members. At the anniversary meeting in 1882, it was decided to enlarge the sphere of action of the Association by the establishment of an Art School, and for the purpose a School Committee was appointed, to whom was intrusted the care of preparing a suitable building, and of conducting the School. The building, No. 18 Chalmers St., overlooking Washington Square, was purchased and remodelled, so as to fit it for the purposes both of an Art School and for exhibitions, at a cost of about $5,000. On Nov. 1, 1882, the Art School was opened, with Mr. F. W. Engel as principal, and with upwards of 150 pupils, and the session closed on June 1, 1883, with full classes in all departments. During the spring of the year a number of ladies who were interested in the Association gave a series of entertainments at the Academy of Music, and held a grand bazaar, from which sufficient money was realized to pay off all indebtedness of the Association for its building, and leave the sum of $1,500, which was invested in bonds for the benefit of the School. During the month of May an exhibition of paintings was held, consisting largely of works of American artists sent from New York, and representing about 100 artists, out of which 13 of the best were sold, being about one-tenth of the number sent, for $3,500 at catalogue prices. The present session of the School opened with full classes, under the direction of Mr. Geo. S. Burnap, as principal, and there is now every prospect that the Art School will become a permanent institution, and will do much good work in cultivating a taste for, and an appreciation of the beautiful, and in preparing many young ladies to earn a comfortable support for themselves in a manner congenial to their tastes and past surroundings. The present income of the Association, from subscribing members, tuition fees, and interest on bonds, is $2,300 annually. The admission to exhibitions is free to members; others 25 cents.—*Art School.* —The object of the school is to discover, encourage and instruct those who have a talent for Modelling, Drawing, Coloring, or Designing. Pupils will be helped and directed to fit themselves for profitable employment in one or the other of the constantly multiplying departments of Art Work. Any who display exceptional ability for Painting or Statuary, will be assisted in the studies requisite to attain distinction. Pupils may be of both sexes, and are taught together.—Classes and fees : First Drawing Class, $1 dollar per month ; Advanced Drawing Class, $2 per month ; Oil Painting, $6 per month ; China Painting, $2 per month. School term from first Monday in Oct. to last Friday in May ; there are Morning, Afternoon, and Evening classes.—Teachers : George S. Burnap, Principal ; Miss Edith G. Matthews, Assistant ; Miss Della Torré, China Painting.—A public exhibition of the work of the school is held at the close of the school year, when certificates and prizes in money are awarded to deserving students.—Annual meeting of the Association, first Tuesday in June.

21. Charlestown, Mass.

NAVAL LIBRARY AND INSTITUTE.—U. S. Navy Yard.—Organized 1842 ; incorporated 1859.—Officers: Pres., Com. O. C. Badger, U. S. N. (*ex officio*, Commandant of the Yard); V. P's., Rear Adml. G. H. Preble, U. S. N., Dr. H. Lyon ; Sec. and Treas., Lyman H. Bigelow ; Librarian and Curator, Alex. M. Massie.—Collections: Library of about 3,800 vols.; shells, minerals, ancient arms, models of ships, and mementoes ; two paintings by Salmon, "Boston Harbor" and "City of Shields, England;" several portraits in oil, by Flagg, Cole, and others ; water colors, crayons, engravings, etc.; a marble head of a youth, found at Palmyra, Syria; a fragment from Tarsus; a Roman mosaic, from Oudima, Africa ; wood carvings, etc.—Open every week day from 9 A. M. to 3 P. M.

PUBLIC LIBRARY.—City Hall, City Square.—Libr., Cornelius S. Cartee.—This is one of the branches of the Boston Public Library. It owns a number of portraits (Washington, by Frothingham after Stuart ; Jackson, by A. C. Hoit after Vanderlyn; Richard Devens, Commissary General in the Revolutionary Army, painted by Henry Sargent in 1798, bequeathed to the Library by his descendant, Miss Charlotte Harris); John Pope's "Webster delivering his address on the completion of Bunker Hill Monument"; "The Landing at Plymouth Rock," an early work by S. F. B. Morse, who was a native of Charlestown, and a plaster bust of Dr. James Walker, by Dexter.

22. Chicago, Ill.

ART GUILD.—239 Wabash Ave.—Organized, Sept., 1882 ; incorporated, Dec. 7, 1882.— Officers : Pres., J. W. Root, 56 Eighteenth St.; Sec. and Treas., L. J. Millet, 320 Michigan Ave.— Objects: Mutual assistance and entertainment of persons actively engaged in the pursuit of some one of the recognized fine arts or persons known as patrons, or critics of art.—Present number of members (painters, architects, sculptors, musicians, and decorators), 42. Initiation fee, $25 ; annual dues, $20 ; non-resident members, one-half the usual fees.—The Club holds exhibitions of the works of its members, as well as loan exhibitions. At its meetings, papers on art, etc., are read by members. The entertainments consists in musical receptions, or in character receptions, such as a "Japanese night," a " White and Gold Night," etc., in which case the decorations of the rooms are in keeping with the titles.—Annual meeting, last Saturday in November.

ART INSTITUTE OF CHICAGO.—(Formerly *Chicago Academy of Fine Arts.*)—Cor. Michigan Ave. and Van Buren St.—Organized and incorporated, May 24, 1879.—Officers, 1883-4 : Pres., C. L. Hutchinson ; V. P., Edson Keith ; Treas., L. J. Gage ; Sec., N. H. Carpenter.— Objects : The founding and maintenance of Schools of Art and Design, the formation of Collections of objects of art, and the cultivation and extension of the arts of design by any appropriate means.— Members are of three classes, Governing, Honorary, and Annual. The Governing Members only, chosen by the Board of Trustees, have the right to vote or be eligible to the office of Trustee ; initiation fee, $100 or more ; annual dues, $10. Honorary Members, also chosen by the Board, from among persons who have rendered eminent services to the institution, or who have claim to the rank of artists or patrons of art ; no dues ; no vote. Annual Members, $10 p. a.; no vote. All members are entitled to admission with their families to all exhibitions, receptions, etc., and are eligible to appointment upon committees, other than the Executive Committee.—Present number of members : 104 Governing, 311 Annual.—The association has no floating debt. Its bonded debt is $60,000, amply secured by mortgage on its real estate.—The Institute owns the property it at present occupies, and effected its removal from its former quarters in Dec., 1882. The land, 54 x 170 feet, with the building originally upon it, cost $45,000, and another building has been erected alongside of the old one, at a cost of $22,000. This new building is only part of a larger building which the association hopes ultimately to erect. Among the sources of revenue are the rentals received for those parts of the building which are not, at present, needed by the Institute.—*Exhibitions*, etc.: The Institute has an annual loan exhibition of paintings, the second of which opened in January, 1884, and its galleries are kept open throughout the year, filled with loan objects of various kinds. It has also held several receptions. The use of the galleries has been given to the Art League and the Bohemian Art Club for their exhibitions. The fee at the exhibitions, to others than members, is 25 cents. The number of visitors in 1883 was about 15,000, of whom 4,004 paid an admission fee.— *The Museum :* the only acquisitions so far made toward a permanent collection or museum, are two paintings, " The Beheading of St. John," by Chas. Sprague Pearce, and " Les Amateurs," by T. Alexander Harrison. Both these pictures were purchased and presented to the Institute by a number of gentlemen, who clubbed together for the purpose.—*The School :* " The School," says the last report, " has now been in successful operation for four years. In almost every respect it will compare favorably with any in the country. It has done and is doing excellent work, under a competent corps of instructors. Excluding rent, the School has been self-supporting for two years past. [Receipts of the School for the year, $6,588.71 ; expenditures, $6,539.48.] Tuition fees have been placed at the smallest possible sum that will cover actual expense of tuition. The equipment of the School has been largely increased and improved during the year ; still there is much room for further improvement. We are in need of more casts, of more costumes for life models, and of a greater variety of subjects for use in the still-life classes."—Classes : Costume Model ; Water Color ; Nude Life ; Painting from Still Life ; Drawing from the Flat and Cast ; Composition ; Perspective ; Artistic Anatomy ; Children's ; Saturday Sketching ; Evening Life ; Evening Antique Class. Three Terms : Fall, Oct. 1-Dec. 22 ; Winter, Jan. 2-March 22 ; Spring, Mch. 31-June 21.—Instructors : A. J. Rupert (Costume, Nude); C. A. Corwin (Costume, Still Life, Composition); L. C. Earle (Water Color); J. H. Vanderpoel (Drawing); Miss C. D. Wade (Drawing and Children's Class) ; N. H. Carpenter (Perspective) ; Dr. S. V. Clevenger (Artistic Anatomy).—Fees : Matriculation fee of $2, applied to the purchase of books for the library, open to students. Full term, every day each week, $25, with fractional rates for less time ; Evening Life Class, $10 a term, or $4 a month ; Evening Antique Class, $8 a term, or $3 a month ; Children's Class, $10 a term for two days a week, or $6 for one day.—Pupils (both sexes, taught together, except in Nude Life Class) can enter the elementary classes at any time. Advanced students can enter the classes to which their proficiency entitles them. Number of pupils for school-year 1882-3 359 ; average number enrolled, 147 ; average daily attendance, 80 ; fall term, 1883 : average daily attendance, 105 (58 in day classes, 47 in evening classes).—An exhibition of students' work is held at the end of each term. Prizes are awarded at the close of the school year.—Annual meeting of the Governing Members, first Tuesday of June.

BOHEMIAN ART CLUB.—Life Room of Art Institute.—Organized 1880.—Officers :

Mrs. Theo. Shaw, 2124 Calumet Ave.; Sec., Miss Emma L. Trip, 712 W. Monroe St.; Treas., Miss Eva Webster, 327 Fulton St.—Objects : Mutual improvement, and promotion of good feeling among local artists.—Members : Ladies only. Candidates must submit an original drawing or sketch from life or nature. Initiation fee, $3, and annual dues. Present number of members, 23 active, 3 honorary.—Meetings every Saturday. Annual exhibitions, the last of which was held at the Art Institute, Apr. 3-10, 1883. The next is to be held Mch. 14-24, 1884, at the same place.—Annual meeting, first Saturday in October.

CHICAGO ACADEMY OF DESIGN.—Monroe St., American Express Building.—Organized 1867 ; incorporated under special charter, March 10, 1869.—Officers : Pres., Enoch Root ; V. P., Paul Brown ; Sec. and Business Manager, John F. Stafford ; Treas. (pro tem.), R. W. Wallis.—Objects : The founding and maintenance of Schools of Art for the cultivation of the Arts of Drawing, Painting, Sculpture, Architecture, Engraving, and Design, and for the formation of a Gallery of objects of Art.—Membership : Academicians, artists elected from among the Associates, in whom is vested the governing power ; Associates, students of art ; Honorary Academicians, artists, or contributors of not less than $500 (perpetual, with power to name successor) ; Fellows, for life, contributors of $100. Present number : 55 Academicians, 9 Honorary, 60 Fellows.—Previous to the great fire of 1871, the Academy was in promising condition, and had a building of its own on Adams St. Its property was (and still is) free from taxation by special act of Legislature, and the schools were reported to be prosperous and amply equipped. The fire, however, swept away every vestige of the property, and the insurance proved worthless. Quarters were indeed rented, and schools opened, but the financial panic operated against them, and they closed in debt. Renewed efforts are now being made, aided by the City government and many citizens, to give efficiency to the valuable charter of the Academy, and to obtain a grant of land from Congress, on the tract known as Dearborn Park. The building to be there erected is to contain free Art Schools, a free Gallery, studios (from the rental of which part of the revenue is to be derived), and an observatory 255 feet above the street level, reached by elevator, and open to visitors on payment of a small fee. The Academy is out of debt. For the present, however, it has but limited quarters.—*Art Schools :* Classes in Landscape, Figure, Flower and Historical Painting, Drawing and Composition, with all necessary facilities for the rapid and thoroughly practical training of artists and amateurs in the best technical methods.—Director of Schools : J. F. Gookins.—Term begins Sept. 29, 1883 ; classes open three days in the week, from 9 A.M. to 12 M., and 1 to 4 P.M. Fees, $20 per month. Each pupil receives individual instruction.—Pupils, both sexes, may join at any time, and begin to work in color or black-and-white, as they may choose. [Attendance not given.]—Annual meeting, first Thursday in November.

CHICAGO ART CLUB.—Rooms 35 and 36 Ayer B'ldg., 70 Monroe St.—Organized Oct. 3, 1881.—Officers : Sec., Alfred Payne (address at Club rooms) ; C. F. Schwerdt, Treas.—Objects : Advancement of its members in the knowledge of correct principles and practice in art, and furthering their interests generally, by providing for exhibitions, art receptions, etc.—Members must be of proved ability in the practice of pictorial, plastic, or other form of art. Present number, 27. Most of the members are of the older generation of Chicago artists.—The Club purposes to hold semi-annual exhibitions. Such an exhibition was held in the spring of 1883, at the Stevens' Art Gallery, followed by an auction sale, but the fall exhibition was omitted, in consequence of absence from the city of active members.—Annual meeting, second Monday in January. [Title wrongly given in last year's issue as *Chicago Artists' Club.*]

CHICAGO ART LEAGUE.—Art Institute.—Organized March, 1879.—Officers : Sec., J. H. Vanderpoel, Art Institute ; Treas., Fred Voss.—Objects : To benefit the artists of Chicago, and to furnish headquarters where members can assemble for the general discussion of art.—Membership : Candidates must submit an oil study from nature. Present number of members, 20. The members are all young professional artists. Initiation fee, $5 ; monthly dues, $1.25.—The Club holds annual exhibitions in February. The third, comprising over 100 works, was held, Feb. 25 to Mch. 10, 1883, at the Art Institute. The fourth will take place, Feb. 25 to Mch. 10, 1884, also at the Art Institute.

CHICAGO CHAPTER OF THE AMERICAN INSTITUTE OF ARCHITECTS.—Rooms 31 to 35, 80 Dearborn St.—Organized Dec. 13, 1869.—Officers : Pres., A. Bauer,

85 La Salle St.; V. P., T. D. Cleaveland, 175 La Salle St.; Sec., S. A. Treat, 80 Dearborn St.; Treas., J. R. Willetts, 94 La Salle St.—Objects : To unite in fellowship the architects of Chicago, and to promote the efficiency of the profession.—Present number of members, 19.—Annual meeting, in October.

CHICAGO POTTERY CLUB.—Works, 795 West Congress St.—Organized, Feb. 27, 1883.—Officers: Pres., Mrs. Philo King; Treas., Mrs. V. B. Jenkins ; Sec., Mrs. Jno. B. Jeffery, 3141 South Park Ave.—The Club consists of about twelve ladies interested in ceramic art, who were compelled to send their work to Cincinnati for firing, as the facilities were lacking in Chicago. These ladies paid for the building of the kiln, and guarantee the salary of the potter. There are about as many honorary members, who merely pay a fee for the privilege of working in the pottery. The Club has engaged Mr. Jos. Bailley, formerly of the Rookwood Pottery, Cincinnati, as its super- intendent, and takes orders for decorative ware of various kinds, as well as for firing and glazing. Mrs. Jenkins has a studio at the works, where pupils are received.

CHICAGO SOCIETY OF DECORATIVE ART.—Rooms 6, 7 and 8, 170 State St. After Apr. 1, 1884, at the Art Institute.—Organized May 24, 1877.—Officers : Pres., Mrs. B. F. Ayer, Hyde Park, Ill.; Rec. Sec., Mrs. A. T. Galt, 550 Dearborn Ave.; Cor. Sec., Mrs. R. H. McCormick, 124 Rush St.; Treas., Mrs. John A. Yale, 108 Pine St.—Objects: To create a desire for artistic decoration, and for a knowledge of the best methods of ornamentation ; to provide train ing in artistic industries, and enable decorative artists to render their labor remunerative.—Any person may become a member by an annual payment of $5. Present number of members, about 200.—The Society is prepared to maintain classes in embroidery. Miss S. Smith, teacher, but there were no pupils at the time this report was sent (Dec., 1883).—Exhibitions are held annually, and there are to be three lectures this season.—Annual meeting, held at the Palmer House, third Tuesday in May.

ILLINOIS ART ASSOCIATION.—145 Ashland Ave.—Organized and incorporated, Sept. 15, 1882.—Officers: Pres., Jos. M. Rogers ; Sec., S. P. McConnell.—Objects: The collec- tion, exhibition, and distribution of works of art.—Present number of members, about 100.—The Association has a capital of $25,000. It holds annual exhibitions in November, and has also held a Black-and-White exhibition. The sales at the exhibitions so far held (two Annual, Nov., 1882, and Nov. 1883, Black-and-White, May, 1883), amounted to $11,846. The Association has made as yet comparatively few purchases. It owns, through purchase and gift, 14 paintings, valued at $6,400. Eight of these are foreign pictures, bought directly from the artists. The others are works of local artists. The exhibitions, as well as the collection of the Association, are open only to members and invited guests.

INTERSTATE INDUSTRIAL EXPOSITION OF CHICAGO.—Exposition Build- ing.—Officers: Pres. A. F. Seeberger ; Sec., John P. Reynolds ; Treas., J. Irving Pearce. Art Com- mittee : Jas. H. Dole, Chairmn.; Chas. L. Hutchinson, Watson F. Blair, Chas. D. Hamill, Harry D. Spears ; Miss Sara T. Hallowell, Sec.—The Eleventh Annual Exhibition of this association was held from Sept. 5 to Oct. 20, 1883. The Art Department connected with these exhibitions has grown in excellence and importance from year to year, and the sales are considerable. At the Exhibition of 1881, 65 works of art, valued at $30,075, were sold, out of 382 exhibited ; 1882, 54 works out of 329, value, $19,296.60 ; 1883, 36 works out of 502, value $17,835.—The Exposition Company also owns a small nucleus of a permanent collection, in the shape of a number of casts from antique statuary.

PERMANENT EXHIBITIONS of works of art, both foreign and American, will be found at the *Stevens Art Gallery,* 24 and 26 Adams St.

23. Cincinnati, O.

ART STUDENTS' LEAGUE.—54 West 4th St.—Matt. Morgan, Principal and Manager. [This " League " seems to be a private school, and according to the rule adopted for this Directory has no place here. Attention is, nevertheless, called to it, on account of the valuable " European

Scholarship " of $1,200, to be expended in study abroad, which it offers as a prize. For details, see circulars issued by the League.]

CINCINNATI CHAPTER OF THE AMERICAN INSTITUTE OF ARCHITECTS.

—55 W. 4th St.—Organized, Jan. 10, 1870.—Officers: Pres., A. C. Nash; Sec., Chas. Crapsey, 46 Wiggins Block.—Present number of members: 10 practising, 8 honorary.—The students and draughtsmen in the several offices are organized into a class for the study of architecture collectively. This class meets every Thursday night, and each Saturday afternoon the members visit works in process of construction.

CINCINNATI INDUSTRIAL EXPOSITION.

—Officers, B'd of Comm.: Pres., W. W. Peabody; V. P's., Hugh McCollum, Oliver Kinsey, Jno. E. Bell; Sec., Wm. H. Stewart; Treas., Benj. E. Hopkins; Chairm. Art Comm., Lawrence Mendenhall; Supt. Art Dept., Emery H. Barton, 17 Emery Arcade.—An exhibition of works of art is connected with the yearly expositions held by this Association. At the Eleventh Exposition, which took place from Sept. 5 to Oct. 6, 1883, there were sold 28 pictures, valued at $4,141.50.

CINCINNATI MUSEUM ASSOCIATION.

—Temporary rooms, Music Hall.—Incorporated Feb. 15, 1881.—Officers: Pres., M. E. Ingalls; Treas., Julius Dexter; Sec., R. H. Galbreath; Director, A. T. Goshorn.—Objects: Establishing and maintaining in Cincinnati a Museum, wherein may be gathered, preserved, and exhibited valuable and interesting objects of every kind and nature, and for the further purpose of using the contents of such Museum for education, through the establishment of classes and otherwise, as may be found expedient. The formation of the Museum is to be based on the general plan of the South Kensington Museum. It will include departments in art, science, natural history, etc., and instruction in the subjects illustrated by the objects deposited in the Museum. The opportunities for art education are to be the first to be made available.—The contributions toward the general fund, begun by Mr. C. W. West with a subscription of $150,000, amounted at the date of the First Annual Report, March 6, 1882, to $316,501, contributed by 455 subscribers. Mr. C. W. West has also endowed the institution with an additional fund of $150,000, which, as at present invested, yields $10,500 annually. The city of Cincinnati has ceded to the Association a tract of 19.71 acres of land in Eden Park, which it is to occupy free of all taxes, assessments, etc., so long as it maintains thereon a building or buildings devoted to the objects stated, as nearly free from all costs and charges to the public as may be consistent with keeping it in repair, etc. The rest of the grounds, not occupied by the buildings, are to be maintained as a free park at the expense of the Association. The buildings to cost not less than $50,000.—The Association consists of 148 stockholders, who are not allowed to hold more than one share, of $25, bearing no dividend or interest, each. [" The plan of organization of the Cincinnati Museum Association," says the Report, " adopted by the subscribers to the fund, gave to each subscriber the option of becoming a shareholder in the corporation. One hundred and forty-eight subscribers in this manner became shareholders, and represent the entire number of shares of the corporation." The manner of becoming a shareholder is not, however, indicated in the Report.] No share can be transferred without the consent of the Association, and the shares of deceased members revert to the Association. It is provided, however, that the Association shall at all times keep placed in the ownership of proper persons the full number of 148 shares, and to that end shall, within 30 days after becoming the owner of a share, dispose of it to such person as the Trustees may elect. Any 25 resident freeholders in Cincinnati may require an investigation of the Museum management and affairs, through one or more experts.—The Trustees, ten in number, are elected by the stockholders, two being renewed each year. The Mayor of the city is, ex-officio, a member of the Board, and two other members may be appointed by the Common Council.—The Museum building now in course of erection in Eden Park (Jas. W. McLaughlin, architect), is in the Florentine-Romanesque style, and will be one of the finest in the country. [See illustration.] Ground was broken, Sept. 21, 1882, and the building is to be completed by Oct., 1885. Temporary rooms in Music Hall were opened to private view on Feb. 10, 1882, and have since been open to the public from 10 A.M. to 4 P.M. daily, Sundays excepted. Admission, 25 cents. The Trustees have accepted as gifts valuable art treasures from Mr. Joseph Longworth (a large number of drawings by Lessing, etc.), the Women's Art Museum Association (an older organization, now dissolved, which began the agitation for an Art Museum), Mr. George Hoadley (Turner's " Liber Studiorum "), Mrs. Eliza Longworth Flagg, Mrs. S. N. Pike, the Ninth Cincinnati Exposition, and others. Later acquisitions of importance are, the Hillingford Collection of arms and armor ; 210 pieces of reproductions of metal vessels, etc., in the South Kensington, Russian and other Continental Museums ; a collection of Peruvian antiquities ; a large collection of Cashmere shawls, given by the late Joseph Longworth, and a collection of etchings, from the same donor. The temporary exhibition includes part of the sketches, etc., by Lessing, above alluded to ; the " Liber Studiorum " of Turner ; a ceramic display exhibiting the progress of the art in Cincinnati, from the first experiments by Miss McLaughlin to the latest work of the Rookwood Pottery ; and a loan collection of painting, bric-à-brac, armor, etc. The only catalogue so far issued is one of part of the Lessing collection and of the " Liber Studiorum." Price, 25 cents.—The Museum has received an endowment of $15,000 annually from the Longworth estate, which is to be applied to the maintenance of the Art School formerly connected with the University of Cincinnati, but lately transferred [in 1884] to the Museum Association.—Annual meeting, first Monday in March.

CINCINNATI POTTERY CLUB.—Organized 1879.—Officers : Pres., Miss M. Louise McLaughlin ; Sec., Miss Clara C. Newton, 207 Eastern Ave.; Treas., Miss Alice B. Holabird.— Object : Painting pottery in under-glaze, and modelling in relief upon wet clay objects in pottery.— Number of members limited to 15 ; no vacancies.—An Annual Reception is held in May. The Club used to have rooms at the Rookwood Pottery, but at present has no room. Monthly meetings are held at the residences of the members.

ETCHING CLUB.—Officers : Pres., Dr. D. S. Young ; Sec., Emery H. Barton, 117 Emery Arcade. [This Club used to hold regular meetings, to which invitations were issued, etched by its members. It has, however, been dormant for some time, although it is still in existence, and is likely to be more active again as soon as a suitable place can be found for meetings. The Club gave a collection of fifty etchings to the Cincinnati Art Museum.]

HISTORICAL AND PHILOSOPHICAL SOCIETY.—Cabinet of Indian curiosities and Mound Builders' relics. [No reply to repeated requests for information.]

OHIO MECHANICS' INSTITUTE OF THE CITY OF CINCINNATI.— Organized 1828 ; incorporated Feb. 9, 1829.—Officers : Pres., Thomas Gilpin ; V. P., Jas. Dale ; Rec. Sec., W. B. Bruce ; Treas., Hugh McCollum ; Clerk, John B. Heich ; Comm. of School of Design, W. B. Bruce, Wm. H. Stewart.—*The School of Design* connected with the Institute was established in 1856. Aim : The teaching of mechanical, architectural, and artistic drawing for the instruction of apprentices.—Departments and Teachers : Prin., John B. Heich ; Mechanical Dept., in charge of Ernest Lietze, Geo. Wadman, Bert L. Baldwin ; Architectural, Wm. W. Franklin, W. S. Burrows ; Artistic, W. R. McComas, Alb. J. Kaiser ; Original Designing, W. R. McComas, Alb. J. Kaiser ; Modelling in Clay, C. L. Fettweis ; Geometry and Mathematics, Jas. B. Stanwood. Full course, 3 years. Sessions, Tuesday and Friday of each week, from 7 to 9 P.M. The Life Class, organized four years ago, because there was no adequate opportunity for such study in the city at that time, has been discontinued as no longer necessary, and in a great measure out of the particular line of tuition applied to the industrial arts.—Tuition free ; pupils must provide materials and instruments.—Pupils, males only : Mechan. Dept., 117 ; Arch., 58 ; Artistic, 78 ; Modelling, 12 ; Geom. and Math., 15 : total, 280 for the season of 1881-2.—Bronze medals are awarded the first year ; silver medals the second ; gold medals or the badge of the Institute the third. " Honorable Mentions " and " Degrees of Merit " are also given. Pupils who have attended for three consecutive years receive certificates attesting their attendance.—The School of Design is eventually to be developed into a *School of Technology*, and the first move toward the realization of the plan, in conjunction with other bodies, was made in 1881. [From last year's issue. No reply to repeated requests for later information.]

UNIVERSITY OF CINCINNATI.—Incorporated April 16, 1870.—Officers : Chairm. of B'd of Directors, Saml. F. Hunt ; Clerk of the B'd, T. B. Disney, N. E. cor. 3d and Main Sts.; Rector, Thomas Vickers, B. D.—Upon its organization the Board received an estate left in trust for the city by Chas. McMicken in 1858. Since then the endowments have been increased by important donations from the Cincinnati Astronomical Society, Joseph Longworth, John Kilgour, and by a bequest from the Rev. Sam'l J. Browne. The University has also received assistance from the city.—It consists of three departments: The Academic, or Department of Literature and Science; the School of Design or Art Dept.; and the Observatory, or Astronomical Dept. In the first and last of these departments no drawing is taught, with the exception of what is necessary in connection with engineering.—*The Art Department* was organized in 1869, as "The McMicken School of Art and Design," with one teacher and 30 pupils. Aims: The Directors desire practical results from the Art School, so that those who pass through it shall be fitted for the active duties of life, and especially for the branch of art chosen as a profession. A thoroughly graded course has been adopted, with a view of graduating such students (with a Diploma from the University) as shall have proved themselves worthy of the honor at the end of the curriculum.—Courses of Study: Drawing, Perspective and Pictorial Design, in Black-and-White, extending from elementary drawing to drawing from the living model, and original pictorial composition, 5 grades; Oil Painting; Decorative Design, 4 grades; Water-Color Painting, from the elements to compositions from life subjects, 4 grades; Sculpture, 4 grades; Wood Carving for Decorative Purposes, 4 grades. Full course, 5 years. Day and night classes in session from beginning of September to end of May.—Teachers: Principal, . Thos. S. Noble; Decor. Design and Water Color, Wm. H. Humphreys; Drawing and Perspec., Rebecca R. Whittemore-Gregg, Martha Jane Keller; Drawing, Nettie Wilson; Sculpture, Louis Thos. Rebisso; Carving, Benn Pitman.—Students, both sexes, must be not less than thirteen years old, and must satisfy the principal that they are capable of pursuing the studies of the school to advantage. Application for admission to be made to the Clerk of the B'd of Directors. Attendance during season 1882–83: Drawing and Design, day classes, 136 female, 13 male; night classes, 18 female, 93 male: total, 260 (154 female, 106 male). Decorative Design, 27 f., 10 m.; Pen Drawing, 26 f., 3 m.; Water Color, 22 f., 1 m.; Oil Painting, 7 f.; Sculpture, 19 f., 7 m.; Carving, 28 f., 1 m. Grand total of attendance, 411 (283 f., 128 m.). The number of individual students was however, only 274, as in the statement of attendance those pupils who attended several classes are counted more than once.—Fees: To *bona fide* residents of Cincinnati the instruction is free. Non-residents, $60 p. a. for day classes, $30 p. a. for night classes. All pupils pay $5 p. a. in the day classes, $3 p. a. in the night classes, for the use of models, etc. Materials must be furnished by the pupils.—Collections: Plaster casts from the antique, ornaments, natural fruits and flowers, etc.; autotypes from drawings of celebrated masters; library of books of reference.—At the close of the academic year a public exhibition is held of such work of the students as may seem meritorious to the Faculty. The work done in the various grades is classified into three orders of merit, and the diplomas given at the end of the fifth year are graded accordingly. Students who have completed three years with credit are entitled to a certificate stating their qualifications. [This Art School has since been transferred, in January, 1884, to the control of the Cincinnati Art Museum Association. For the present, its organization is to remain as here reported.]

24. Cleveland, O.

CLEVELAND ACADEMY OF ART.—Rooms 25 and 27 City Hall.—Founded as the Art Club, 1876; incorporated Dec. 15, 1881.—Officers: Pres., W. J. Gordon; V. P., Hon. G. M. Barber; Sec. and Treas., W. H. Eckman.—Objects: To establish and maintain a School of Art, to afford facilities for the acquirement of a practical knowledge of the arts, and to procure, for the use and benefit of members and others, such appliances and material as may be necessary to further this purpose; to create and maintain a Gallery of Art.—The members of the corporation consist of the original incorporators (of whom there were 34), and of the following: 1. Members: initiation fee, $100; annual dues, $5; entitled, with the actual members of their families, to admission to the Gallery and to all exhibitions. 2. Individual members: initiation fee, $25; annual dues, $2; entitled to same privileges for themselves only. 3. Life Members, contributing $500; entitled, with their families, to all the privileges of the corporation, during life, excepting instruction. 4. Honorary Life Members, contributing $1,000; entitled, with their families, to all the privileges of the corporation during life. Artists, in lieu of the membership fee, may present a work of art, subject to acceptance, of a value not less than $100, and shall not be subject to annual assessments.—A committee of five, known as Curators, three of whom must be artists, appointed by the Trustees, is charged with the management of all exhibitions, and everything pertaining to them. The Committee on Instruction, five in number, also appointed by the Board, must consist entirely of artists. It is placed, however, under the supervision of the Board, and the rules and regulations made by it for the use of the property of the Academy must be approved by the Board before they can be enforced. The president is *ex-officio* a member of all committees, with a right to vote.—*Classes of the Academy.*—Aims and methods. The manner of instruction is based upon the principle that the student must work out the problem for him or herself, and that only such instruction, direction, and guidance should be given as will enable him or her to avoid the repetition of inevitable errors, abundant, repeated, and close criticism of the work by those amply qualified, accomplishing more practical and lasting results than constant direction, which tends to make the student dependent, weakens his individuality, and breeds mannerism.—Term begins Sept. 10, 1883, and continues until June 1, 1884, with sketching parties during the following summer months. Day Classes: Oil painting, portraiture, landscape, drapery, and still life ; Drawing from casts and draped model in charcoal and crayon ; Modelling ; Etching ; Wood Engraving ; Architectural, ornament, and furniture drawing ; Conventional and decorative drawing. Evening Classes: Sketch ; Cast ; Life ; Composition. Lectures on Artistic Anatomy, Perspective, etc.—Instructors : A. M. Willard, Sketch and Composition Classes ; John W. Bell, Oil Painting, Landscape ; De Scott Evans, Drapery and Figure Painting in Oil ; C. M. Buxbaum, Modelling in Clay ; Miss Sally Rayen, Oil Painting and Drawing, Landscape, Flowers, and Still Life ; Charles Heiss, Wood Engraving; Otto S. Ruetenik, Architectural Ornament and Furniture Drawing ; Geo. C. Groll, Conventional and Decorative Drawing ; Adam Lehr, Painting in Oil, Landscape, and Still Life ; Geo. L. Grossman, Charcoal Drawing ; John S. Jennings, Cast Drawing ; Miss May Remington, Oil Painting, Landscape, Still Life, and Wood Carving; Otto H. Bacher and Joseph R. De Camp, Oil Painting and Etching.—Tuition Fees : Membership Fee, $1 ; Day Classes, except Modelling, $5 a month, one day each week ; Modelling Class, $25 a quarter, two days in each week. Evening Classes, $5 for the entire term. Free admission to the classes may be secured upon satisfactory representation being made to the Board of Trustees.—Public receptions, which have been very popular, are held on the last Monday of each month, day and evening.—"*The Sketch Book,*" issued monthly by the Cleveland Academy of Art," illustrated, editor W. H. Eckman, was published during the year 1883. Subscription $2.50 per year.—Annual meeting, third Thursday of December.

EAST CLEVELAND ART ASSOCIATION.—Pres., Mrs. S. E. Stone.

WESTERN RESERVE AND NORTHERN OHIO HISTORICAL SOCIETY.
—Museum of antiquities, principally relating to the West, including a fine collection of curiosities taken from the mounds on the Mississippi River, near Memphis ; Babylonian and other Oriental antiquities. [No reply to repeated inquiries.]

WESTERN RESERVE SCHOOL OF DESIGN FOR WOMEN.—Fourth floor of
City Hall B'ldg.—Organized, Oct. 2, 1882, by Mrs. Sarah M. Kimball, assisted by eight other ladies; incorp., Nov. 13, 1882.—Officers : Pres., Henry C. Ranney; V. Ps., R. K. Winlow, Mrs. S. M. Kimball, 1265 Euclid Ave.; Rec. Sec., George Hoyt; Cor. Sec., Mrs. Clara Kimball Sheridan; Treas., Mrs. E. C. Pechin, 303 Prospect St.—Object : To establish and maintain a School of Art and Design for Women, in which shall be taught the principles of art and design as practically applied to artistic and industrial pursuits, and also the collection and exhibition of works of art and virtu.— The membership of the corporation which manages the school consists of two classes, active and honorary: Active, who alone have the right to vote, the original incorporators, and others approved by Committee on Membership; initiation fee, $3 ; annual dues, $3. Honorary, any person who shall pay $25. There is also a class of members, known as Founders, limited to 100, who pay $100 each. [Privileges of this class not given in documents sent.]—There are two terms, from Sept. 10, 1883, to Feb. 1, 1884, and from Feb. 4 to June 30, 1884. The curriculum of the school includes: Lectures on Ornamentation, Botanical Analysis, Art Anatomy, Perspective, Technical Design, Etching, Wood Engraving, Lithography, Wood Carving, Modelling, Glass Painting, Landscape from Nature. The course of study is divided into eight stages : 1. Elementary; 2. Fruit and Flowers; 3. Ornament; 4. Detail of Figure ; 5. Detail of Face ; 6. Antique Busts ; 7. Statues ; 8. Portraiture.—Instructors : Harriet J. Kester, Principal, Painting from Cast in Monochrome and Perspective ; R. Way Smith, Landscape from Nature ; De Scott Evans, and H. J. Risler, Drawing from Life in Color, Drapery

in Color; Miss Louisa F. Randolph, Ornamentation and its Analysis; S. R. Spencer Gray, Etching ; Dr. Charles Parker, Art Anatomy ; George R. Lindsay, China Decoration, Design. Teachers of other specialties not yet appointed.—Tuition fees, $20 per term of 20 weeks; $5 per term extra to those requiring special instruction in any one of the industrial arts ; $10 extra to those desiring instruction from more than one master in the higher branches. Two perpetual free scholarships have been granted to Mrs. Sarah M. Kimball, in consideration of the untiring and important personal attention she has given the institution. Other free scholarships may be secured by the payment of $1,000.—Pupils may be of both sexes, and are taught together. Number of pupils, first term of second year, 60. —Ten prizes are given, and an annual exhibition is held in June.—It is the desire of the incorporators to erect a special building for the school, and Mrs. Kimball has already expressed her willingness to donate, as the nucleus of a museum in connection with the school, her collection of artistic and other interesting objects.—The first Tuesday evening in each month during the school session, the founders give receptions alternately at their residences, inviting the instructors. The second Tuesday of each month, the managers give receptions at the school rooms, inviting the pupils, etc.—Annual Meeting, first Monday in October.

25. Columbia, Mo.

MISSOURI STATE UNIVERSITY.—Founded 1820; organized 1840.—Officers of the B'd of Curators: Pres., Hon. Jas. S. Rollins, LL.D.; V. P., Jerre C. Cravens ; Sec., Robt. L. Todd ; Treas., Robt. Beverly Price. Officers of the Faculty: Pres., Sam'l Spahr Laws, A.M., M.D., LL.D.; Sec., J. C. Jones, A.M.; Libr. and Proctor, J. H. Drummond, A.B.—The departments of instruction are: 1. The Academic Schools of Language and Science. 2. The Professional Schools of Agriculture, Pedagogics, Engineering, Art, Law, Medicine, Mining and Metallurgy. Girls are admitted to the University in a special Ladies' Department, Mrs. O. A. Carr, Prin. —The University forms part of the State system of public instruction. Its income is derived from tuition fees ($20 to $50 p. a.), appropriations by the legislature, and from lands granted by the U. S.—In the four Academic courses (Course in Arts, in Science, in Letters, and Girls' Course in Fine and Domestic Arts), the study of art is made a condition of graduation, the University of Missouri being the only institution in the U. S. in which this is the case. In the Girls' Course the study of drawing has to be taken completely. The work of this department is not confined to the art phase, but comprehends the study of form in general, i. e., the elements of scientific and pictorial representation In a college course the educational feature of the work must receive more prominence than mere manual training, hence the latter is limited on the one hand to drill in the use of the compass and the straight-edge, and exercises in the tracing of curves through fixed points ; on the other to surface representation, i e., gradating of light and dark. Students are also encouraged to carve suitable examples out of soft substances. No copies are used ; all the exercises are conducted by dictation on the blackboard. The lessons thus learned must be put into practice by the students by drawing from objects at home, the work to be submitted when completed. It is stated that this system has given very good results. The subjects taught include descriptive geometry, shades and shadows, perspective, ornament, the laws of decoration and design, the forms of architecture, the laws of the beautiful, the theory of color, and object drawing practised at home, as already explained. Lead pencil and water colors are the only media used. Professor of Art Dept., Conrad Diehl. The attendance in the Art Dept. for the year 1882-3 was 179, exclusive of the classes in Botany, the students in which practise drawing in connection with their studies. The enlargements and improvements now in progress, by special authority of the legislature, and which will be completed within 1884, will afford admirable accommodations for an Art Gallery, and increased facilities for the Art Department.—Catalogues may be obtained by addressing " The Librarian of Missouri University," Columbia, Boone Co., Mo.

26. Columbus, O.

COLUMBUS ART ASSOCIATION.—15 E. Long St.—Organized, Nov., 1878.—Officers : Pres., Mrs. Ezra Bliss, Hubbard and Park Ave.; 1st V. P., Mrs. Saml. Galloway; 2d V. P., Mrs. Edward Orton ; Treas., Mrs. T. C. Mendenhall, State University Grounds; Sec., Mrs. Wilson Gill, 40 Broad St.—Object : To further and encourage the study of the Arts, theoretically and practically, through the medium of lectures, teachers, books, pictures, models, and in all the most approved methods of the present day, so as to bring within the reach of all persons so desiring, the means of knowledge and of improvement in the Arts.—Members : Ladies only ; annual dues, $2. Honorary members, not entitled to vote, ladies or gentlemen, $5 annually.—Present number of members, 79 regular, 22 honorary.—The Association maintains an Art School (see below) and a Fine Art Library, and arranges lectures and readings at its meetings.—Annual meeting, first Tuesday in November.

COLUMBUS ART SCHOOL.—15 E. Long St.—Organized, Jan., 1879, by the Columbus Art Association, and still maintained by it. The Art School depends for its support on the receipts from regular and honorary Art Association membership fees, tuition fees, donations, and bequests.— Teachers and Classes: Prof. W. S. Goodnough (161 Hamilton Ave.), Director, Evening Drawing Classes, Free-hand, Architectural, and Machine Drawing ; Miss Dora M. Norton, Drawing, Elementary and Advanced Life Classes, Decorative Design, Water Color, Oil Painting ; Miss Fanny Heyl, China Painting ; Miss Stella Hall, Art Needle-work ; Miss Henrietta Jamison, Saturday Drawing Class ; C. Brower Darst, Curator, Wood Carving. There is also a Life Sketch Class, and it is proposed to organize classes in Sheet Brass and Leather work.—Tuition fees vary from $14 to $3 per term according to subject; single lessons from 30 to 75 cents, according to subject. There are three terms, which, for the season of 1883-4, begin Oct. 9, 1883, Jan. 7, and April 9, 1884.—Persons of any age may enter any of the classes at any time, but those entering others than the Drawing •Classes, are expected to have some knowledge of drawing. Number of students from Oct. 16, 1882, to May 1, 1883, 236 (191 female, 45 male). Total number of students for the five years since the founding of the school, 1,072.—Certificates and Diplomas : A course of study has been arranged for each class. On passing through this course satisfactorily, a Certificate is given. A Diploma is granted to students obtaining Certificates in Drawing, Life, Water Color and Oil Painting Classes, or to those taking Certificates in Drawing, Design, and either China Painting, Art Needle-work, or Wood Carving. The taking of the prescribed course in each class for the Certificate is optional with students. Those taking the prescribed course are known as Regular Students; others are classed as Special Students. [Number of certificates and diplomas awarded not given.]—An exhibition of the work of the students is held in June.—There is a large collection of casts, models, copies, and photographs, which is constantly being increased.—Pupils have access to the Art Library of the Association.

27. Contoocook, N. H.

NEW HAMPSHIRE ANTIQUARIAN SOCIETY.—Officers, 1883-4 : Pres., Hon. Isaac A. Hammond, Concord, Me.; Curator, M. S. Davis.—Collection of antiquities of North American Indians, ancient and modern coins, etc. At the annual meeting of 1883, the curator reported 2,149 articles added to the collection during the year. At the same meeting a number of addresses were delivered, one of them, by Mr. D. C. Blanchard, of New York, on " Problems in American Archæology." It is said that the Society contemplates the erection of a building in which to arrange its collections.—Annual meeting in June. [From newspaper notices. No reply to repeated requests for information.]

28. Dayton, O.

LADIES' DECORATIVE ART SOCIETY.—Officers : Pres., Miss C. Brown ; V. P.'s, Mrs. E. M. Wood, Mrs. O. M. Gottschall, Mrs. I. B. Thresher; Treas., Mrs. David Houk ; Rec. Sec., Mrs. W. F. Gebhart ; Cor. Sec., Mrs. James A. Robert.—The Society is in a transition state. It has, in fact, resolved itself into an Amateur Art Club for practical work. The Art School was kept up vigorously until June, 1883, but has since been given up. The Society has a kiln where members fire their own work.

29. Decatur, Ill.

DECATUR ART CLASS.—Officers : Pres., Mrs. A. T. Hill; V. P., Mrs. R. L. Walston; Sec., Miss Mary Wilder ; Treas., Mrs. R. J. Gallagher.—Objects and Methods : The object of the Class is study. A Topic Committee is elected every three months, whose duty it is to assign topics for study and subjects for the papers to be read. The subjects of study are not confined strictly to art. The meetings are held weekly.—Number of members limited to 20. The Class is full.—The association is a member of the Central Illinois Art Union.—Annual meeting, first Saturday in November.

YOUNG LADIES' ART CLASS.—Officers : Pres., Miss F. Shellabarger: V. P., Miss J. Rogers ; Sec., Miss Lillie A. Brown.—Objects and methods : The class is a social organization for the study of the history of art. At the weekly meetings, essays on art topics are read by the members. The subjects are chosen by the essayists.—Number of members, 15 active. The Class is a member of the Central Illinois Art Union.

30. Denver, Col.

ACADEMY OF FINE ARTS ASSOCIATION.—Discontinued.

NATIONAL MINING AND INDUSTRIAL EXPOSITION ASSOCIATION.—
Organized, 1882.—Officers : Pres., H. A. W. Tabor ; Sec. and General Manager, W. A. H. Loveland.—An Art Department is connected with the yearly exhibitions arranged by this Association. The exhibition of 1883 was held July 17 to Sept. 30.

UNIVERSITY ART CLUB.—University of Denver, cor. 14th and Arapahoe Sts.—Officers : Pres., Miss Ida de Steiguer, University of Denver ; V. P., Mrs. Frank Church, 59 S. 14th' St. ; Sec.. Mrs. Sidney Short, University ; Treas., Mrs. Alfred Wolf, University.—Membership, March, 1883, about 50. [No reply to repeated requests for more detailed information.]

UNIVERSITY OF DENVER.—14th and Arapahoe Sts. Incorporated 1880, under the auspices of the M. E. Church.—Officers B'd of Trustees : Pres., Gov. John Evans ; V. P., J. W. Bailey ; Sec., Earl Cranston ; Treas., J. A. Clough ; Chancellor, David H. Moore, A.M., D.D.—No drawing is taught in the Preparatory Courses, and in the other courses only in the Scientific (Free-hand, in the Sophomore year), and the Mining Engineering (in the Freshman and Sophomore years and one term of the Junior year).—*The College of Fine Arts* connected with the institution confers the degree of Bachelor of Painting. The technical work done in the Maryland Institute is the model in this department. In addition thereto there are at least two recitations per day in related branches, including modern languages, natural science, and belles-lettres. The time required for the completion of the course and obtaining the degree will depend upon the talent and application of the student. The studio is supplied with designs and casts, and the work is done by the most thorough and advanced methods. A furnace for burning decorated china adds greatly to the efficiency of the department. Wood carving has lately been added, as an art destined to command increasing attention, and to open to women new fields of delightful and remunerative employment.—Principal of the College, Miss Ida de Steiguer.—Tuition from $10 to $15 per quarter of 10 weeks, 2 lessons per week, according to subject.—Number of pupils last season, 75.

31. Detroit, Mich.

ART ASSOCIATION.—An association, known as the *Detroit Art Loan Association*, organized Feb. 27, 1883 (with the following officers : Chairm., W. H. Brearley ; Sec., Fred. E. Farnsworth ; Treas., John L. Harper), held a very large and successful Loan Exhibition, in a building especially erected for the purpose, in Detroit, during the months of September and October, 1883, the sales at which were reported at about $20,000 for 87 oil and water color paintings, 79 prints, and 37 miscellaneous articles. The exhibition was organized in the hope that it might lead to the establishment of a permanent art building, to be used as a Gallery and for a School of Design, and this hope seems in a fair way of being realized. [The further history of this enterprise belongs to the year 1884. At last accounts, the sum of $40,000 had been raised for the purchase of a site for a building, and a meeting had been called for Feb. 27, 1884, at which further steps were to be taken towards the organization and incorporation of a permanent Art Association.]

DETROIT ART CLUB.—Randall's Art B'ldg.—Organized and incorporated, 1879.—

Officers : Pres., L. T. Ives, 490 Brush St. ; Sec., R. C. W. Dillaway, Detroit Art Store ; Treas., R. C. Wilby, 97 Jefferson Ave.—Objects : Sketching, and improvement in all art matters.—Present number of members, 100. There are two classes of members, those belonging to the Sketching Class, and general.—Art talks, lectures, etc.—Annual meeting, in November.

DETROIT SKETCHING CLUB.—15 Burns Block.—Pres., Julius Jahn.—Object : Full knowledge of sketching from life.—Present number of members, males only, 18. Dues, $3 quarterly.—The Club was organized by Mr. Fred. Wolfenden, and Mr. W. B. Conely, at whose studio it meets, and who is also its teacher.—Annual meeting, in October.

DETROIT WATER COLOR SOCIETY.—Organized March 22, 1883.—Officers : Pres., Gari J. Melchers ; Sec. and Treas., Wm. Mylne, 255 Jefferson Ave. ; B'd of Control, G. J. Melchers, H. C. Bullock, L. H. Robertson, Miss C. Roberts.—Object : The advancement of the art of water color painting.—Members : Resident, artists of Detroit and vicinity (at present 18), in whom is vested the governing power ; non-resident, artists elsewhere (at present 1) ; honorary, connoisseurs (at present 6). Initiation fee, $3. By an amendment, passed Jan. 16, 1884, it was resolved to assess an annual fee of $3 on active members, and to raise the fee for honorary membership to $10.—The Society exhibited a collection of 57 pictures at the Detroit Art Loan Exhibition, Sept.-Oct., 1883, and held an exhibition at Sigler & Stratton's Art Store in Dec., 1883. Two exhibitions are to be held annually hereafter in May and November.—Annual meeting, first Saturday of March.

32. Elgin, Ill.

ELGIN ART ASSOCIATION.—42 Chicago St.—Organized 1877 ; incorporated 1880.— Officers, 1883 : Pres., J. S. Wilcox ; V. P., Mrs. V. S. Lovell ; Treas., S. E. Weld ; Rec. Sec., Miss Laura Davidson ; Cor. Sec., Geo. E. Bowen.—Objects : Painting, sculpture and decorative work.—Present membership, about 60. Art qualification not necessary. Yearly fee, $3.—Monthly meetings, readings, musical entertainments, etc.—At the Seventh Annual Exhibit (admission 15 cents, season tickets, $1 50), 148 objects were shown consisting of paintings, studies, and art needlework.—*Art School :* The Association maintains classes in Landscape, L. H. Yarwood, teacher ; Flower and Pottery Painting, Mrs. H. H. Denison, teacher ; Figure and Object Drawing and Painting, Prof. Sammons ; Sculpture and Modelling, Mrs. V. S. Lovell.

33. Fordham, N. Y.

ST. JOHN'S COLLEGE.—Conducted by Jesuit Fathers.—Prof. of Painting and Drawing, Stephen J. Shaughnessy.—The Art Class meets twice a week. Instruction is given in Instrumental, Elementary and Free-hand Drawing from copy and from the round ; painting in water colors ; oil-painting (when the time at the disposal of the pupil permits). The importance of sketching from nature is inculcated, by having the most advanced pupils make out-of-door studies in summer. Exhibition of students' work in June, when prizes are awarded. These studies are optional.

34. Hartford, Conn.

CONNECTICUT HISTORICAL SOCIETY.—Wadsworth Athenæum Building, 206 Main St.—Incorporated 1827.—Officers : Pres., J. Hammond Trumbull ; Treas., John F. Morris ; Rec. Sec., W. I. Fletcher ; Cor. Sec., Chas., J. Hoadly ; Auditor, Rowland Swift.—The Society owns a considerable number of portraits of Connecticut worthies of the last and first half of this century, most of which have only an historical interest. The collection includes, however, at least one picture by Blackburn, and two fine specimens of S. F. B. Morse. There is also a large collection of relics, in which the famous chest of Elder William Brewster, of the " Mayflower," has the first place.—Admission free.

CONNECTICUT SCHOOL OF DESIGN.—Chartered May, 1872.—Officers : Pres., J. W. Stancliff, 17 Bellevue St.; V. P., C. Conrads ; Sec. and Treas., T. S. Steele.—This association, which was organized upon the dissolution of a previously existing society, known as the Hartford

Art Association, has for its object the establishing of a school of art, and the holding of exhibitions and sales. The by-laws provide that there shall be two classes of members, the first professional artists, either natives or residents of Connecticut, the second honorary members. The Society began under apparently favorable circumstances, but for some years past it has been dormant, although the organization is still kept up. The classes and exhibitions have been discontinued, and the casts owned by the School loaned to the Society of Decorative Art.—According to latest report there is some prospect of the resumption of work in the year 1884.

SOCIETY OF DECORATIVE ART.—303 Main St.—Organized June, 1877.—

Officers: Pres., Miss Mary D. Ely, 668 Main St.; V. P's., Miss Alice Taintor, Mrs. George A. Jones; Cor. Sec., Mrs. Charles D. Warner; Rec. Sec., Miss M. L. Collins; Treas., Mrs. F. G. Whitmore.—Objects: The promotion and diffusion of a knowledge of art among women; their training in artistic industries, and eventually the establishment of rooms for the exhibition and sale of women's work.—Any person may become a member of the Society by an annual payment of $1; present number of members, 138.—The first classes in Drawing, Painting, and Art embroidery were opened on Jan. 17, 1878, the few ladies who organized the Society pledging themselves to pay the teachers in case the sum received from pupils proved insufficient. They also assumed the rent of the studio, at $300 a year, the furnishing and care of it, and all incidental expenses for medals, etc. The Conn. School of Design kindly loaned the Society several valuable imported casts of the best works of art. Miss Taylor, Miss Wheelright, and Miss Knowlton, of Boston, all of them pupils of Hunt, were the first teachers, followed by Miss Townsend, of Albany, who gave instruction in water color and china painting, and Mrs. Whiting, of Hartford, in embroidery. The pupils made good progress under these teachers, and the classes were self-supporting, and have continued so ever since. The tuition fees at that time were $6 for 12 lessons in charcoal drawing, $12 for 12 lessons in water color, china painting, or embroidery. In October, 1878, the services of Prof. J. Wells Champney, of New York, were secured, and he has been very successful in instructing and bringing forward his pupils in drawing, painting in oil and water-colors, and sketching from life. The price at present for his tuition is $15 per 12 lessons, the lessons occupying most of the day on Wednesdays, as there are two sessions, morning and afternoon.—There are no free scholarships, but through the kindness of ladies connected with the Society, instruction has been given to several pupils, three of whom are now able to support themselves by furnishing designs to manufacturers.— On April 3, 1880, the Society held its first Exhibition and Sale, for the benefit of ladies capable of doing artistic work, and dependent on their own exertions for support. Five other sales have followed, and the Society has paid in all $1,835 to contributors of this class, throughout the State, who otherwise would have had no market for their work, outside of a limited circle of friends. Thus many of the original aims and objects of the Society have been accomplished, and every day brings evidence of the stimulus it has given to art in Hartford and its neighborhood.—The financial condition of the Society is satisfactory, in so far as no debts have been incurred. But this condition could not have been secured except by the untiring energy of ladies of the Board of Managers, who have provided attractive entertainments at private houses and elsewhere, as a means of replenishing the treasury. The membership fees, $1 a year, and the small excess from tuition fees would be wholly inadequate to make the Society self-supporting, and it has, as yet, asked no aid from the public and received no valuable donations.—Annual meeting, first week in January.

WADSWORTH ATHENÆUM.—206 Main St. Founded 1842.—Officers: Pres., Calvin Day; 1st V. P., Wm. R. Cone; 2d V. P., Roland Mather; Sec., J. Hammond Trumbull; Treas., J. F. Morris: Auditor, E. B. Watkinson.—This is a private association, named after Daniel Wadsworth, who gave the ground on which the Athenæum stands, and contributed freely toward the erection of the building and the acquisition of the works of art it contains. The collection known as the The Wadsworth Gallery is rich in paintings by Trumbull, of whose work it has thirteen specimens, among them several replicas of the well-known Trumbulls of the Yale Art Gallery, such as the "The Battle of Bunker Hill," etc., and including his first essay in painting. There are also six landscapes by Thomas Cole, including his "Mount Ætna"; Vanderlyn's "Death of Miss M'Crea"; three early works by F. E. Church; and portraits by Stuart, Sully, Ingham, and Jewett. Among the works by foreign artists, the most noticeable are Lawrence's full-length portrait of Benj. West, and an admirable portrait of a gentleman by Raeburn, painted about 1824. In the

lower hall there is a collection of statuary, including several of the best works of F. S. Bartholomew, of Hartford (" Eve Penitent," "Shepherd Boy," " Sappho "), and all his working models in plaster.—There is a catalogue of the paintings, but it is antiquated and insufficient, having been reprinted in 1863 from the original edition of 1844.—Admission, 25 cents. The Gallery is open, *for the present*, on week days, from 9 A.M. to 12 M., and 2 to 5½ P.M. in summer, to 4 P.M. in winter. Intending visitors from a distance will find it to their advantage to inquire in advance, by postal card, regarding time of opening and closing. [See Illustration.]

35. Hingham, Mass.

HINGHAM ART CLUB.—Discontinued.

36. Indianapolis, Ind.

ART ASSOCIATION OF INDIANAPOLIS.—Cor. of Meridian and Circle Sts.—Organ., May, 1883; incorp., Oct. 11, 1883.—Officers: Pres., Albert E. Fletcher; V. P.'s, Mrs. Jos. A. Moore, Mrs. S. J. Fletcher, John M. Judah; Rec. Sec., Mrs. May Wright Sewall; Cor. Sec., H. B. Palmer; Treas., Miss Anna Dunlop. Heads of Groups: Colorists, Thos. E. Hibben; Etchers, Mrs. M. A. Pratt; Literary Students, Miss Belle Sharpe.—Objects and Methods: To cultivate art in all its branches. To this end, the Association will hold loan exhibitions, provide means for art instruction, secure lectures on art, and in time establish a permanent gallery.—Members: Annual, $10 per year; Life, $100; In Perpetuity, $500. Present number of members, 109. Various groups have already been organized within the membership of the organization, viz.: Etchers, Colorists, and Literary Students.—The Association held its first Loan Exhibition, from Nov. 7 to 30, 1883, the catalogue of which showed 460 entries, including foreign and American paintings, etchings, etc. This exhibition (free to members, 25 cents to others, 10 cents to school children on Saturdays) was visited by about 5,000 persons. Eight works were sold for $850.— Annual meeting, second Wednesday in April.—[*The Art School* of the Association was opened Jan. 10, 1884. Its aim is to secure a thorough grounding in the principles of drawing. Special emphasis is laid on form and perspective. Instructor, Chas. F. Macdonald. Tuition fee, $10 per month, or $24 per term of three months. Number of pupils, 30; both sexes; taught together.]

INDIANAPOLIS CHAPTER OF THE AMERICAN INSTITUTE OF ARCHITECTS.—[Application for a charter was made towards the end of the year 1883. No definite information received so far.]

37. Ithaca, N. Y.

CORNELL UNIVERSITY.—Incorporated April, 1865; opened Oct. 7, 1868.—The University is supported by the income arising from the land scrip granted to the State under the act of Congress of July 2, 1862, the interest on an endowment of $500,000 by Mr. Ezra Cornell, and the tuition fees charged.—Officers of the B'd of Trustees: Chairm., Henry W. Sage; Sec., Wm. R. Humphrey; Acting Treas., Emmons L. Williams. Officers of the Fac.: Pres., Hon. Andrew Dickson White, LL.D.; Registrar, Rev. Wm. Dexter Wilson, D.D., LL.D., L.H.D.; Acting Libr., Geo. Wm. Harris, Ph. B.—*Free-Hand Drawing* (Edwin Chase Cleves, B.S., Assoc. Prof. of Free-Hand Drawing) is obligatory with students of agriculture, architecture, civil engineering, mechanic arts, mathematics, and natural history; elective in all other courses. The work embraces a thorough training of the hand and eye in outline drawing, elementary perspective, model and object drawing, drawing from casts, and sketching from nature. The effort is, not to make mere copyists, but to render the student familiar with the fundamental principles. The course is largely industrial, and the exercises are arranged, as far as possible, with special reference to the drawing required in the work of the different courses. The department has a large collection of flat copies, geometrical models, casts from antique busts and parts of the human figure (see Collections below), studies from nature, and examples of historical ornament.—*The Course in Architecture* (Rev. Chas. Babcock, A.M., Prof. of Arch.; Chas. F. Osborne, Asst.) extends over four years, and leads to the degree of Bachelor of Architecture. It is so arranged as to give the student instruction in all subjects which he should understand in order to enter upon the practice of the art. Its object is not merely

7

to develop the artistic powers of the student, but to lay that foundation of knowledge without which there can be no true art.—The Register for 1883-4 enumerates 21 students in architecture. Tuition fee (in all departments), $25 a term ; three terms a year. There are 128 Free State Scholarships, particulars concerning which see in the Annual Register, to be had on application to the treasurer of the University. Several new scholarships were established in 1883 from a fund provided by Mr. Cornell and Messrs. John McGraw, H. W. Sage, Hiram Sibley, and Andrew D. White, of the B'd of Trustees. Women are admitted on the same terms as men, except that they must be seventeen years old.— *The White Architectural Library* contains over 1,000 volumes, and the photographic gallery nearly 2,000 prints (see Collections), all accessible to the student. Several hundred drawings and about 200 models have been prepared to illustrate the constructive forms and peculiarities of the different styles.—*Museum and Collections :* The University owns the following valuable collections, mostly donations by Pres. White and others : 1. A considerable collection of casts, by Brucciani, of London; a collection of 78 casts from the sculptures and carved work of Lincoln Cathedral (lately presented). 2. About 4,000 casts of medals, medallions, and gems, principally from specimens in the Berlin Museum, with considerable additions from Italian collections ; also a number of galvano-plastic casts of the more important medals in the Berlin Museum. 3. About 2,000 large photographs illustrating the history of architecture and sculpture. Of these about 60 are devoted to Athens and other places in Greece ; 30 to Herculaneum, Pompeii, and the Greek cities of lower Italy, such as Pæstum, etc. ; 200 to Rome ; 40 to Ravenna ; 100 to Venice ; a still larger number to Florence ; 60 to Siena ; 40 to Genoa ; 40 to Orvieto ; 150 to France ; and so on through Germany, England, Spain, and Portugal. Also photographs of modern European terra cotta work. 4. Special collections of large colored sheets, showing stained-glass decoration at sundry cathedrals. 5. A framed set of the Arundel Society's publications. 6. Sundry articles of art workmanship, and a considerable number of bronze reductions of noted statues, by Barbedienne. 7. A considerable number of original pictures by modern artists, such as Eastman Johnson, Bellows, Hazeltine, Meyer Von Bremen, Wagner, Ambros, Hamman, Hiddeman, etc., bought by Prof. and Mrs. Fiske, and by Pres. White. 8. A collection, now embracing six or eight specimens, but constantly increasing, of copies of noted modern pictures and portraits. Pres. White gave a commission to the late Mr. C. C. Burleigh, who attracted considerable attention in Berlin as a copyist, and in this country through the specimens of his work sent to the Exhibitions of the Pennsylvania Academy at Philadelphia, to reproduce a number of important paintings, including Piloty's " Galileo in Prison," at Cologne ; portraits of Frederic the Great and his sister, as children, at Charlottenburg ; a portrait of Thomasius, from the University Collection at Halle ; two portraits of Grotius, from Amsterdam ; Becker's " Coronation of Ulrich von Hutten," at Cologne ; Gallait's " Last days of Egmont," at Berlin ; and Piloty's " Wallenstein and Seni," at Munich. All of these, save the last two, had been completed before the premature death of Mr. Burleigh, and the series will be continued as soon as a competent artist can be found to continue the work. There are also various portraits of professors and benefactors of the institution. Many of these objects are still packed away for want of space, or scattered through the University buildings and the houses of the professors ; but the authorities hope to have them all visible to the public in the Museum within a few months. The copies of modern paintings, alluded to above, are not so much intended for a gallery of fine art as for the large historical lecture-room which the authorities of the University likewise propose to have ready at no distant day. The most valuable part of the whole collection for purposes of study will doubtless be the medallions, medals, and gems. These are carefully catalogued, the gems according to the Winckelmann catalogue, published in Berlin, to which the numbers are made to correspond. [In his Annual Report, presented to the Board of Trustees on June 20, 1883, President White urges the necessity of providing a special gallery for statuary, original pictures, casts, copies, drawings, engravings, photographs, etc., to illustrate the history of art, and especially classical archæology and history; and to contain the collections enumerated above, as well as those lately bequeathed to the University by the late Mrs. Jennie McGraw-Fiske (consisting of statuary in marble and bronze, original paintings, tapestries, wood-carvings, ornamental work in brass and iron, specimens of ceramic art, and rare embroideries). President White points out, also, that a beautiful building, likewise bequeathed by Mrs. Fiske, might easily be converted into an appropriate gallery. It is well known, however, that the will of Mrs. Fiske has since been contested, and that the suit is still pending.]

ITHACA BRANCH OF THE NEW YORK SOCIETY OF DECORATIVE

ART.—Cornell Library B'ldg.—Organized, 1878.—Officers: Pres., Mrs. J. C. Gauntlett; 1st V. P., Mrs. Chas. Schaeffer; 2d V. P., Miss Minnie McChain; Treas., Mrs. D. M. Stewart; Rec. and Cor. Sec., Miss Mary E. Humphrey.—Objects: The promotion and diffusion of a knowledge of decorative art among women, and their training in artistic industries.—Members: Active, who must present some work of theirs for inspection, and pay $1 initiation fee, and $1 annually thereafter; Associate, having no vote, annual dues $1; Honorary. Present number of members of all grades, 60.—The Society has organized classes in drawing, wood carving, etc., and opened a salesroom, where work by members or by outside contributors is exhibited, and orders received.—*An Annual Art Bazaar* is held in November, which is quite successful, both as regards the quality of the work displayed and the appreciation of the public.

38. Jacksonville, Ill.

ART ASSOCIATION.—Young Men's Christian Association.—Instituted Dec. 17, 1873; incorporated 1875.—Officers: Pres., J. H. Woods, (P. O. Box 1032); V. P's., Mrs. Mary J. Dewees, Miss Mattie E. Morse; Treas., Henry H. Hall; Sec., Miss Lucy E. Sturtevant.—Objects: The study and appreciation of the Fine Arts, especially of the arts of design, by the formation of a public collection of art-treatises, pictures, engravings, photographs, casts, models, and such other material as may aid in this; and furthermore by lectures, essays, and discussions on art subjects.—The annual membership fee is $1. The membership has varied from 25 to 80, the proportion of ladies to gentlemen being about as five to one.—The Association was organized in the parlor of the Ill. Female College, and owes its existence to the happy thought of Mrs. Ella O. Browne, at the time teacher of art in the College.—Eight monthly meetings are held during the months of October to May inclusive, the present place of meeting being the lecture hall of the Young Men's Christian Association. The exercises at these meetings have consisted of the reading of essays by the members, selected readings, lectures by persons from other cities, discussions, and sometimes the reading of a collection of notes and gossip upon current art news, local and foreign. Whenever possible, photographs have been exhibited to illustrate the subject in hand. The range of subjects covered by these essays, etc., has been very wide, and the list of lecturers includes some names well known in the literature of art. In addition to the regular monthly meetings, fortnightly meetings have been held, since January, 1874, of a few of the members, mostly ladies, who desire to give more time to a thorough study of the history of art. Architecture has been the chief topic at these meetings.—A collection of works of art, begun some years ago, contains 50 autotypes, heliotypes, and engravings, and three paintings. A library has been started, for the increase of which an annual appropriation is made.—Beginning with 1875, an Annual Loan Exhibition has been given, made up of works owned by citizens, productions of pupils and teachers in the four art schools in the city, drawings by pupils in the Public Schools, and paintings, engravings, etc., loaned by artists and dealers in St. Louis, Chicago, New York, and elsewhere. The duration of these exhibitions, the last of which was held Feb. 19 to 24, 1883, has varied from three to five days; single admission, 25 cents; season tickets from 50 cents to $1. The receipts of the nine exhibitions have been in every case greater than the expenses, the net proceeds varying from $20 to $200. The Tenth Exhibition is to be held from Feb. 18-23, 1884. —Annual meeting, first Tuesday in December.—The Association is a member of the Central Illinois Art Union.

39. Le Roy, N. Y.

INGHAM UNIVERSITY.—Organized at Attica, in 1835; removed to Le Roy, Genesee Co., N. Y., in 1837; chartered as a Collegiate Inst., 1852; as a University in 1857. Claims to be the pioneer Female College in point of time.—Officers: Chancellor, Rev. E. B. Walsworth, D.D.; Director of the College of Fine Arts, L. M. Wiles, A.M.—Drawing and painting were taught in this institution as early as 1842. *The College of Fine Arts* at present connected with it owes its existence to Col. Stanton (d. 1867), the husband of the founder, who, in 1870, erected the Art Conservatory in his honor. The Art College, which is a wing of the same building, was erected in 1875.—Aim: To educate those who desire the accomplishment, or wish to follow art as a profession, and to prepare instructors for private and public schools.—Teachers: Prof. L. M. Wiles, A.M., Painting; Miss R. M. Shave, A.P., Drawing; Miss A. Palmer, A.P., Assistant.—There are several courses, as follows: I. Under-Graduate Course; Outlines of single objects; elements of linear perspective; study of light and shade, advancing to drawing from the antique; painting from life and still-life, with landscape during the season suitable for out-door study. Those who desire to graduate from this department are required to produce a complete original picture, the materials of which have been studied from life and composed in conformity to the requirements of art. If approved by the Faculty and the Councillors of the University, it is accepted by them, and finds a permanent place in the collection of graduating pictures. Lectures on technical matters and on the history of art by Prof. Wiles during each session. 2. Post-Graduate Course : For those who have completed the Under-Graduate Course, and desire to prosecute the study of art as a specialty, a Post-Graduate Course has been formed in which they can receive a thorough training in the principles of High Art. Lectures in Artistic Anatomy, Analysis of Expression, and Philosophy of Art will be given, with practical instructions in drawing from the living Model in order to inculcate as far as possible, the princi-ples of Idealism in Portrait, Figure and Landscape Painting. 3. Summer Class : For the benefit of teachers and others who find it more convenient to attend during the usual vacation, a Summer Term of six weeks, opening in July, has been arranged under Prof. L. M. Wiles. The University year has two terms, 20 weeks each. The terms of the Art College are the same, only each term is divided into two sessions of 10 weeks each, to accommodate outsiders.—Tuition fees : Regular Courses ; Full session of 10 weeks in any department, $50. Summer Course : $1 per day, during 5 days of the week.—Although the University is for young ladies only, young men are admitted to the Art College. This College has been improved during the past year by the annexation of a stone structure of two stories, affording an additional painting room and a large room for the life classes and for lecturing purposes. Number of students in actual attendance at the close of the year, 1883, 52.—*The Art Conservatory* contains an inexhaustible store of materials for both artistic and scientific study, consisting of a museum of natural and artificial curiosities, and a gallery of paintings, valued at more than $50,000, and comprising Col. Staunton's best pictures, the graduating pictures painted by students, and some of the best works of eminent foreign and native artists.—An Annual Exhibition is held in June.

40. Licking, O.

LICKING COUNTY PIONEER HISTORICAL AND ANTIQUARIAN SO-CIETY.—See *Newark, O.*

41. Lincoln, Ill.

LINCOLN ART SOCIETY.—Private residence of Col. R. B. Latham.—Organized 1876.—Officers, 1883-84 : Pres., John Scully ; V. P., Mrs. R. B. Latham ; Sec., Miss Pegram ; Cor. Sec., Mrs. C. M. Lutz ; Lib., Miss M. Latham ; Treas., Miss R. Latham.—Objects : The study of art, and promotion of interest in same. The society is not a working class, but many of the members are professional artists.—Membership limited to 30. Annual dues, $1. The Society is full.—Meetings are held weekly, at which lectures are delivered and papers read, by members and others, followed by discussions, etc. A loan exhibition was held in 1879. The Society also has an art library. It is a member of the Central Illinois Art Union.

42. Louisville, Ky.

LOUISVILLE INDUSTRIAL EXPOSITION.—This corporation was dissolved Aug., 1883, and its property sold. Its last exhibition was held in 1882. (See *Southern Exposition*)

POLYTECHNIC SOCIETY OF KENTUCKY.—Fourth Ave.—Organized Dec. 16, 1876; Incorporated Apr. 10, 1878.—Officers : Pres., Bennett H. Young ; V. P., N. Bloom ; Sec., Dr. E. A. Grant : Treas., W. T. Grant ; Com. in charge of Art Gallery, Geo. H. Moore, R. J. Mennefee, E. A. Grant.—Objects : Of the Society, the cultivation and diffusion of knowledge ; of the Art Gallery, the cultivation and diffusion of a knowledge of the principles of art and a pure artistic taste.—Members : Citizens of Kentucky only are eligible to active membership. Present number, 28 life members (who pay $100 once), 600 annual members (who pay $5 a year), 150 corresponding members (citizens of other States, ladies and minors, who pay $3 a year). There are also 3 honorary members, and 1 fellow, which is also an honorary degree.—The financial resources of the Society are derived from its property (8 stores, an Opera House, lodge rooms, offices, etc., donations, subscriptions and membership dues.—Free scientific lectures are given weekly in winter and there are also scientific class lectures, classes for mutual instruction, etc. With the Society are connected Academies of Law, of Medicine, of Geology and Mineralogy, of Art, of Debate, of History, etc. There is a library of 33,000 vols. (rich in illustrated art works), cabinets of about 50,000 specimens (natural history, archæology, ethnology), and a collection of scientific apparatus, worth, probably, $5,000. (Art Classes and Gallery see below). The library and collections are open free week days. Members of the Society may take books home, and strangers have the same privilege, by depositing the value of the book, and paying a small fee.—*Art Classes:* Classes in drawing, painting, etc., which meet from one to four times per week. Instructor, J. A. Pritchett. Fees vary, but are in most classes free to members, and very low to all. There are no scholarships or medals, but prizes are sometimes offered by citzens to stimulate effort in young men and women.— *The Art Gallery:* The Society owns four superb marbles (among them an original "Hebe," by Canova and a copy of the "Venus de Medici," by Joel T. Hart), and about 60 paintings, of which 20 are by recognized American artists, the rest by amateurs, or historically interesting only. Of the paintings, eleven, by Messrs. A. Bierstadt, Wyant, Wm. Hart, F. Schuchardt, Harry Chase, M. De F. Bolmer, Carl Brenner, J. M. Tracy, J. C. Nicoll, Henry A. Loop, and Kruseman Van Elten, were bought, from a fund subscribed by citizens of Louisville, out of the exhibition of the American Art Union, which formed part of the Southern Exposition (see below). The art gallery is not yet organized, but definite plans are now under consideration. As soon as it has taken shape, it will be opened free to the public on certain days.—Annual meeting of the Society, second Monday in April.

SOUTHERN EXPOSITION.—Officers : Pres., B. Du Pont ; Gen. Man., J. M. Wright ; Ch'man of Art Com., F. D. Carley.—This Association held an industrial and art exhibition, from Aug. 1 to Nov. 10, 1883, which was claimed to be the largest and most important exhibition ever held in the country with the only exception of the Centennial Exhibition. The catalogue of the art department (in charge of Mr. Chas. M. Kurtz), contained 468 entries, embracing paintings, statuary, etchings, tapestries, ceramics, etc., etc. Contributions of works of art had been sent from all parts of the country, as an offering of good will to the South. Out of the exhibition of the American Art Union, which was included in the art department, a number of pictures were bought as a nucleus of a permanent art gallery. (See *Polytechnic Society*.)—[It is said that this Association is to be perpetuated, and that it is to hold other exhibitions. No reply to inquiries.]

PERMANENT ART GALLERY.—See *Polytechnic Society*.

43. Lowell, Mass.

LOWELL ART ASSOCIATION.—Organized 1878.—Officers : Pres., Thos. B. Lawson ; V. Ps., E. W. Hoyt, Miss E. O. Robbins ; Treas., Geo. T. Carney ; Clerk, Frank N. Chase.— Object : To increase a knowledge of art and to develop a taste for it, by exhibitions, lectures, readings, or other suitable means.—Members pay an entrance fee of $1, and may be assessed $2 annually. Honorary members may also be elected.—The Club has held a number of exhibitions of the works of local artists, both professional and amateur ; also loan exhibitions, and the following special exhibitions : Two of etchings, ancient and modern ; one of an entire set of Piranesi ; one each of engravings and photographs from the works of Michelangelo, Raphael, Correggio, and Turner ; and one upon the contents of the Vatican, with brief lectures upon each subject. Receptions are held during the cooler months for conversation and the exhibition of novelties and designs for manufactures.—As the city maintains day and evening schools for drawing, modelling, and designing, the Association has made no effort to establish classes.—Annual meeting, first Tuesday in October.

44. Madison, Wis.

STATE HISTORICAL SOCIETY OF WISCONSIN.—State Capitol.—Organized Jan., 1849 ; reorganized and incorp , Jan., 1854.—Officers : Pres., Hon. John A. Rice ; Cor. Sec., Lyman C. Draper, LL.D. ; Rec. Sec., Robt. M. Bashford ; Treas., Hon. A. H. Main ; Libr., Daniel S. Durrie.—Membership : 20 life members ($20), 65 active members ($2 annually), 10 honorary, 300 corresponding.—The *Picture Gallery* owned by this Society contains about 120 pictures in oil and in crayon, and some portrait busts. The latest published catalogue, of Jan. 1, 1878, enumerates 113 paintings, mostly portraits and a few landscapes ; and 14 busts. There is also a cabinet of antiquities, coins, curiosities, and Revolutionary relics.—The Gallery and the Library of the Society, the latter containing 105,000 books, pamphlets, and documents, are open, free of charge, every week day, except public holidays, from 9 A. M. to 12 M., and from 2 to 5 P. M.; during the session of the Legislature also evenings, from 7 to 9 P. M.—The Reports and Collections, published by the Society, of which 9 vols. have so far been issued, occasionally contain papers of interest to archæologists. There has also been published a catalogue of the library, 2 vols., with 3 supplementary vols., and a fourth is to be issued in 1884.—Annual meeting, in January.

45. Madisonville, O.

MADISONVILLE LITERARY AND SCIENTIFIC SOCIETY.—[This Society is actively engaged in archæological researches. See *Peabody Museum*, 15th Annual Report, p. 63. No reply to repeated inquiries.]

46. Malden, Mass.

MIDDLESEX INSTITUTE.—Frank S. Collins, Sec.—Objects : The study and advancement of science.—The Institute gave a Loan Exhibition, March 27 to 31, 1883, the catalogue of which enumerated 289 works, including oil paintings, water colors, etchings, etc. Exhibitions are not, however, a regular feature of the work of the Institute, and no other has since been held.

47. Manchester, N. H.

MANCHESTER ART ASSOCIATION.—Court House.—Originated Sept., 1871 ; organized under State law, Oct., 1874.—Officers : Pres., Moody Currier ; Sec., Marshall P. Hall ; Treas., John M. Chandler ; Auditor, A. G. Stevens.—Objects : To promote knowledge and skill in art and technology among its members, and among artists and artisans, by the establishment of an art library, collection of paintings, statuary, models, and other works of art or science.—The members, at present about 300, are of both sexes.—Initiation fee, $1; annual assessments, not above $2.—*Classes* are formed to some extent in winter, the demand being chiefly for mechanical and architectural drawing. The Association owns a collection of over 50 casts, from life and from antique and modern sculptures, which is at the service of the students. Life classes have also been formed occasionally. A small fee is charged, which goes to the teachers. Lectures, illustrating the principles of art, are given occasionally.—*The Library* contains several hundred volumes, mostly manuals and text-books of value to the practical student. It increases steadily, and is also supplied with American and European art journals.—*An Annual Exhibition* is held in April, lasting usually three or four days. The exhibits largely represent industrial art, supplied by the manufacturers of the city. Oil and water color paintings, loaned by owners or contributed by artists, are also shown, and a division is assigned to amateur work.

48. Maysville, Ky.

HISTORICAL AND SCIENTIFIC SOCIETY OF MASON CO.—Collection of Indian antiquities. [No reply to repeated inquiries.]

49. Melrose, Mass.

MELROSE ART CLUB.—Organized Feb. 10, 1880.—Officers : Pres., Moses S. Page ; V. P., Miss Emma A. J. Bugbee ; Sec., Miss Alice Goss ; Treas.. John C. Maker.—Objects : The study and practice of art.—The members, of both sexes, are mostly amateurs, with a few professional artists. Present number, 108.—A series of lectures on topics connected with art, is delivered during the winter season of each year at the private residences of the members.—Exhibitions are held, once in two years.—The Club has come to be one of the popular institutions of the town. It has supplied a want that many had long felt, and has encouraged its members in the study and practice of art.—Annual meeting, in May.

50. Middlebury, Vt.

MIDDLEBURY HISTORICAL SOCIETY.—Philip Battell, Sec.—This Society gives its attention to collections of art and archæology only incidentally. Its specialty is local history, and something has been collected in that department.

51. Milwaukee, Wis.

LADIES' ART AND SCIENCE CLASS.—Milwaukee College.—Organized 1874.—Officers for 1883–4: Pres., Mrs. T. A. Chapman; Treas. and Sec., Mrs. H. M. Finch; Exec. Comm., Mrs. J. Hiles, Mrs. J. E. Follett, Mrs. J. G. Flint, Mrs. S. Marks.—This Association of Ladies, formed at Milwaukee College eight years ago, for the purposes of study, instruction, and discussion, grew in interest till, in 1878, it was deemed wise to assume a more definite character, on the simple plan indicated in the following Principles of Organization: 1. The Class shall be vitally connected with Milwaukee College. 2. It shall be annually organized by a ballot choice of a President, a Treasurer, and an Executive Committee of four ladies. 3. The annual fee for membership and all privileges shall be $5. 4. The funds thus accruing shall be expended by the Board of Officers in the following manner, viz.: a. Payment for the use of the College Hall as a session-room, and of the Library as a reading-room, a sum not to exceed $12.50 per week, during the season of meetings and Library study; b. The balance remaining after the payment for the use of the Hall and Library, and other merely incidental expenses, not including any salaries or fees of teachers, lecturers, or officers, shall be annually expended before Oct. 1, for books, pictures, casts, and other such treasures or improvements, which shall be the permanent property of the College.—Present number of members, 262.—The Class meets Tuesday afternoon of each week, and the members have daily use of the special library and reading-room of the College. Excellent lantern views, eighteen feet in diameter, are almost constantly employed in the weekly session. Every important building, statue, painting, or other object studied, and many of the details are illustrated on the screen, while the subject is under discussion. The following topics indicate the course of study pursued last year: Cities of Greece; Sicily; Southern Italy; Modern Rome; Northern Italy. For the year 1883–4 the following will be the subjects of study: The Cities of Switzerland and the Passes of the Alps; Cities of Germany, Austria, Holland, and Belgium.

MILWAUKEE COLLEGE.—Chartered 1851 as the "Female Normal Institute and High School;" corporate name changed to "Milwaukee Female College," in 1853; present name assumed in 1876. The College, nevertheless, remains an institution for girls only.—Officers of B'd of Trustees: Pres., Wm. P. McLaren; V. P., Hoel H. Camp; Treas., John Johnston; Sec., W. W. Wight. Pres. of the College: Chas. S. Farrar, A.M.—The College has a Primary Department, a Preparatory Department, and a Collegiate Department. In all of these departments, drawing and painting are elective studies, but lessons in "Art Criticism" form part of the regular study in the first semester of the Senior Year in the Collegiate Department.—The instruction in the *Department of Art* (Miss Frances Farrar, teacher) embraces drawing in pencil, pen, crayon, or charcoal; painting in oil or water colors, and modelling in clay or wax. The practice consists in drawing or painting from copies, from still-life, and natural forms. Particular attention given to sketching from nature, for which the students are taken to selected points affording picturesque objects and motives for landscape studies. Large studios are provided, especially designed and furnished for the purpose.—Drawing and Sketching, tri-weekly, $15 per quarter; Painting in Oil or Water Colors, tri-weekly, $20.—Students in Art Department, season of 1883–4, 40; students in Art Criticism, 12. (See Ladies' Art Class above, which the students can enter.)

MILWAUKEE INDUSTRIAL EXPOSITION ASSOCIATION.—Exposition Building.—Officers: Pres. and Gen'l Manager, John Plankington; 1st V. P., Fred. Pabst; 2d V. P., John R. Goodrich; Treas., John E. Hansen; Sec., R. P. Jennings; Art Committee, Jos. McC. Bell, W. S. Howard, Frank G. Siller; Supt. of Art Dep't., W. S. Howard.—This Association holds annual Expositions, and in connection therewith an Art Exhibition. At the third of these exhibitions, Sept. 6 to Oct. 20, 1883, there were exhibited 629 oil and water color paintings, engravings, statuary, etc. The sales amounted to $14,394.25 for 54 works.

MILWAUKEE MUSEUM OF FINE ARTS FOR THE STATE OF WIS-CONSIN.—423 Milwaukee St.—Incorp., July 1, 1882.—Officers for 1884: Pres., Mrs. Alexander Mitchell; 1st V. P., Wm. H. Metcalf; 2d V. P., Chas. L. Colby; 3d V. P., Mrs. Jas. M. Pereles; Sec., Wm. W. Wight, 102 Wisconsin St. ; Treas., Wm. Plankinton, 82 & 84 West Water St. ; Cura-tor, Wendell Stanton Howard.—Objects: To cultivate and advance art in all its branches, by the establishment of a public collection of works of art and a School of Design.—Members: Patrons, contributors of $500 or more; Fellows in Perpetuity, contributors of $250 ; Fellows for Life, con-tributors of $100 ; Annual Members, $10 yearly ; Honorary Fellows. Present number of members: 4 Patrons, 4 Fellows in Perpetuity, 12 Fellows for Life, 112 Annual Members. All these members together, except the Honorary Fellows, elect the Board of Directors.—The Museum began its activity by opening a Loan Exhibition of a few select works of arts, mostly foreign, in the Exposition Building, in September, 1882. The formal opening of the Museum, as such, took place in the same building on the evening of Dec. 15, 1882. The removal to its present temporary quarters was effected on Nov. 1, 1883, and the rooms were opened on the evening of Dec. 7, 1883. Several offers have been made to provide the Museum with a building, one of which, by Mr. Frederick Layton, has been accepted. Mr. Layton has purchased land on the corner of Mason and Jefferson Sts., but this is now occupied by a church society, and will not be surrendered until the fall of 1884.—The collec-tions of the Museum are small as yet, and the pictures, etc., shown at its rooms, are mostly loans. Admission is free to members always, and free to the public on Wednesdays. Other days, admission fee, 25 cents.—*The Art School* of the Museum was opened Jan. 2, 1884, with Antique, Life (costumed model), Still-Life, and Water Color Classes. Terms : Matriculation fee, $2 ; tuition fee, $21 per term, or less for shorter time. There are two terms, January to March, and April to June. Names of teachers not given.—Annual meeting of the corporation, last Wednesday in June.

52. Minneapolis, Minn.

ARCHITECTURAL ASSOCIATION OF MINNESOTA.—Officers: Pres., E. B. Bassford, St. Paul ; V. P., Isaac Hodgson, Minneapolis ; Sec., D. W. Millard, of St. Paul ; Rec. Sec., Fred. G. Corser, Minneapolis ; Treas., J. Walter Stevens, St. Paul. [According to the *American Architect* of Jan. 27, 1883, the officers above given were elected at the annual and regular meeting of the Association, held at Minneapolis on January 2, 1883. No reply to repeated inquiries for later information.]

ARCHITECTURAL LEAGUE OF MINNEAPOLIS.—Organized, Jan., 1884.—Officers : Pres., Geo. E. Bertrand ; V. P., H. W. Jones ; Sec., Francis W. Fitzpatrick, 22 Boston Block ; Treas., Walter S. Parker.—Objects and methods: To improve the social relations of the students of architecture in the city; to facilitate their study of both the artistic and scientific elements of the profession, and to create a more just and elevated public appreciation of art. The means that have been and are to be taken to secure the above are : the providing of a suitable apart-ment wherein are to be collected designs, models, pictures, casts, specimens, etc.; regular meetings of the members for discussion and interchange of ideas ; the forming of Clubs among the members for modelling, sketching, etc.; such other means as may be considered the most efficient for the study of architecture and the general culture in art.—Members: There are four classes, Fellows, having studied architecture at an Institute of Technology or in an office for at least three years ; Juniors, who have not yet completed such a course of study ; Associates, practising architects, artists, engravers, engineers, etc.; Honorary Members. The governing power is vested in the Fellows. Present number of Fellows, 24.

MINNEAPOLIS SOCIETY OF FINE ARTS.—Organized and incorporated, Jan., 1883.—Objects: To advance the knowledge and love of art through the exhibition of works of art, lectures upon subjects pertaining to art, the acquisition of books and papers for the formation of an art library, and such other means of æsthetic and general culture as come within the province of similar associations.—Officers: Pres., Wm. W. Folwell; V. P., A. B. Nettleton; Sec., Miss Frances A. Shaw, 906 Sixth Ave. S.; Treas., Mrs. Frederick Payne.—Members : Annual initiation fee, $5 ; annual dues, $2 ; Patrons, contributors of $500 ; Fellows in Perpetuity, contributors of $250 ; Fellows for Life, contributors of $100. Present number of members, 130.—The first Loan Exhibition of the Society was held at 421 Washington Ave. S., from Nov. 20, 1883, to Jan 2, 1884. The catalogue enumerated 1,777 objects, including oils, water colors, engravings, etchings, ceramics, curiosities, bronzes, and statuary. Eight oil paintings were sold for $1,050. The net proceeds of the exhibition amounted to $1,537.95. Number of visitors, nearly 3,000.—At a meeting of the Society, held in Feb., 1884, it was resolved : 1. To procure suitable rooms in which to open a permanent exhibition and a school of art, according to the best academic methods, the income from tuition to go toward expenses ; 2. to procure a site for a permanent museum and studio building, and plans for the structure on a scale worthy the purpose and the coming greatness of the city ; 3. to raise funds for the building, and to erect and equip, if not the whole, then some complete portion of it.—Mrs. Adsit, of Milwaukee, in May, 1883, gave before the Society a course of twelve lectures on etching and engraving, and another course was to be delivered by Mr. Wm. M. French, of Washington, during the month of Feb., 1884.—Annual meeting, second Wednesday in October.

53. Montpelier, Vt.

VERMONT HISTORICAL SOCIETY.—State House.—Incorp. 1838.—Officers : Pres , Hon. E. Walton, Montpelier ; V. P.'s, Hon. Jas. Barrett, Rutland ; Rev. Wm. H. Hazen, Northfield, Hon. E. A. Sowles. St. Albans ; Rec. Sec., C. W. Porter, Montpelier ; Cor. Sec's, Hon. G. G. Benedict, Burlington. Z. S. Stanton, Roxbury; Treas., Hiram Carleton, Montpelier ; Lib., Hiram A. Huse, Montpelier.—Objects : To discover, collect and preserve whatever may relate to the natural, civil, literary and ecclesiastical history of the State of Vermont.—Members : Resident, Corresponding, Honorary. Present number, 150. Resident members, initiation fee, $2 ; annual dues, $1.—The library of the Society is accessible, free to strangers on application ; the collection of historical and Indian relics, etc., free.—The Society has published two vols. of " Collections," 1870 and 1871, and various addresses, proceedings, etc., beginning with the year 1846.—Biennial meeting, Tuesday preceding third Wednesday of October in years of even date.

54. Nashua, N. H.

NASHUA HISTORICAL SOCIETY.—Historical Hall, Telegraph Block.—Organized March, 1870.—Officers : Pres., O. C. Moore ; V. P., John H. Goodale ; Sec., H. B. Atherton ; Historiographer, D. W. King.—Objects : The collection and preservation of the local, general, and natural history of Nashua and its vicinity ; the promotion of the intellectual culture of its members ; the dissemination of historical, scientific and useful information throughout the community.—Collection of minerals and other natural history specimens, and relics of local historical interest. Admission free.

55. Nashville, Tenn.

HISTORICAL SOCIETY OF TENNESSEE.—Valuable collection of Indian antiquities ; cabinet of coins; extensive museum of articles of historical interest, including a large number of portraits of the historical characters of the State. [No reply to repeated inquiries.]

NASHVILLE ART ASSOCIATION.—Organized Jan. 18, 1883 ; incorp. June, 1883.— Officers : Pres., Dr J. P. Dake ; V. P., Gen. G. P. Thruston ; Treas., J. L. Weakley ; Sec., D. H. Rains (Nashville Banner, 22 N. Cherry St.).—Objects and methods : The cultivation of a taste for the fine arts, and the encouragement of better rewards for artists of merit, by means of (1.) stated meetings for discussion, etc. ; (2.) public meetings devoted to lectures, etc. ; (3.) the acquisition and preservation of works of art ; (4) the securing of rooms for meetings and exhibitions ; (5.) the institution and management of classes in drawing, painting, and decoration, so far as contemplated and as practicable under the liberal provision made by the late Mr. Samuel Watkins.—Members : At present 150 ; initiation fee, $2 ; annual dues, $2. Honorary members may also be elected.— The Association is to give one general exhibition and sale of works of art each year, and minor exhibitions and sales, as may be deemed advisable. No such exhibitions have as yet been held. At the monthly meetings, works of art are shown and criticised by a committee, papers read, discussions held, etc. There are no collections as yet, and no classes.—The Association was organized with the view of carrying out one of the provisions of the will of the late Mr. Samuel Watkins, a wealthy gentleman who left a considerable sum of money for the erection of the Watkins Institution, in which, when completed, arrangements will be made for it. At present the meetings are held in the studio of Mrs. Dr. W. A. Barry, cor. Church and High Streets.—Annual meeting, second Friday in April.

NASHVILLE CHAPTER OF THE AMERICAN INSTITUTE OF ARCHITECTS.—[An application for a charter was addressed from Nashville to the American Institute of Architects toward the end of the year 1883. No particulars received so far.]

56. Newark, N. J.

ESSEX ART ASSOCIATION.—21 West Park St.—Organized Apr. 16, 1883.—Officers: Pres., J. K. Hoyt. "Newark Daily Advertiser:" V. P.'s, W. C. A. Frerichs, 760 Broad St., John A. McDougall, 744 Broad St., J. J. Spurr, 44 Clinton St.; Sec., Henry M. Crowell, 673-5 Broad St.; Cor. Sec., John J. Hubbell, 800 Broad St.; Treas., Dr. Chas. A. Meeker, 27 Fulton St.,—Objects : To establish an industrial art school ; to hold annual loan exhibitions and eventually to establish a permanent art gallery ; to offer opportunity for study to artists, together with such social advantages as the rooms of the Association may afford.—Membership limited to 1,000 ; present number, 400. Initiation fee, $1 ; annual dues, $3.—Three exhibitions are to be held each year. At the first, held from Nov. 7 to 28, 1883, a collection of paintings, drawings, etchings, etc., was shown, and 20 works were sold for $2,000. The next exhibition is to be held from Mch. 15 to Apr. 1, 1884.—*The Art School* of the Association was reported to be in process of formation, under the direction of Prof. John W. Bolles, at the beginning of the year 1884.

NEW JERSEY HISTORICAL SOCIETY.—757 Broad St.—Organized Jan., 1845; incorp. 1846.—Officers : Pres., Rev. Samuel M. Hamill, D.D.; Cor. Sec., Wm. A. Whitehead ; Lib., F. W. Ricord.—The collections of this Society are almost exclusively papers relating to the history of the State of New Jersey.—Annual. meeting, third Thursday of January.

57. Newark, O.

LICKING COUNTY PIONEER HISTORICAL AND ANTIQUARIAN SOCIETY.—Court House.—Organized 1867.—Officers : Pres., Isaac Smucker ; V. P.'s, M. M. Munson, Jas. H. Brown, David Wilson ; Rec. Sec., C. B. Giffin ; Cor. Sec., E. M. P. Brister ; Treas., Enoch Wilson.—Objects : To write up the early pioneer history of Licking County ; to make known the character and extent of the Mound Builders' work in the county, and to collect a cabinet of Mound Builders and Indian relics, coins and curiosities.—Members must be pioneer citizens. Contributions voluntary. Women free. Present number of members, 131. There are besides these 75 Antiquarian and 174 Corresponding members.—The collections embrace (besides a small library) Mound Builders' and Indian relics, coins, and curiosities, to the number of about 2,000. Visitors admitted free.—The Society has published 140 Pioneer Papers and Historical Sketches, and 12 Pioneer Pamphlets.—Annual meeting, July 4.

58. Newburyport, Mass.

NEWBURYPORT DRAWING AND PAINTING CLUB.—Public Library B'ldg.— Organized Jan. 5, 1881.—Officers : Pres., Luther Dame ; Sec., Mrs. L. M. Knapp ; Directors, W. H. Swasey, Miss S. M. Stone, W. S. Drown, Miss S. P. Tenney, Miss S. B. Balch.—Present number of members, 30.—Private exhibitions are given once a month. A public exhibition was held Oct. 26 to 28, 1882. Lectures have also been arranged by the Club.—Annual meeting, Jan. 1st.

59. New Haven, Conn.

CONNECTICUT MUSEUM OF INDUSTRIAL ART.—Old State House.—Organized 1876.—Officers : Pres., Francis Wayland ; Sec , Treas., and Manager, Prof. Wm. P. Blake.—

Objects : To promote industrial and applied art in industry and manufactures, particularly the artistic advancement of the industries of Connecticut.—Membership, annual, $10 a year ; life, payment of $100. Number not given.—Collections : Ceramics, metal work, woodwork, glass, costumes, furniture, textiles, laces, embroideries, tapestries, etc.—Open week days ; admission 25 cents, except on Saturdays, when the fee is 10 cents.—Number of visitors, 800 to 1,000 annually.—There are no schools at present, for want of funds to pay expenses. The Museum is much in debt, and the receipts at the door are given to the janitor. The other expenses are now, and have been, chiefly paid by the secretary.

NEW HAVEN ART CLUB.—Room 31, Hoadley B'ldg.—Organized Oct. 17, 1883.—

Officers : Pres., Robert R. Wiseman, 31 Sylvan Ave. ; V. P.'s, Fred. F. Langzettel, Room 19, 308 Chapel St., and Miss Sara B. Gilbert, 667 Chapel St.; Sec., C. C. Benham, 553 Howard Ave.; Treas., Wm. F. Hopson, Room 11, 270 Chapel St.—Objects : For the benefit of artists and others connected with, or interested in art ; For study, mutual improvement, and advancing a knowledge and love of art in the community, and for social intercourse among its members.—Members must be artists, or in some way connected with art matters as collectors, critics, etc. Present number, 38 (29 male, 9 female). Initiation fee, $5 ; annual dues, $12.—An annual exhibition is to be held of work by members, supplemented by contributions from others.—Meetings are held four times a week for study from life : for gentlemen, Tuesday and Thursday evenings ; for ladies, Friday and Saturday afternoons. The club room is well supplied with casts. No instruction is given.—The quarters of the Club, although fairly adapted for the purpose of study, are somewhat limited. As soon as feasible, it desires to enlarge its membership to 100, and to secure a gallery for exhibition purposes, in connection with library, reading room, study rooms, reception room, etc.—Annual meeting, last Thursday in June.

NEW HAVEN COLONY HISTORICAL SOCIETY.—Old State House.—Sec., Thos.

R. Trowbridge, Jr.—The collection of this Society contains many interesting and valuable Revolutionary and other relics and curiosities, including a number of portraits, busts, engravings, etc. Among the portraits, that by John Trumbull of his father, Gov. Jonathan Trumbull, and a couple by S. F. B. Morse, of Mr. and Mrs. David C. De Forest, are especially noteworthy. Those interested in the history of engraving in America will find, besides a number of other old prints, several specimens of the rude work of Amos Doolittle, b. 1745, d. 1832, including the "Battle of Lexington," etc.—Open free on week days. A printed catalogue of the collection can be had on application.

YALE COLLEGE.—Incorporated 1701.—Pres. of the Corp. and of the Fac., Rev. Noah

Porter, D.D., LL.D., 31 Hillhouse Ave.; Sec., Franklin B. Dexter, M.A., 178 Prospect St.; Treas., Henry C. Kingsley, M.A., 23 Hillhouse Ave.—Instruction in Instrumental Drawing (Fred. R. Honey, instructor, 14 Lincoln St.; assistant in Drawing, Alton W. Leighton, M.D., 129 College St.), and in Elementary and Free-Hand Drawing (Prof. J. H. Niemeyer, instructor) is given in the Sheffield Scientific School in the Introductory Freshman Year, and in the Engineering Courses. It is not included in the Courses in Chemistry, Agriculture, Natural History, and Biology, and in the Studies preparatory to Mining and Metallurgy, and the Select Studies Preparatory to other Higher Studies. In the Undergraduate Academical Department all the art instruction provided for is an Optional, four exercises a week, through the second term of Senior year, under Prof. Weir, in Drawing and Painting and the Principles and Means of Art, and Prof. Hoppin, in the History of Art ; fee, $18 for three months.—*The Yale School of the Fine Arts*, a separate department of the College, was founded by the late Aug. Russell Street, who erected the Art Building, which was opened in 1866. Faculty : The President of the College ; John F. Weir, N.A., M.A., Prof. of Painting and Director of the School, 58 Trumbull St.; Rev. Jas. M. Hoppin, D.D., Prof. of the History of Art, 47 Hillhouse Ave.; John H. Niemeyer, M.A., Prof. of Drawing, 8 Art School. Instructors : Fred. R. Honey, in Geometry and Perspective, 14 Lincoln St.; John P. C. Foster, M.D., in Anatomy, 109 College St.; Harr. W. Lindsley, Ph.B., in Architecture, Cutler Building.—Aim : (1) To provide thorough technical instruction in the Arts of Painting, Sculpture, and Architecture ; (2) to furnish an acquaintance with all branches of learning relating to the History, Theory, and Practice of Art.—The courses of instruction, covering three years, provided under the heads of Practice and Criticism, may be regarded as distinct or correlative, embracing that technical and theoretical knowledge of art which is no less desirable for the critic than for the artist. In the departments of Drawing and Painting the practice of the studio is based upon the study of human form, from the antique and the living model, supplemented by lectures on Form and Proportion, Color, Chiaroscuro, and Composition. Drawing is continued, without interruption, through the first half of the course, or until the student evinces that proficiency which will warrant advancement. Painting is continued through the remainder of the course. Students are encouraged to remain in the school and pursue advanced studies after the three years' course is completed. Perspective and Anatomy are taught in the form of lectures. Lectures are also given on the History and Philosophy of Art, and kindred subjects. Besides the Department of Drawing and Painting, there are also special Departments of Sculpture, and of Architecture, and a class in Etching.—Two Exhibitions of the work of the students are held annually, one from June 1 to October 1, containing the work of the students during the previous session ; the other, in January, containing the work of the summer vacation. Both free to the public. Prizes may be competed for, both in Drawing and in Painting, at the close of the course. Diplomas are only awarded to those who remain through the full course, and pass the requisite examinations.—Tuition fee, $36 for three months. Art students are admitted free to all the lectures delivered in the school, to the collections, and to the special library provided for the Art Department.—The school is opened to pupils of both sexes of fifteen years or over. Special art students in regular attendance last term, 50 (14 male, 36 female) ; students in drawing from the Sheffield Scientific School, 84.—The term begins Oct. 1 and ends May 31. All applications for admission to be made through the Director before Oct. 1. No conditions of admission, save as to age and general good character.—"While the Faculty are sensible," says the report for 1882, "of having done their utmost to advance the interest of the school. . . . they have labored under the disadvantage of an insufficient income. The school is burdened with a debt [incurred, for the most part, for the completion of the building, and like necessary expenditures], the payment of the interest of which has absorbed about half the income received through tuition fees, and thus rendered further development for the present impossible, unless some means of relief can be provided. . . . With the discharge of this debt the school would be able to maintain its effective and progressive course without further assistance." The Professorship funds with which the school is endowed amount to $75,000.—*The Art Collections* embrace the "Jarves Gallery of Italian Art," numbering 120 paintings, dating from the 11th to the 17th centuries ; the "Trumbull Gallery" of works by John Trumbull, numbering 54 pictures ; a collection of portraits and works of contemporaneous art, about 100 in all ; and an excellent collection of about 150 casts from the antique, etc. The "Trumbull Gallery," which is unique for the study of this talented painter of the Revolutionary epoch, contains some of his most important earlier works, such as the small pictures of "The Battle of Bunker Hill," "The Death of Montgomery," "The Battle of Princeton," etc., and the beautiful little portrait heads which he painted as studies for his larger works. Other important works by American artists, owned by Yale College, are Smybert's "Family of Bishop Berkeley," Allston's "Jeremiah and the Scribe," Morse's "Dying Hercules," portraits by Stuart, Jarvis, Elliott, and others, and sculptures by Bartholomew, Augur, Powers, etc.—There are no funds for additional purchases. The proceeds of the exhibition, which is occasionally varied by transient loan collections, are applied to the incidental expenses of the school.—Gallery open every week day, including holidays, from 9 A.M. to 12½ P.M., and 1½ to 6 P.M., June till end of Oct. ; for the rest of the year only from 1 to 5 P.M. Admission 25 cents. The catalogue has been out of print for some time, as it does not pay.— *The Peabody Museum of Natural History,* the gift of George Peabody of London, besides its Natural History specimens, has also a collection in Archæology and Ethnology. So far as the collections are arranged, this Museum is open to the public every day, Sundays excepted, in term-time.

60. New London, Conn.

NEW LONDON COUNTY HISTORICAL SOCIETY.—23 State St.—Incorp. July 6, 1870.—Officers : Pres., Chas. Aug. Williams, New London ; V. P's., Francis B. Loomis, New London, Ashbel Woodward, Franklin ; J. Geo. Harris, Groton ; Sec., Wm. H. Starr, New London ; Treas., Wm. H. Rowe, New London.—Objects : Collecting, preserving, and publishing historical and genæological matter relating to the early settlement and subsequent history, especially of New London County.—Members, about 100 annual ($1 a year) ; 15 life ($10)—Collection of historical relics, Indian curiosities, etc., unclassified. Rare books and manuscripts.—Annual meeting, last Monday in November.

61. New Orleans, La.

SOUTHERN ART UNION AND WOMAN'S INDUSTRIAL ASSOCIATION.—
203 Canal St.—Chartered May 26, 1880.—Officers: Pres., Robert Mott, 17 Carondelet St.; 1st V. P., Gideon Townsend; 2d V. P., Adam Thompson; Treas., Milton C. Randall, 47 Carondelet St.; Sec., W. S. Mitchell, M.D., 47 Carondelet St. Chairm. Woman's Ind. Assoc., Mrs. H. W. Connor; Sec., Mrs. Clarence Fenner.—Objects: To advance, develop, and encourage art and æsthetic culture in all branches, and to foster feminine skill in all departments of art and industry.—Members (ladies and gentlemen): The original incorporators and any one thereafter elected. Ordinary members, $10 p. a.; life members, one payment of $100. Honorary members may be nominated by the president. Present number of members, about 200.—This Association combines the features of a general Art Society with those of the Ladies' Decorative Art Societies elsewhere established. It has a salesroom, in which the work of contributors is sold on commission, and which is to be used also as a medium for the exchange of works of art.—The *School of Design*, established by the Union, has classes in Drawing and Painting from the flat, cast, and living model (day and evening), Water-Color Painting, Linear Perspective, and Architectural Drawing (day and evening), Painting on China and Silk, Kensington Embroidery, etc., also drawing classes for children. The tuition fees range from $4 to $6 per month. Instructors: Miss H. Winant, A. Perelli, A. Molinary. The Association is indebted to Miss Mason, of Boston, for a gift of $2,000 to be expended in salaries for teachers, etc.— A Free Circulating Library has also been inaugurated, originally by the generosity of Mrs. Field. It is worked under a system of rules drawn up by Mr. Geo. W. Cable, and the committee find it quite difficult to supply the demand for books, although donations (which are earnestly solicited) are continually coming in from all quarters.—Among the other objects of the Union are the holding of exhibitions and auction sales, the gathering of a nucleus for an Art Museum, and the publication of an Art Journal.—The executive committee of the Union has been placed in charge of the Art Dep't of the coming Exposition (see below.)—Annual meeting, first Monday in May.

WORLD'S INDUSTRIAL AND COTTON CENTENNIAL EXPOSITION.—
Officers: Pres., Edmund Richardson; 1st V. P., Albert Baldwin; 2d V. P., Wm. B. Schmidt; Sec., Samuel Mullen; Treas., Thos. H. Hunt; Director-General, E. A. Burke; Commissioner-General, F. C. Morehead.—With this Exposition, which is to be held from December, 1884, to May, 1885, under the joint auspices of the United States, the National Cotton Planters' Association, and the City of New Orleans, there will also be connected an Art Department, to which the artists of the world are invited to contribute. All matters pertaining to this department have been placed in the hands of the Executive Committee of the Southern Art Union (see above), whose secretary is W. S. Mitchell, M.D., 47 Carondelet St.

62. Newport, R. I.

NEWPORT HISTORICAL SOCIETY.—Collection of Indian and local curiosities and antiquities. [No reply to repeated requests for information.]

REDWOOD LIBRARY AND ATHENÆUM.—Bellevue Ave., cor. Redwood St.—
Originated 1730; incorporated 1747; edifice erected 1748; enlarged 1858.—Officers: Pres., Dr. Henry E. Turner; V. P., Wm. Gilpin; Treas., Job T. Langley; Sec., Wm. P. Sheffield, Jr.; Libr., Benj. F. Thurston.—This library (26,053 vols. according to last printed report) is owned by an association of stockholders, but non-stockholders may acquire the right to use it by becoming annual subscribers.—*Art Collections:* The Library owns a number of busts, and between two and three hundred oil paintings, including many portraits of American celebrities, mostly the gift and the work of Charles B. King, an American artist, b. Newport, R. I., 1786, died Washington, D. C., 1862. Besides these there are works by Stuart, Thos. Sully, J. G. Chapman, etc. One of the most interesting objects is the "Portrait of Mrs. Wanton," the wife of Joseph Wanton, governor of R. I. from 1769-75. This portrait is by Robert Feke, one of the earliest native American painters of

whom there is any record.   Many of the canvases are copies from paintings by the old masters.
Mr. King left to the Library also a *Collection of Prints* which is thus described in the Report for
1862 :   " Seven quarto volumes contain prints classified as Historical, Religious, Classical, Landscape,
Portraits, Costumes, and Miscellaneous.   Seven other volumes are of folio size, generally of large
dimensions, and are also arranged with reference to their subjects.   They include many works of
the old masters ; a copy of Raphael's Bible, in fifty-two plates ; some original etchings from Rembrandt ; a series from Rubens, illustrating the life and destiny of Marie de Medicis ; nine prints from
the paintings of Titian, . . . and a large number of other works from the Italian, Dutch, and other
schools.   In portraiture will be found many of great value : those from Vandyke and Reynolds alone
making two volumes.   The collection is especially rich in English engravings, published in London
in the beginning of this and the latter part of the last century, and presents examples from the works
of Reynolds, Gainsborough, West, Romney, Stubbs, Copley, Cosway, and other noted artists of the
time, with some fine specimens of the costly line engravings issued by Boydell."   Many of these
prints were obtained by Mr. King while he was a student of the Royal Academy in London, and a
very large proportion of them are said to be early impressions.—Open free to visitors every week
day.--Annual meeting of the stockholders, third Wednesday in August.

RHODE ISLAND CHAPTER OF THE AMERICAN INSTITUTE OF AR-
CHITECTS. —See *Providence*.

63. New York, N. Y.

AMERICAN ART UNION.—44 East 14th St.—Incorp. May 11, 1883.—Officers for
1883-4 : Pres., D. Huntington, P.N.A.; V. P., T. W. Wood, V.P.N.A.; Sec., E. Wood Perry,
Jr., N.A.; Treas., Frederick Dielman, N.A.—Objects : The promotion of interest in the fine arts
by means of the establishment of galleries for the exhibition and sale of works of art, the holding of
art exhibitions in different parts of the country, the publication of engravings and other artistic productions, the publication of an art journal, the acting as agent for others in the purchase of works
of art, the establishment of an artists' benevolent fund, and the promotion of social intercourse
between its members.—Members : Active and honorary. Professional artists only can become active
members.   Initiation fee, $10, for which the member receives a share of stock, which is not trans-
ferable.   Honorary members are chosen from amateurs and friends of art.   Present number of members : Active, about 150 ; honorary, 52.   (Subscribing members, see below.)—Exhibitions : The Art
Union has opened permanent exhibition rooms at the address given, and has thus far held two exhibitions in other cities, one in Buffalo, N. Y., at the Fine Arts Academy, in June, 1883, the other at
Louisville, Ky., in connection with the great Southern Exposition, which opened Aug. 1, 1883.
One of the objects of the Society is to act as a medium between the several exhibition associations
of the country and the artists, *i. e.*, to furnish such associations meritorious collections of pictures
without giving them the trouble of dealing with individual artists, and, on the other hand, to obtain
for the artists guarantees of sales to an amount proportionate to the number and value of the pictures exhibited.   Correspondence on this subject must be addressed to the secretary.—Publications :
The Association publishes a monthly journal, the *Art Union* (Mr. Chas. M. Kurtz, editor), illustrated with etchings and phototypes, the first number of which appeared in January, 1884.   Subscription price, $3 p. a.   It has also published an etching, " The Reprimand," by Walter Shirlaw,
after Eastman Johnson (13 x 16 inches), which is issued only to subscribing members for 1884.—Subscribing members : Any person may become a subscriber to the American Art Union upon the payment, annually, of $5.   In return he will receive : A season ticket to the permanent exhibition of the
Union ; the etching of the year (mentioned above), the monthly *Art Union* journal for the current
year ; an interest in the works of art purchased by the Union during the year.   One half of the subscriptions received is to be set apart for such purchases.   The method of disposing of, or distribut-
ing the works thus acquired has not yet been decided upon.—The Union has appointed the following
agents or honorary secretaries, who are authorized to receive subscriptions : Henry D. Williams
(Williams & Everett), 508 Washington St., Boston, Mass. ; Jas. S. Earle & Sons, 816 Chestnut St.,
Philadelphia, Pa. ; Leonard B. Ellis, 76 William St., New Bedford, Mass. ; Evarts Cutler, New
Haven, Conn.; S. M. Vose, Westminster St., Providence, R. I.; James D. Gill, Springfield, Mass.;
J. F. Ryder, 239 Superior St., Cleveland, O.; William Morris, 19 and 21 Post St., San Francisco,

Cal. ; D. D. Benson, Main St., Buffalo, N. Y. ; S. Boyd & Co., 100 Wood St., Pittsburgh, Pa. ; J. V. Escott & Sons, 521 Fourth Ave., Louisville, Ky. ; T. J. Stubbs, Portland, Me. ; Bement & Davenport, Elmira, N. Y. ; D. M. Dewey, Rochester, N. Y. ; W. H. Baumgras & Co., 17 Vanderbilt Square, Syracuse, N. Y. ; Henry B. Pettes, Sixth and Olive Sts., St. Louis, Mo. ; V. G. Fischer, 529 Fifteenth St., Washington, D. C. ; Wm. Scott & Son, 363 Notre Dame St., Montreal, Canada.

AMERICAN ETHNOLOGICAL SOCIETY.—60 Wall St.—Officers : Pres., Alex. J. Cotheal ; Libr., Henry T. Drowne.—The Archæological Collections of this Society have been deposited in the American Museum of Natural History. The Peruvian Antiquities, presented to the Society by one of its presidents, the late George Folsom, are in the custody of the New York Historical Society.

AMERICAN MUSEUM OF NATURAL HISTORY.—Manhattan Square, Central Park, 77th St. and 8th Ave.—Incorporated Apr. 6, 1869.—Officers: Pres., Morris K. Jesup, 197 Madison Ave.; V. Ps., Robert Colgate. D. Jackson Stuart ; Sec., Hugh Auchincloss, 17 W. 49th St. ; Treas., J. Pierpont Morgan, 219 Madison Ave. ; Supt., Prof. Albert S. Bickmore.—The revenues of this Museum are derived from donations and dues paid by members, etc. The cash donations, as per last report, amounted in all to $229,018 ; but large donations have also been received in the shape of collections. The present building, which comprises only about one-twelfth of the contemplated structure, was put up and is partially maintained by the city. The Museum is not devoted to the study of the lower orders of nature only, but embraces also anthropology, with its various subdivisions.—*The Archæological Department* is arranged on the gallery of the second hall or principal floor. Some of its component parts may be enumerated as follows : The most complete collection of the Ethnology of the Pacific Islands to be found anywhere. All that is left of the Squier and Davis Ohio and Mississippi Valley Collections, incl. some 60 specimens of which figures are given in "Smithsonian Contributions to Knowledge," Vol. I. All the collections made by Squier in Peru, Nicaragua, etc. The whole collection of Chas. C. Jones, Jr. (author of "Antiquities of the Southern Indians," Appleton, 1873), bought for the Museum for $7,500. A very large collection illustrating the ethnology of British Columbia, gathered by Dr. J. W. Powell, Supt. of Indian Affairs in that part of the Dominion of Canada, and presented by Mr. H. R. Bishop, of New York. The largest collection, outside of France, of prehistoric relics from that country, particularly the Somme Valley. English, Irish, and Swiss prehistoric collections. A number of minor collections are incorporated with those named. Besides these collections, all of which are on exhibition, there is a still larger collection of stone implements from various parts of the United States, east of the Rocky Mountains, owned by Mr. Andrew E. Douglass ; and a similar collection from the same area, together with the best collection of stone implements ever gathered on the Pacific Coast, owned by Mr. Jas. Terry. These private collections are in separate rooms in the building, and are accessible by application to the owners, addressed at the Museum. Together with those on public exhibition, these two collections equal in value and variety all other collections of stone implements.—The Museum also owns a few pictures, illustrating scientific subjects, among them an Arctic scene by Wm. Bradford.—No catalogue, but the objects are labelled. The Museum publishes Annual Reports and Scientific Bulletins, which can be had by students on application. A consulting library, in the Superintendent's office, is also at the service of students.—Open free week days, including holidays, all the year round from 9 A.M. to half an hour before sunset. Mondays and Tuesdays are called reserved days for students, but all visitors are admitted on giving name and address.—The Museum is accessible by the Eighth Ave. horse cars, and the Harlem trains on the Sixth Ave. Elevated Railroad. Approaches for carriages and pedestrians have been made from the Fifth Ave. side of Central Park at 77th and 81st Sts. Visitors to the Park can also take the ferry at the Terrace, which will land them near the 77th St. entrance on 8th Ave.—Annual meeting of the corporation, second Monday in November.

AMERICAN NUMISMATIC AND ARCHÆOLOGICAL SOCIETY.—Room 25, University B'ldg.—Founded 1857 ; incorp. 1865.—Officers for 1884-5 : Pres., Daniel Parish, Jr. V. P.'s, Robert Hewitt, Jr., Andrew C. Zabriskie, John M. Dodd, Jr. ; Sec., Wm. Poillon, 61 Bethune St.; Treas., Benj. Betts; Lib., Richard Hoe Lawrence; Curators, Chas. Henry Wright and Henry De Morgan.—Objects : The encouragement and promotion of the sciences of numismatology and archæology; the formation of a library and cabinets relating to the study of these and kindred interests; the publication and dissemination of information relating thereto.—Members: Resident members, who must reside in the U. S., initiation fee, $5; annual dues, $5. Life members, one payment of $30. Corresponding members, of which there are two classes, for two years, and permanent. Honorary members, limited to 50. Number of members in 1883: Honorary, 28; Permanent Corresponding, 52; Corresponding for two years, 10; Resident. 61; Life, 43.—The income of the Society is derived from fees, donations, and the interest on several small funds.—The society has published, besides the proceedings of its annual meetings and a number of papers and essays, a "Catalogue of the Numismatic Books in the Library of the American Numismatic and Archæological Society, with a subject index to the important articles in the American Journal of Numismatics, and other periodicals to the end of 1882" (N. Y., 1883, 4+31 pp., large 8vo.), and "A Guide to the Gold and Silver Coins of the Ancients, exhibited in electrotype by the American Numismatic and Archæological Society. From the English edition by Barclay V. Head, British Museum" (N. Y., 1884, 12+128, 12mo).—Collections: Library; cabinet of about 3,000 coins, medals, etc. A collection of electrotypes ("Guide" mentioned above) from the finest specimens of the coins of the ancients in the British Museum (published by the authorities of the Museum named), has lately been bought by a number of gentlemen, and placed by them on exhibition (1884) at the rooms of the Society. This collection numbers 793 specimens and illustrates the period from B. C. 700 to the beginning of the Christian era.—The public is admitted free upon application to officers or members.—Annual meeting, second Tuesday in March.

AMERICAN WATER COLOR SOCIETY.—Office 51 W. 10th St.—Organized 1868. —Officers for 1884-5: Pres., Thos. W. Wood, 51 W. 10th St.; Sec., Henry Farrer, 51 W. 10th St.; Treas., Jas. Symington, 58 W. 57th St.—Object: To advance the art of painting in Water Colors.—Members: Resident, professional artists living in the city, or its immediate vicinity; initiation fee, $25; no further dues. Non-Resident, professional artists living at a distance. Honorary, amateurs and connoisseurs. The two classes last named pay no fees, cannot vote, and can hold no office except that of treasurer, to which an Honorary member may be elected. There are at present 67 Resident, 28 Non-Resident members; total, 95, of whom 3 are ladies. No Honorary members.—The holding of exhibitions, strictly confined to Water Colors (although etchings have also been exhibited), is the only public activity of the Society. These exhibitions are the most important of their kind in the country. The Seventeenth Annual Exhibition was held at the National Academy of Design from Feb. 4 to Mch. 1, 1884. The by-laws provide that "the Board of Control shall examine all works (except those made by members) sent for place in the Annual Exhibition, and order the return of such as in their judgment do not possess sufficient merit."—Annual meeting, third Wednesday in March.

ARCHITECTURAL LEAGUE OF NEW YORK. — Organized 1881.— Officers: Pres., D. W. Willard, 57 B'way; V. P., J. P. Riley; Treas., J. B. Robinson; Rec. Sec., C. I. Berg, 76 E. 54th St.; Cor. Sec., A. W. Brunner, 24 W. 45th St.—Objects: To promote the artistic, scientific, and practical efficiency of the profession, and the means of accomplishing this end shall be: The reading of essays; lectures upon topics of general interest; competitions in architectural design; exhibitions of members' work; formation of a library; formation of a collection of drawings, photographs, and casts; establishment of a travelling studentship; and any other means calculated to promote the object of the Association.—Members: Active, engaged in Architectural work; present number, 30; initiation fee, $5, and dues $1 per month; finable for non-attendance. Honorary members may also be elected.—Many of the sketches by members have appeared in the "American Architect," principally designs for the regular problems which are set by the Committee on Current Work. These problems are given at each meeting, and each member is expected to send in a sketch. All the designs are hung up in the League's rooms, and the criticism of prominent architects upon them is invited. Nothing has as yet been done toward the establishment of the travelling studentship.—Annual meeting, first Tuesday in October. [The League has given up its rooms for the present, and is somewhat in a state of inactivity, although still in existence.]

ART CLUB OF NEW YORK.—Rooms of American Art Association, 6 East 23d St.—

Organized 1876 ; incorp. 1880.—Officers for 1884 : Pres., Wm. Sartain, 152 W. 57th St. ; Sec., Bruce Crane, 58 W. 57th St. ; Treas., B. N. Mitchill, 58 East 13th St.—Objects : Promotion of social intercourse among artists.—Members, at present, 86 must be professional artists.—The Club has held one exhibition, so far, at the American Art Galleries, from Feb. 12 to 23, 1883, at which 101 works by members were exhibited.—Annual meeting, first Thursday in December.

ARTISTS' FUND SOCIETY OF NEW YORK.—Instituted 1859 ; chartered 1861.—

Officers : Pres., Thos. Hicks, 6 Astor Pl. ; V. P., Alfred Jones, care Am. B'k Note Co. ; Treas., John L. Fitch, 51 W. 10th St. ; Sec., G. H. Yewell, 578 Fifth Ave. ; Honorary Medical Adviser, F. N. Otis, M.D.—Members at the time of election must reside in New York or vicinity. Present number, 71, including the elect, not yet qualified. Annual dues, $75.—The Society has three funds : 1. The Widows' Fund for the relief of widows and orphans of members. 2. The Relief Fund for the relief of disabled members. 3. The Benevolent Fund for the relief of artists, or the widows and orphans of artists, not members. The first two are maintained by the annual dues, the last is maintained by donations.—The Society holds an Annual Exhibition and Sale to which members may contribute. Out of the proceeds the dues of the contributors are paid. If the work contributed by a member brings less than $75, he must make up the amount; if it brings over $100, the surplus is turned over to him. The Twenty-Fourth Annual Sale was held in January, 1884. The services of the auctioneer at these sales are given gratis.—This Society claims to be the most successful benevolent organization in existence of those maintained by artists only.

ART STUDENTS' LEAGUE OF NEW YORK.—38 W. 14th St.—Founded June

2, 1875 ; incorporated Feb. 8, 1878.—Officers : Pres., Wm. St. J. Harper, 11 E. 14th St.; V. P's., Miss A. R. Miles, D. C. Beard ; Cor. Sec., G. Fitz Randolph ; Rec. Sec., R. M. L. Walsh ; Treas., A. Teggin. The majority of the Board of Control must be students actually at work in the Life Classes ; one of the Vice-Presidents must be nominated by the ladies.—Objects : The establishment and maintenance of an Academic School of Art, which shall give a thorough course of instruction in drawing and painting ; the cultivation of a spirit of fraternity among Art Students.—The active members must be artists and students who intend to make art a profession ; applicants for membership are required to work three months in the Life Class before they can be elected. Present number of members, over 100. Honorary members may also be elected. The fixing of the annual membership fee is left to the Board of Control.—Classes (opened for the season 1883-4 on Oct. 1; close May 31, 1884): Drawing and Painting from Life ; Painting from Draped Model or Still-Life ; Drawing from the Head ; Drawing from the Antique ; Costume Classes ; Sketch Class ; Composition Class ; Lectures on Perspective ; Lectures on Artistic Anatomy. Both sexes taught together, except in the Life Classes. The Classes are open for study from the life and the antique, every day in the week, morning, afternoon, and evening, during eight months in the year.—Instructors : Drawing and Painting, Morning Life Class, T. W. Dewing ; Drawing and Painting, Evening Life Classes and Evening Antique Class, Wm. Sartain ; Drawing and Painting, Afternoon Life Class, and Class in Drawing from the Head, C. Y. Turner ; Drawing and Painting, Afternoon Life Class, Walter Shirlaw ; Painting Classes, Wm. M. Chase ; Drawing, Morning and Afternoon Antique Class, and Afternoon Head Class, Geo. de Forest Brush ; Artistic Anatomy, J. S. Hartley ; Perspective, Fred. Dielman.—Tuition fees : For students not members of the League, the fees vary from $120 for the full term of eight months, six full days each week in the Painting Class, downward, according to time and subject.—Students of both sexes can enter any class immediately, upon submitting specimens of work which show the necessary proficiency. The requirements are as follows : Applicants for admission to the Life Classes must submit a drawing of a full length nude figure from cast or life ; for the Painting Class, a painting from life, or a drawing from life, with a painting from still life ; for Class in Drawing from the Head, a drawing of a Head from cast or life ; for the Antique Class, a drawing from cast : for the Composition Class, an original design ; for the Costume Class, a drawing of a figure from life in costume ; for the Sketch Class, a sketch from life. Number of students, season 1882-3 : Life Classes, 170; daily average, 108 (41 ladies). Painting Classes, 59 ; monthly average, 35 (majority ladies). Antique Class, 162 ; average, 103. Sketch Class, average 50. Composition Class, average 74. Costume Class, 64. Total number of students entered during the season, 410, an increase of 96 over the previous season.—The collections belonging to the League consist of casts, studies, etc., and a library.—The peculiar feature of this school is that it is entirely under

8

the control of the students, through the Board of Control elected by the members of the League. Practically, therefore, the students themselves appoint their teachers. The League has all along been remarkably successful, and the season of 1882-83 was the most prosperous the Society has known since its organization. The treasurer in his last report estimated that the total cost of maintaining the classes would be about $14,000 for the school year. The total receipts, including surplus from last year, will exceed $15,000, an increase of $4,000 over the preceding season. The surplus now amounts to $5,000, and is held as a reserve fund to guarantee the permanence of the school.—Occasional exhibitions and receptions are given during the season, at which the work of the instructors is exhibited, together with other works of art. For further information and circulars address "The Art Students' League of New York," 38 W. 14th St., New York.—Annual meeting, in April.

ASTOR LIBRARY.—34 Lafayette Pl.—Founded and endowed by John Jacob Astor ; incorporated Jan. 18, 1849.—Officers : Pres., Alexander Hamilton ; Sec., Henry Drisler, 48 West 46th St.; Treas., John Jacob Astor ; Supt., Robbins Little ; Libr., Frederick Saunders.—The Library has no special art collections, but is very rich in works on archæology, architecture, the industrial arts, decoration, etc.; books of reference on art, and art manuals ; illustrated works on the great galleries of Europe, etc. All the more important art journals of Europe are regularly received.—The Library is for reference only, and under no circumstances can books be taken away.—Open daily except Sundays and holidays, from 9 A.M. to 5 P.M. from April to the end of July, and from the beginning of Sept. to the end of Oct.; to 4.30 P.M. in Nov.; to 4 P.M. in Dec., Jan., and Feb.; and to 4.30 P.M. in March. Closed from end of July to beginning of Sept.

CENTURY CLUB.—109 East 15th St.—Organized Dec., 1846.—Officers : Pres., Daniel Huntington, P.N.A., 49 East 20th St. ; 1st V. P.. Gilbert M. Speir ; 2d V. P., Henry C. Potter ; Sec., A. R. Macdonough, 19 Madison Ave.—This Club was formed by members of the old "Sketch Club," a private social Club composed of artists, literary men, and art amateurs of the day. It remains true to its artistic traditions, counting not only a large number of artists among its members but taking a lively interest in everything pertaining to art. The Club has a valuable permanent collection, in which the following painters and sculptors are represented : A. Bierstadt, Eug. Benson, H. C. Bispham, J. F. Cropsey, Thos. S. Cummings, T. Colman, C. P. Cranch, F. O. C. Darley, W. P. W. Dana, A. B. Durand, C. T. Dix, Paul Duggan, J. W. Ehninger, Chas. L. Elliott, Regis Gignoux, F. Guenet, H. P. Gray, R. Swain Gifford, W. J. Hays, Thos. Hicks, D. Huntington, R. W. Hubbard, E. L. Henry, W. J. Hennesey, Winslow Homer, A. C. Howland, Geo. Hess, C. C. Ingham, Jones, J. A. Jackson, Eastman Johnson, J. F. Kensett, Louis Lang, E. Leutze, Lancret, H. A. Loop, W. J. Linton, Wm. S. Mount, E. J. Man. L. R. Mignot, Jervis McEntee, H. D. Martin, Powers, C. S. Reinhart, Rondel, T. P. Rossiter, Jas. A. Suydam, R. M. Staigg, J. B. Stearns, Launt Thompson, E. Terry, G. Trumbull, Jr., L. Voelkert, J. F. Weir, M. Waterman, T. W. Wood, W. Whittredge. Besides these originals, there are also a number of engravings, casts, photographs, etc. As the Club is not open to strangers, the collection can only be seen upon personal introduction by a member. For the monthly meetings held during the winter season, loan collections of works of art are gathered, and these remain on view the Sunday and Monday following the Saturday on which the meeting is held. To these exhibitions visitors are admitted on presenting the card of a member. [A paper by Mr. John Durand entitled "Prehistoric Notes of the Century Club," replete with information concerning some of the older organizations out of which the Century Club sprung, was printed for distribution among the members themselves in 1882.— No reply to repeated requests for later information.]

CHAMBER OF COMMERCE.—63 William St. ; after May 1, 1884, Nassau, bet. Cedar and Liberty Sts.—Sec., George Wilson.—The Chamber owns a number of portraits, including some good specimens of the work of early American artists, as follows :—Matthew Pratt : full length of Lt.-Gov. Cadwallader Colden, painted for the Chamber in 1772 (the price paid to Pratt for this portrait was £37) ; J. S. Copley : Henry White (copy by an unknown artist) ; John Trumbull : full length of Alex. Hamilton, first Sec. of the Treasury, painted in 1792, and DeWitt Clinton ; Henry Inman : DeWitt Clinton ; H. P. Gray : Joshua Bates (copy after Eddis), and Isaac Carow (from a miniature) ; D. Huntington : John Murray (after Trumbull), Robert Lenox (after Jarvis), John C. Green (replica), John

Sherman, Sec. of the Treas., and S. B. Ruggles; Thos. Hicks: Elias Hicks (replica), John Alsop (copy from unknown original). John Cruger (from a miniature), Thomas Tileston, Pelatiah Perit (replica); Vinc. Colyer: Theophylact Bache (copy of a crayon by St. Memin); T. P. Rossiter; Jas. Boorman, Jas. Brown, Jas. G. King; Fagnani: Richard Cobden and John Bright, both from life. Unknown artists: Wm. Walton, Duke of Bridgewater, Jonathan Goodhue (marble bust).—The rooms of the Chamber are open, free to all visitors, on week days during business hours.

CHARCOAL CLUB.—14 and 16 W. 14th St. (at the Gambier Gallery). —Organized April 12, 1882.—Officers: Pres., Chas. Volkmar, 139-145 W. 55th St. ; Treas., Alf. Trumble, 238 6th Ave. ; Sec., Geo. R. Halm, 263 W. 25th St.—Objects : To secure the artistic improvement of its members by sketching and drawing from draped and nude models, still-life, etc., and to promote social intercourse.—Members : Active members, limited to 21, who must practice art as a profession ; Honorary members, unlimited. Initiation fee, $10 ; monthly dues, $2, for both classes. Honorary members excluded on study nights, nor can they vote or hold office. Present number, 16 active, 7 honorary.—Meetings in winter, every Tuesday evening. In summer, one Sunday each month to be devoted to an excursion for sketching and out-of-door enjoyment. The social meetings, every fourth week, to be inaugurated by a half-hour address or paper to be read by a member on some art subject.

CITY HALL.—Broadway, opposite Murray St.—The Governor's Room, in the old City Hall, contains a collection of portraits of governors of the State, mayors of the city, and national celebrities which are well worth seeing, on account of the artistic and historical interest attaching to them. Among the painters whose work is represented here are John Trumbull (1756-1843), Vanderlyn (1776-1852), J. W. Jarvis (1780-1840), Samuel Waldo (1783-1861), S. F. B. Morse (1791-1872), Geo. Catlin (1796-1872), Henry Inman (1801-1846), C. L. Elliott (1812-1868), H. P. Gray (1819-1877), Weimar, A. H. Wenzler, W. H. Powell, Whitehorne, Mooney, Spencer, Robt. W. Weir, Wm. Page, D. Huntington, Thos. Hicks, F. B. Carpenter, J. H. Lazarus, and Mrs. Anna Lea Merritt. Many of these artists are represented by several specimens : Vanderlyn by four, Inman by six, Elliott by five, including one of his best larger works, the portrait of Gov. Bouck, dated 1847. The canvas by Morse is the full-length portrait of Lafayette, which he was commissioned to paint when the Marquis visited the United States in 1824 on an invitation by Congress.—The Governor's Room is open free to visitors all the year round, except on Sundays and holidays, from 10 A.M. to 4 P.M.—The city owns a number of other interesting portraits, but as they are hung in the Mayor's office, and other rooms in constant use, they are not generally accessible.

COLLEGE OF ARCHÆOLOGY AND ÆSTHETICS.—120 E. 105th St.—Incorporated 1880.—Officers: Chancellor, Hon. Amos K. Hadley, 346 E. 125th St. ; Vice-Chan. and Dean, Rev. J. W. Henry Canoll ; Censors, Anson N. Brockway, M.D., Jas. Wotherspoon Graff; Registrar, Wm. B. Randall ; Directors, A. K. Hadley, J. W. H. Canoll, Erastus H. Benn, Dr. Richard Kunze, Wm. B. Randall.—Faculty : Rev. J. W. Henry Canoll, Æ. LL.D., Professor of the Analogies of the Fine Arts and Teacher of English Versification ; John Silva-Beer, Teacher of Ethnographic Tenets ; Carina Canoll, Teacher of Textile Handicrafts ; H. A. Van Note, Demonstrator of Ancient Domestic Arts ; Teachers of Music, Modelling and Painting, temporarily employed.—This institution comprises : 1. The Philosophical Department, composed of the Fellows (electors) and Colleagues (associate members), who meet in sections for the reading and discussing of original essays and the presentation of facts relating to the history and the technicalities of the fine arts and various handicrafts. 2. The Polytechnic Department, in which the strictly æsthetic arts are taught, including modelling, music, English versification, and literary criticism.—The College is self-supporting, and makes no appeals to the public for financial aid. Its Museum and principal offices are at 120 E. 105th St., where free lectures are frequently given. The Museum is open to the public, without charge, on Thursday evenings. It contains collections of ancient and modern pottery, numerous idols and religious symbols, antique books and manuscripts, laces and mediæval tapestry, mosaics, cameos, and gems. It affords peculiar advantages in studying the analogies of the arts.—Life Members, constituting the Fellows of the College, are elected only on especial nomination ; tickets, $100. Colleagues, entitled to all the privileges of the Philosophical Department, are elected on nomination of the Dean. The securing of an annual matriculation ticket is thereafter required, for which the fee is $1. Corresponding Members, having the privilege of presenting essays for discussion and requiring reports thereon, entitled also to replies to questions on art technics, are elected to annual membership. They are required to take a matriculation ticket, for which the fee is $3.— Pupils are admitted to the Polytechnic Department on application to the Dean. Fees in all branches of this department are moderate. The canons of the College prohibit the exactment of dues, fines, and assessments. They require that, as far as may be practicable, the institution shall be an unostentatious, liberal school of the æsthetic arts and cognate literature.—Inquiries and applications should be addressed to the Dean, Prof. Canoll, 120 E. 105th St. [From written information furnished by Prof. Canoll. There are no printed catalogues or reports.]

COLUMBIA COLLEGE.—Officers B'd of Trustees: Chairm., Hamilton Fish, LL.D., 251 E. 17th St.; Treas., Gouvern. M. Ogden, 9 W. 10th St.; Clerk, Gerard Beekman, 5 E. 34th St.; Pres. of College, Fred. A. P. Barnard, S.T.D., LL.D., L.II.D., 63 E. 49th St.; Dean of the Faculty, Chas. F. Chandler, Ph.D., M.D., LL.D.—*The School of Mines,* E. 49th St., cor. Madison Ave., established in connection with this College in 1864, offers six courses of study, viz.: Mining, Engineering, Civil Engineering, Metallurgy, Geology and Palæontology, Analytical and Applied Chemistry, and Architecture. Drawing, Alfred D. Churchil, A.M.,M.S., E.M., Ph.B., instructor, in its practical application to the subjects involved, is taught throughout the whole of each course (four years), with the exception of that in Chemistry, in which it is omitted in the third year.—*The Course in Architecture* was established in the year 1881, under the direction of Prof. Wm. R. Ware, B.S., formerly of the Massachusetts Institute of Technology, of Boston. This course is intended for those only who wish to pursue the study of architecture in the most thorough manner, and no students are received who do not propose to take the entire four-years' course, with all the literary and scientific studies which may be laid down for the training of a scientific and thoroughly educated architect. (For a detailed exposition of the course, see the "Circular of Information," issued by the School of Mines.)—The school is well supplied with drawing models for the use of students, comprising both flat models and plaster casts; the Olivier models, forming all mathematical surfaces by silk threads, and admitting of a variety of transformations; other models, illustrating general and special problems of descriptive geometry, shades and shadows, and stone cutting; drawings of machines and parts of machines for studying and copying; and models of machines and of details of building construction. There have recently been added a considerable number of architectural drawings executed in French and German schools, and an extensive collection of photographs of architectural subjects. Besides the general library of the college, most of the departments have special collections of books for the use of their own students.

COOPER UNION FOR THE ADVANCEMENT OF SCIENCE AND ART.—

7th St., cor. 4th Ave.—Founded in 1857 by Mr. Peter Cooper, and since sustained by his generosity, and a few small donations by others. Total expenditures, from organization to end of last term, $1,603,614.17.—Officers: Pres., left vacant by Mr. Cooper's death; Treas., Wilson G. Hunt, 331 Broadway; Sec., Abram S. Hewitt, 9 Lexington Ave.; Curator, J. C. Zachos; Clerk, I. J. Byrnes.—Besides its Free Library (about 16,000 vols., for reference only), Free Reading Room, Free Lectures, Free School of Telegraphy, Stenography, and Type-writing for Women, and Free Night Schools of Science, the Cooper Union maintains several Art Schools.—*The Free Art School for Women.* (Clerk, Mrs. M. B. Young.) Aim: To afford instruction in the Arts of Design to women, who, having the requisite taste and natural capacity, but are unable to pay for instruction, intend to apply the knowledge acquired in the institution to their support, either by teaching or pursuing Art as a profession.—Classes: Elementary drawing from objects; Cast drawing; Life drawing from draped model; Normal designing class; Oil painting; Retouching and coloring photographs; Porcelain painting; Wood Engraving; China Painting. The classes are in session from the beginning of October to end of May. Hours of study from 9 A.M. to 1 P.M. daily, except Saturdays and Sundays. Pupils may remain for practice until 4 P.M.—Teachers: Mrs. Susan N. Carter, Prin.; R. Swain Gifford, N.A., Oil painting; John P. Davis, Wood engraving; Miss Clara Wilson, Normal drawing; Wm. Sartain, A.N.A., Life and cast drawing; Miss Ella Ward, Miss M. C. Reid, Cast drawing and composition; Mrs. M. C. B. Ellis, Crayon photographs; W. W. Scott, Photo-color; Miss M. A. E. Carter, China painting; Wm. H. Goodyear, Lecturer on art.—Tuition free; pupils must provide their own materials, etc. Orders for wood engraving and other work, to be executed by the students and graduates, are taken at the school, and the earnings go to the students who have done the work.—Students: Females only; ages from 16 to 35. Written reference must be given as to character, fitness, and inability to pay. For formalities of application, see circular to be obtained at the office of the Cooper Union. Pupils in the wood engraving class not taken for less than three years. Number of students, season of 1882–3: Applied for admittance, 1,450; admitted, 275 (and 32 in wood engraving class); remained at end of term, 202 (and 28 in wood engraving class).—Money prizes varying from $5 to $60, silver and bronze medals, honorable mentions, etc., are awarded at the Annual Exhibition in May. Certificates are given for drawing, painting (of two grades in these studies), normal drawing, and photo-crayon.—*Afternoon or Amateur School:* This department forms an exception to the rest of the institution, as the students are required to pay.—Classes: Elementary, cast and life drawing, from draped model, $15 for 30 lessons of 2½ hours each; Oil painting, $15 for 20 lessons, 2 hours each; China painting, $3, 6 lessons; Designing class, $15, 30 lessons; Wood engraving (for particulars apply to Mrs. M. B. Young, Clerk of Women's Art School). The profits derived from this school go towards the maintenance of the free classes.—Ladies only admitted as students.—*The Free Night School of Art:* Aim: Practical instruction, bearing on some useful employment in which the arts of design and drawing are the principal or accessory occupations.—Teachers and subjects taught: Mechanical drawing, J. A. Saxton, A.M., and Edm. Maurer; Architectural drawing, Edw. C. Miller and Emil Maurer; Perspective, Benj. Braman; Cast drawing, Wm. W. Scott; Form drawing, Geo. W. Maynard; Ornamental drawing, Max Eglau; Figure and rudimental drawing, H. Plumb; Decorative designing, R. Wasserscheid; Modelling, Nic. Rossignoli.—The classes are in session from 7.30 to 9.30 P.M. Term begins Oct. 1, ends Apr. 15.—Tuition free, but pupils must provide materials.—Students, male only, must be at least 15 years old. For formalities of application, see " Rules and Regulations," to be obtained at the office of the Cooper Union. Number of students, season of 1882–3: Admitted during the term, 1,797; remained at close of term, 903.—Honorable mentions and prizes, and certificates of two grades, are awarded at the end of the term. A reception and exhibition of drawings deemed worthy of showing is given in May.—The teaching in the classes is supplemented in all the departments by lectures delivered by the instructors and others.—A small gallery of photographs is provided for the use of the female students, comprising excellent examples from the early masters, Giotto, Cimabue, etc., and from Holbein, Velasquez, Titian, etc. A set of the Elgin marbles and of various Greek statues, and Florentine bas-reliefs from originals by Donatello, Della Robbia, and others, fill the long corridor on the floor occupied by the Women's School with most inspiring examples of the art work of other times. A small library has also been specially gathered for the use of the school.—In their last annual report, dated May 26, 1883, the trustees say that there is an overwhelming demand for the privileges of the Institution, which has, however, reached the limit of its usefulness, with the space at its command, and the money available for its support. Its income is mainly derived from two sources: from rents received from portions of its building [see illustration], and from an endowment of $200,000 provided by the late Mr. Peter Cooper during his lifetime. For the first time during the last year the expenses materially exceeded the receipts by the sum of $3,548.54. This deficiency was provided for out of a special donation of $30,000, made by Mr. Cooper for general expenses, and of which there still remains a balance sufficient to pay the debts of the corporation. By the terms of his will, Mr. Cooper gave another $100,000 to the Institution, the interest on which will be sufficient, in addition to his previous endowments and the rents, to defray the ordinary expenses, upon the scale of usefulness which is provided for by its present organization. The children of Mr. Cooper have also notified the Trustees that, in accordance with what they understood to be his final wishes, they will contribute during the coming year (1883–4), the sum of $100,000 in addition to the bequest already mentioned. To be able, however, to enlarge the Institution, and to give up the whole of its building to purposes of instruction, the Trustees believe that an additional endowment of $1,000,000 would be required. " This statement is made," continues the report, " because some suggestions have appeared in the public journals, that it would be well to signalize the great change which has taken place in the loss of its founder and benefactor, by raising a fund which would enable his designs to be carried out to their final completion. The Trustees think it is a proper time for them to say that Mr. Cooper never expected to be able, of his own means, to accomplish the full realization of his plans, and would gladly have welcomed any addition to the funds of the Institution from any source whatever. If, therefore, it should occur to any one, in the disposition of his means, to make a gift to the Cooper Union, the Trustees desire it to be understood that such gifts will be gladly received ; and that in the enlargement of the School of Design for Women, in the establishment of a Reference Library on a larger scale, and particularly in the creation of an Art Library, designed especially for the use of the pupils of the School of Design, and of a Museum of Art and of mechanical models, containing specimens useful to the formation of taste and embodying examples of special excellence, there is abundant opportunity for endowments to the extent of a million of dollars ; and this sum, sooner or later, the Trustees hope to secure for the Institution."

GENERAL SOCIETY OF MECHANICS AND TRADESMEN OF THE CITY OF NEW YORK.

—Mechanics' Hall, 18 E. 16th St.—Organized, Nov. 17, 1785 ; chartered, March 14, 1792.—Officers, 1884 : Pres., John H. Rogers, 405 E. 83d St.; 1st V. P., John H. Waydell, 21 Old Slip ; 2d V. P., Chas. Galloway, 818 Greenwich St.; Treas., Jas. J. Burnet, 89 E. 10th St.; Sec.,Thos. Earle, Mechanics' Hall ; Chairm. School Comm.,Wm. C. Smith, 36 N. Moore St.; Sec., School Comm., Jos. E. Macfarland, 401 W. 21st St.—This wealthy Society, organized, as its name indicates, by mechanics and tradesmen, for the purposes of benevolence, founded a *School for the Instruction and Improvement of Apprentices*, in which reading, writing, and arithmetic were taught, at a time when the public-school system was as yet undeveloped. Upon the establishment of these institutions, the course of instruction in the School of the Society was changed, and it is now simply a *Free Drawing School.*—John C. Babcock, Supt., 64 College Pl.; Teachers: Henry Van Kuyck, Free-Hand drawing ; E. F. Randolph, Elementary class ; C. Otto Ficht, Advanced class ; Jos. Crampton, Mechanical drawing ; Jas. H. Monckton, Machine drawing ; W. S. Purdy, Architectural drawing ; Miss Lucy Stone, Ladies' class.—Term, 6 mos., begins in October and ends in March.—Four sessions weekly, from 7 to 9 P.M.—Tuition absolutely free ; materials supplied at cost.—Pupils last term, about 250 males, and 60 females. Conditions of admission, good character, and working at some trade as an apprentice or journeyman.—Aim : To make mechanics more proficient in their trade by means of the art of drawing, and to train designers for the art industries.—The School is reported to be in a very prosperous condition. In the Ladies' Class, which has been in existence only about eight years, drawing from objects and designing are the principal studies ; but these studies are also encouraged in the male classes.—Besides its School, the Society maintains a Free Library (about 60,000 vols.), a valuable Technical Reference Library, and Reading-Room, and during the winter season arranges courses of lectures for its members and their families. Free Scholarships in Columbia College and in the University of New York are in the gift of the Society.—The last report represents " the condition of the school as prosperous and satisfactory in every branch. For many years the average attendance has not been as high as at present, and by a careful discrimination of the numerous applicants, the benefits of the School are conferred almost exclusively on persons learning a useful trade. . . . Our limited accommodations compel us to refuse many deserving applicants for instruction in our School, but we cherish the hope that at a future day we shall, with the generous help and fostering care of our Society, be enabled to extend the usefulness of this branch of our institution in a manner worthy of the memory of its founders."—For a full history of the Society, see "Annals of the General Society of Mechanics and Tradesmen of the City of New York, from 1785 to 1880." Edited by T. Earle and C. T. Congdon, New York, 1883.

GOTHAM ART STUDENTS.

—17 Bond St.—Organized Dec. 28, 1879 ; incorp. Nov. 6, 1880.—Officers, 1884 : Pres., John S. Sharp, 401 Lexington Ave.; Sec., Louis J. Weyprecht, 12 Stanton St.; Treas., Herm. Engel, Jr., 20 Barrow St.—Object : The advancement of art.—Members (males only) : Active (all of whom must participate in the exercises of the Club), at present, beginning of 1884, 26 ; honorary, at present, 8. The dues and fees depend upon the expenses and strength of membership of the Society. At present they are as follows : Initiation fee, $3 ; monthly dues, $5 in winter, $1 in summer. Non-members are admitted to the classes on payment of $6 a month in winter, and $2.50 in summer. There are 3 such students at present.—This is a working organization of practical men, designers, lithographers, carvers, engravers, etc., and the aim of the classes is to provide thorough instruction in drawing and painting for artisans and those wishing to follow art as a profession. The original intention of the Society was to afford a chance to study during the summer months, when the other schools are closed. The rooms are open, therefore, all through the year, but the instructor, Mr. Walter Shirlaw, directs the classes only from Oct to May. Candidates must submit a drawing from life or cast.—Classes : Life, Monday, Wednesday and

Friday evenings; Costume Sketch Class, Tuesday evenings ; Composition Class, Thursday evenings ; Sunday Class, generally from draped model, from 8.30 A.M. to 12.30 P.M., for three or four Sundays.—Exhibitions of paintings and studies, accompanied by lectures by the professor, are held twice a month.—It is proposed to add a Cast Class, Reading Room, and Library, as soon as possible, and to have regular exhibitions of the work of students and artists fresh from foreign schools.

KIT-KAT CLUB.—23 East 14th St.—Organized Jan. 30, 1882.—Officers: Pres., Philip Cusacks ; Cor. Sec., Lafayette W. Seavey ; Treas., John Durkin.—Objects : To afford to professional artists opportunity to study from the living model and still-life, and provide a social rendezvous for its members and their friends.—Members, professional artists, and art patrons, limited to 50. Present number, 22. Initiation fee, $5 ; monthly dues, $1.50.—The Club has regular meetings twice a week, but the members have keys, and can use the studio at any time.

LADIES' ART ASSOCIATION.—24 W. 14th St.—Founded 1867 ; incorporated 1877. —Officers : Pres., Mrs. F. H. Marsily; V. P.'s, Mrs. L. B. Hinton, 3 Park Pl.; Mrs. L. A. K. Clappe, Hastings-on-Hudson, N. Y.; Treas., Miss E. C. Field ; Sec., Miss Alice Donlevy.— Objects : To promote the interest of Women Artists, and to found a central point of union and reference for its members ; to provide instruction (1) for those already engaged as teachers of drawing and painting in schools and colleges, (2) in painting on porcelain and those departments of decoration which prove the most readily remunerative as a profession, (3) for boys and girls up to the age of fifteen in art industrial education, (4) for artists in study from life and nature ; to enlarge facilities for non-residents, whose stay in New York is limited, and whose study needs direction ; to provide a way for students to pay for art education by the Labor-Note System ; to secure a building in which studios connected with apartments may be hired to members.—Members : Active, i. e., professional women artists ; Associates, i. e., women art students ; Subscribing Members, any lady or gentleman interested in art ; dues, $5 annually for all members. Teachers of any specialty may become Subscribing Members on payment of 30 cents a month. Strangers may be introduced to the privileges of the rooms by members for $1 per month. There are also Honorary Members. Candidates for active membership must submit an original work of art to the Executive Committee.—The Association is supported by the dues of members, the tuition fees paid by the pupils, and donations.— Classes and Teachers : Modelling, Children's Class, Miss Clio Hinton ; Drawing from Cast and Fruit Painting, Annie Morgan ; Painting in Oil from Still-Life, Heads, Figures (from Copy and from Life), Sketch Class from Life (Charcoal or Pencil), J. Roy Robertson : Landscape Painting, A. Hochstein ; Pastel, Mrs. Favarger Newell; Modelling, Mrs. L. B. Hinton ; Perspective, Miss E. C. Field ; Teachers' Class (Principles of Form and Color, Decorative Design), Children's Class (Industrial Art), Miss Alice Donlevy ; Crayon Portraits, Mrs. Bianca Bondi Robitscher ; Wood Engraving, Miss A. T. Crane and Miss I. D. Kyle ; Botanical Drawing, S. J. Knight ; Embroidery and Wood Carving, Miss Laura Grimsgaard ; Porcelain Painting, Mrs. Potin and Miss C. S. Post. Lessons have been given to deaf mutes, and a deaf mute is preparing herself to teach. Opportunities for summer study, either independently or under a teacher, are afforded to those who wish to utilize part of their vacation.—Students : Female only, except in the Children's Class. Number of students last season about 40 (and 100 at the Brooklyn Branch, which see).—The tuition fees vary according to subject and time. Those who cannot pay are admitted on the Labor-Note System, an arrangement peculiar to this Association. Under it the student binds herself to do a certain amount of work for the Association, within a certain time, as an equivalent for the tuition given. Three scholarships have been established by Mrs. W. Jennings Demorest, Mrs. Edward Moran, and Mrs. Jane Russell.—Lectures on a variety of subjects are delivered during the winter season, and at the monthly meetings art matters are discussed, and technical questions submitted to specialists.—The erection of a Studio Building for Women is one of the principal objects of the Association. The first step towards the carrying out of this idea was taken on May 1, 1881, when a large room was hired, to be used as a class-room, while the apartments formerly occupied by the Association in the same building were let as studios to ten ladies.—The Association owns a small collection of books on art and education, illustrated books, casts, photographs, etc. A new feature, lately introduced, is a Loan Collection of paintings and studies, which are loaned as copies, against payment of a small fee, to schools, classes, and private individuals.—One of the rooms of the Association was opened in June, 1883, as a permanent gallery, for the sale of original pictures by members and those connected with the Association.—An exhibition of the work of members, teachers and students was held in December, 1883.—Annual meeting, in May.

LENOX LIBRARY.—1001 Fifth Ave., 70th and 71st Sts.—Founded by the late Mr. James Lenox, who erected the building at a cost of about $1,000,000, endowed the institution with $250,000, and gave nearly the whole of the collections at present contained in it. Opened to the public in 1877.—Geo. H. Moore, Sec. and Supt.—*The Art Gallery*, according to the last printed catalogue, autumn, 1882, contains 147 paintings, 18 works of sculpture, and 59 paintings on porcelain, enamels, mosaics, etc. (these latter exhibited in the rooms on the ground floor). The following are some of the artists represented in the collection. American artists: A. Bierstadt, Geo. L. Brown, J. G. Chapman, F. E. Church, Thos. Cole, J. S. Copley, A. B. Durand, W. J. Hays, G. P. A. Healey, D. Huntington, H. Inman, J. W. Jarvis, J. F. Kensett, Chas. R. Leslie (8 specimens), S. F. B. Morse, Wm. S. Mount, G. S. Newton, Jas. Peale, Rembrandt Peale, Gilbert Stuart (5 specimens), John Trumbull, John Vanderlyn, Thos. Ball, Thos. Crawford, Hiram Powers. European artists, old : Andrea del Sarto, Le Brun, Jacob Ruysdael, Solomon Ruysdael. European artists, modern : F. de Brackeleer, Sr., Sir A. Calcott, Wm. Collins, John Constable, Paul Delaroche, Leon y Escosura, Thos. Gainsborough, Sir Francis Grant, Carl Hübner, José Jimenez, Sir Edwin Landseer, J. B. Madou, Geo. Morland, J. L. E. Morgenstern, Wm. Mulready, M. Munkaczy ("Milton dictating to his Daughters," presented to the Library by Mr. Robert Lenox Kennedy), Peter Nasmyth, Sir Henry Raeburn, Sir Joshua Reynolds, David Roberts, H. Salentin, J. M. W. Turner (3 specimens), P. Van Schendel, Eug. Verboeckhoven, Horace Vernet, C. Wauters, Sir David Wilkie (7 specimens), Ed. Zamacois, E. Barrias, John Gibson, C. D. Rauch, Sir John Steell, etc.—*The Library* is exceedingly rich in incunabula and old illustrated books, valuable to the student of the history of engraving. A large number of these, together with a collection of old illuminated MSS., are exhibited in cases in the rooms on the lower floor.—Open to the public, until further notice, every Tuesday, Friday, and Saturday, except during the month of August, from 11 A.M to 4 P.M. No person admitted without a ticket, which will be mailed to applicants free of charge. Address the Superintendent by postal card, at the Library.—Catalogue for sale ; price 15 cents.

LOTOS CLUB.—147 Fifth Ave.—Pres., Whitelaw Reid ; Sec., Thos. W. Knox ; Treas., F. A. Brown ; Art Committee, Montague Marks, Ch'man, Wm. S. Macy, and Douglas Taylor.— The Club arranges exhibitions of works of art at some of its receptions during the winter. The chief events of the past year were the receptions given in honor of Dr. Francis Seymour Haden, when a very fine collection of his etchings was exhibited, and of Mr. Hubert Herkomer, on the occasion of the presentation by him to the Club of his life-size portrait of the president, Mr. Whitelaw Reid.

METROPOLITAN MUSEUM OF ART.—Central Park, Fifth Ave., and 82d St.— Inaugurated at a meeting held Nov. 23, 1869. Chartered Apr. 13, 1870.—Officers for 1884-5 : Pres., John Taylor Johnston, 8 Fifth Ave. ; V. P.'s., Wm. C. Prime, 38 E. 23d St., D. Huntington, 49 E. 20th St. ; Treas., Henry G. Marquand, 21 W. 20th St. ; Sec. and Director, L. P. di Cesnola, 107 E. 57th St.; Libr., Wm. L. Andrews, 16 E. 38th St. ; Curator, W. H. Goodyear.—Objects : Establishing and maintaining a museum and library of art, encouraging and developing the study of the fine arts and the application of arts to manufactures and practical life, advancing the general knowledge of kindred subjects, and to that end furnishing popular instruction and recreation.— Members : The original incorporators, the Patrons and Fellows, and all persons duly elected, are life members of the corporation ; new life members are elected by the corporation upon nomination of the Trustees. Annual members and Honorary Fellows may also be elected by the Trustees. The contribution of $1,000 entitles the contributor to be a Patron in perpetuity, with the privilege of appointing a successor ; §500, a Fellow in perpetuity, with privilege of appointing a successor ; $200, a Fellow for Life. Any person giving twice the value of the amounts named in works of art, if accepted, may be elected to either of the above degrees by the Trustees. Annual members pay $10 a year. Number of members, etc., Dec. 31, 1883 : Patrons, 211 ; Fellows in Perpetuity, 139 ; Fellows for Life, 116 ; Honorary Fellows, 37 ; Annual Members, 1,139. Assessments may be laid on members of the Corporation, not to exceed $50 annually, as determined from time to time by the Trustees. (Such an assessment was laid in 1873.)—The government consists of the officers, 21 Trustees, and, *ex officiis*, the President of the Department of Public Parks, the Comptroller of the

City of New York, and the President of the National Academy of Design. The officers are elected annually from among the members. The Trustees serve for seven years, and three are elected annually, also from among the members.—The Museum is dependent for support on the annual membership fees, which, up to Dec. 31, 1883, amounted to $44,879.50 in all ; the receipts at the door on the two pay days, which, up to the same date, amounted to $43,244.16 (including the proceeds of the Centennial Exhibition held for the benefit of the Museum in 1876) ; the appropriations made by the city of New York ; and donations in cash (by Patrons, Fellows, etc.) and in works of art. The receipts for catalogues, etc., are offset by the cost of making and printing them. The city, authorized by act of Legislature of Apr. 5, 1861, put up the building now occupied by the Museum (which is only a small part of the structure as it is eventually to be) at a cost of nearly $500,000. This building, which remains the property of the city, is given rent-free so long as the Museum fulfils the conditions of its charter. The collections remain the property of the corporation, which can vacate the building at any time, upon giving due notice. The city was also authorized to expend certain moneys in keeping the building in repair, in installing the collections therein, and in maintaining them. Up to Dec. 31, 1883, the city had expended upon the Museum, for these purposes the sum of $194,745.57. These appropriations, however, are not sufficient for current expenses, and are precarious, as they can be withheld or reduced at any time. The building having already become too small for the collections, the Legislature, in 1881, passed a bill authorizing the city to expend $240,000 additional, in four yearly installments of $60,000 each, in extending it ; but this bill failed to receive the approval of the governor. Another bill, subsequently passed and approved by the governor, authorized the expenditure of $60,000 ; but the Board of Apportionment declined to place the amount in the tax levy, and the act is no longer operative. The total of paid-in subscriptions to the funds of the Museum, according to the last Report, amounted, on Dec. 31, 1883, to $488,681.80. The works of art donated up to Dec. 31, 1883, are valued at $203,549.50. There is no endowment for purchases, and whenever a new acquisition is to be made, the friends of the Museum must be appealed to.—Of the purchases made by the Museum, the most important are as follows: A collection of 175 paintings, mostly by Flemish and Dutch artists of the 16th and 17th century, but including also some old Italian, French, and German pictures, costing about $145,000 ; Kensington reproductions, $3.160.76 ; Cesnola Collections of Cypriote Antiquities, $130,750.71 ; MacCallum Collection of Laces, $2,445 ; Collection of Babylonian Cylinders, $496.71 ; Avery Collection of Oriental Porcelain, $35,000 ; Collection of Antique Glass, $15,000 ; King Collection of Antique Engraved Gems, $6,000. Some of these collections were purchased with funds specially donated for the purpose, as for instance the Antique Glass, for which the money was supplied by Mr. Henry G. Marquand, while Mr. John Taylor Johnston provided the means to buy the King Collection of Gems. The following are some of the larger donations of works of art, with the names of the donors.: Collection of Central American Pottery, etc., N. Y. Chapter of Amer. Inst. of Arch. ; Thirty-eight oil paintings, the last summer studies executed by John F. Kensett, Thos. Kensett ; Collection of Greek Vases, etc., Samuel G. Ward ; Collection of Japanese Coins, etc., J. Carson Brevoort ; 85 Water Color Paintings by Wm. T. Richards, Rev. E. L. Magoon, D.D.; Collection of Ancient American Pottery, Collection of old Venetian Glass, Set of Electrotype Reproductions, by Elkington & Co., of London, of the Russian art objects selected by the South Kensington Museum (cost, £3,800), Henry G. Marquand ; Collection of old Venetian Glass, etc., J. J. Jarvis ; Collection of 690 Drawings, etc., by old masters, Corn. Vanderbilt ; Collection of Architectural Casts, Rich. M. Hunt ; Collection of Peruvian Pottery, W. W. Evans ; Collection of Egyptian Casts, and Collection of Ancient Coins, Jos. W. Drexel; Miscellaneous Collection of works of art, valued at $50,000, bequeathed by Stephen Whitney Phœnix ; Collection of Casts of ivories, Alph. Duprat ; Collection of works of art (statues, paintings, prints, porcelains, medallions, etc.), having special reference to Washington, Franklin, Lafayette, etc., Wm. W. Huntington, etc. Besides these more extensive collections, the list of donations registers the gift of many smaller ones, and a large number of single pictures, statues in bronze and marble, objects of industrial art, etc. Among the acquisitions of the year 1883, is to be noted, also, the bequest of the late Mr. Levi S. Willard, who left to the Museum, a considerable portion of his estate, estimated at about $75,000, for the purchase of a collection of models, casts, photographs, engravings, etc., illustrative of the science and art of architecture, the collection to be made under the direction of the N. Y. Chapter of the American Institute of Architects.—The library is as yet small, but has now an endowment fund of $7,000, and a friend of the Museum has agreed to contribute $75 each year for subscriptions to periodicals.—The Museum has published a series of twelve etchings by Jules Jacquemart from paintings in his possession, and some of the antique jewelry of the Cesnola collection has been reproduced by Tiffany & Co. Photographs of some of the objects in the Museum are for sale at the door.—Besides the permanent exhibition of the collections owned by the corporation, there are two Loan Exhibitions each year, of paintings, and objects of industrial art, etc., loaned by private owners. The plan of lending for exhibition in different cities selections from the cabinets of the Museum, which, according to the Seventh Report, has been approved by the Trustees, has not yet been carried into execution.—The Museum was opened in a temporary gallery, 681 Fifth Ave., on Feb. 21, 1872. The year following it removed to a more commodious building, 128 W. 14th St. The transfer of the collections to the present building was accomplished in March and April, 1879; the opening occurred March 30, 1880.—The total number of visitors for the six years from 1873 to 1879 was 353,421. During the last year of the Museum's occupancy of the 14th St. building, there were 26,137 free, and 3,795 paying visitors. From the day of the opening of the new building, to April 30, 1881, a period of thirteen months, the visitors are given as 1,191,796 free and 8,577 paying. From figures obtained at the Museum, the number of visitors, which are now counted automatically by means of turn stiles, footed up 206,673 free and 16,992 paying, total 223,665 for the year ending Dec. 31, 1883 (last week estimated).—The Museum publishes nine catalogues, or "hand-books," which are for sale at the door, to wit : 1. Pictures by Old Masters. 2. Potteries of the Cesnola Collection. 3. Sculptures of the Cesnola Collection. (4 has been dropped.) 5. Oriental Porcelains. 6. Loan Collection. 7. Collection of Casts from Ivory Carvings. 8. Vanderbilt Collection of Drawings. 9. Engraved Gems. 10. General Guide to the Museum. Price 10 cents each.—The Museum is open daily, legal holidays included, except Sundays, and from April 15 to May 1, and Oct. 15 to Nov. 1, from 10 A.M. to one-half hour before sunset.—Admission on Mondays and Tuesdays, 25 cents ; on other days free.—(*Technical Schools of the Museum*, see below).—Annual meeting of the Corporation in February.—" Our property at the beginning of the year 1884," says the last report, presented at the annual meeting, held Feb. 11, 1884, " including works or objects of art, endowments, furniture, cases, etc., (valuation of objects of art being made at the time of acquisition), is estimated at $676,571.89. We owe no debt, and enter on the year 1884 with a small balance in the treasury. It has been only by the strictest economy, and the executive ability of the Director, that we are enabled to report this sound financial condition of the Museum. His labor and that of the staff employed under him would furnish ample employment for a very much larger force. The division of the Museum into departments is rapidly becoming a pressing necessity. This plan can, of course, never be fully realized until our income is much larger. But the rapid increase of our possessions, entailing largely increased responsibility, labor, and expense, demands the most serious consideration of members at the present moment. . . . . It has been forcibly argued that the Museum would rest on more solid foundation if it were located in its own private building, and its revenues, to some extent, augmented by a charge for admission at its door. There is no doubt that a mistaken idea that this is one of the public institutions of the city supported by the public, has diverted from it much substantial aid which it would have received in accessions to its membership and gifts toward its increase. But while the contributions of the city to its support form but a part of the expenses of keeping it open as a free Museum to the people, it must not be forgotten that a regular charge for admission would be a final abandoning of that one desire which has always animated the members of making our institution a free gift to all classes of people . . . . Our position may be stated in brief terms under two heads : 1st. We have vastly more works of art than can be exhibited in the present building in Central Park. 2d. Our income is not sufficient for a proper discharge of the duties of the Museum in its present condition, much less for its necessities in the immediate future. . . . . The variable and precarious character of our income will be seen from the financial statement. The necessities of the institution are visible. It is certainly unnecessary for us to enlarge on this plain statement of facts. We need a larger building, and an endowment which will insure a permanent income. Embarrassing as the position is in which the trustees now find themselves, they look with entire confidence to the continued unanimity of purpose and abundant self-sacrifice which members have displayed in the past. The work you have already accomplished is without parallel in the history of such institutions. The reward for past labor is ample in present success, in the enjoyment and benefit conferred on crowds of visitors, in the evidence of good accomplished. Other rewards for past and future labor and sacrifice no member of the institution asks or expects." [No view is given of the building occupied by the Museum, as the architectural effect of its exterior lines would be misleading, because it is only a section of a much larger build-ing, and many of its present exterior walls will eventually become interior sub-divisions. From the plan herewith published, which was prepared for the Park Department, in accordance with the views of the Trustees, by Messrs. C. Vaux and J. W. Mould, architects, the extent and general design of the proposed building may be readily comprehended. The present building covers an area of about 24,000 square feet, and the building, when completed, will cover an area of about 250,000 square feet. This provision for the future places the Museum in a favorable position with reference to its inevitable extension. Most similar buildings stand upon ground which is narrowly limited, and even when completed will be of such insufficient dimensions that the growth of the collections housed in them must soon be arrested. The plan of the Metropolitan Museum building, in accordance with the character of the great city of which it is to be an ornament, is calculated for a growth of genera-tions. No ample site for such a structure could have been found outside of the Park, even in New York, as the city is so laid out that any building over 200 feet wide would interfere with a long line of streets. As the tract set apart for this purpose forms no part of the characteristic Park landscapes, it was considered suitable for the erection of a popular art Museum building that would admit of an arrangement of architectural gardens on a liberal scale in connection with it. And the plans of the Park Department contemplate the laying out of such gardens in the future.]

NATIONAL ACADEMY OF DESIGN.—E. 23d St., cor. 4th Ave.—Instituted 1826 ; incorporated 1828.—Officers : Pres., Daniel Huntington, 49 E. 20th St. ; V. P., Thomas W. Wood, 51 W. 10th St. ; Cor. Sec., T. Addison Richards, National Academy ; Rec. Sec., H. W. Robbins, 51 W. 10th St. ; Treas., Alfred Jones, Am. B'k Note Co.—Objects : The cultivation and extension of the arts of design.—Members : Academicians, limited to 100, at present 96 ; Associates, also lim-ited to 100, at present 82, of whom 3 are ladies; Fellows for Life, contributors of $100 to the Fellowship Fund, at present 620 ; Fellows in Perpetuity, contributors of $500 to Fellowship Fund, 95 at present living.—*The Schools of the Academy* consist of an Antique School and a Life School. Aims and methods : In the Schools of the Academy, the principles and practice of art are taught chiefly through the study of the antique sculpture and the living model, both nude and draped, by means of lectures upon anatomy, perspective and other subjects, through portrait, sketch, and com-position classes, and in such other ways as may from time to time be provided.—The schools are open from the first Monday in October until the middle of May, daily, Saturdays and Sundays ex-cepted, from 8 A.M., with morning, afternoon, and night sessions, either or all of which may be attended by the students. The life class begins on the third Monday of October.—School Com-mittee, 1883-4 : S. J. Guy, N.A., E. W. Perry, Jr., N.A., Carl L. Brandt, N.A.—Classes and Pro-fessors : Antique and Life Schools, L. E. Wilmarth, N.A., and Edgar M. Ward, N.A. ; Painting Classes, W. H. Lippincott; Art Anatomy, J. Wells Champney, A.N.A. ; Perspective, Fred'k. Diel-man, N.A. ; Composition and Sketch Classes, L. E. Wilmarth, N.A. ; Modelling Class, J. Q. A. Ward, N.A.—*All* students must first enter the Antique School. Qualifications : Fair practice in study from plaster cast, to show which a shaded crayon drawing of part of the human figure must be exhibited to the School Committee. Students in the Antique School may be advanced to the Life School on showing to the Council an approved drawing of a full length statue made in the Antique School, during the current session. Oil and water colors, as well as crayons, may be used in the studies in both the Antique and Life Schools, when permitted by the professor. The duration of the course of study depends entirely upon the capacity and the progress of the student.—Students of both sexes are taught together, except in the Life Classes. Total number, season of 1881-2, 190 (males 120, females 70). Number in each class : Antique, all students ; Life, 50 ; Sketch, 40. Reported at about the same for the season of 1882-3. The capacity of the classes is limited to 200.—All students are required to pay an annual entrance fee of $10, and must provide their own materials. Other-wise the instruction is free, except in the Painting and Modelling Classes, in each of which there is a charge of $10 per month.—The " Elliott Medals," silver and bronze, are awarded in the Antique School ; the " Suydam Medals," silver and bronze, in the Life School. Honorable mention is also accorded. A fund of $5,000 was given to the Academy in 1883 by the late Julius Hallgarten, the interest of which is to be used for school prizes at the discretion of the Council. An exhibition of the drawings which are specially made in competition for these prizes, and of other selected work by the students, is usually held in the Lecture Room of the Academy, near the close of the session.— *Collections :* The Academy owns the portraits of all its Associates, and one work by each Academician, the presentation of these on election being one of the conditions of admission. It is also in possession of a collection of foreign and American pictures (bequeathed to it by Jas. A. Suydam, an American artist who died in 1865), and numerous other works of art. None of these are accessible, however, and most of them are packed away for lack of room. The Academy has, besides, an excellent collection of casts for the use of its schools, and a library.—*Exhibitions :* A most important part of the activity of the Academy is found in its Exhibitions, which have been held regularly since its organization, and of which there used to be two each year, one in spring, the other in winter. The Winter Exhibition was abandoned some years ago, but has been revived again lately in the shape of a Special Autumn Exhibition, held in Oct. and Nov. Beginning with the year 1884, a number of prizes are to be given at the Spring Exhibitions. Three of these, to be known as the *Hallgarten Prizes*, of $300, $200. and $100 each, provided for out of an endowment by the late Julius Hallgarten, are to be awarded to the painters of the best three pictures in oil colors, painted in the United States by American citizens under 35 years of age. A fourth prize to be known as the *Clarke Prize*, of $300, provided by Mr. Thos. Clarke, of New York, is to be awarded to the painter of the best American figure composition. The awards are to be made by a vote by ballot of all the exhibitors of the season, at a meeting held for the purpose during the third or fourth week of each exhibition.— The building [see illustration] occupied by the Academy, which is its property, was built from the plans of Mr. P. B. Wight, and opened to the public in 1865.—For a history of the institution see Thos. S. Cummings, N.A., " Historic Annals of the National Academy of Design." Phila. : Geo. W. Childs. 1865.—Annual meeting, second Wednesday of May.

NEW YORK CHAPTER OF THE AMERICAN INSTITUTE OF ARCHITECTS.—Bryant B'ldg., 55 Liberty St.—Organized 1867.—Pres., E. H. Kendall ; V. P.'s, Geo. B. Post and C. W. Clinton ; Sec. and Treas., A. J. Bloor, Bryant B'ldg., 55 Liberty St.—In accordance with the terms of the will of the late Levi Hale Willard, who bequeathed the bulk of his property, estimated at about $75,000, to the Metropolitan Museum for the formation of an architectural collection, under the direction of a commission appointed by the N. Y. Chapter of the Am. Inst. of Architects, Messrs. Napoleon Le Brun, A. J. Bloor, and Emlen T. Littell, were chosen such commission at a meeting held in April, 1883.—Annual meeting, in November.

NEW YORK ETCHING CLUB.—Organized Nov., 1877.—Officers : Pres., Henry Farrer, 51 W. 10th St.; Sec. and Treas., J. C. Nicoll, 51 W. 10th St.; Exec. Comm., F. S. Church, 58 E. 13th St., Thos. Moran, 9 E. 17th St., F. Dielman, 51 W. 10th St.—Object : To advance the art of " Free-Hand Etching."—Members : Resident, etchers resident in the city, or its immediate vicinity ; initiation fee, $10 ; annual dues, $3. Non-resident, etchers living at a distance ; can neither vote nor hold office, and are exempt from fees. Present number of members, 29 (22 resident, 7 non-resident), one of whom is a lady.—The only public activity of the Club, so far, has been the holding of exhibitions, the last of which took place in conjunction with that of the American Water Color Society, at the Academy of Design, from Feb. 4 to Mch. 1, 1884. Of these exhibitions catalogues are published, illustrated with etchings by the members. Three such catalogues have so far been issued ; price, $1 each.—Annual meeting, second Friday in April.

NEW YORK HISTORICAL SOCIETY.—170 Second Ave.—Instituted 1804.— Officers : Pres., Aug. Schell ; 1st V. P., Hamilton Fish ; 2d V. P., Benj. H. Field ; For. Cor. Sec., Wm. M. Evarts ; Dom. Cor. Sec., Edw. F. de Lancey ; Rec. Sec., Andrew Warner ; Treas., Benj. B. Sherman ; Libr., Jacob B. Moore ; Chairm. of Comm. on Fine Arts, A. B. Durand. Members : 481 resident, 641 life, 610 corresponding, 210 honorary ; total, 1,942.—*Art Gallery and Museum of the N. Y. H. Soc.:* Besides a very valuable library (abt. 70,000 vols., not counting the pamphlets, maps, newspapers, and MSS.), the Society owns the following collections bearing upon Archæology and Art : 1. The Abbott Collection of Egyptian Antiquities, 1127 numbers ; 2. A Collection of Paintings, 791 numbers, comprising the Bryan and the Dürr Collections of Old Masters, the Luman Reed Collection, the Collection of the former New York Gallery, and a large number of single pictures donated by artists and others [the Bryan and Dürr Collections afford the best and most complete illustration of the History of Painting, from Christian Byzantine Art down to that of our own time, to be found in the country, many of the specimens, all of them presumably originals, being of excellent quality ; the History of Painting in the U. S., from early colonial times to about the middle of this century, is nowhere else so abundantly illustrated, especially as regards portraiture] ; 3. A Collection of Sculptures, principally American, 57 numbers ; 4. The Lenox Collection of Nineveh Sculptures, 13 pieces ; 5. A Collection of American Antiquities ; 6. The nucleus of a Print Collection, about 250 choice engravings, mostly by modern Italians, such as Raphael Morghen, Volpato, etc., made by Luman Reed, the generous art patron of New York during the first half of the century, and a volume containing all the engraved work of Asher Brown Durand.—The rooms are open daily, from 9 A.M. to 6 P.M., except on Sundays, legal holidays, and during the month of August. —The Historical Society is a private association, but its policy is very liberal, and visitors, especially strangers, can easily gain access by application to the librarian at the building, or by a card or note of introduction from a member. No admission fee. Catalogues may be obtained at the desk in the library.—The Society owns the building in which it is located. It is very prosperous, having no debts, no mortgages on its building or collections, and no outstanding bills. It has several funds, amounting in all to $74,050, some of which were given for special purposes, such as the publication of works of history, etc. The building [see illustration], erected as a Library, and not as an Art Gallery, is unfortunately but ill suited to the display of paintings, etc., and it is therefore the desire of the Society to provide, as soon as possible, another building, offering the requisite exhibition facilities.—Annual meeting, in January.

NEW YORK TRADE SCHOOLS.—First Ave., 67th and 68th Sts.—These schools are not intended to be either a charitable or money-making institution. The charges for instruction are designed to cover the actual cost of the instruction given. Manual instruction is given by skilled mechanics, under the supervision of the manager of the schools. Each member of the classes is advanced as rapidly as thorough instruction will allow.—Classes : Plumbing (evening class, 3 evenings weekly ; Nov. to Apr., $3 per month, or $10 per course ; day class, commencing in Dec., $25 for the course) ; Brick Laying (Nov. to Apr., 3 evenings weekly; $3 per month, $12 for course); Face Brick (twice a week, 3 months, commencing in Dec., $12) ; Pattern Making for Moulders and Machinists (Nov. to Apr., 3 evenings weekly ; $3 per month, $10 for course) ; Plastering (Dec. to March, 3 evenings weekly ; $5 per month, $12 for course); Fresco Painting (Nov. to Apr., 3 evenings weekly ; $2.50 per month, $10 for course) ; Stone Cutting (Nov. to Apr., 3 evenings weekly ; $3 per month, $10 for course) ; Turning, Scroll Sawing and Wood Carving (Nov. to Apr., 3 evenings weekly; $3 per month, $10 for course).—The charges for instruction include the use of tools and materials. The workshops are open during the day for those who wish to practice, without extra charge.

NEW YORK TURNVEREIN.—Turnhalle, 64-68 East 4th St.—Officers : Pres., Max Zebe ; Chairm. of School Comm., Jacob Heintz ; Sec. of School Comm., Gustav Scholer, 235 Sixth Ave.—The School of the Turnverein was established in 1852, at first for gymnastic exercises only, to which reading and writing in German, singing, bookkeeping, drawing, modelling, and needlework were added later. The aim of the school is : 1. Thorough and harmonious development of the body by gymnastic exercises ; 2. The preservation of the German language and German customs ; 3. Technical and artistic education by means of free-hand drawing, geometrical drawing, perspective, and modelling in clay.—The sessions of the classes begin at four o'clock in the afternoon, and there is also a Sunday school. Most of the pupils are boys and girls who attend the public schools or young people already engaged in earning a living. The total number of pupils, in November, 1883, was 1,095, of whom 265 were girls. The pupils pay 50 cents a month for instruction in gymnastics, which is obligatory. All other subjects are elective, and are taught free. The school is supported by the small tuition fee charged, and by the interest on an invested fund of $9,000 (the Jacob Uhl fund) created by Mrs. Ottendorfer.—*The Drawing and Modelling Classes* are in charge of H. Metzner, 212 East 83d St. (who is also the Principal of the whole school), assisted by F. Eifler, R. Singer, and G. Gruenewald. There are 17 classes in Free-Hand Drawing (5 of these for girls and 2 for young men), and one each in Geometry, Perspective, and Modelling. Number of pupils in drawing, abt. 650 boys and 250 girls ; in modelling, 20, all grown up. The Classes in Needle-Work are attended by 220 girls. In the lower Drawing Classes, wall charts are used, prepared by the principal, and showing in the first stage straight and curved lines, angles, triangles, and squares, and thence progressing to simple geometrical forms, simple vessels, natural leaves, etc. These are succeeded by ornaments from the flat, and object drawing from geometrical models. In the higher classes, ornament drawing in advanced stages is continued, and figure drawing is added. The more talented pupils draw from casts. All the drawing is done in lead pencil or crayon. The school owns a collection of about 600 models and casts, including antique busts, reliefs, statues, etc., which were bought of the widow of the late sculptor Plassman.

PERMANENT EXHIBITIONS.—Permanent exhibitions are to be found at the galleries of the art dealers, of whom the following are among the most important :—*The American Art Gallery*, Kurtz Building, 6 E. 23d St., Madison Sq., James F. Sutton, Thos. E. Kirby, R. Austin Robertson, Proprietors. American Works of Art only ; admission to gallery, 25 cents ; open from 9 A.M. to 6 P.M., in winter also from 8½ to 10 P.M.—*S. P. Avery*, 86 Fifth Ave., near 14th St. Mostly foreign works of Art ; open free from 9 A.M. to 6 P.M. ; closed from end of July to beginning of Sept.—*Cottier & Co.*, 144 Fifth Ave. Principally decorative art work and furniture ; also paintings, etc., mostly foreign ; open free.—*L. D. Crist*, successor to *Adolph Kohn*, 166 Fifth Ave. Foreign paintings : open free.—*M. Knoedler & Co.* (Goupil & Co.), 170 Fifth Ave., corner 22d St. Foreign and American paintings, etc. ; admission to gallery, 25 cents.—*Wm. P. Moore*, 290 Fifth Ave. and 11 Pine St. Foreign and American paintings, decorative art objects, furniture, etc. ; open free.—*Gustav Reichard & Co.*, 226 Fifth Ave. Foreign and American paintings, etc. ; open free.—*William Schaus*, 749 Broadway. Foreign paintings, etc. ; open free.

SALMAGUNDI SKETCH CLUB.—Organized 1870 ; incorporated Feb. 23, 1880.—Officers for 1884-5 : Pres., Joseph Hartley, 301 W. 4th St. ; V. P., G. W. H. Ritchie, 109 Liberty St. ; Rec. Sec., W. H. Shelton, 1 Union Square ; Cor. Sec., F. M. Gregory, 19 University Pl. ; Treas., A. C. Morgan, 1074 Madison Ave.—Object : The encouragement of originality in its members, by the frequent submission of original sketches to mutual criticism ; and the advancement of the interests of art in black-and-white by public exhibitions.—Members : Active, artists, either professional or amateur ; candidates must submit an original work, which, on election, becomes the property of the Club ; entrance fee, $10 ; monthly dues, $1. Honorary, who need not be artists ; annual dues, $5. Present number of members, 40 active, 2 honorary.—Every active member is expected to furnish a sketch at each weekly meeting, illustrating a subject previously selected by majority vote. Whoever fails to do so, without good reason, at four successive meetings, may be dropped.—A yearly reception is given by the Club, to which gentlemen only are invited.—The Annual Black-and-White Exhibitions of the Club are held in December. The sixth took place at the American Art Gallery, Dec. 1-21, 1883. The by-laws provide that "the Art Jury [one of the standing committees] shall decide what works shall represent the Club, and what works shall be admitted to the exhibitions."—Annual meeting, first Friday in March.

SOCIETY OF AMERICAN ARTISTS.—Organized 1878.—Officers : Pres., A. H. Thayer, Cornwall-on-Hudson, N. Y. ; V. P., Walter Shirlaw, 51 W. 10th St. ; Sec., Edwin H. Blashfield, 58 W. 57th St. ; Treas., J. Carroll Beckwick, 58 W. 57th St.—Object : The advancement of the Fine Arts.—Members : Active only. Present number, 76, of whom 4 are ladies.—The principal public activity of the Society is the holding of exhibitions, the seventh of which will open at the National Academy of Design on May 26, 1884. The Society has taken action also in favor of the abolition of all duty upon works of art, and in 1883 circulated a petition to Congress advocating the passage of a bill embodying its views. A Selection Committee of six is elected each year. This Committee, in conjunction with the Hanging Committee of three, decides upon the admittance of works of art to the annual exhibition. The Hanging Committee, Selection Committee, and Board of Control, constitute together the Exhibition Committee.—The Society has been offered the use of the Grosvenor Gallery, London, for an exhibition of the works of its members, and it has voted to avail itself of the courtesy, in the months of Sept. and Oct., 1884.—Annual meeting, first Saturday in May.

SOCIETY OF AMERICAN EMBROIDERERS.—Officers : Pres., Mrs. T. M. Wheeler, 115 E. 23d St. ; Sec., Miss Caroline Townshend, 115 E. 23d St.—The exhibition of embroideries which formed part of the Pedestal Fund Loan Exhibition at the National Academy of Design, in Dec., 1883, was held under the auspices of this Society. It is not yet, however, fully organized, and the officers, for the present, are only acting officers.

SOCIETY OF AMERICAN WOOD-ENGRAVERS.—Organized Feb. 14, 1882.—

Officers: Treas., J. G. Smithwick, care Harper & Bros. ; Sec., Robert Hoskin, Cranford, N. J. No president; chairman elected at each meeting.—Object: The advancement of Art in Wood-Engraving.—Members: None but actual wood-engravers; but any member of five years' standing, who may relinquish engraving after that time, may remain in the Society. Assessments may be levied, or dues established, by a two-thirds vote of all the members. The by-laws require every member, upon election, to subscribe $25 toward the general fund, subject to the call of the Treasurer. Present number of members, 13.—The Society proposes to publish a portfolio of proofs from blocks specially engraved by the members for the purpose.—Annual meeting, first Thursday in December.

SOCIETY OF DECORATIVE ART.—28 E. 21st St.—Organized March, 1877 ; incorporated March, 1878.—Officers for 1884: Pres., Mrs. Wm. T. Blodgett, 11 E. 12th St.; V. P's, Mrs. H. G. De Forest, Miss Robbins, Mrs. Wm. F. Bridge, Mrs. B. F. Corlies ; Treas., Geo. C. Magoun, 10 E. 37th St ; Sec., Miss Catherine G. Van Rensselaer ; Asst. Sec., Miss M. E. Waller ; Supt. and Bookkeeper, Miss K. Stewart.—Objects : The reception, exhibition, and sale of artistic and decorative work ; the promotion of decorative art, and instruction in artistic and decorative work and industries.—The membership of the Society consists of Voting, Associate, and Honorary Members. The Voting Members, who alone have the right to vote, and whose number is limited to 30, consist of the original incorporators, and such others as may be elected by the Board of Managers. Any person may become an Associate Member by an annual payment of $5. Besides the members, there are also " Annual Subscribers," who are accorded the privilege, in proportion to the amount of their subscription of nominating a pupil or pupils to the free classes, and of designating needy women to be helped through the " Workers' Aid Committee " (see below). According to last published report, there were, on Dec. 31, 1882, 409 such subscribers.—The activity of the Society consists in the maintenance of classes, of a lending library, and of sales and work rooms for the taking and execution of orders and the sale of articles sent by " contributors" (i.e., needle-women, artists, etc., all over the country) ; the holding of sales at well-known summer resorts ; the arrangement of competitions and exhibitions, etc.—*Classes :* Artistic embroidery (pay class, $5 for 6 lessons ; free class for professional students, nominated by subscribers) ; Painting on China : Underglaze, teacher, Miss M. V. Meade ; Limoge, Mr. Chas. Volkmar (mostly paid pupils, $2 a lesson) ; Water color, decorative work only, teacher, Miss M. V. Meade (paying pupils only, individual lessons, $1.50 ; in classes of not over six, $1 per lesson) ; Object drawing in charcoal and pencil for children and young people : Teacher, Miss Amanda Brewster ($8 for 12 lessons of 1½ hours each). Classes are also held during July, August, and September at various summer resorts. Of free pupils there were 135 in 1883, and the more competent graduates have found instant and remunerative employment.—According to the forthcoming annual report for 1883, a distinct and successful branch of the work during the past year has been the establishing of free classes of instruction, in plain and fine sewing, free-hand drawing, and modelling in clay, among the poor children and mission schools of the city, including the Boys' Club, at the Wilson Mission, 125 St. Mark's Place; Trinity Mission, 30 State St.; The Sheltering Arms, 129th St. and 10th Ave.; St. Barnabas House, 304 Mulberry St., and others. The object of these classes is not to make artists, but to train hand and eye, and to quicken the observation and perception, so that the pupils may become good artisans and useful working girls. The children taught are from 9 to 15 years of age. As soon as possible free classes will be formed in wood carving, hammered brass, mosaic, and other work, and the society earnestly asks the support and encouragement of the public, as upon its support must depend the development of the work undertaken.—*The Lending Library* is used as a means of instructing distant workers, to whom books, patterns, designs, etc., are sent by mail—an advantage which is highly appreciated by them. The report for 1882 acknowledged a gift of $150 for the Library, and expressed the hope that it might prove a suggestion to others.—*The Sales-Rooms and Work-Rooms* are reported to have been prosperously active during the year (1883). The articles offered for sale by 3,349 contributors or outside workers in 1883 numbered 6,249, and of these 3,606 were accepted, the rest declined. Contributors whose articles are rejected may, by request, receive special criticism and advice. A commission of 10 per cent. is charged on the sales of contributed articles. The payments made to contributors during the year 1883, for work sold for them on commission, amounted to $16,515.88. During the six years of its existence the society has paid altogether to contributors and in salaries and daily wages, $191,509.56. The orders received by the society in 1883, numbered 3,661 for stamping and prepared work, and 350 orders for finished work, including an order for the furnishing and decoration of an entire house in Newport.—*The Workers' Aid Committee* furnishes materials and designs, and stamps and prepares work, which, under certain conditions, is sent to women in any part of the United States. This work, when finished, is returned to the Society for sale, and, when sold, the proceeds are sent to the person who executed it, less the bare cost of the materials.—*Competitions and Exhibitions.* The last exhibition held by the Society, in May, 1881, was one of Competitive Prize Designs, in connection with a Loan Exhibition, at which $1,300 were distributed in prizes.—This Society was the first to conceive the idea of combining education in decorative art with honorable aid to struggling and deserving women, and is the parent society of the various associations of like title now existing in the U. S. and Canada. At the same time the Society has had a considerable share in the development of the minor arts, and the general refinement of taste in the United States. All its operations are carried on in the interest of its pupils, workers, and contributors. Its income is mainly derived from membership dues and annual subscriptions, tuition fees, profits on materials sold and orders executed, and commissions on sales. "The success of the work thus far," says the forthcoming report of the President, for 1883, thus repeating the words of a former report, "has been almost entirely due to the personal efforts of the working members of the Society, some of whom, since its foundation, have given daily to its advancement much time, thought and active labor. It has had no large donations, no legacies, no capital, nothing but the determination to succeed in the work of educating women in marketable art industries which inspired its organization a little more than six years ago."—The Society solicits orders for interior household decoration, and feels that it may be of especial use to people distant from large centres, in giving suggestions and aid in decorating and furnishing houses, etc.—Annual meeting, last Tuesday in January.

TECHNICAL ART SCHOOLS OF THE METROPOLITAN MUSEUM OF ART.

—214 E. 34th St.—Officers: Museum Comm. on Art Schools and Industrial Art: Robt. Hoe, Jr., 11 E. 36th St.; Wm. L. Andrews, 16 E. 38th St.; D. O. Mills; J. T. Johnson, 8 Fifth Ave.—These schools have lately been reorganized, with Mr. Jno. Ward Stimson as General Manager. The following extract, from the circular of the schools, explains their aim : "The necessity for these Industrial Art Schools has become more and more apparent to the trustees of the Metropolitan Museum. For many years our artisans and mechanics have shown great lack of artistic taste and knowledge, and were practically destitute of originality in design. As a natural consequence, bad forms, improper treatment and handling of material, false construction and tasteless decoration, are found in most of our industrial work. Yet it is as easy to make a tasteful as a tasteless work, if those who originate and execute are made familiar with forms of beauty, and taught the principles of color and design, adaptation and construction. The trustees are satisfied from general observation and from experience in particular cases, that there is ample dormant talent among the working youths of this city, which, if encouraged and developed, would furnish to New York a noble class of mechanics and artificers. Foreign talent is not essentially superior to American. In European capitals, like London, Paris, and other cities, the opportunities for development, through Industrial Schools which receive national encouragement, bring out and educate the talent that otherwise might have remained unknown, thus raising the standard of taste in their communities and becoming the means of enriching their nation and manufacturers as well as securing superior wages to workmen who obtain these advantages. Experience showing that it is possible to secure a more thorough and advanced education at the School than at the shop where there is frequently small time for instruction in theory or detail. It is therefore proposed to furnish facilities not hitherto attainable in this country to Artists and Artisans ; to provide thorough technical instruction in Painting, Decoration, Designing, Modelling, Carving, Free-hand, Architectural, Instrumental and Perspective Drawing ; also in Carriage Drafting and Construction as a specialty, and to furnish an acquaintance with the Theory and Practice of the Arts."—Classes and Teachers : Color, Composition and Decoration, Jno. Ward Stimson (twice a week, 1–4 P.M., $10 the season) ; Free-Hand Drawing, from Life and Antique, Jno. Ward Stimson (3 times a week, 1–4 P.M., $10) ; Sculpture and Modelling, A. Locher (evening class, 3 times a week, 7.30–10 P.M., $10 ; Day Class, 3 times a week, 9–12 A.M., $10) ; Architectural, Instrumental, and Furniture Designing, Ernest Gilles (3 times a week, 7.30–10 P.M., $10); Perspective, Anatomy, and Drawing from Flat, Frost Johnson (twice a week, 7.30–10 P.M., $5) ; Mechanical Drawing, E. Volz (3 times a week, 7.30–10 P.M., $5); Carriage Drafting and Construction, J. D. Gribbon (3 times a week, 7.30–10 P.M., $5). The class last mentioned is under the auspices of the Carriage Builders' Association. A new feature in it is the introduction of the Chatauqua Correspondence System of Instruction, for the convenience of young men residing elsewhere than in New York. A course of Lectures on the Philosophy, History, and Development of Art is given in January and February. Full school course, from October to May.—Special privileges are accorded to the pupils of these schools. They are admitted free to the illustrated lectures, to the School Library, and to the opportunities of the Metropolitan Museum for study and consultation. The fees charged are only intended to cover the cost of materials used. The school has an endowment fund of $50,000. and receives $1,200 a year from the Carriage Builders' Association. "It is known to members," says the last published (13th) report, of the Metropolitan Museum "that the endowment fund of $50,000 does not furnish a sufficient income for the maintenance of the schools, which make necessarily a large annual draft on our Treasury. The total expense of the year [1882] has been $8,841.76. Trustees have themselves contributed $2,550 toward the estimated wants of the school for the present season."— Number of students at the close of the year 1883, about 100. There are accommodations for 800 to 1,000.

TILE CLUB.—58½ W. 10th St.—Organized fall of 1877.—This Club is a rather informal association of artists, musicians, etc., without constitution or by-laws and even without officers. The Club meets every Wednesday evening during the winter season, when part of the evening is devoted to the decoration of tiles, plaques, etc. The members act as hosts in turn, the host of the evening providing the tiles and materials, as well as the plain fare which the traditions of the Club allow, receiving in return the artistic product of the evening's labors. The Tile Club has been made famous by the articles descriptive of its summer excursions, written and illustrated by members, which have appeared in "Scribner's Monthly," and by "Harper's Christmas Pictures and Papers, done by the Tile Club and its Literary Friends," published in 1882. [No reply to repeated requests for later information.]

UNION LEAGUE CLUB.—No. 1 E. 39th St.—Pres., Wm. M. Evarts ; Treas., Geo. F. Baker ; Sec., David Milliken, Jr.; Ch'man Com. on Art, C. B. Custer.—At the monthly meetings, held from October to April or May, pictures are sent in by the members or by artists, and ladies are admitted to see them, on tickets supplied by members, on the two days following each meeting. The club has a collection of about seventy paintings, comprising many portraits of former members, and men eminent in war, statesmanship and literature. Receptions are occasionally given to which guests are admitted on invitation.

YOUNG MEN'S CHRISTIAN ASSOCIATION.—52 E. 23d St., cor. 4th Ave.— Officers for 1884-5 : Pres., Wm. W. Hoppin, Jr.; V. P., Cornelius Vanderbilt ; Secretaries, R. R. McBurney and Jas. McConaughy; Rec. Sec., Henry C. Vedder; Treas., Fredk. A. Marquand; Libr., Reuben B. Poole.—The association owns and is the depository of a number of paintings, which have been distributed throughout the various rooms, but are accessible to all visitors. Prominent among them are, the series of the three large allegorical landscapes, "The Cross and World," by Thos. Cole; a mountain gorge with a waterfall, by Kensett, a very good specimen ; "Peace and Plenty," an immense landscape by Geo. Inness, dated 1865 ; Rossiter's portrait group, "American Merchants"; and three pictures by Federigo Nerly (Friedrich Nehrlich), a German artist.—The Library (over 30,300 vols.), for reference only, contains a very good and quite extensive collection of books on the various branches of art, with a preponderance of architecture and the decorative arts; illustrated works on the great European galleries ; illustrated art journals, etc. It possesses also the nearest approach to a *Collection of Prints* to be found in any public institution of the city of New York, including a collection of 8,000 engraved portraits, many of them by celebrated engravers and in good impressions, arranged in 35 folio volumes begun by John Percival, Earl of Egmont, and completed by John T. Graves, purchased for $1,600 ; a collection of imitations of drawings in aqua tint, etc., such as were so popular in the last century ; several volumes with old Dutch etchings, etc.—Lectures are delivered on a variety of subjects during the winter. The course for the winter of 1883-4, included three lectures on Greek Sculpture, by Prof. J. M. Hoppin, of Yale. —The rooms of the Association, as well as the Library, are open week days, including holidays, from 8 A.M. to 10 P.M. ; Sundays from 1½ to 10 P.M. Admission free.—Annual meeting in January.

9

64. Northampton, Mass.

SMITH COLLEGE.—Founded by Miss Sophia Smith, of Hatfield, Mass., who bequeathed for that purpose property amounting now to over $500,000.—Officers: Pres. of B'd of Trustees and of Fac., Rev. L. Clark Seelye, D.D.; Treas. Hon. Geo. W. Hubbard.—Object: To furnish to young women means and facilities for education equal to those afforded in colleges to young men. The College is not intended to fit woman for a particular sphere or profession, but to perfect her intellect by those methods which philosophy and experience have approved, so that she may be better qualified to enjoy and do well her work in life, whatever that work may be. It is to be a Woman's College, aiming not only to give the broadest and highest intellectual culture, but also to preserve and perfect every characteristic of a complete womanhood.—No preparatory department is connected with the institution. The standard of admission and the standard of instruction are in accordance with its legitimate collegiate work.—The study of art in any form is not obligatory in the College, but this study has been made as truly a part of the collegiate course as the other electives with which it is associated, and the students are admitted gratuitously to the Hillyer Art Gallery and to all lectures in the *School of Art*, which forms a separate department. The aim of this School is to furnish practical and theoretical instruction in the principles of the arts of design—drawing, painting, and sculpture, including the elements of the architectural styles and decoration. Its privileges are accorded to all regular students who may elect to use them. Special students are also admitted. The regular course of study covers four years, and diplomas are awarded to students who complete the course. The study of art through drawing is continued until the student has attained sufficient power to justify her in taking up the special studies which she may choose. Such special studies are Painting in Oil or Water Color, Sculpture, Architecture, Decoration and Etching. Teacher: John H. Niemeyer, M.A., of the Yale Art School.—Terms: One lesson a week, $30 a year; $20 a half-year. To special students, $40 and $25.—Number of students, January, 1884, 28, of whom 18 were special.—*The Hillyer Art Gallery.*—The collections owned by the College embrace several hundred autotypes, illustrating the history of painting in chronological sequence; a very complete collection of casts from the antique, from architectural details, etc.; and a collection of original oil paintings, embracing the works of the most distinguished American painters. Through the generosity of the late Mr. Winthrop Hillyer an Art Gallery has been erected, 180 by 50 feet, designed exclusively for the collections and for studios. The building has been constructed with special reference to the exhibition of works of art, great pains having been taken to avoid cross lights. The lower floor, devoted to sculpture and studios, is 18 ft. high, with the exception of a long corridor, which is 20 ft. high. In the upper story there are galleries for oil paintings (26 ft. high, and 25 by 54 ft. in dimension) and for the exhibition of architectural specimens. These are surrounded by a corridor 12 ft. wide arranged for the exhibition of smaller pictures, and to give opportunity for a free circulation of air through the entire building. Mr. Hillyer also endowed the Gallery with a fund of $50,000.

65. Norwalk, O.

FIRELANDS HISTORICAL SOCIETY.—Cabinet of Indian and other relics. [No reply to repeated requests for further information.]

66. Norwich, Conn.

NORWICH FREE ACADEMY.—Incorp. May 5, 1854.—Principal, W. Hutchison.—The Academy prepares for college, scientific schools and business. An *Art Department* was added in October, 1883. The aim of instruction is improvement of taste and skill in execution. Present number of pupils (both sexes taught together), 15. Tuition fees, $20 for 12 weeks for painting, $15 for charcoal. Instructor, Prof. J. Wells Champney.

67. Peoria, Ill.

LADIES' ART SOCIETY.—[No reply to repeated requests for information. The following is taken from the report made at the meeting of the Central Illinois Art Union (to which the

society belongs) on May 16, 1883. Officers: Pres., Mrs. E. W. Edwards ; V. P., Mrs. Mary Mc-
Clure; Sec., Miss A. M. Dodge; Treas., Mrs. A. Blair; Cor. Sec., Miss F. M. Blanchard.—
Members, 30 active, 7 honorary.—*The Art Classes*, which meet weekly, with a lesson each session,
occupy three rooms. Six additional cases were bought during the year for the use of the drawing
class. The lives and masterpieces of the artists from Fillipino Lippi to Salvator Rosa in the Italian,
and from Van Eyck to Teniers in the Dutch school, were made the subject of study during the year,
in the history of art.—*A Woman's Exchange* was opened under the auspices of the society in Oct.,
1882, and has met with satisfactory results, although it is but in its infancy and will require the
aid of subscribers, patrons, and chiefly consignors, to enable it to extend its sphere.—A Loan Exhibition was in contemplation for June, 1883.]

68. Philadelphia, Pa.

ACADEMY ART CLUB.—1104 Walnut St.—Organized March, 1883. — Officers: Pres.,
Geo. F. Stephens, 1338 Chestnut St. ; V. P., Miss S. H. Macdowel, 2018 Race St. ; Treas., D. W.
Jordan, 1020 Chestnut St. ; Sec., C. Few Seiss, 1328 Spring Garden St.,— Objects: The promotion
of artistic work, and the common artistic interests of its members. — Active members are elected
from students of the Pennsylvania Academy only.— Present number, 50 resident, 1 non-resident, 1
honorary. — The Club meets every Tuesday evening during Academy season.

ACADEMY OF NATURAL SCIENCES.— S. W. cor. 19th and Race Sts. Organized
March 21, 1812 ; chartered March 24, 1817. — Officers : Pres., Jos. Leidy, M.D., 1302 Filbert St. ;
V. Ps., Thos. Meehan, Germantown, and Rev. H. C. McCook, D.D., 125 N. 21st St. ; Rec. Sec.
and Libr., Edw. J. Nolan, M.D., 830 N. 20th St. ; Cor. Sec., Geo. H. Horn, M.D., 874 N. 4th
St. ; Treas., Wm. C. Henszey. — The *Museum* of the Academy is mainly filled with specimens illustrating zoölogy, botany, mineralogy, etc., although anthropology, including archæology, ethnography, and ethnology, is also within its province. The archæological and ethnographic collections
are as yet limited, but are constantly increasing by gifts. The following are the more important
components of these collections as at present constituted : The Peale collection of stone implements,
made by Franklin Peale, one of the sons of Chas. Willson Peale ; Prof. S. S. Haldeman's collection
of stone implements, pottery, etc. ; a small collection of Egyptian and Greek antiquities ; the Poin-
sett Collection of Mexican antiquities, mainly pottery and small sculptures ; a collection of Peruvian
pottery, and some specimens of Nicaragua pottery presented by Dr. J. F. Bransford. The latest addition of special importance is the fine collection of antiquities which came into possession of the
Academy by bequest of the late Wm. P. Vaux. The specimens number (counting arrow heads and
small implements by trays) 2445, and are arranged in groups according to locality. They consist of
stone axes, hatchets, celts, hammers, pestles, balls, shovels, hoes, arrows, spear and lance heads, dis-
coidal and chunker stones, ceremonial implements, copper and bronze axes, mound pottery, and
several pieces of Mexican, Peruvian, Costa Rican, Roman and Carthaginian antiquities. — The
Library, which is quite extensive, includes a valuable collection of works on Roman, Greek and
French antiquities, among which is a complete set of Piranesi. A series of portraits of presidents
and benefactors of the Academy is hung in the Library. — Open daily, except Sundays and holidays,
from 9 till sunset. Admission to Museum, 10 cents ; students admitted free on application to the
secretary, Dr. E. J. Nolan, or to the curator in charge, Prof. Angelo Heilprin. The archæological
collections are not in the main museum, but can be seen on application to the officer in charge.
The Vaux Collection, by the terms of the bequest, is kept separate from the main archæological department, and is arranged in five upright and five horizontal cases, in one of a suite of rooms devoted
to the exhibition of a superb collection of minerals received from the same source.—Mr. Jacob Bin-
der is the special curator of these collections.—None of the archæological collections are included
in the " Guide to the Museum " (published in 1876), for sale at the door.

ARTISTS' FUND SOCIETY OF PHILADELPHIA. — Incorporated April 29,
1835.—Officers: Pres., I. L. Williams, 1334 Chestnut St. ; V. P., Geo. C. Lambdin, 1520 Chestnut
St. ; Sec., F. DeB. Richards, 1520 Chestnut St. ; Treas., Samuel Sartain, 210 Franklin St.—Objects:
The relief of such artists or their families as may be, by the by-laws, entitled to pecuniary assistance,
and such modes of promoting the cultivation of skill, the diffusion of taste and the encouragement

of living professional talent in the arts of painting, sculpture, architecture, and engraving, as may best conduce to the primary purpose of benevolence.—There are four classes of members (both sexes): Members of the Board of Control (initiation fee $50, in cash or in a work of art; annual dues, $3), professional artists who have resided in or near Philadelphia for one year; Associates, gentlemen and ladies residing in Philadelphia or vicinity, who shall pay an annual contribution; Life Members, who pay $100 on election; Honorary Members, distinguished non-resident artists.—All the powers of the body are vested in the Board of Control. — The society has two funds, the Benevolent Fund and the Trust Fund. The former is sustained by dues, sales of works of art contributed by members and others, interest on investments and donations. Appropriations may be made from this fund for the relief of sick and disabled members, and the heirs of deceased members are paid a certain percentage out of it. The Trust Fund consists of voluntary contributions which are placed to the credit of the member contributing. The interest derived from this fund goes to the Benevolent Fund, but the principal is paid over to the heirs of the contributor on his or her death.—In its earlier years, under the presidency of John Neagle, this society included a large majority of the resident artists among its members, and up to the year 1845 furnished, with some few exceptions, all the annual exhibitions opened in Philadelphia. Its last annual exhibition in 1845 was held in conjunction with the Penn. Academy of Fine Arts, the Society having, in the year 1840, made an arrangement with that institution, by which they had erected a separate exhibition gallery in front of the building of the Academy. After the fire in the Academy in 1846, the Society led a very quiet life until 1864, when occasional receptions and exhibitions were gotten up. In the year 1866 the suite of galleries on the second floor of 1334 Chestnut St. was leased, free exhibitions were arranged, and a series of sales held, the amount realized over $100 on each work sold going to the contributor. The venture was not successful, however, and at the end of its three years' lease, the Society found that the proceeds of the annual sales and the money received from annual contributors (of whom there were then about 100, at $10 each) had been swallowed up by the expenses. Since then all exhibitions have been abandoned, and under its present by-laws, as remodelled in 1877, the society has taken a fresh start, with a good outlook for the future in its social and benevolent features.—Annual meeting, last Wednesday in March.

FAIRMOUNT PARK ART ASSOCIATION.—524 Walnut St., room 18.—Incorporated Feb. 2, 1872.—Officers: Pres., A. J. Drexel, S. E. cor. of 39th and Walnut Sts.; V. P., Chas. H. Rogers, York Road; Treas., Jas. L. Claghorn, 222 N. 19th St.; Sec., John Belangee Cox, 524 Walnut St.—Objects: To embellish Fairmount Park with fountains, statues, busts, and similar ornaments, such as good taste shall dictate, and the Commissioners of the Park sanction.—Members (both sexes): Annual, $1 initiation fee and $5 p. a.; Life, $1, and one payment of $50; Honorary. Present number: Honorary, 7; Life, 185; Annual, 710.—The income is derived from membership dues and donations. Funds in hand according to the last printed report: General Fund (applicable to purchase of works of art), $7,224.11; Permanent Fund, $13,715.34; Meade Memorial Fund, $30,877.06; Garfield Memorial Fund, $13,457.71.—The Association has thus far presented 17 works of art to the Park, and has voted to contribute $5,000 to the Meade Memorial Fund, of which it is the Trustee. It has also created a fund for the erection of a Garfield monument in Fairmount Park.—During its existence of eleven years, the association has expended for works of art, fountains, etc., $28,348.25. It has just given (close of 1883) commissions amounting to $15,000.—Annual meeting, second Thursday in November.

FRANKLIN INSTITUTE OF THE STATE OF PENNSYLVANIA FOR THE PROMOTION OF THE MECHANIC ARTS.—No. 15 South Seventh St.—Officers: Pres., W. P. Tatham, 1420 Walnut St.; Sec., Wm. H. Wahl, 1436 N. 13th St.; D. S. Holman, Actuary.—*Drawing School of the Institute.* Aims and Methods: The main feature of the School has been the teaching of such drawing as would be useful in the workshop and applicable to construction as well as to ornamentation, and thus a large part of the instruction has been devoted to the geometrical principles of drawing, but the demonstration and application of these principles have always been made to conform with the practice of the best engineers and architects, while proper manipulation and correct technicalities have been rigidly enforced, so that the student would learn how to properly use his hands and his instruments; how to give clearness and beauty to his work, and at the same time obtain a knowledge of geometrical forms and their projections, intersections

and developments, and finally learn to make working drawings of machine or architectural con-
structions. In this course, the use of copies has been almost entirely avoided, the student being
required to make his drawings accurately to scale, either from free-hand sketches, or from the drawing on the blackboard by the preceptor, who spends part of his time there and part with the student
in giving individual instruction and criticism. Importance is attached to the free-hand sketches of
the student, and the value of this accomplishment is always kept in view. The class of exclusively
free-hand drawing begins by copying from the flat, and gradually advances to drawing from casts.—
Classes and Teachers, etc.: Junior Classes, teachers, Geo. S. Willits and E. E. Claussen ; Intermediate Class, Carl Barth; Senior Mechanical Class, Wm. H. Thorne, Principal; Architectural Class
and Free-Hand Class, Edw. S. Paxson. Two terms of 16 weeks each ; Winter from Oct. to Jan.;
Spring from Jan. to May. The next Winter term begins Oct. 2, 1884. Hours of attendance, Tuesday and Thursday evenings from 7¼ to 9½ P.M. The full course extends over two years, but special
subjects may be selected by sufficiently advanced pupils. Students are required to do home work.—
Pupils : Winter Term, 1882-3, 210 ; Spring Term, 1883, 194.—Tuition Fee, $5 per term of 16
weeks. Pupils must provide their own apparatus and materials. Twelve free scholarships, from
the B. H. Bartol Fund, are awarded each year to pupils who have successfully completed their first
term. Students also have the free use of the library of the Institute.—Certificates are given to those
who have completed the full course of two years.—This Drawing School has been in operation for
more than half a century, and the Institute is now so crowded for room that a subscription has been
set on foot for a building fund of $200,000.—For tickets to the School and further information apply
to D. S. Holman, Actuary, at the rooms of the Institute.

HISTORICAL SOCIETY OF PENNSYLVANIA.—1300 Locust St.—Organized,

Dec. 2, 1824. Incorp. June 2, 1826.—Pres., John Williams Wallace ; V. P.'s, John Jordan, Jr.,
Horatio Gates Jones, Geo. de B. Keim, Aubrey H. Smith, William M. Darlington, Craig Biddle ;
Sec., Wm. Brooke Rawle ; Cor. Sec., Gregory B. Keen ; Treas., J. Edward Carpenter ; Lib., F. D.
Stone.—Objects : The collection of material for the elucidation of the history of Pennsylvania in
particular, and of America in general.—Life membership, $50 ; annual members, $5.—The Society
publishes " Memoirs " and the " Pennsylvania Magazine of History and Biography."—*Collections :*
Portraits, paintings, and engravings of historical interest, Indian and other antiquities. Free to
the public. A catalogue was published in 1872.—Annual meeting, second Monday in May.

INDEPENDENCE HALL AND NATIONAL MUSEUM.—Old State House, Chest-

nut, bet. 5th and 6th Sts.—In the Old State House of Pennsylvania, the Second Continental Congress, sitting in the east room on the first floor, adopted the Declaration of Independence on July 4,
1776. This room, since known as *Independence Hall*, was restored to its original state as far as possible about ten years ago, and upon its walls was placed a collection of portraits, all of them absolutely authenticated, of the men who signed, voted upon, or debated the Declaration in this very
chamber. A large number of these portraits are originals by Chas. Willson Peale, which formerly
belonged to his Museum, others are copies after Copley, Trumbull, Stuart, etc. A descriptive catalogue, price 25 cents, is for sale at the Hall.—The western room, on the same floor, formerly the
Judicial Hall of the Colony of Pennsylvania, is occupied by the *National Museum*. Besides many
relics of great interest and value, illustrative of the history of Pennsylvania, this Museum contains
also a number of paintings, among them " Penn's Treaty with the Indians" and a portrait of Chief
Justice Allen, both by Benj. West, and quite a large number of crayons by Sharpless, including portraits of Mr. and Mrs. Washington, John Adams, Jefferson, Madison, and other personages of distinction. There is no catalogue of this Museum.—Open free, all the year round except Sundays,
from 8¼ A.M. to 5 P.M.—The statue of Washington in front of the building is by J. A. Bailly.

LADIES' DECORATIVE ART CLUB.—1512 Pine St.—Organized Dec., 1881.—

Officers : Pres., Chas. G. Leland ; Sec., Mrs. James Mifflin ; Treas., Miss Elizabeth Robins.—The
great aim of this Club is to have its members taught something serious in the way of Design and Art,
a little deeper than the present fashion of making something merely pretty. All facilities and help
will be given for the production of objects of art for purposes of sale or otherwise, and opportunity
given to those who wish systematic study, with a view to making art a profession.—Membership limited to 150 (the Club is full); terms, $30, which entitles members to one lesson a week in each

department of the school maintained by the Club.—Classes and Teachers : Preliminary Drawing, Designing in Monochrome, and several Minor arts, Chas. G. Leland ; Painting from Still-Life, Casts, Flowers, Living Models in Costume, etc., J. Liberty Tadd ; Modelling from Still-Life, Fruit, Flowers, the Living Model, etc., J. Liberty Tadd ; Different Styles of Pottery, Limoges, High or Low Relief, Underglaze Painting, etc., J. Liberty Tadd ; China Overglaze Painting, Miss B. S. Paul ; Wood Carving, H. Uhle ; Repoussée Brass, J. Liberty Tadd.   Term from Oct. 15 to June 1.—The Club occupies an entire house devoted to the different classes, a salesroom for the work of members, library, etc.   Lectures and exhibitions are also to be provided.

NUMISMATIC AND ANTIQUARIAN SOCIETY.—S. W. cor. 18th and Chestnut

Sts.—Instituted Jan. 1, 1858, as the Numismatic Society of Philadelphia ; present name adopted in 1865.—Officers for 1884 : Pres., Eli K. Price, LL.D., 709 Walnut St.; V. P.'s, Daniel G. Brinton, M.D., Wm. P. Chandler, Edwin W. Lehman, Lewis A. Scott ; Cor. Sec. and Treas., Henry Philips, Jr., 320 S. 11th St.; Rec. Sec., R. Stewart Culin ; Historiog., Chas. Henry Hart ; Curator of Numismatics, Robt. Coulton Davis, Vine, cor. N. 16th St.; Curator of Antiqu., Edwin Atlee Barber ; Libr., Thos. Hockley, 603 Walnut St.—Object : To encourage and promote numismatic science and antiquarian research.—Members : Resident (initiation fee, $5, diploma fee, $1, annual dues, $5, or $50 in commutation of all fees); Corresponding ; Honorary.—Besides a Library, the Society has also a cabinet of coins and medals, Grecian, Mexican, and other American antiquities, pottery, engravings, etc., which is open to members only.   The bulk of the coins and medals, however, have been placed on exhibition at the Pennsylvania Museum of Industrial Art, Memorial Hall, Fairmount Park, together with similar collections belonging to the Library Company of Philadelphia, and the American Philosophical Society.   For some description of these collections see Henry Phillips, Jr., " Notes upon the Collection of Coins and Medals," etc., Phil., 1879 (reprinted from the Proceedings of the American Philosophical Society), and " Additional Notes upon the Collection of Coins and Medals," etc. (read before the American Philosophical Society, Oct. 3, 1879) which can be obtained at Memorial Hall.—The Society publishes yearly reports of its proceedings.   According to the last of these reports, the accessions to the collections of coins and antiquities during the year 1883 numbered 674.   The Numismatic and Antiquarian Society of Philadelphia is the oldest of its kind in the U. S.—Annual meeting, first Thursday in January.

PENNSYLVANIA ACADEMY OF THE FINE ARTS.—N. Broad, cor. Cherry St.

—Organized Dec., 1805 ; incorporated March 28, 1806.—Officers : Pres., James L. Claghorn, 222 N. 19th St.; Treas., Edward H. Coates, 116 Chestnut St.; Sec., Geo. Corliss ; Chairm. of Comm. on Instruction, Edward H. Coates ; Curator of the School and Libr., H. C. Whipple.—Objects : To promote the knowledge and enjoyment of, and cultivation in, the Fine Arts in the city of Philadelphia, by the establishment of schools and other methods of instruction ; by books and other publications ; by the establishment of a gallery, or galleries, of paintings or sculpture ; and by such other methods as in their judgments may seem proper.—Membership is confined to the stockholders, at present over 1,100, who elect the President and a Board of Directors.   Liberal patrons of the Academy and distinguished friends of art may be elected Honorary Members by the Board ; distinguished artists may be elected Professional Honorary Members in the same way.   Present number of Honorary Members, 96.—The funds with which the Academy has been established were raised entirely by subscription.   Its capital is limited to 10,000 shares at $100 each, and of these 4,382, representing a value of $438,200, have been subscribed and paid for.   The income is limited to admission and tuition fees, and donations.   The Academy has also the following invested funds, given for specified purposes : Temple Trust Fund, $60,000, half the interest to be used for purchases at the exhibition of the Academy, the other half for general expenses ; Phillips Bequest, $12,000, for the maintenance of the Phillips Collection ; Charles Toppan Prize Fund, $8,000, for school prizes (see below) ; and Mary Smith Prize Fund, $2,000, for a prize of $100 to be given to the best painting by a resident Philadelphia lady artist at the yearly exhibition.—*Exhibitions.*   Two or more exhibitions are held every year.   The regular Annual Exhibition is held in autumn.   At the exhibition of last autumn (1883) 10 works, valued at $3,815, were sold, out of 518 works exhibited by 315 artists.   For prizes awarded at this exhibition see pp. 16 and 17, in the paragraph on " Prizes and Competitions."—*Collections.*   The edition of the Catalogue of the Permanent Collection of the Academy, for 1881, enumerated 259 paintings and 60 pieces of sculpture (not including the casts used in the schools), acquired mostly by donation and bequest ; the catalogue for 1883 shows an increase of these numbers to 273 and 113 respectively. Some of the pictures bear the names of old masters, and among the later acquisitions there are a number of large canvases by well-known European artists, such as Wittkamp, Janssen, Bouguereau, Kaulbach, Hermans, etc. The interest centres, however, upon the paintings by American artists, in which the collection is very rich, standing, in this respect, next to that of the N. Y. Historical Society, and rather surpassing it in variety of subject. Among the artists represented may be named : Stuart, Trumbull, Sully, West (" Death on the Pale Horse," " Paul and Barnabas," "Christ Rejected "), Allston (" Dead Man Restored to Life "), the Peales, Vanderlyn (" Ariadne "), Leslie, Neagle, Shaw, Doughty, Mount, Inman, Rothermel, Schüssele, Leutze, May, Gray, Huntington, etc. Generous patrons have lately begun to increase the collection by works of American artists of the younger generation bought at the exhibitions held at the Academy. In this way have been acquired the paintings by Robert Wylie, Picknell, R. Koehler, presented by Mr. Jos. E. Temple, and Dana, presented by Mr. Atherton Blight. The sculptures also include many works by earlier American artists, such as Rush, Frazee, Clevenger, etc. The latest additions to the Temple Collection, presented by Mr. Temple in 1882 and 1883, comprise 7 pictures by de Pratere, Charles Hermans, Alex. Struys, Alex. Thomas (these four Belgian artists), Burr H. Nichols F. A. Bridgman, and Milne Ramsey. Pictures by Geo. Cole, W. T. Trego (of Philadelphia), and Carolus Duran, were presented respectively by Messrs. Thos. Mellor, Fairm. Rogers, and P. Haldeman. By bequest of the late Henry Seybert, the Academy is to receive, also, $2,000 and such a selection from his paintings, engravings, books, etc., as his executors may choose.—*The Phillips Collection of Engravings*, left to the Academy by its former owner, with the fund alluded to above, contains about 60,000 impressions, and is the largest public collection of its kind in the U. S. —Besides these collections there is a *Library* of works on art of about 1,000 volumes.—Open every week day throughout the year, from 9 A.M. to 6 P.M.; admission 25 cents. Sundays, open free, from 1 to 6 P.M., on tickets obtainable at the Academy during the week. Strangers from out of town are admitted without tickets. Catalogues, 10 cents.—*Schools of the Academy.* Aims: The Academy does not undertake to furnish detailed instruction, but rather facilities for study, supplemented by the occasional criticism of the teachers ; and the classes are intended especially for those who expect to be professional artists.—Instructors : Director, Thomas Eakins ; Asst. Prof. of Painting and Drawing, Thomas Anshutz ; Prof. of Artistic Anatomy, W. W. Keen, M.D. ; Demonstrator of Anatomy, Fred. R. Wagner.—The Course of Study is believed to be more thorough than that of any other existing school. Its basis is the nude human figure. In the anatomical department, the advanced students dissect. Animals are also dissected from time to time, and living horses and other domestic animals are used as models in the modelling room. Classes : Men's Life (day and evening) ; Women's Life (day and evening) ; Antique (day and evening) ; Portrait ; Sketch ; Lectures on Art Anatomy; Dissecting Room Study. Lectures are also given on Perspective and Composition. School Year from first Monday in October to last Saturday in May.—Any person of good character, of either sex, and over fifteen years of age, will be admitted as a student. Number of students in actual attendance Dec., 1883, 128 (70 men, 58 women).—Tuition fees : Full season, all privileges, $48 ; one month, all privileges, $8 ; Antique Class, one month, day and night, $4 ; Night Life Class, one month, $4.—The only prizes given in the school are the Charles Toppan Prizes of $200 and $100 respectively. Competitors must be students of two years' standing, and the terms of the fund especially provide that drawing shall be first taken into account by the examiners.—The Schools of the Academy are amply furnished with the necessary casts, etc., and the accommodations provided for them are admirable. Correspondence on matters connected with the Schools should be addressed to H. C. Whipple, Curator.—The Pennsylvania Academy of Fine Arts is the oldest institution of the kind in the U. S. For some details of its history see " The First American Art Academy," reprinted from " Lippincott's Magazine " (not dated), in which may also be found representations of the former building of the Academy erected in 1806, and burned in 1844. The second building, erected after the fire of 1844, was demolished in 1870. The elegant structure at present owned and occupied by the Academy is the work of Messrs. Furniss & Hewitt. [See illustration.]

PENNSYLVANIA MUSEUM AND SCHOOL OF INDUSTRIAL ART.—

Museum, Memorial Hall, Fairmount Park ; School, 1709 Chestnut St.—Incorp. Feb. 26, 1876.— Officers of Board of Trustees for 1884 : Pres., Wm. Platt Pepper, 1730 Chestnut St. ; V. P.'s, Frederic Graff, 1337 Arch St., Thos. Dolan ; Treas., J. H. Dingee, Jr.; Sec. and Curator, Dalton Dorr, 1722 Walnut St.   The Governor of the State and Mayor of the City are *ex officiis* members of the Board, upon which the State Legislature, the City Councils, and the leading scientific and artistic bodies of the city are also represented.—Object : The establishment of an institution like the South Kensington Museum and School in London.—Members (both sexes) of the corporation according to last report, Dec. 31, 1882 : Patrons, who have paid at one time $5,000 or upwards, 9 ; Life, who have paid $100 at one time, 205 ; Annual, who paid $10 for 1882, 85 ; total, 299.—*The Museum.* The building occupied, rent free, by the Museum, is the Memorial Hall [see illustration], erected as an art gallery for the Centennial at the joint expense of the State of Pennsylvania and the city of Philadelphia.   The income of the Museum is limited to membership dues, tuition fees from the pupils of the school, and donations.   For three years a yearly appropriation has been made by the City Councils of $10,000 for the maintenance and repair of the Hall, which is given on condi- tion that the Museum shall be open free to the public.   Until this appropriation was made, the annual receipts, including the admission fees then charged, were so insufficient that the necessary repairs could not be made, and the building was rapidly going to decay.   The sum of $50,000 has been raised towards an endowment fund.   The need, however, of increasing this sum fivefold, not only remains, but is more urgent now than ever before, if the educational work of the School is to be developed, and permanency is to be given to the Museum.   There are no funds for purchases, and the constant growth of the collections is due to gifts and deposits on loan.   The total cost of the collections, according to the balance-sheet of Dec. 31, 1882, amounts to $49,364.84.   In addi- tion to this, however, are the collections obtained by gift or bequest, which greatly exceed in value the cost of the objects purchased, but do not appear in the balance-sheet.—The nucleus of the pres- ent collections was formed by purchases made at the Centennial Exhibition with funds subscribed for the purpose, to which were added donations by exhibitors at the same exhibition.   Very valuable donations have since been made by private individuals (Wm. S. Vaux, bequest of Greco-Italian and ancient American pottery ; the Moore Memorial, given by Mrs. B. H. Moore, in memory of her husband, consisting of over 1,700 objects in pottery, enamels, metal work, etc.), and the collections have been largely increased by loans.   The character of the Museum is distinctively art-industrial and technical, covering a wide range of time and of nationalities.   A few paintings by American and foreign artists are included in the Moore Memorial.—A " Guide to the Museum " (price 5 cents), giving a general idea of the collections and their location in the building, is for sale at the door, where may also be obtained a catalogue of the " Indian Collection " and " Notes on the Collection of Coins " (by Henry Phillips, Jr.), deposited in the Museum by the Numismatic and Antiquarian Society.   Photographs of objects in the Museum can likewise be bought at the catalogue stand.   A slip inventory of the collections has lately been completed, and the preparation of a series of descrip- tive catalogues has been begun this year.—During the three years, 1878, '79, '80, when an admission fee was charged, the total number of visitors was only 42,000.   From Jan. 1, 1881, when the en- trance fee was abolished, to Dec 31, 1883, the number of visitors was 463,734.—Open daily through- out the year, Sundays and holidays included, from 9.30 A.M. to 5.30 P.M. in summer, and 4.45 P.M. in winter, except Monday mornings.—*The School.*   Aim : To furnish such instruction in drawing, painting, and modelling as is required by designers and workmen in the various construc- tive and decorative arts, and to serve as a training-school for teachers of these branches.—The course of study embraces drawing and painting from models, casts, draperies, and still-life ; plane and descriptive geometry ; projections, with their application to machine drawing and to building con- struction ; shadows, perspective ; modelling and casting ; historical ornament and original design. Instrumental drawing is taught by means of class lessons or lectures, and lectures are also given upon anatomy, structural botany, historical ornament, the harmony of color, etc.   The complete course of study embraces three years, but graduates may continue in the school for advanced study.—Teach- ers : L. W. Miller, Principal ; H. F. Stratton, Assistant ; W. W. Keen, M.D., Lecturer on Anatomy —Tuition Fees : Day Class, $18 per term of 18 weeks ; Night Class, three times a week, $5 per term of 18 weeks.   Two terms each year.   The attendance of regular students is required only on four days of the week, from 9 till 1 o'clock.   The Board of Trustees have placed at the disposal of the Board of Public Education five free scholarships.   Graduates may continue in the School for ad- vanced study without payment of fees, on condition that they will devote a certain amount of time to teaching in the School.—Students (both sexes) must be not less than fifteen years of age.   No pre- vious knowledge of drawing is necessary.   Number of students, 1882-3, 79 (51 males, 28 females).—

Certificates are given upon the completion of the Course in Drawing, in Painting, and in Modelling. Those who have received the three certificates are awarded the full diploma of the School.—An exhibition of the work of the students was made in the Rotunda of Memorial Hall during the summer vacation, and a series of drawings, illustrating the course of study, has been placed permanently in the North Corridor.—Annual meeting of the corporation, third Monday in January. [The Eighth Annual Report, presented at the meeting held in January, 1884, reports substantial progress in several directions. The Endowment Fund now amounts to $55,650. Annual members added during the year, 35. " But even with the additional revenue derived from these sources," says the report, " the income of the Institution has not been sufficient to meet its current expenses, and the indebtedness has been increased from $8,450 to $10,100. To secure this indebtedness, debenture bonds for $10,000 have been issued, and the income of all sums received for the Endowment Fund in excess of $50,000 pledged for its extinguishment. We do not deem it prudent that this debt should be made any larger. It will be necessary, therefore, to at once obtain a sum of say $2,500, sufficient to meet its estimated current expenses, if the Institution is to be continued on its present basis during the coming year. There certainly need be no difficulty in doing this, if only the individual members will interest themselves in its accomplishment."]

PERMANENT EXHIBITIONS of works of art, both foreign and American, will be found at the galleries of *Messrs. Jas. S. Earle & Sons*, 816 Chestnut St., and *Mr. Chas. F. Haseltine*, 1516 Chestnut St.

PHILADELPHIA CHAPTER OF THE AMERICAN INSTITUTE OF ARCHITECTS.—15th and Chestnut Sts.—Founded Nov., 1869.—Officers : Pres., Jas. A. Windrim ; 1st V. P., John McArthur ; 2d V. P., T. P. Chandler, Jr.; Sec., Edwd. Hazlehurst ; Treas., Samuel Huckel, Jr.—Objects : To bring the architects of Philadelphia into close relationship ; to benefit them mutually, and to promote the general cause of art and the practical efficiency of the profession ; to further the education of architectural students by providing lectures, etc.; to establish and maintain an architectural and general art library and reading room ; to organize a museum of constructive and art models, as well as of building materials and appliances.—Members : Professional, Non-Professional, Junior.—The chapter has competitions, etc., at stated intervals.

PHILADELPHIA SCHOOL OF ART NEEDLE-WORK.—1602 Chestnut St.— Founded 1879 ; incorporated 1881.—Officers : Pres., Mrs. T. Dundas Lippincott, 509 South Broad St.; Secr., Mrs. Caspar Wister, 1303 Arch St.; Treas., Miss Fanny Clark, 2037 DeLancey Pl.— Principal, Miss Frances Tate Lawe, formerly of the Royal School of Art Needle-Work, London.— Orders are taken in the Salesroom, to be executed by the pupils taught in the School. Originally started with a contributed fund of $1,800, the school has since been self-supporting. For the year ending Mch. 8, 1883, the receipts, of which $7,195.47 went to the workers, exceeded the expenses by $1,206.66, with a stock of materials, etc., on hand, valued at $4,805.70. Those desirous of entering the school as workers are required to pay an entrance fee of $10, which entitles them to the necessary instruction, and a place in the workroom at the first vacancy.—Instruction to others, daily, from 10 A.M. to 4 P.M., 12 lessons, $10 ; 6 lessons, $5 ; 1 lesson, $1.

PHILADELPHIA SCHOOL OF DESIGN FOR WOMEN.—S. W. cor. Broad and Master Sts.—Founded 1847 ; incorp. 1853.—Officers of B'd of Directors: Pres., Jas. L. Claghorn, 222 N. 19th St.; V. P., John Sartain, 728 Sansom St.; Sec. and Treas., F. O. Horstmann, 3925 Chestnut St.—Object : The instruction of women in decorative art, and the various practical applications thereof to industrial pursuits. Particular attention is given to those who may wish to adopt teaching as a profession.—The corporation consists of Life Members, who have paid $50 or more at one time ; and Annual Members, who pay $5 p. a. Number of Life Members, according to last report, 129 ; Annual Members, not given.—This School was founded in 1847 by Mrs. Sarah Peter, wife of the British consul at Philadelphia. It then passed into the care of the Franklin Institute for a short time, until it assumed corporate existence under its present charter. Its income is derived from the contributions of members, tuition fees, an annual appropriation made by the State Legislature, and donations. It has never been attempted to render it self-sustaining, since that could only be done by raising the tuition fee to an amount which would impair its usefulness. Aid, therefore,

is solicited, particularly for its free department. Any person contributing $1,000, has the privilege of sending a free student during his or her lifetime.—The School is organized into seven classes : A. Preparatory course. B. Ornament, with its subdivisions. C. Landscape. D. Human figure (including the study of antique statuary, draperies, etc.). E. Modelling. F. Wood engraving, drawing on wood, lithography, and etching. D. China decorating. The regular course occupies three years. The various technical courses are taken by students who wish to devote their whole attention to a thorough preparation for special professional employment. A standard of admission is required for these special courses. Those who do not meet the requirements, enter the preparatory course, for which no previous knowledge of drawing is required. Regular courses of lectures on art subjects are delivered before the School, and art literature has been made an additional study.—Teachers : Miss Elizabeth Crossdale of South Kensington, Principal ; Chas. Page, Designing, Modelling, and Lithography ; Peter Moran, Landscape in Oil and Water-Colors, Still Life, Etching ; Stephen J. Ferris, Drawing from Life in Charcoal, Oil, or Water-Colors, and Drapery ; Herm. Faber, Antique Drawing, Anatomy and Composition ; Geo. P. Williams, Wood Engraving ; Albrecht Jahn, China Decorating ; Geo. C. Lambdin, Flower Painting in Oil ; Emma W. Fullerton, Perspective ; Mary M'Allister, Light and Shade, Time Sketching, Drawing from Nature, Object Drawing, and Water Colors ; Sara C. Pennypacker, Geometry, Free-Hand, Analysis of Plant Form, and Elementary Design. Lectures on Historic and Decorative Art are also given.—Tuition, $20 per term of five months ; two terms each year. To those requiring preparation for special classes, $5 per term extra ; to those desiring instruction from more than one master in the higher branches, $10 per term extra. In consideration of the appropriation made by the State, ten pupils are accepted annually from the advanced classes of the Philadelphia Girls' Grammar and Normal Schools. Eleven perpetual free scholarships have also been established by patrons of the School, who have given $1,000 each. Another scholarship, founded by Mrs. Wm. J. Horstmann, is awarded annually, as a prize. —Students, female only. must be at least thirteen years of age. Number of pupils, season of 1882-3, 293.—The Diploma of the School is granted to those students only who complete the subjects of study, and pass the examinations in Classes A, B, C, and D. Certificates as teachers are given upon examination.—Besides the scholarship awarded annually, as mentioned above, three gold medals founded by Mr. Geo. W. Childs and Mr. Jas. L. Claghorn, are given each year.—The spacious, building at present occupied by the School, the former Forrest Mansion [see illustration], was purchased 1880 for $45,000, and $60,000 have since been expended upon it for improvements. It embraces a well-lighted gallery for the statues possessed by the School, with school-rooms adapted to the special needs of each class, a large lecture-room, and a conservatory, with ample grounds, to which the students can resort for recreation. The copies of masterpieces of art, casts of ornaments, drawings, library, etc. (of which a partial list is given in the Report), obtained at a cost of $5,000, are, so it is claimed, superior in number and arrangement to those possessed by any similar institution in the country.—Annual meeting of the corporation, fourth Monday in June.

PHILADELPHIA SKETCH CLUB.—1328 Chestnut St.—Organized Nov. 20, 1860, as " The Crayon Sketch Club "; present name adopted Dec. 3, 1861.—Officers : Pres., H. T. Cariss, 1328 Chestnut St.; V. P., C. F. Spooner, 1520 Chestnut St.; Sec., Geo. Wright, 1520 Chestnut St. ; Treas., Geo. D. McCreary, 137 South 2d St.—Objects, etc. : Social intercourse among artists, students of art and amateurs, and artistic practice. The association is distinctively a students' club, and efforts have always been made to maintain this character. At each weekly meeting impromptu sketches, single figures in action, are made from subjects given out by the Executive Committee. Besides these, monthly studies are required, from subjects announced in advance, as essays in composition and treatment of subject, and annual studies, from subjects chosen by the Club, or by the artist, as may be determined.—Members : Artists, art students, and amateurs are eligible ; students and amateurs must submit sketches for approval by the Committee. Present number of members, 85 —Prizes : In former years money prizes were occasionally given by individual members or friends of the Club ; latterly, the prizes have consisted of a photograph or a photogravure from a modern picture for the best original monthly study, and an autotype from an old master for the best original study submitted at the annual meeting in January.—The Club arranged an Exhibition of Works of American Artists at the Academy in the winter of 1865-6, and published, in 1874, " The Sketch Club Portfolio," a collection of designs, without text, in monthly parts. From 1873-76, after the demolition of the old Academy of Fine Arts, and before the opening of the new building, a Life

Class for drawing from the nude was conducted under the auspices of the Club, with Mr. Thos. Eakins as instructor. Lectures on anatomy were delivered before the class in the winter of 1874-5. This class (open to males only) was a great success, and the applications from non-members, who were admitted on payment of a small fee, were so numerous that many had to be refused.—A peculiar feature of this Club is its *Relief Trust*, of which Messrs. Geo. D. McCreary, 137 South 2d St., and W. Moylan Lansdale, 700 Walnut St., are the Trustees. This fund, applicable to the relief of members only, in case of sickness or where assistance is needed to pay burial expenses, is sustained by a small annual assessment and by donations. In case the Club ceases to exist, it is provided that the fund shall be paid over to the Academy, to be applied by that institution to the relief of artists and students, or to the Pennsylvania Hospital.

PHILADELPHIA SOCIETY OF ARTISTS.—1725 Chestnut St.—Incorp. June 24, 1879.—Officers: Pres., Jas. B. Sword, 1520 Chestnut St.; Sec., Newbold H. Trotter, 1520 Chestnut St.; Treas., F. De B. Richards, 1520 Chestnut St.—Objects: The establishment of a gallery or suitable rooms in the City of Philadelphia for the exhibition and sale of works of painting and sculpture, and to give such encouragement as may best promote and advance the interest of art.— Members: Active (professional painters and sculptors whose works are of a high order of merit, and in whom is vested the governing power), Associate (professional musicians and readers), Contributing (life, $25, or annual, $5 a year), and Honorary (professional painters and sculptors). Active members pay $5 initiation fee, and such dues as shall be prescribed. Present number: Active, 37; associate, 6; life. 31; annual, 248.—The Society holds several exhibitions each year. At its Fifth Annual Exhibition, which was held from Jan. 21 to Feb. 23, 1884, 240 works were exhibited by 131 artists.—Annual meeting, third Saturday in March.

PHILADELPHIA SOCIETY OF ETCHERS.—Organized June, 1880—Officers: Pres., Peter Moran, 1322 Jefferson St.; Sec., J. Neely, Jr., 617 Market St.; Treas., Stephen J. Ferris, 1523 Chestnut St.—Objects: The advancement of the art of etching; social intercourse at the monthly studio meetings; and a quarterly exchange of etchings among the members.—Present number of Resident Members, 8; Non-resident, 9; Honorary, 7.—The First Exhibition of the Society, held at the Penns. Academy of Fine Arts, from Dec. 27, 1882, to Feb. 3, 1883, was a very interesting affair, and contained a good representation of European as well as American work. Of the latter there were 356 plates by 45 artists. The fine quarto catalogue of the exhibition (price $1) was illustrated with etchings by F. S. Church, P. Moran, J. Simpson, H. Farrer, S. J. Ferris, T. Moran, J. Pennell, and B. Uhle.

SOCIAL ART CLUB.—1811 Walnut St.—Officers: Pres., Caspar Wister. M.D., 1303 Arch St.; V. Ps., Geo. S. Pepper, 1819 Walnut St., Francis W. Lewis, M.D., 2016 Spruce St.; Treas., J. Rochman Paul, 903 Pine St.; Sec.. Thos. DeWitt Cuyler, 704 Walnut St.—Objects: The promotion of literary, artistic, and antiquarian tastes among the citizens of Philadelphia, and such kindred purposes as the Club may from time to time determine, by establishing and maintaining a library and reading room, and a collection of works of art and antiquities, either by loan or otherwise.—Membership, limited to 400: Resident members, who alone have the right to vote, $100 initiation fee, and $50 annually; non-resident, $50 and $30. No person under twenty-three years of age can become a member.—Annual meeting, second Monday in March.

SPRING GARDEN INSTITUTE.—N. E. cor. Broad and Spring Garden Sts.—Organized and incorp., 1851.—Officers for 1883-4: Pres., John Baird, 1705 N. Broad St.; V. P., Isaac C. Price, 1825 Mt. Vernon St.; Treas., W. Hobard Brown, 1911 Park Ave.; Sec., Addison B. Burk, 1024 Brown St.; Ch'man Comm. on Drawing Schools, Jas. H. Windrim, 817 N. Broad St.—Object: the moral and intellectual improvement of young persons.—Members: Stockholders, $10 per share, each share subject to $2 annual tax; stockholders *in perpetuo*, $50 free of further tax; stockholders for life, $30 free of further tax. There are also Annual Subscribers (adults), $6 p. a., and Junior Subscribers (minors), $4 p. a. These subscribers have the use of the library, and the right to attend a night class two sessions per week. Membership as per last report (April, 1883): In Perpetuo, 43; Life, 730; Stockholders, 97; Annual Subscribers, 8; Junior Subscribers, 20. (This does not include the students in the night classes and drawing schools, who have also the privileges of subscribers).—

The work of the Institute is thus stated : 1. Library (13,000 vols.) and Reading Room. Open from 10 A.M., to 10 P.M. Books loaned to members. Public admitted free to the use of the books, etc., in the library and reading-room. 2. Lectures and entertainments, one each week, from October to March. Free, except for reserved seats, and in special cases. 3. Evening Drawing Schools in Mechanical, Free-hand, and Architectural Drawing and Modelling. Fee nominal. 4. Day School, for instruction in Drawing, Oil and Water Color Painting, Stained Glass, China Painting, etc. Paid. 5. School in Mechanical Handiwork. Afternoon and night classes for teaching the proper handling of tools, vise and machine-tool work. A nominal fee, sufficient only to defray actual expenses, is charged the pupils,—*The Art Schools.* Teachers: Prof. Wm. A. Porter (of South Kensington, for six years master of the Art School in Worcester, England), Principal; Free-hand Drawing and Painting, Prof. Wm. A. Porter, Kate M. Bessinger, Chas. Feurer, Chas. Grafly, J. E. Reddie; Mechanical Drawing, W. H. Miller; Architectural Drawing. Thos. V. Lonsdale.—Aim : To give thorough instruction in drawing and the higher arts of painting, in all its branches, with a view to fit the pupils, at any stage of the instruction, to do useful work in the mechanic arts, or, if they complete the course. to become draughtsmen, architects, designers, artists, or teachers of drawing. —Day Classes : For the pupils in these classes there is a fixed course of instruction, covering a period of three years, and grade certificates are issued at the close of each year, testifying to the advancement of the pupil. The full certificate is that granted to Art Teachers, and cannot be gained in less than three years. The subjects are the usual ones, including painting from life. A kiln is provided for the students of china and glass painting. In connection with the school is an Art Library, free to the pupils. There are two terms, Sept. to Feb., and Feb. to June. Fees, $20 per term, or $40 p. a. Five sessions per week, 9 A.M.-2 P.M., and one hour (optional) for additional practice. There are more applicants than can be accommodated.—Night Schools : These are entirely distinct from the day classes. They are intended for the education of young men and women who have no leisure during the day, and for those who have had no previous instruction. The course of study, in Mechanical, Architectural, and Free-hand Drawing, is particularly adapted for mechanics and others who require a practical training, and the teachers are practical draughtsmen and designers. There is one term, from Oct. to Apr. Fees, $4 per term for minors ; $6 per term for adults. Two lessons per week, 7½-9½ P.M. At the close of the term in April an exhibition of the work of the pupils is held, and such prizes are awarded as may be provided by friends of the Institute.—*The Mechanical Handiwork Schools.* Aim : The education of young men in mechanic arts, and to supply the learning necessary for producing complete machines which the numerous sub-divisions of work in manufactories does not allow. Teachers : Lieut. Robert Crawford, U. S. N., Supt.; John Hall, Thos. Williams, Geo. R. Allen, Thos. Henshaw, Thos. Chase. There are afternoon classes and night classes. The school year consists of three quarters, and the full course in the night classes occupies two years. Fees : For full course students, first year, $15 per quarter; second year $25 per quarter; afternoon students, $9 per quarter; night students, mechanical handiwork, $5 per quarter; course of 6 lectures in steam engineering, $3; 10 lectures, $5. The schools have all the necessary accommodation of shops, tools, machinery, etc., and the instructors are skilled mechanics of wide experience. —According to last published report (Apr., 1883), the number of pupils in the Drawing Schools was 472, in the Mechanical Handiwork School 181, total 653. Towards the end of the year 1883 the total was reported at about 800.—The income of the Institute, from rent of lecture hall, etc., in its building, membership and subscribers' fees, sale of reserved seats at lectures, profits on occasional paid entertainments, advertisements in the " Journal " published by it, tuition fees, etc., is not quite sufficient to meet expenses, although all the work of management is done gratuitously. It is the desire of the Institute, therefore, to raise an Endowment Fund of $50,000. A donation of $5,000 towards this fund, from "A Friend of Art," through Mr. Chas. D. Reed, was received in 1883-3, and another of $1,000 from Mr. Wm. Singerly, which, with $7,000 previously received, carried the Endowment Fund up to $13,000.—Annual Meeting, second Thursday in April.

69. Pittsburgh, Pa.

PITTSBURGH SCHOOL OF DESIGN FOR WOMEN.—Y. M. C. A. Building, Penn Ave. and 7th St.—Incorporated 1865.—Officers for 1883-4 : Pres., Chas. J. Clarke ; Treas., Geo. A. Berry ; Sec., John B. Jackson ; Ch'man of School Comm., J. G. Siebenbeck.—Object : The systematic training of young women in the practice of art, and in the knowledge of its scientific principles, with the view of qualifying them to impart to others a careful art education, and to develop its application to the common uses of life, and its relation to the requirements of trade and manufactures.—The course lasts from two and a half to four years, depending on the industry of the student. It begins with drawing from the flat, from lines to the entire human figure ; progresses to drawing from models and casts, the study of composition and design in ornament, perspective, color, etc., and ends with painting in oil and water-color from nature, and such other work as may be necessary in connection with design. To those who do not wish to follow the full course, instruction is given in any special branch. Special instruction given to ladies in oil and water colors.—Teachers : Annie W. Henderson, Prin.; Olive Turney, Drawing and Painting ; Agnes D. Jamison, Drawing : May E. Kelly, Drawing and Geometry.—There are two sessions of five months each ; classes meet daily except Saturday and Sunday. Besides these regular classes there are also Saturday classes for women, and in connection therewith a class for boys from 8 to 15 years of age.—Fees for session of 5 months : Elementary Course, $15 ; Figure and Landscape, in oil, each, $25 ; Saturday Painting Class, $12.50 ; Saturday Drawing Class, $10 ; China Decorating, $20.—A number of free scholarships have been founded by contributors to the funds of the school.—An annual exhibition is held in January, and bronze, silver, and gold medals may be competed for at the close of each school year. The school also gives diplomas.—Number of students in attendance at date of last printed Report, Sept. 1883 : Women's Classes, 132 ; Boys' Class, not given.—The receipts from tuition, at present rates, do not meet more than 50 per cent. of the necessary current expenses of the School, the institution relying on the intelligent liberality of its friends to sustain it. But it is earnestly hoped that the marked usefulness of the School during the past years, and the growing interest felt in its success, will lead to more and more liberal support from contributors, in order that the charge for instruction and the use of the facilities of the School may be reduced from year to year, and, if possible, be made free to all. The School removed from its former quarters, Bank Block, 173 Wood St., to the larger rooms at the address above given, on Apr. 1, 1884.

WESTERN PENNSYLVANIA NUMISMATIC SOCIETY.—[No reply to repeated requests for information.]

70. Pittsfield, Mass.

LADIES' ART ASSOCIATION.—8 South St.—Organized 1880.—Officers : Pres., Mrs. Theodore Pomeroy ; V. P.'s., Mrs. J. M. Stevenson, Mrs. C. B. Redfield ; Treas., Miss F. W. Stevenson ; Sec., Miss M. W. Redfield.—Objects : 1. To raise the standard of woman's work ; 2. To find a good market for it, and to do away with the unpleasantness and trials ordinarily connected with the disposal of work ; 3. To aid, by establishing new industries, and by showing what is salable and desirable ; 4. To establish free classes, that may help to direct many into desirable ways of earning a livelihood.—Any person may become a member by paying an annual fee of $1.—The salesroom established by this Association has been quite successful. During the season from June 1, 1881, to Jan. 1, 1882. it paid to contributors, over and above all commissions and expenses, $1,071.21. The articles taken on sale from members and outside contributors (commission, 10 per cent) comprise all sorts of artistic and decorative work, old furniture, etc., and home-made cake, preserves, jellies, etc. Orders are also taken.—All correspondence to be addressed to Mrs. M. C. Buell, the lady in charge.—Annual meeting, last Wednesday in April.—[From last issue. No reply to repeated requests for later information.]

71. Plymouth, Mass.

PILGRIM SOCIETY.—Pilgrim Hall, Court St.—Organ. and incorp., 1820.—Officers : Pres., Hon. Th. Russell ; Treas., I. N. Stoddard ; Sec., Wm. S. Danforth ; Lib., J. Lasinby Brown. —Objects : To commemorate the Pilgrim Fathers.—Membership is secured by the payment of $5. There are upward of 10,000 members. Financial resources : Admission to the Hall, and the interest on a small fund.—The collections of the Society occupy the whole of the building owned by it (Pilgrim Hall), and consist of paintings (" The Embarkation of the Pilgrims," copied by Edgar Parker from the original by Weir ; " Landing of the Pilgrims," by Chas. Lucy ; " The Mayflower Arriving in Plymouth Harbor," by W. F. Halsall), portraits (by Stuart, Greenwood, Trumbull, etc.), engravings, old books and documents, Pilgrim and Mayflower relics (including the sword of Miles Standish, etc.), Indian relics, and curiosities. Admission 25 cents; free to members.

72. Portland, Me.

MAINE HISTORICAL SOCIETY.—City Hall Building, Congress St.—Incorp. 1822.— Libr. and Curator, Hubbard W. Bryant, 218 Middle St.—This Society was recently removed to Portland from New Brunswick, Me. The library and cabinet are open to the public daily from 2 to 5 P.M. The Indian implements, relics, and portraits are well worth the attention of visitors.

PORTLAND ART LEAGUE.—Club House of the Portland Society of Art.—Organized 1883.—Officers: Executive Comm.. Miss Inez A. Blanchard. Emery St., Miss Anna Clark; Posing Com., Miss Talbot, 57 Park St., Miss Crocker, Miss Hones; Sec., Miss Wolhoupter.—Objects: Improvement in art.—Present number of members, 35.—There are two lessons per week, from the living model (head only), and two sketch classes per week; each member posing in turn for the class. The League is open to both sexes, who work together. Teachers: Miss Crocker and Mr. John McDonald. Tuition fees, $5 per month —The League held an exhibition, in May, 1883, of works by New York artists and by its own members; admission fee for non-members, 15 cents.

PORTLAND SOCIETY OF ART.—Deering Place.—Organized and incorporated, 1882. —Officers: Pres., Wm. E. Gould, First Nat'l B'k; V. P.'s, Francis II. Fassett, 93 Exchange St.; Henry B. Brown, 400 Danforth St.; Sec., Geo. D. Rand, 93 Exchange St.; Treas., Thos. J. Little, 31 Exchange St.; Librarian, Hubbard W. Bryant, 218 Middle St.—Objects: To encourage a knowledge and love of art, through the exhibition of art works and lectures upon art subjects; the acquisition of an art library and works of art, such as paintings, statuary, and engravings, and the establishment of an art school and museum.—Members: Annual, initiation fee, $5, annual dues, $3; life, $25 (in money or works of art, at the option of the Board of Management); Honorary. Number of members, Feb., 1884. 225.—The society holds one General Exhibition yearly, Spring and Fall Exhibitions of Local Art, and occasional exhibitions of engravings and etchings. The exhibitions are free to members and such friends as they may supply with complimentary tickets; others 25 cents admission.—The new club house of the society [see illustration] was opened with a reception on the evening of Feb. 14, 1884. It contains an exhibition room, 32 x 20 feet, a smoking room, and a reading room, and cost a trifle less than $2,200, exclusive of the land.—The Portland Art League (see above) has the use of the rooms for its classes and exhibitions.—Annual meeting, last Wednesday of January.

73. Portland, Oregon.

SOCIETY OF DECORATIVE ART OF CALIFORNIA.—This is a branch of the San Francisco Society, which see.—Agent: Mrs. Moeller, cor. 9th and Taylor Sts.

74. Poughkeepsie, N. Y.

VASSAR COLLEGE.—[Instruction in Drawing, Painting, etc., is given in this College. Henry Van Ingen, instructor. No response to repeated requests for information.]

75. Princeton, N. J.

COLLEGE OF NEW JERSEY (Princeton College).—Officers: Pres. of the B'd of Trustees (in the absence of the Governor of the State, who is president *ex-officio*) and of the Fac., James McCosh, D.D., LL.D.; Clerk of the B'd of Trustees, Elijah R. Craven, D.D.; Treas., Rev. Wm. Harris, A.M.; Clerk of the Fac., Henry C. Cameron, Ph.D., D.D.; Lib., Frederic Vinton, A.M.; Registrar, Henry N. Van Dyke, A.M.—According to the last published catalogue (1883-4), the only department in which drawing is taught is the John C. Green School of Science, which is connected with the college; Frederick N. Wilson. C.E., Prof. of Descriptive Geometry, Stereotomy, and Technical Drawing; F. C. Roberts, Instructor in Topographical and Map Drawing.—The pupils in the General Course in Science are regularly engaged in the drawing room in the Freshman year (Elements of Industrial Drawing, Projections, and Descriptive Geometry), Sophomore year (Descriptive Geometry, Shades, Shadows, and Perspective), and Junior year (Free-Hand Drawing). No provision for drawing is made in the senior year. Additional courses in drawing are given to the classes in Civil Engineering, as follows: Sophomore year, Structure Drawing; Senior year, Stereotomy (Stone-Cutting). Topographical and Map Drawing (from surveys) is taught in each year of the Engineering Course. There is, however. a course of lectures on art subjects every winter, which is open to the whole College. Such lectures have been delivered by Gen. L. P. Di Cesnola, Wm. C. Prime, LL.D., Prof. John F. Weir. and Prof. C. E. Norton. For the endowment of a *School and Professorship of Art*, the sum of $50,000 has been received from the residuary legatees of the late Mr. Frederick Marquand ; and Messrs. Wm. C. Prime, LL.D., and Allan Marquand, Ph.D., have been appointed Professors of the History of Art. Money is now collecting for the purpose of erecting a suitable fire-proof building for the reception of collections owned by or promised to the College. The history of art is an elective study. A course on architecture will be delivered first by Prof. Marquand, and will embrace Egyptian, Moorish, Romanesque and Gothic buildings, which will be selected and studied from an historical, æsthetic and structural point of view. (This course is at present deferred in consequence of the illness of Prof. Marquand, contracted while making researches in the service of the College.)— *The E. M. Museum of Archæology,* Prof. Wm. Libby, Jr. Vice-Director, is classified in the three general departments of Geology, Palæontology, and Archæology. The Archæological Department contains an extensive collection of specimens of pre-historic implements of the palæolithic age, from Switzerland, France, Denmark, etc. ; remains of the mound builders ; Peruvian pottery ; a series of models of Cliff ruins of the Southwest, and a large collection of recent Indian relics. It is open to all visitors every secular day.

PRINCETON SKETCH CLUB.—Studio in one of the College buildings.—Organized, Nov., 1881, by a number of professors and students.—Sec.,Prof. Henry F. Osborn, Sc.D.—Objects : To secure good instruction in free-hand drawing and water-color painting, and to promote the interest in art matters in the College.—Members, limited to 20, must be connected with the College as teachers or students.—The meetings during 1882-3 were under the direction of Mr. Jno. Ward Stimson, of New York. For the winter of 1883-4 the Club was inactive, owing to the illness of Prof. Marquand. In the fall of 1884 it will undoubtedly be reorganized with his coöperation.

76. Providence, R. I.

BROWN UNIVERSITY.—Officers for 1883-4 : Pres. B'd of Fellows and of the Faculty, Rev. Ezekiel G. Robinson, D.D., LL.D. ; Chancellor, Hon. Thos. Durfee. LL.D. ; Sec. of the Corp., Rev. Samuel L. Caldwell, D.D. ; Treas., Arnold B. Chace, A.M.—In the course for the degree of A.B., Civil Engineering is an elective study in the Junior and Senior classes. In the course for the degree of Ph.B. including an ancient language, Mechanical Drawing (2 hours a week) is compulsory in the Freshman class ; Shades and shadows (3 hours a week) in the first half of the Sophomore class ; Surveying is an elective study in the second half of the Sophomore class, Civil Engineering in the Junior and Senior Classes. In the course for the degree of Ph.B. not including an ancient language, Mechanical and Free-hand Drawing (6 hours a week) are compulsory in the Freshman class ; Shades and Shadows (3 hours a week) in the first half, and Surveying (3 hours a week) in the second half of the Sophomore class ; Civil Engineering is an elective study in Junior and Senior classes. In the Department of Practical Science, the necessary practice in Instrument and Free-Hand Drawing is required, as a matter of course, in the Civil Engineering course ; in Botany, "great stress is laid upon the importance of drawing from nature, and students are taught to make illustrative sketches." No mention is made of drawing in the Catalogue of the University in connection with the study of Chemistry, Physics, Zoölogy, Geology, and Agriculture. Prof. of Mathematics and Civil Engineering, Benjamin Franklin Clarke, A.M.— *The Museum of Natural History and Anthropology,* in Rhode Island Hall, Prof. John Whipple Potter Jenks, A.M., Curator, contains (besides a very large collection of specimens illustrative of natural history) Indian implements and relics (1000 specimens), implements and curiosities of other uncivilized peoples (1000), and coins and medals (3000).— *The Library,* for the use of those connected with the University only, consists of 55,278 bound vols.. and 17,000 unbound pamphlets. The last report of the President (June 21, 1883), states that valuable additions have lately been made to it in the department of fine arts.—*Portrait Gallery*: Through the liberality of the friends of the College, many portraits have been presented to it, most of which are deposited in the picture gallery in Rhode Island Hall. The collection includes portraits of benefactors of the University, of some of its former officers, and of men conspicuous in the annals of Rhode Island. This collection has been greatly enriched in late years by portraits presented through a committee appointed by the Alumni " for the purpose of procuring and placing within the walls of Brown University, the portraits of her Presidents, professors, distinguished graduates and benefactors."—During the warm weather, beginning towards the latter part of May, the public is freely admitted to the Museum and Portrait Gallery, each Saturday, from 2 to 5 P.M.

PROVIDENCE ART CLUB.—35 North Main St.—Organized Feb. 19, 1880; incorp. Apr. 15, 1880.—Officers for 1884: Pres., John Howard Appleton; V. P., Geo. W. Danielson; Treas., Albert L. Calder; Sec., Courtl. B. Dorrance.—Objects: To unite and promote the interests of the artists of Rhode Island, and to cultivate and combine social interests with those of art.— Members, of both sexes: Professional, artists by profession; Associates. not practical artists. Initiation fee, $6; annual dues, $6, payable by all members alike, all of whom are entitled to vote. (From Jan. 1, 1885, the fees and dues are to be $15 and $10 respectively.) Number of members, Dec. 31, 1883, 240.—Lectures on art and other subjects, concerts, etc., are given during the winter, and two or more exhibitions are held yearly. Four exhibitions were held the past year (1883), one of Dr. Haden's Etchings in February (607 visitors); the Fourth Annual in April (905 visitors); the Autumn Local Exhibition in October (472 visitors), and a Water Color Exhibition in December (162 visitors). Free to members; others 25 cents.—The club maintains a class for sketching from the living model, for members only (both sexes); fee $1.—The club has voted to create a capital or building fund.—Annual meeting, first week in January.

PROVIDENCE ATHENÆUM.—Incorporated 1836.—Officers, 1883-4: Pres., Augustus Woodbury; V. P., Royal C. Taft; Treas., Stephen H. Arnold; Sec., Wm. M. Bailey, Jr.; Lib., Daniel Beckwith.—The Athenæum is a private library (number of vols., 1883, 42,014), owned by an association of stockholders. Non-stockholders may, however, obtain its use as Annual Subscribers, and strangers can be introduced by stockholders.—The *Art Collections* of the Athenæum are small, consisting of three busts and eight paintings. Among the latter are portraits of James Gates Percival, by Alexander; Washington Allston, by Chester Harding; and John Hampden, by James Gandy, an English artist of the 17th century, said to have been a pupil of Van Dyck. There is also a "Cavalier of the Time of Charles I.," by Van Dyck; a "Girl Reading," by Sir Joshua Reynolds; and Edward G. Malbone's celebrated miniature, "The Hours," on ivory, 6 by 7 inches. (Some of these pictures were stolen in 1881, but were subsequently recovered.)—The library is open every week day from April 1 to Oct. 1 from 9 A.M. to 7 P.M., and from Oct. 1 to April 1 from 10 A.M. to 9 P.M. Transient visitors are admitted on application.—Annual meeting of the association, in September.

RHODE ISLAND CHAPTER OF THE AMERICAN INSTITUTE OF ARCHITECTS.—Organized Nov. 10, 1875.—Officers, 1883-4: Pres., A. C. Morse, Wilcox B'ldg.; V. P., Alfred Stone, 65 Westminster St.; Sec., E. I. Nickerson, 65 Westminster St. (P. O. address, Box 1031); Treas., Jas. Fludder, Newport, R. I.—Objects: United efforts for the honorable practice of the profession, and mutual improvement.—Membership is conditioned upon honorable practice of the profession and residence in the State of Rhode Island. There are three classes: Members (subdivided into two classes, professional, who are or have been practising architects, and non-professional, lovers of the fine arts generally, or amateurs in architecture); Junior Members (architects' assistants, draughtsmen, and students of architecture); Honorary (not architects, who shall contribute $100). Initiation fee of Members, $5; of Juniors, $2.50. The annual dues vary, according to the relations held by the payer to the Am. Inst. of Arch. The governing power is vested in the members. Number of members, Jan., 1884: Members, 14 (13 professional, 1 non-professional); Juniors, 2.—The society owns a library of architectural works.—Annual meetings, first Wednesday in October, at Narragansett Hotel.

RHODE ISLAND HISTORICAL SOCIETY.—College Hill, opp. Brown University.
—Organized 1822; incorp. June, 1882.—Officers: Pres., Wm. Gammell; V. P's., Francis Brinley,
Newport, R. I., and Chas. W. Parsons; Sec. and Lib., Amos Perry; Treas., R. I. Everett.—
Objects: To preserve and utilize the materials for local history, and in general to cultivate a taste
for historical pursuits.—Members: Resident (at present about 275), initiation fee $5, annual dues,
$3; Life (20), payment of $50; Corresponding; Honorary.—Financial resources: Members' dues,
income of a small fund, and $500 a year from the State.—The Society publishes "Collections" (6
vols. so far) "Annual Proceedings," and occasional publications.—Besides a library, the Society has
a Cabinet, comprising a number of paintings, portraits, engravings, maps, and curious articles of
historical interest. Among these is a large view, in excellent condition, of the East side of Providence,
as it appeared from the old fort on Federal Hill in 1809. This was painted by Worrall, of the
Boston Theatre, and was used as a drop scene in the old Providence Theatre from 1812 to 1832.—
Annual meeting, second Tuesday of January.

R. I. SCHOOL OF DESIGN.—Hoppin Homestead Bldg., 283 Westminster St.—Organized and incorp., 1878.—Officers: Pres., Hon. C. B. Farnsworth; V. P., Hon. Rowland Hazard;
Treas., Henry R. Chace; Sec., Miss Sarah E. Doyle.—Object: To furnish such instruction in
Drawing, Painting, Modelling, and Designing, as required by artisans generally, that they may more
successfully apply the principles to the mechanical arts and industries; the systematic training of
students, enabling them to become successful art teachers, and the general advancement of art
culture.—This School was originated by an association of which any person may become an annual
member by the payment of $3 a year, or a life member upon the payment of $100. Present number
of members, 70. The income consists of tuition fees, membership dues, donations, and a yearly
appropriation of $500 by the State.—The Course of Instruction embraces Elementary Free-Hand
Drawing and Design; Free-hand from copy, models, and casts, in pencil, crayon, stump, India ink,
and charcoal; Geometrical and Applied Design; Perspective; Architecture; China Painting, etc.
Students who finish a complete set of drawings included in the course of instruction, to the satisfac-
tion of their teachers and the committee of management, are given a certificate.—Instructors: E.
Rose, 32 Hammond St.; E. W. Hamilton, G. W. Whitaker, W. Woodward, E. Woodward.
Curator: Miss H. C. Hall.—Tuition fees: Day Students, $20 each term (two terms a year);
Evening Students, $6; Children (Saturday Class), $4; China Painting, $9 for 12 lessons; Special
Classes, special terms.—Number of pupils, both sexes, season of 1882: Day pupils, 36; evening,
111; Saturday, 50; total, 197.—An annual exhibition is held in June. Various courses of lectures
on art and other subjects are given during the year.—Annual meeting of the association, second
Wednesday in June.

77. Quincy, Ill.

QUINCY ART ASSOCIATION.—[The notice of this association, given in the first issue
of the "Directory," was made up, as stated at the time, from documents dated 1879, no response
having been received to requests for later information. It has since been learned that the society
was disbanded in December, 1880.]

78. Richmond, Va.

RICHMOND ART ASSOCIATION.—819 East Main St. (up stairs).—Organized 1877;
incorp. 1884.—Officers: Pres., M. I. Dimmock; Sec., A. D. Grocer; Treas., L. R. Price.—Objects:
Cultivation of the taste for art in the community and instruction in same.—Members: Active, initiation fee, $1, annual dues, $10, which includes instruction in drawing; Associate, $5. Present num-
ber of members, about 50.—Supt. of Classes, W. L. Sheppard; Instructress, Miss Alicia Laird.—
An annual exhibition of pictures, etc., loaned, and of the work of the students, is held in May.

VIRGINIA HISTORICAL SOCIETY.—Westmoreland Club House.—Organized Dec.
29, 1831; chartered Mch. 10, 1834.—Officers: Pres., Alex. H. H. Stuart, Staunton, Va.; V. P.'s,
Conway Robinson, Washington, D. C., W. W. Corcoran, Washington, D. C., Wm. Wirt Henry;
Cor. Sec. and Libr., R. A. Brock; Rec. Sec., Geo. A. Barksdale; Treas., Robt. T. Brooke.—Present membership: 32 Honorary, 65 Corresponding, 55 Life, 482 Annual: total, 634. Annual dues,

10

$5 ; no entrance fee ; life membership, $50.—The Society, besides a number of engraved portraits, relics, etc., has a collection of twenty-eight portraits in oil, including the following : Pocahontas (two), Earl of Essex, Capt. George Percy, Lord Culpepper, George Washington, Martha Washington, Patrick Henry, Peyton Randolph, George Mason, Thomas Jefferson, Lafayette, Arthur Lee, Edmund Pendleton, John Marshall, Duke de Lauzun, Gerard, Edmund Randolph, John Randolph of Roanoke, Hugh Nelson, Comm. Oliver H. Perry, Gov. Wm. B. Giles, Black Hawk, and Rev. M. D. Hoge, D.D.—The portraits may be inspected any week day between 9 A.M. and 3 P.M., when the Librarian is in attendance.—The Society has a library of about 14,000 vols. It has recently published two volumes of documents relating to the history of Virginia.

79. Rochester, N. Y.

POWERS ART GALLERY.—Powers Building.—Established by D. W. Powers in 1875. —Manager : Chas. C. Burns.—One of the objects of this Gallery is to show, in copies, and explain the noted paintings of the old masters side by side with the best examples of recent art.—This Gallery contains over 1.000 paintings, in oil and water-colors, arranged in thirty rooms, comprising copies after Allori, Andrea del Sarto, Boucher, Biliverti, Bassano, Battoni, Ann. Caracci, Correggio, Carlo Dolci, Ferrari, Guercino, Guido, Gargiuoli, Honthorst, Mad. Le Brun, Raph. Mengs, Michelangelo, Murillo, Carlo Maratti, Raphael, Leopold Robert, Sassoferato, Titian, Tintoretto, Paul Veronese, Joseph Vernet, etc. Pictures by the following are catalogued as originals : Bonifacio, Boucher, Carletto Cagliari. Canaletto, Polidoro da Caravaggio, Caravaggio, Honthorst, Sigmund Holbein. P. Liberi, Pieter de Laar, Salvator Rosa, Rosa da Tivoli, Tiepolo (6 entries), Zuccarelli, etc. There are also modern European pictures by O. Achenbach, Bruck-Lajos, Breling, C. Becker, Bouguereau, Chierici, Diaz, Delacroix, Dubufe, Carl Hoff, Kowalski. Knaus, Leon y Escosura, Meissonier, Carl Müller, Meyer von Bremen, Pallizzi, Pecrus, Piot, Romako, Riedel, Roybet, Anton Seitz, Hugo Salmson, Schenck, Carl Sohn, Simler, Schreyer, Trayer. F. Voltz, Vibert, Worms, Zimmermann, etc. The American artists represented are Wm. H. Beard, A. F. Bunner, J. J. Enneking, J. M. Falconer, R. Swain Gifford, S. R. Gifford, Edw. Gay, D. Huntington, Eastman Johnson, Geo. McCord, Geo. H. Story, T. W. Wood, etc. The sculptures include " The West Wind," by Thos. Gould, and " Joy," by Thos. Ball. [The very confused catalogue contains many names of artists unknown to fame, some of which are no doubt rendered unrecognizable by the outrageously careless spelling. This is a private Gallery, but the public is admitted on payment of 25 cents.]

ROCHESTER ART CLUB.—80 Arcade B'ldg.—Organized 1877 ; incorporated Mch. 4, 1882.—Officers : Pres., Harvey Ellis, 140 and 141 Powers B'ldg ; V. P., John Z. Wood, 10 Chestnut St.; Sec., Horatio Walker, 48 Elwood B'ldg; Treas., Jas. Somerville, 79 Arcade B'ldg.— Object : The cultivation and advancement of the Fine and Industrial Arts and the promotion of social intercourse among its members.—Members are of three classes : Resident, artists of Rochester and vicinity (5 at present), in whom are vested all the powers of the Club ; Non-resident, artists at a distance (7 at present) ; and Honorary, amateurs and connoisseurs (23), neither of which last two classes can vote or hold office. Resident and Honorary members pay an initiation fee of $10.— Every [resident ?] member must submit a specimen of his own handiwork for exhibition in the rooms of the Club within two months after election, and is liable to forfeiture of membership upon failure to contribute to the Annual Exhibition.—This association had its origin in the meetings, begun in 1872, of a few artists for the purpose of drawing from life, but the Club was not actually formed until 1877. At the beginning of the year 1882 it was reorganized under the present constitution, and incorporated. The Club holds annual exhibitions in May. The first exhibition was held in 1879. The (illustrated) catalogue of the fourth, held from May 21-26, 1883, enumerated 211 works, by 77 artists.—Classes maintained by the Club : Drawing from Cast, from Draped Figure, and from the Nude (for gentlemen only) ; Wood Engraving, Water Color and Oil Painting. The Painting Classes meet Saturday afternoons, all others, evenings.—Instructors : Jas. H. Dennis, Harvey Ellis, John Z. Wood, Jas. Somerville, Horatio Walker.—The classes are open to both sexes, who are taught together, except in the Nude Life Class, which is for gentlemen only. Number of students, December, 1883, 50.—Tuition fees vary according to time and subject.—Annual meeting, last Tuesday in May.

ROCHESTER ART EXCHANGE.—191-195 Powers Bldg.—Organized Feb. 2, 1880.—Pres., Miss Lois E. Whitney, Lake Ave.; V. Ps., Miss Mary Butts, Mrs. D. W. Powers, Miss Cunningham, Mrs. M. B. Anderson, Mrs. Wm. S. Kimball; Treas., Mrs. Elmer Smith, So. Washington St.; Sec., Miss Belle Clark, 5 Oxford St.; Cor. Sec., Miss Belle Watson, 252 Clinton St.—Objects: To provide for the exhibition and sale of decorative art work of any description, which shall be of sufficient excellence to be accepted, and for training in artistic industries.—Any person may become a member by an annual payment of $1.50. All persons desiring to place articles on sale, must become members. Number of members, Jan., 1884, about 300.—The activity of this association is similar to that of the Decorative Art Societies organized in other places. A commission of 10 per cent. is charged on the amount of sales made for contributors.—*Classes :*—Two free classes in Charcoal Drawing, Rev. Jas. H. Dennis, teacher (Aim : To give pupils skill in decorative industries ; three money prizes, usually of $10, $7, and $5. awarded yearly) ; Water Colors, Miss Jeffreys (50 cents per lesson) ; Brass Hammering, Mr. Hoffman ($1 per lesson) ; Kensington Embroidery, Mrs. Graham (50 cents per lesson ; there is also a number of free students in this class). In the free drawing classes, the pupils are of both sexes, in the others females only.—An exhibition is held in May.—Since Feb. 1, 1881, the society has paid to consignors and teachers, $7,336.31. The results of the free classes have been very gratifying. Many of the pupils in these classes have become self-supporting, by filling positions where artistic training is demanded, a number of them earning from $6 to $10 a week. In all of these cases the pupils had no art knowledge previous to becoming students in the free classes of the Art Exchange. The work of the society is not self-supporting, of course, and it therefore asks for increased patronage and a more extended list of membership.—*The Housekeepers' Exchange,* for the sale of preserved fruits, cakes, jellies, pickles, etc., is a branch of the Exchange, added about a year ago. It has been found to pay.—Annual meeting of the Association, first Monday in February.

80. Salem, Mass.

ESSEX INSTITUTE.—Plummer Hall, 134 Essex St.—Incorporated 1848.—Officers : Pres., Henry Wheatland ; V. Ps., Abner C. Goodell, Jr., Daniel B. Hagar, Fred. W. Putnam. Robt. S. Rantoul ; Sec., Geo. M. Whipple ; Treas., Geo. D. Phippen ; Aud., Richd. C. Manning ; Libr., Wm. P. Upham ; Curator of Archæology, Fred. W. Putnam ; Curator of Painting and Sculpture, T. F. Hunt.—The Essex Institute was formed by the union of the Essex Historical and the Essex County Natural History Societies. Its objects embrace Science, History, Horticulture, and Art.—Present number of members, about 340. Membership is secured by election and payment of an annual fee of $3. Life membership, $30.—The *Art Library* consists of 330 vols. of the choicest selection, including the best current issues upon painting, sculpture, architecture, ceramic decoration, etc., and is constantly increasing. (The whole number of volumes in the library of the Institute, June, 1881, was 53,900.)—The *Art Exhibitions* began in Feb., 1875, with a collection mostly of copies of paintings by the old masters, which was succeeded in November by a Second Exhibition of Paintings, in connection with the first ceramic display ever attempted in the city. In December of the same year an Exhibition of Antique Articles was held, gathered from the rich stores of colonial furniture, etc., still owned in Salem. Other exhibitions were held in June, 1879, April, 1880, May, 1881, May, 1882, and May, 1883, and are to be continued annually. The exhibits are confined almost entirely to the work of local artists and amateurs, and include paintings, drawings, etchings, embroidery, ceramic decoration, etc. The sales at these exhibitions amounted to $150 in 1881, to $195.15 in 1882, and to $224.50 in 1883.—The *Art Collections* consist of about 80 paintings, a very considerable collection of busts of men of local reputation, many rare and choice engravings and prints, large and well-arranged collections of coins and medals, and the best existing collection of relics and curiosities illustrative of the history, characteristics, arts, and industries of Essex County. Among the paintings are two portraits of Governor Endicott (1588-1665), copied from likenesses painted from life ; a portrait of Rev. John Rogers, by Smibert ; portraits of Timothy Fitch and wife, by Copley ; a portrait of Alexander Hamilton, by Trumbull ; and others by Jas. Frothingham, Chester Harding, Francis Alexander, etc. ; several old views in and about Salem, and a few old Dutch and Flemish pictures.—A place is also given to art in the *Lectures* arranged by the Institute during the winter season.—Open free, every week day, excepting holidays, from 8.30 A.M. to 1 P.M., and from 2.30 to 6 P.M. in summer, to 5 P.M. in winter. A guide, entitled "Plummer Hall : Its Libraries, its Collections, its Historical Associations," is for sale at the

office. price 15 cents. This guide contains a descriptive list of the paintings. There is no catalogue
of the other collections, which are labelled.

PEABODY ACADEMY OF SCIENCE.—East India Marine Hall, 161 Essex St.—
Founded and endowed with $100,000, in 1867, by George Peabody, of London.—Officers: Pres., Wm.
C. Endicott ; Treas., John Robinson ; Director, Edward S. Morse.—Objects : To maintain a museum
and disseminate useful scientific knowledge throughout the county of Essex.—The Museum contains,
on the Western side of the main floor, a collection illustrating the orders of the animal kingdom,
arranged in their proper sequence from the lowest form to that of the highest. The most striking features are the Corals, Reptiles, Birds, and the Australian Marsupials. This collection was chiefly derived
from the Essex Institute, in 1867. On the Eastern side are arranged the Ethnological collections,
principally received from the East India Marine Society, which are subdivided according to races or
countries. These collections rank among the very highest in importance in America, and are
especially rich in South Sea Island implements, cloths, models, idols, domestic utensils, etc. ;
and Chinese, Japanese, and East Indian life-sized models of native characters, besides the boats,
clothing, utensils, implements of war and of domestic use from these countries, and from Africa,
Arabia, and North and South America. The collection from Japan and Corea is the finest on exhibition in the country. It was formed by the Director during a recent visit to Japan, and has just
been added to the Museum. The gallery is devoted to the Natural History and Archaeology of
Essex County. Nearly every species of the flora and fauna is represented by preserved specimens,
the collection of birds and that of native woods being especially fine. The Academy has also the
best local collection of prehistoric implements and utensils of stone, bone, and clay to be found in
Essex County. There is also to be seen at the Academy a collection of portraits, 16 in all, of old
East India merchants and shipmasters.—The Academy publishes scientific memoirs and annual
reports.—Open free to all, every week day, from 9-12 A.M., and 2-5 P.M. Number of visitors, 1882,
36,676 ; from Jan. 1 to Dec., 1883, 34,545.

PUBLIC BUILDINGS.—At the *Court House*, Federal St., cor. Washington, may be seen
the portrait of Chief Justice Shaw, one of the best works of the late Wm. M. Hunt; the portrait of
Judge Lord by Frederic P. Vinton, and a portrait of Judge Putnam. In the *City Hall*, Washington
St., in the Aldermen's Room, there is a portrait of Washington, copied by Frothingham from an
original by Stuart, and a portrait of Hon. Leverett Saltonstall, the first mayor of Salem. In the
Council Chamber is another Washington, copied from an original by Stuart, by his daughter, Miss
Jane Stuart; and a portrait of Lafayette, copied by Chas. Osgood from the original by Morse in the
City Hall at New York.

SALEM ART CLUB.—[Discontinued.]

81. Salt Lake City, Utah.

LADIES' ART CLUB.—Organized 1876.—This is an informal reading circle, limited to
seven members (ladies). Its object is, to become informed on subjects of art; its meetings are held
every Tuesday morning, except in July and August, in the parlors of the members.—The club has
so far given three entertainments or exhibitions. The first, complimentary to friends, was an exhibition of engravings and etchings loaned by a collector in San Francisco. The second, also complimentary, was a conversation on ceramics, illustrated by a collection, held in Independence Hall.
The third, Feb. 12 and 13, 1883, was a public exhibition of prints, 267 numbers, from the collection
of the Club, representing the masterpieces of Christian painting, from Cimabue downward. This
exhibition was given for the benefit of the Ladies' Literary Club, the funds to be ultimately applied
to the establishment of free drawing classes, for which purpose $50 were donated also from another
source.—The Club has no officers, the hostess at each meeting acting as chairwoman.

82. San Francisco, Cal.

BOHEMIAN CLUB.—430 Pine St.—Organized Feb. 23, 1872; incorp. April 1, 1883.—
Officers: Pres., W. H. L. Barnes ; V. P., A. S. Bender ; Sec., Peter Robertson; Treas., C. P. Gor

don.—Members, limited to 500, professionally connected with literature, art, music, or the drama, or deemed eligible by reason of their love or appreciation of these objects. Initiation fee, $100; dues, $3 per month. The Club is full.—The convivial meetings held on the last Saturday evening of every month, are known as "High Jinks," for which certain subjects are announced in advance. Every "Jinks" subject is illustrated by a painting by one of the artist members. Once a year a "Midsummer High Jinks" is held in the woods.—Annual meeting. second Tuesday in April.

NAHL COLLECTION.—This is a private collection consisting of 133 paintings, 78 of which are "Old Masters"; 390 original drawings by "Old Masters"; old engravings; old and rare books ; cameos; Egyptian curios, etc., etc.; and a set of casts from cameos and cut stones. [For some further account of the collection, of which a printed catalogue has been published, see p. 24.] —On exhibition, for the present, on Wednesdays and Saturdays, in a large hall connected with the studios of the owner, Mr. H. W. Nahl, 318 Kearny St.

SAN FRANCISCO ART ASSOCIATION.—430 Pine St.—Organized Mch. 28, 1871. —Officers : Pres., Col. A. G. Hawes ; 1st V. P., F. Marion Wells, 757 Mission St.; 2d V. P., Horace Fletcher, 520 Commercial St.; Sec., Joseph D. Redding ; Asst. Sec., J. Ross Martin ; Treas., Lovell White.—Objects : The promotion of painting, sculpture, and the fine arts in general, and the establishment of a School of Design.—The membership, both sexes, unlimited, consists of Life Members, who pay $100 ; Contributing Members, initiation fee $2, monthly dues $1 ; and Honorary Members. Present number of members : 152 Life ; 406 Contributing ; 9 Honorary. Members are elected by the Board of Directors.—The resources of the Association consist of the dues of members, and the tuition fees of the pupils in the School of Design, averaging $421 a month.—The *California School of Design*, which is maintained by the Association, has the following classes. Regular : Crayon Drawing, antique and portrait, $24 per term of three months (three terms each year), or $10 per month ; Oil Painting, still-life and portrait, $30 per term, or $12 per month. Special : Portrait Class, $5 per month ; Sketch Class, $2 per month ; Landscape Class (study from nature, excursions in the country every Wednesday), $4 per month. The special classes are open without charge to all regular pupils who are sufficiently advanced. The Director gives semi-weekly lectures to pupils and such members of the Association as choose to attend, on anatomy, perspective, color, etc.—Director, Virgil Williams ; Assistant, W. E. Rollins.—Pupils must be 14 years or over. Both sexes are taught together. Average number, 86.—Two prizes, the Avery Gold Medal for excellence and progress in oil painting, and the Alvord Gold Medal for the best full-length crayon study from cast, are awarded to pupils of the regular classes at the end of each school year. Pupils who intend to teach art are entitled to a certificate from the Director, specifying the course of study pursued and the medals received, and giving the opinion of the Director as to the qualifications of the recipient.—*Exhibitions.* Annual Exhibitions are held of works of local artists, and of work done by pupils of the schools ; also occasional loan exhibitions, including foreign paintings, etc. At the Nineteenth Exhibition, April, 1883, 145 works were shown by 73 artists.—[From newspaper reports, it appears that the school is in much better condition than ever before. It is clear of debt, and the prospects are improving. Receipts, for past year, $4,760.80, against $4,174.75 expenditures. There were 30 applicants during the year for free scholarships, most of which had to be refused. Endowments of free scholarships are, therefore, called for. It is claimed that the collection of casts and other material is not surpassed by any in America, and that the school is the best in the United States, west of New York.]—Annual meeting of the Association. in March.

SAN FRANCISCO CHAPTER OF THE AMERICAN INSTITUTE OF ARCHITECTS.—240 Montgomery St.—Organized Jan. 20, 1881. (Now in process of incorporation.) - Pres., John Wright, 418 California St.; V. P., Wm. Curlett, Phelan Block ; Sec., G. H. Wolfe, 240 Montgomery St.; Treas., H. C. Macy, 120 Sutter St.—Objects : Mutual benefit and improvement of members.—Members, January, 1884, 46 (38 fellows, 5 draughtsmen, 3 students).— Meetings are held regularly every month, and lectures are given several times during the year.—The chapter has opened *Classes* in Perspective (G. H. Sanders, teacher), Drawing from the Flat (A. Pissis), Modelling (F. Marion Wells), Geometry (J. Gash), and Carving (J. Bryant), to which only students of architecture in the employ of San Francisco architects are admitted. No charge whatever is made for instruction.—Annual meeting of the Chapter, first Friday in September.

SOCIETY OF DECORATIVE ART OF CALIFORNIA.—300 Stockton St.—

Organized Jan., 1881.—Officers: Pres., Mrs. I. L. Baker; V. P's., Mrs. C. Cushing, Mrs. R. Balfour, Mrs. I. Gerstle, Mrs. J. L. Rathbone; Treas., Mrs. F. M. Brown; Rec. Sec., Mrs. J. G. Kittle; Cor. Sec., Mrs. R. Kaufman.—Objects: to establish rooms for the exhibition and sale of women's work; the diffusion of a knowledge of decorative art among women, and their training in artistic industries.—Annual membership, $5; Life membership, $100. Present number of members, Annual, 100; Life, 29.—The income of the Society is derived from dues, donations, tuition fees, commissions on sales and orders (10 per cent.), interest on life-membership fund, and the proceeds of exhibitions.—*Classes:* Art Needle-Work, Miss E. M. Smith, Graduate of South Kensington, teacher ($5 for 6 lessons; $1 a single lesson in class; $2.50 a private lesson of two hours). Number of free pupils, 100. The classes in Design, etc., were discontinued, as they did not pay expenses. Classes in embroidery were formed during the summer (of 1882) in San Jose, San Rafael, and Portland, Oreg., in which there were 35 free and 15 paying pupils.—The Society held a very successful Art Loan Exhibition in April. 1881. including paintings, engravings, and objects of industrial art of all kinds, the proceeds of which netted $3,453.21. In November, 1882, a Competitive Exhibition of Designs and Embroideries was held, at which 67 articles were entered for competition and 10 prizes awarded [See p. 16].—The Society has established an agency at Portland, Oregon (Mrs. Moeller, agent, cor. 9th and Taylor Sts.), which is in a flourishing condition. A second agency in Seattle, Washington Territory, was discontinued at the beginning of 1884.—The Second Annual Report, Jan., 1883, gives the number of contributors at 241; number of articles contributed, 1,110, of which 164 were rejected; payments to contributors, $1,873. The Workroom and Order Committee report during the past year (1882), 1,112 orders received and executed; increase in receipts, $2,000 over 1881. Nearly $3,000 was paid out in salaries to teachers, and to workers. "Although the Society has not flourished in one department [classes] as the Managers had reason to hope," says the report, "they feel encouraged in their general work. and trust that another year's effort will accomplish still more satisfactory results."—Annual meeting, in February.

83. Saratoga Springs, N. Y.

MOUNT McGREGOR ART ASSOCIATION.—Incorporated 1883.—Pres., W. J. Arkell; Sec. and Treas., W. H. Finehout.—The Association held an exhibition from June 15 to Sept. 15, 1883, from which 14 pictures were sold (out of 155 exhibited by 109 artists) for $9,700.— [This Association appears to be a private undertaking. The exhibition is held at Mount McGregor, ten miles north of Saratoga. It is reported that 22,000 persons visited the mountain during the summer of 1883.]

84. Springfield, Ill.

SPRINGFIELD ART SOCIETY.—Organized about 1875.—Officers: Pres., Charles Ridgely; V. P's., Miss Virginia Stuart, C. L. Conkling; Sec., Mrs. Paul Selby; Treas., Geo. H. Souther.—Objects: The improvement of its members in the knowledge of art and its history, and the promotion of a general interest in art matters.—Number of members, about 50.—The meetings are held fortnightly at the residences of the members. The Programme of Study is published in advance, and the topic for each evening is assigned to a member, who, as leader, divides the subject into several subdivisions, and calls upon as many other members to assist. Lectures and exhibitions are also arranged occasionally.—The Society is a member of the Art Union of Central Illinois.— Annual meeting, first Tuesday in October.

ART UNION OF CENTRAL ILLINOIS.- Organized May 26, 1880.—Officers 1883-4: Pres., Charles Ridgely, Springfield; V. P's., one from each society; Sec., Mrs. W. T. Wells, Decatur; Treas., Miss May Latham, Lincoln.—The credit of originating this association belongs to Mrs. Col. Latham, of Lincoln. At her instance, the Art Society of Lincoln, in the spring of 1880, extended invitations to several similar associations to send delegates to an informal meeting at the place named.. About twenty representatives of half a dozen societies responded, and spent a pleasant and profitable day or two in a highly artistic atmosphere, with several essays, a few speeches, and much social converse. The whole affair was so thoroughly enjoyed, that in order to insure its repetition a formal organization was agreed upon. The constitution, adopted at the second meeting, held in Springfield in 1881, and slightly amended since, is here given entire : " I. The name of this Association shall be *The Art Union of Central Illinois.* II. It shall be composed of representatives from the Art Societies of Central Illinois; each Society to be represented by five delegates. III. The officers shall be a President, one Vice President from each Society, a Secretary, and a Treasurer. IV. The term of office shall be one year. V. The officers shall be nominated at the annual meeting by a committee of one from each Society, chosen by their delegates. VI. The Secretary of the Union shall be chosen from the place where the next annual meeting is to be held. VII. Honorary members may be elected at any meeting by a unanimous vote. VIII. Regular meetings of the Union shall be held annually on the third Wednesday in May. Special meetings may be called by the President, at the request of representatives of a majority of the Societies. IX. The place of holding the annual meeting shall be chosen by the committee on nominations, subject to the approval of the Union. X. At the annual meeting a paper shall be presented by each Society, the reading of said paper not to occupy more than thirty minutes. XI. When deemed practicable, a Loan Exhibition shall be held in connection with the annual meeting. XII. The Secretary of each Society shall send to the Secretary of the Union, on or before the first of May, each year, a full report of the work of the Society during the year, embracing names of officers· number of meetings, lists of topics, essays, readings, lectures, or other exercises, of works of art procured, of books used, and such other information as may be valuable in the study of art. XIII. The Secretary of the Union shall make an annual report compiled from the reports of the Societies, and summarizing their work. XIV. Other Art Societies may be admitted to the Union on the vote of three-fourths of the delegates present at any annual meeting. XV. This Constitution may be amended at any meeting of the Union by the unanimous vote of the delegates present; or at any regular meeting by a two-thirds vote, provided that the amendment has been proposed at a previous meeting."—The Union is composed of the following nine Societies : *Historical and Art Society* and *The Palladen*, both at Bloomington ; *Art Class* and *Young Ladies' Art Class*, both at Decatur ; *Art Association*, Jacksonville ; *Art Society*, Lincoln ; *Art Society*, Peoria ; *Art Society*, Springfield ; *Art Club*, Champaign. (For details, see the special account given of each Society.)—The fourth annual meeting of the Union was held at Jacksonville, May 16 and 17. The fifth will be held at Decatur, on the third Wednesday of May, 1884.—The Union has published its " Proceedings" for 1883, in pamphlet form, including a synopsis of the meetings previously held. [Although this association is not localized in Springfield, it is inserted under this heading, as the president of the year lives here.]

85. Springfield, Mass.

SPRINGFIELD ART ASSOCIATION.—Evangelist Bl'dg., State St., cor. of Chestnut. —Organized Jan., 1879.—Officers 1883-4: Pres., Elisha Morgan ; V. Ps., P. P. Kellogg, W. W. Colburn, Chas. Bill ; Treas., W. F. Ferry ; Clerk, Louis C. Hyde.—Objects : To furnish opportunities for education that shall be of value, not merely as a pleasant accomplishment, but as a preparation for industrial and artistic pursuits, enlarging in a practical way the means of dignified and honorable self-support for young men and women. --Members pay $5 annual dues, which entitles them to free admission to all lectures and exhibitions given during the year, and to the privilege of using the rooms and casts at any time, when the regular classes are not in session ; each additional member of family, $2. Number of members, both sexes, Dec., 1883, 62.—*Art School :* R. Lionel De Lisser, instructor. The Association maintains the following day-classes : Elementary, Intermediate, Antique, and Life and Painting. There are also evening classes of the first three grades, and an evening class in Drawing from the Living Model (draped). Terms—per quarter of three months, two lessons per week. Day Elementary or Intermediate, $18 ; Antique, $24 ; Life and Painting, $30 ; Evening Classes, $12. Terms made also per month or single lesson. The managers hope to make the school self-supporting the present season (1883-4). At the end of each term there will be an exhibition by the pupils. The pupil showing the best work in each of the day classes for the season, at the last exhibition, will receive a quarter's tuition free.—The Association arranges lectures and holds receptions and exhibitions. At the last exhibition held from Dec. 17-29, 1883, of which an autographic illustrated catalogue was published, 48 works were shown by 40 artists.—Annual meeting, first Monday in June.

SPECIAL EXHIBITIONS of "Pictures selected from the Studios of American Artists" are held annually in February at *Gill's Art Galleries*, Jas. D. Gill, Prop., cor. Main and Bridge Sts. Admission, 25 cents. For the rest of the year the Gallery is open free.

86. St. Johnsbury, Vt.

ST. JOHNSBURY ATHENÆUM.—Founded 1870; opened 1871.—Officers: Horace Fairbanks, Edw. T. Fairbanks, Andrew E. Rankin, Franklin Fairbanks, Trustees; Mrs. Abbie McNeil, Libr.—The Athenæum building contains a library (about 10,500 vols.), a lecture hall and an *Art Gallery*. The paintings, of which there are about 50, and the statuary gathered in this gallery, have been selected with a view to forming a collection of choice specimens of representative artists. The following are among the more prominent paintings: "The Domes of the Yosemite," by A. Bierstadt ; "Woods of Assohochan, Catskills," Jervis McEntee ; "On the Plains, Colorado," W. Whittredge ; "South Mountains, Catskills," S. R. Gifford ; "Under the Elms," Jas. M. Hart ; "Hiding in the Old Oak," J. G. Brown ; "The Emigrant Train, Colorado," Saml. Colman ; "Marine, after a Storm," M. F. De Haas ; "Sheep," Verboeckhoven ; "Italian Girl," Kaulbach ; "St. Ursula," Gabr. Max ; "View in Holland," Achenbach ; "Up for Repair," Guez ; "The Halberdier," J. Baufain Irving ; "Autumn on the Delaware," J. F. Cropsey ; "Cattle." Hartmann ; "Aspasia," Coomans. There are also some copies from Raphael, Carlo Dolci, and Van Dyck. In the same hall have been placed a number of standard illustrated works on art, including Ruskin, Mrs. Jameson, Owen Jones, Lübke, etc. ; Robert's "Egypt and the Holy Land," the "Musée Français," "Musée des Antiquités," etc.—The institution was founded and is sustained by Mr. Horace Fairbanks.. It has a permanent endowment fund of $30.000.—The Library and Reading Rooms are open free daily, Sundays excepted ; the Art Gallery is open free on Tuesdays and Fridays. Hours from 9 A.M. to 12 M., and from 2 to 6 P.M.

87. St Louis, Mo.

MISSOURI HISTORICAL SOCIETY.—O. W. Collet, keeper of the Museum. [According to the report on "Public Libraries," published by the U. S. Bureau of Education in 1876, p. 348, one of the objects of this society is the establishment of "a cabinet of antiquities, relics, etc." In answer to repeated requests, detailed information was refused, on the ground that the society "has nothing whatever to do with art."]

PEN AND PENCIL CLUB.—Organized 1870.—Officers: Pres., W. R. Hodges, 2115 Walnut St. ; V. P., Mrs. M. J. Lippman ; Sec. and Treas., Mrs. A. C. Walker, 2809 Washington Ave.—Object: Art and literary culture. Meets at the residences of members. Present number of members, about 40. [The Club still exists, but has been dormant the past year.]

PERMANENT EXHIBITIONS of works of art will be found at the *Pettes Leathe Art Rooms*, cor. Sixth and Olive Sts.

PUBLIC SCHOOL LIBRARY.—In the reading room of this Library are to be seen 3 oil paintings (Conrad Diehl's "Macbeth," and two copies from Rembrandt) ; 21 engravings and 151 autotypes, giving a synopsis of the history of art from Cimabue and Giotto down to Corot and Rousseau, and 10 casts of antique statuary. These works (together with an original copy of Claude's "Liber Veritatis," donated by Mr. Jas. E. Yeatman) were placed permanently in the Library by the *St. Louis Art Society*, upon its dissolution in 1879. [The Society named was organized in 1872 and incorporated in 1873, "for the promotion of art interests, and to form a collection of art works." It consisted of 178 active and 20 honorary members. and had rooms in the Polytechnic Building, cor. Seventh and Chestnut Sts. It held a loan exhibition, arranged lectures, readings, etc., and maintained an art school, under the direction of Mr. Conrad Diehl. These details were kindly communicated by Mr. J. R. Meeker, a former president of the Society.]

SALMAGUNDI SKETCH CLUB.—Eighth and Chestnut Sts.—Organized Nov., 1883. —Officers: Ch'man of B'd., J. R. Meeker ; Sec. and Treas., F. W. Ruckstuhl.—Objects: The development of the creative faculty, and to cultivate sociability among artists.—Members : Active, must be able to sketch well ; Associate, $6 a year. Present number, 25 Active, 50 Associate.—Annual meeting, first Thursday in November.

ST. LOUIS ACADEMY OF SCIENCES.—Collections illustrating the archæology of the country. The Archæological Section of the Academy published " Contributions to the Archæ-ology of Missouri.—Part I. Pottery." (Salem : Geo. A. Bates, 1880.)—[No reply to repeated requests for more detailed information.]

ST. LOUIS ART SOCIETY.—See *Public School Library.*

ST. LOUIS CHAPTER OF THE AMERICAN INSTITUTE OF ARCHI-TECTS.—[The Institute received an application for a charter from St. Louis toward the end of 1883. No details as yet.]

ST. LOUIS KÜNSTLER VEREIN. (St. Louis Artists' Society.)—27 and 29 S. Fourth St.—Organized Feb. 19, 1878.—Officers : Pres., Herm. Marquardt, 106 S. 8th St.; V. P., Chs. Stoelting, 106 S. 8th St.; Sec., Adolph Schenk, 27 and 29 S. 4th St.; Financ. Sec., Christ. Hert-wig, 714 Franklin Ave.; Treas., L. Hock, 217 S. 2d St.—Object : Harmonious co-operation among artists in the social and practical relations of life, and more especially the encouragement of the art of the country.—Members : Active, professional artists, initiation fee, $4, monthly dues, 50 cents ; Passive, amateurs and connoisseurs, initiation fee, $6 ; monthly dues, 50 cents. Active members may pay initiation fee and dues in works of art. If a work of art offered for this purpose is valued at more than $50 by the Committee whose duty it is to pass upon it, the member offering it acquires life membership. Present number, 37 active and 28 passive members.—On the third Saturday of each month some one of the members delivers a lecture, and this is followed by a discussion. Most of the members are German, and all the proceedings are conducted in German.—Annual meeting, in January.

ST. LOUIS SCHOOL AND MUSEUM OF FINE ARTS. (Art Department of Washington University).—Officers : Pres. B'd of Control, J. G. Chapman ; Director, Halsey C. Ives.—The *St. Louis School of Fine Arts* was organized May 22, 1879. The establishment of an art school upon a broad and permanent foundation has always been part of the plan of Washington University. For more than twenty-five years art instruction has been embodied in the course of studies followed by many of the classes. In 1875 special students were admitted to the Drawing Department, and class and public lectures were given by Prof. Ives on Art History. The same year an evening school was opened. From this time the growth of the department was so marked, and the work of the students had assumed such a degree of importance, that it was deemed advisable to reorganize the Drawing Department. The Directors of the University therefore passed an ordinance on May 22, 1879, establishing it as a special department, the objects of which were set forth as fol-lows : " The object of said department shall be instruction in the Fine Arts ; the collection and exhibition of pictures, statuary, and other works of art, and of whatever else may be of artistic interest, and appropriate for a public gallery or art museum ; and in general the promotion by all proper means of æsthetic and artistic education."—The School furnishes instruction in drawing, modelling, painting, artistic anatomy, perspective and decorative design, including study from the draped and nude model. Full-time students are privileged to take up the study of French, German, and English History and Literature in classes of the Undergraduate Department as regular school work. Ladies are not required to work with University students who come to the School for instruc-tion, but are given places in rooms set apart to the use of art students.—Instructors : Prof. Halsey C. Ives, Director ; Carl Gutherz, Paul E. Harney, Edmund A. Engler, Jno. O. Anderson ; Lecturer on Anatomy, Chas. A. Todd, M.D.; Assist. in Elementary Work, Mary L. Fairchild ; Assist. in Mechanical Drawing in Night School, Hollis B. Page.—There are two terms in the year, from Octo-ber to February, and from February through the rest of the academic year. The rooms are open daily from 9 A.M. to 5 P.M.—Classes for drawing from the antique and from life meet four evenings in the week, from Nov. to May. Students may enter any class upon submitting examples of work showing the necessary skill.—Tuition per term (two terms, Oct.-Feb., Feb.-June), admitting to all classes and lectures, $40 ; various rates per month, according to studies pursued. Saturday Class for Teachers, $10 per term. Evening Classes, $3 per term of 12 weeks.—Students enrolled in the Art School from Jan., 1883, to Jan., 1884, 301 (194 in the day classes, 107 in the night classes). Average attendance in the day classes, 110 ; in the night classes, 103. At the same time there were 350 students from other departments of the University receiving instruction either in the Art School or from its teachers. An exhibition of the work of the School is held in May.—The School is fully equipped with models, casts from the antique, etc. A collection of several hundred autotype reproductions from sketches, studies, and paintings by celebrated masters from the 15th century to the present time may be used by the students upon application to the Director. There is also a collection of 1,041 carbon prints, illustrating the historical development of art, and including the following six divisions : Prehistoric and Ethnographic, Egyptian, Assyrian, Grecian, Etruscan and Roman, Mediæval. The Museum (see below) is free to the students at all times, while open, and an Art Library is being formed for their use. From time to time class and public lectures are given upon the History of Art, for the illustration of which more than 1,400 views are available.—*The Museum of Fine Arts* was founded by Mr. Wayman Crow, in memory of a deceased son. The building, which cost about $150,000, was dedicated and transferred to the Board of Control of the University on May 10, 1881. Subscriptions toward an endowment fund of $100,000 were started at the same time. Of this sum, $30,000 had been secured up to Jan., 1884, and there was a move on foot at that time which it was hoped would lead to the securing of the whole amount. The Museum contains a carefully selected collection of casts from antique and mediæval sculptures ; several works in marble and in bronze ; a collection of paintings, rare engravings, etchings, and other objects of art and art industry. Examples are being added, when feasible, with a view to affording the student the best possible opportunity for pursuing the study of art history. The additions in 1883 were, by gift, 11 paintings, a collection of 300 etchings and engravings, one bronze, and two marbles ; by purchase, 66 examples of antique and mediæval sculptures and architectural fragments. At all times since the Museum was opened there has been a sufficiently important collection on exhibition in the Loan Gallery to afford ample material for study. Open daily, except Sundays, from 9.30 A.M. to 5 P.M. Visitors in 1882 : 5,657 (2,157 free, 3,518 paid); from Jan. 1 to Dec. 1, 1883, 8,365 (4,171 free, 4,194 paid). Admission 25 cents. [The following extracts are from the report of 1882 : " The students in the night classes represent nearly all the trades and professions requiring in their practice a knowledge of the principles of drawing. Stonecutters, carpenters, builders, painters, paper-hangers, pattern-makers, machinists, engineers, architects, decorators, teachers, photographers, engravers, dentists, lawyers, and physicians have all been represented in the classes of the evening School. The aim of the School thus far has been to afford students from these different callings such instruction as could be practically applied to their daily work ; the large number of trades and professions represented and the increasing attendance warrants the supposition that the effort has not been in vain..... The School has no income except that derived from the small fee charged each student for tuition. Washington University has given the School free use of rooms with heat and light. There has at no time been a sufficient income from tuition fees to meet the expenses of conducting the School. That it might be continued, the teachers have in many cases volunteered their services ; three have never received payment for their services from the day they began to assist in the work to the present ; one, in addition to services, has given sums of money whenever needed to continue the work. With the beginning of the next session a more extended range of work should be introduced..... To accomplish this and assist in establishing a similar work in the day School, without increasing the tuition fee, not less than $1,500 will be required annually..... With the exception of one gift of $400, for the support of life-class work last year (1880–81), there has been almost nothing done by our citizens for the support of the educational work of the School, except gifts of time and money by teachers and others directly connected with the work. This is certainly to be regretted, when we find how much money is used annually for work of much less magnitude and of a transitory nature. To illustrate : Our Veiled Prophets Exhibition, while it brings money into our city, gives a precarious, or, at best, an ephemeral return for the thousands of dollars put into it. Were a sum of money equal to that expended in one such display bestowed on the School, the result would be felt in our midst not only now, but for years to come."]

ST. LOUIS SKETCH CLUB.—1724 Washington Ave.—Organized about 1877.— Officers : Pres., W. R. Hodges, 2115 Walnut St.; V. P., Halsey C. Ives ; Sec. and Treas., W.

S. Eames, 2930 Washington Ave.—Objects : The cultivation of sociability among artists and members, and the development of the creative faculty.—Members : Regular, who must qualify by presenting a satisfactory original sketch ; Privileged, members of the press, art patrons, and those specially devoted to the advancement of art ; Associate, friends of the fine arts. Only Regular members can hold office or vote. Regular members pay an initiation fee of 50 cents, and the same amount monthly. Associate members are expected to contribute to the support of the Club at pleasure. Present number of members, about 20 Regular and 50 Associate and Privileged.—Meetings are held about once a month, from October to June, when studies and sketches are exhibited. A set of sketches by members of the club was sold some time ago for $500.—Annual meeting, first Wednesday in March.

STUDENTS' SKETCH CLUB.—Organized Feb., 1882, by students at the night class of the St. Louis School of Fine Arts.—Officers for 1884 : Pres., F. M. Chambers ; Sec., W. D. Streetor, 314 Locust St. ; Treas., G. M. Cady.—Members, gentlemen interested or amateurs in art, limited to 15. The club is full.—Meetings are held the second Thursday of each month, at the members' houses, each member entertaining in regular order. The host names a subject, and receives the sketches made in illustration. Any member who fails to present a sketch, or shows careless work, is fined $1. All the sketches must be original ; no copying allowed.—Annual meeting, second Thursday in January.

88. St. Paul, Minn.

ARCHITECTURAL ASSOCIATION OF MINNESOTA.—Pres., E. B. Bassford, St. Paul ; Sec., D. W. Willard, St. Paul. [See *Minneapolis.*]

MINNESOTA HISTORICAL SOCIETY.—State Capitol.—Organized and incorporated Dec. 1849.—Officers : Pres., H. H. Sibley ; Sec., J. F. Williams ; Treas., H. P. Upham.—Objects : To collect materials for the history of the State ; to collect a library of useful works, which shall be free to any one in the pursuit of knowledge ; to disseminate knowledge by means of lectures, addresses, publication of works, etc. ; to collect a museum, art gallery, etc.—Members : Any citizen of Minnesota can become a member on payment of $25 ; present number, 100. There are also 100 corresponding and honorary members.—The society is mainly supported by a grant from the State funds, amounting at present to $6,000 p.a., but receives also some contributions from members.—Publications : Four vols. of " Historical Collections " (a fifth in press), reports, etc. —*Collections :* Library, 22,000 vols., bound and unbound ; a fair collection of pictures, mostly portraits of men well known in the history of the State ; a cabinet or museum of historical and archæological curiosities, Indian implements, weapons, etc. ; also manuscripts, autographs, engravings, coins, currency, etc. All these objects were acquired by gift. [In the fire which destroyed the State Capitol on March 1, 1881, most of the archæological and historical relics, costumes, implements, specimens of pottery, etc., then belonging to the Society were lost. The picture gallery also suffered considerable loss, some pictures being wholly destroyed, and others badly injured.]

89. Syracuse, N. Y.

ARTISTS' LEAGUE.—Organized 1881.—Pres., Prof. N. A. Wells, 5 Harlow Block. [No reply to repeated requests for information.]

ESTHETIC SOCIETY.—Syracuse University.—Organized 1873.—Officers : Pres., D. R. Augsburg ; V. P., R. C. Brown ; Sec., Miss Libbie Hall ; Treas., Miss Grace Comfort ; Critic, Miss Ida Gilzer.—Objects : To promote the artistic, literary, and social culture of its members, for which purpose weekly meetings are held during term time.—Members : Active, who must be regular students in good standing of the College of Fine Arts of Syracuse University (initiation fee, $1 ; yearly dues, 50 cents), at present 20 ; non-active, 60 ; honorary, 12.—An annual exhibition is held in June, of the work done during the year, and popular exhibitions (usually loan exhibitions) are given at irregular times as sources of income to the society. The exhibition held from June 25 to July 14, 1883, to celebrate the completion of the first decennium of the Society was divided into two parts, the

Raphael Exhibit (265 photographs, engravings, etc., from the works of Raphael), and collection of paintings, etchings, etc., comprising quite a number of "Old Masters" (see p. 241.—The Society is making a collection of photographs, engravings, etchings, etc., as fast as its resources will allow. Original work is added by members on graduating, or in Senior Year. An extensive library is also forming.

PORTFOLIO CLUB.—58 West Onondaga St.—Organized 1875, by a number of young ladies, after the meeting of the Women's Congress in Syracuse : incorp. 1878.—Officers : Pres., Mrs. L. P. Brown, 10 Madison St.; V. P., Mrs. E. C. Stearns, Vanderbilt House ; Treas., Mrs. W. N. Nottingham, 141 Warren St.; Sec., Miss Ella J. Barber, 88 Warren St.; Cor. Sec., Mrs. E. C. Stearns, Vanderbilt House.—[Objects not stated in the constitution.]—Members: Active, ladies only, limited to 25 (present number 22); annual dues $1. Honorary, ladies or gentlemen, annual dues, $5. Corresponding members, limited to 20 ; no dues. Fines are exacted for tardiness, etc.— Regular meetings are held every Wednesday afternoon, and three lectures given each year. In January, 1883, Dr. F. Seymour Haden lectured before the club, and an exhibition and sale of his etchings preceded the lecture.—Collections: A small library, and engravings, etchings, and photographs of the most important work of arts.—Annual meeting, last Wednesday in April.

SOCIAL ART CLUB.—Organized Nov., 1875.—Officers : Pres., Mrs. Mary Hicks ; V. P., Mrs. Henry C. Leavenworth ; Sec., Mrs. Louise V. L. Lynch ; Cor. Sec., Mrs. Geo. N. Crouse ; Treas., Mrs. Edwin S. Jenny ; Libr., Mrs. Henry Gifford.—Object : To cultivate the study of art in its various relations, by reading, discussions, essays, and such practical work as may be suggested.—Members, ladies only : Regular, limited to 40, annual fee, $3 : Associates, limited to 15, annual fee, $5.—Honorary members may also be elected. Every vacancy is promptly filled, and applicants are always waiting for admission.—The Club has pleasant rooms, well supplied with pictures, art publications, etc. At the weekly meetings essays are read by members on art and its history. In this manner were studied during the past year, Roman architecture, the ruins of Pompeii and Herculaneum, Etruscan art. Greek and Roman sculpture, Greek and Roman coins, pottery and porcelain, animal forms in ornamental art, Greek and Roman painting, etc. The Club owns a collection of about 200 engravings, wood-cuts, autotypes, heliotypes, photographs, and chromolithographs (published by the Arundell Society, of which the Club is a member), of which 161 are framed. The published catalogue of this collection shows that it illustrates the art history of Europe from the fifteenth century downwards, and includes some valuable engravings by Dürer, Carracci, Calamata, Morghen, Longhi, Desnoyers, F. Müller, and others.—Annual meeting, last Tuesday in October. [From last year's issue. No reply to requests for later information.]

SYRACUSE ART CLUB.—Officers: Pres., Brace W. Loomis ; V. P., Frank Beard ; Sec., Albert W. Curtis. 10 South Salina St.; Treas., James Cantwell.—Present number of active members, 10.—The Syracuse Art Club is founded upon the success of an experimental exhibition held in Syracuse in June, 1883, which was generally conceded to be the best local exhibition ever held in the city. The active membership embraces the leading professional artists and amateurs of Syracuse. The object of the club is to elevate and extend local art. It proposes to accomplish its object by annually throwing open for the enjoyment and study of the public an exhibition of the best work of local artists, good examples of foreign work. and, principally, representative work of leading American artists. The first of these exhibitions will open at the Decorative Art Rooms, No. 45 South Salina St., May 5, and close on the evening of May 19, 1884.

SYRACUSE UNIVERSITY.—Organized 1870.—Officers B'd of Trustees: Pres., Francis H. Root, Delaware Ave., Buffalo ; 1st V. P., Hon. George F. Comstock, LL.D. ; 2d V. P., Erastus F. Holden ; Sec., Rev. D. W. C. Huntington, D.D. ; Treas., Thos J. Leach ; Gen. Agent, Rev. E. C Curtis, 727 Irving St. Officers of Gov't. : Chancellor. Rev. Chas. N. Sims, 646 Irving St. ; Dean of Coll. of Lib. Arts, John R. French, LL.D., 728 Chestnut St. ; Dean of Coll. of Fine Arts. Geo. F. Comfort, A.M., 353 East Ave.—Three colleges are organized and in active operation, viz., the College of Liberal Arts, the College of Medicine, and the College of Fine Arts. Other colleges are to be organized as circumstances permit. All the colleges are open to women on the same terms as men.—The College of Liberal Arts has four courses, Classical, Latin Scientific, Scientific, and Civil Engineering. Students in the Scientific and Latin Scientific Courses are required, and students in the Classical Course may elect, to attend the classes in the College of Fine Arts, two hours a week during one term, in Free-Hand Drawing, Mechanical Drafting, and Architectural Drafting. Students in the Scientific Course are also required to attend classes in Perspective Drawing two hours a week during the first term of the Sophomore year. Weekly lectures are given on .Esthetics during the first term, and on the History of the Fine Arts during the second and third terms of the senior year. The Appliances of the College of Fine Arts are employed to illustrate these lectures. — *The College of Fine Arts*. Opened 1873.—Faculty : Geo. F. Comfort, A.M., 383 East Ave., Dean and Prof. of Æsthetics and the History of the Fine Arts ; Newton A. Wells, M.P., 5 Harlow Block, Prof. of Drawing ; Ward V. Ranger, Instructor in Photography ; Hiram S. Gutsell, A.M., B.P., Instructor in Modelling and Etching ; Geo. H. Liddle, B.P., Instr. in Persp. Drawing and Archit. Drafting ; E. Ely Van De Warker, M.D., 45 Montgomery St., Lecturer on Artistic Anatomy.—This college is ultimately to include all the Fine Arts, that is, in the Formative Arts : Architecture, Sculpture, Painting, Engraving, and the various forms of Industrial Art : and in the Phonetic Arts : Music, Oratory, Poetry, and Belles-Lettres Literature. At present, courses in architecture, painting, and music only have been organized. [The musical members of the Faculty are omitted in the list above given.]—The courses of study already established include systematic and progressive instruction in the theory, history, and practice of architecture and painting, and in those branches of mathematics, natural science, history, language, and philosophy which bear most intimately and directly upon the arts, and without a knowledge of which success in the highest domains of art is impossible. The professors are proficient and practical workers in their several departments, and the students have access to their studios and offices, so that they have opportunity of witnessing works of art in process of completion. The aim is to develop the individuality of the student, rather than to mould his or her talent after the same arbitrary method. The complete course in architecture as well as in painting extends over four years. The subjects taught are as follows : 1. Free-Hand Drawing from the flat, from objects and casts, from nature, from memory, and from original designs ; in the choice of media, lead-pencil, pen, charcoal, crayon, India ink, and sepia, the students are left largely to their own tastes. 2. Architectural Drafting, including instruction in the use of instruments ; the drawing of plans, elevations, sections, ornaments, details, and working drawings ; the principles of taste in their application to architectural composition ; the study of executed works and works in progress, and the sketching of completed buildings ; the use of building materials ; principles and processes of construction ; laws and usages in drawing up contracts and specifications, in making estimates and measurements, and in superintending the erection of buildings. Special instruction is also given in Decorative Art in its relations to architecture, and in Landscape Gardening. 3. Oil and Water Color Painting, including the use of Colors, the principles of technical execution, and the laws of composition. 4. Linear Perspective and the Projection of Shades and Shadows. 5. Modelling. Prominence is given to this study, as a most important means of cultivating a feeling for solid form. 6. Etching, including the printing of etchings. 7. Photography, as a valuable aid to the architect, and more especially to the painter. (Students may also make a special study of Photography.) 8. .Esthetics. Instruction is given by lectures in the general principles of the science of æsthetics, which give the foundation of all the Fine Arts. The principles of Art Criticism, which apply especially to architecture and painting, are treated more at length in separate courses of lectures. 9. History of the Fine Arts. 10. Classical Mythology and Archæology. 11. Christian and Mediæval Archæology. 12. Art Literature, consisting of critical remarks, etc , upon the most important books and periodicals on the subject of art. 13. Related studies, including Mathematics, Natural Science, Languages, History, English Literature, Rhetoric, and Elocution. Essays and a thesis to be preserved in the archives of the college must be presented during the Senior year. The College of Medicine offers excellent opportunity to such students as may desire to make more extensive studies in human and comparative anatomy. [No mention is made of study from the nude in the " Manual " issued by the College of Fine Arts.]—Candidates for admission to the Course in Architecture are examined in English Grammar, Geography, American History, Arithmetic, Natural Philosophy, Algebra as far as the Calculus of Radicals, Plane Geometry, and Free-Hand Drawing, sufficient to represent the progress usually made by students in at least one year of thorough and systematic study. Candidates for admission to the Course in Painting are examined in English Grammar, Geography, American History, Arithmetic, Natural Philosophy, and Free-Hand Drawing, sufficient to represent the progress usually made in at least two years of thorough and systematic study. Special students, or those not proposing to graduate, may enter at any time and take up such branches of study as they are prepared to pursue.—Expenses: Matriculation fee, $5 ; tuition, $100 per year (or $33½ for a single term) ; graduation in each course, $20.—The College confers the degrees of Bachelor of Architecture and of Bachelor of Painting. Special students may receive certificates of progress and proficiency. Every candidate for graduation in architecture is required to leave in the college an original project drawing, with specifications ; and an original graduating painting will be required of candidates in painting. Students who have acquired a complete education as photographic artists, may receive the degree of Bachelor of Painting. Graduates who have pursued professional work for three years after graduation may receive the Master's degree upon presentation to the college of an approved original work in their respective branch, an examination in an approved course of reading in æsthetics and in the history of their respective arts, and the payment of $25. Any person, not a student of the college, who is not less than twenty-eight years of age, and can give evidence that he has fully mastered any course of study in the College of Fine Arts, can obtain the appropriate degree, on passing the requisite examination. The charge for such examination is the same as for one year's tuition, with the usual graduation fee. —An Annual Exhibition of the works produced by the students is held during the last week of each college year.—Students entered for the season 1883-4 : Regular Course in Painting, 30 (5 male, 25 female) ; Special Course in Painting, 15 (all female) ; Regular Course in Architecture, 1 (male) ; Special Course in Architecture, 2 (males). Total, 48 students (8 male, 40 female). The greater portion of the former students are at present engaged in teaching in seminaries and colleges.—The College of Fine Arts has several thousand photographs, including over a thousand on glass for stereopticon use, engravings, and chromolithographs, together with a sufficient number of copies and plaster preparations and casts to answer the demands of the course of instruction. These, with the graduating paintings and drawings, a number of other pictures, and a few busts, form the nucleus of a museum. As a nucleus to a Library of the Fine Arts, a number of valuable books have been gathered, and the Reading-Room is supplied with some of the most important art journals.—In addition to the regular work of the College, much has been done by the Faculty to educate the general public, especially in Syracuse, in art matters. Courses of public lectures are held nearly every winter. During the summer of 1876 a Normal Art Institute was held, lasting six weeks, and attended by teachers from New York and from other States. An extensive Free Loan Exhibition was held at the same time.

90. Toledo, O.

TOLEDO HISTORICAL AND GEOGRAPHICAL SOCIETY.—This Society makes the collection of Indian relics a specialty. [No reply to repeated requests for more detailed information.]

TOLEDO UNIVERSITY OF ARTS AND TRADES.—[No reply to repeated requests for detailed information. Seems to have gone out of existence.]

91. Urbana, Ill.

ILLINOIS INDUSTRIAL UNIVERSITY.—Chartered Feb., 1867.—Officers B'd of Trustees : Pres., Emory Cobb ; Cor. Sec., Prof. T. J. Burrill ; Rec. Sec., Prof. E. Snyder ; Treas., John W. Bunn ; Bus. Agent, Prof. S. W. Shattuck. Officers of Fac. : Regent (President), Selim H. Peabody, Ph.D., LL.D.; Sec., Jas. D. Crawford, M.A.—Aims : To offer freely the most thorough instruction which its means will provide in all the branches of learning, including scientific or classical, useful in the industrial arts, or necessary to the liberal and practical education of the industrial classes. Theory is supplemented by practice, i. e., by work in the shop, the field, the garden, etc.—The University embraces four Colleges : 1. College of Agriculture. 2. College of Engineering (subdivided into the School of Mechanical Engineering, the School of Architecture, and the School of Civil and Mining Engineering). 3. College of Natural Science (School of Chemistry and School of Natural History). 4. College of Literature and Science (School of Modern and School of Ancient Languages). Besides these there are two additional Schools, that of Military Science and of Art and Design.—In the Agricultural Course, free-hand drawing is optional in the first year, architecture required in the third year; in the Mechanical Engineering Course, drawing, including projection and machine drawing, free-hand sketches of machinery, ornamentation, and lettering, is required through the whole course of four years ; in Civil and Mining Engineering, projection drawing, free-hand drawing from landscapes and buildings, lettering and ornamental work, topographical drawing and mapping, and designing and drawing of engineering structures, are practised the first three years; in Chemistry, free-hand drawing is required the first year, to a limited extent, while in Natural History and in the School of Modern Languages, it is optional. In the School of Ancient Languages and in that of Military Science, no provision is made for drawing. — *The School of Architecture.* Prof. of Arch., N. Clifford Ricker, M. Arch.; Peter Roos, Prof. of Industr. Art and Designing ; Jerome Sondericker, B.S., Instr. in Right Line Drawing. The course (four years) embraces the knowledge of theory and principles, of constructive details, and of the ordinary routine work of office practice, so far as these can be taught in a technical school. The technical instruction is given chiefly by lectures, with references to text-books, and is illustrated by sketches, engravings, photographs, and models ; practical applications are made by students. Drawing is practised throughout the course, and, as far as possible, original work is executed. Drawing from casts and modelling in clay give facility in sketching details and correct knowledge of form. In shop practice, joints in carpentry and joinery, cabinet making, turning metal, and stone work are executed, also models at reduced scale of roof and bridge trusses, ceilings, domes, and stairs. The course includes mathematics, mechanics, physics, chemistry, geology, French, political economy, constitutional history, history of civilization, and history and æsthetics of architecture.—Number of students, season of 1882-3. 18, all males.—(An interesting account of the course of instruction in this School of Architecture, by Prof. Ricker, will be found in the fifteenth Proceedings of the American Institute of Architects.)—*School of Art and Design.* Professor Peter Roos.—This School, besides providing instruction in free-hand drawing for the students in other departments, offers to such as have a talent or taste for art the best facilities for pursuing studies in industrial designing or other branches of fine art. Students not seeking a professional training may avail themselves of the two years' course in industrial art, which will qualify any person of ordinary ability who faithfully completes it, to teach drawing and designing in public schools, or to enter professions in which artistic taste and skill are indispensable to success. The course includes drawing from copies and casts, ornamental and decorative design, color, perspective, modelling in clay or wax, drawing landscapes and animals from copy, sketching from nature in charcoal and color, artistic anatomy, and the history of art. A more advanced course is designed for those who wish to become accomplished either as designers, painters, or teachers. In order that the student may acquire thoroughness in his specialty the subject at this stage is divided into two divisions,—decorative and pictorial. The teacher-student must give attention to both branches, and with him theory will necessarily supersede practice. Opportunity is afforded such pupils to teach in the elementary classes. The Advanced Course in Painting takes in copying from pictures and leads up to still-life and landscape from nature, and portrait painting from life in oil and water-colors, and pictorial composition. The Advanced Course in Designing includes the study of the human figure, the application of ornamentation to various manufactures, a knowledge of the processes of manufacture, designs for church decoration, for stained-glass windows, etc.—Students in the School of Art, season of 1882-3, about 100, including 7 special students (ladies).—The tuition is free in all the University classes ; matriculation fee, $10 ; incidental expenses, $7.50 per term.—Degrees are given by the institution, but not in the School of Art. Special students receive certificates, with statement of work done and credits attained.— *The Art Gallery* of the University, established in 1874, the gift of citizens of Champaign and Urbana, is one of the largest and finest of the West. It occupies a beautiful hall, 61 by 79 feet, and embraces 13 full-sized casts from antiques, such as the Laocoön, the Venus of Milo, etc.; 40 statues of reduced size, and a large number of busts, ancient and modern ; bas-reliefs, etc., in all over 400 pieces. There are also hundreds of large autotypes, photographs, and fine engravings, and a gallery of historical portraits, mostly large French lithographs of peculiar fineness, copied from the great national portrait galleries of France.—A large room is devoted to the gathering of a *Museum of Engineering and Architecture*, the materials for which have been constantly accumulating in the various schools of science of the University.—The gallery is open to the public, free of charge, on Thursdays, from 8 A.M. to 5 P.M.; on other days a fee of 10 cents is charged, but strangers from other places are admitted without charge. A printed catalogue of the gallery was published in 1876.—The Illinois Industrial University is the State University of Illinois. It was opened in March, 1868, and in 1871 female students were admitted on the same terms as males. Its property and endowment funds, not including 25,000 acres of land in Minnesota and Nebraska, are valued at about $752,000, the result of Congressional land grants, appropriations by the State of Illinois, and donations, in the shape of bonds, buildings, and farms, valued at over $400,000, by Champaign County. The University is located in the township of Urbana, but its P. O. address is Champaign, Ill.

92. Utica, N. Y.

UTICA ART ASSOCIATION.—Incorporated Jan., 1866.—Officers: Pres., Geo. W. Adams ; V P., Robt. S. Williams : Sec., E. Z. Wright ; Treas., D. N. Crouse ; Cor. Sec., Benj. D. Gilbert.—Object : The holding of exhibitions, and, eventually, the establishment of a permanent gallery of art in Utica.—Present number of members, 40.—It is the intention of the Association to hold annual exhibitions, but this has not been strictly adhered to, eight exhibitions only having been held so far. The last of these opened at the City Library Building on Jan. 16, 1882, and contained 262 works by 157 artists. The Association has been quite prosperous, and its efforts to effect sales for its contributors have resulted, since its organization, in the disposal of works of art valued at over $100,000.—For two years the Association has not been able to obtain a suitable building in which to hold an exhibition. The project of erecting a structure for the purpose has therefore been discussed quite freely among the members.

93. Vineland, N. J.

VINELAND HISTORICAL AND ANTIQUARIAN SOCIETY.—Collection of local curiosities. [No reply to repeated requests for more detailed information.]

94. Waltham, Mass.

WALTHAM PENCIL AND BRUSH CLUB.—Pond St.—Organized April, 1882.— Officers : Pres., Geo. E. Johnson ; V. P., Henry Buncher ; Sec. and Treas., W. B. Rutter.—Objects: Advancement of the members in art from the comparison which club membership affords ; to assist the artistic feeling in the community, and to meet for practice in drawing from model, etc.—The only condition of membership is that applicants shall be possessed of the artistic impetus. Present number of active members, 25.—The Club intends to hold an exhibition each year, as a rule, of the works of members. This year, however, outside contributions are to be admitted, and possibly there will also be a loan department of works owned in town.

95. Washington, D. C.

CORCORAN GALLERY OF ART.—Pennsylvania Ave., cor. 17th St.—Chartered May 24, 1870 ; opened to the public, 1874.—Officers B'd of Trustees : Pres., Jas. C. Welling ; V. P., Chas. M. Matthews ; Sec. and Treas., Anthony Hyde ; Curator, Wm. MacLeod ; Asst. Cur. and Lib., F. S. Barbarin.—This gallery, including ground, building, contents, and endowment fund, is the free gift of Mr. Wm. W. Corcoran to the public. In the deed to the Trustees, dated May 10, 1869, the object of the institution is stated as "the perpetual establishment and encouragement of Painting, Sculpture, and the Fine Arts generally," with the condition that "it should be open to visitors without charge two days in the week, and on other days at moderate and reasonable charges, to be applied to the current expenses." The cost of the building [see illustration] and ground was $250,000 ; the pictures and statuary contained in the museum at its opening were valued at $100,000. The institution is maintained by an endowment fund of $900,000, yielding an annual income at present of over $50,000.—The gallery has an excellent collection of casts from the antique, and from Renaissance and modern sculptures ; a collection of 107 bronzes by Barye, said to be the largest in existence ; an extensive collection of ceramics and art-industrial objects, ancient, modern, Oriental and European ; a series of Kensington and other electrotype reproductions ; and a number of original works in bronze and in marble, among the latter Vela's celebrated statue of "The Last Days of Napoleon I. ; " " The Greek Slave," " Genevra," " Proserpine," by Hiram Powers ; " Penseroso," and " Endymion," by W. H. Rhinehart, etc. The collection of paintings, about 200 in all, gives a tolerably good chronological view of American art within certain limits, as will be seen by the following partial list of artists represented : Gilbert Stuart, Rembrandt Peale, Thos. Sully, J. Vanderlyn, Henry Inman, Chester Harding, Saml. Waldo, C. L. Elliott, T. P. Rossiter, Geo. A. Baker, D. Huntington, G. P. A. Healy, B. C. Porter, Thos. Le Clear, Thos. Doughty, Alvan Fisher, Thos. Cole, J. F. Kensett, S. R. Gifford, R. Gignoux, A. B. Durand, F. E. Church, W. Whittredge, A. Bierstadt, Wm. MacLeod, J. F. Cropsey, J. R. Tilton, Jas. M. Hart, Geo. Inness, John R. Key Wm. S. Mount, E. Leutze, H. P. Gray, Eastman Johnson, Louis Lang, Geo. H. Boughton, J. G. Brown, F. A. Bridgman, R. A. Brooke, W. T. Richards. Besides these works of native artists, there are European pictures by Bail, Barye, Begas, Emile Breton, Cabanel, Chialiva, Chierici, Comte, Bouder, Detaille, Blaise Desgoffe, De Brackeleer, Faed, Ed. Frère, Gérôme, Hildebrandt, Japy, Kaemmerer, Leroux, Moretti, C. L. Müller, Erskine Nicol, Portaels, Preyer, Priou, Robbe, Salmson, Ary Scheffer, Schreyer, Vely, O. Van Thoren, Ziem, Heilbuth, etc., and a few old paintings attributed to Murillo, Van Dyck, Canaletti, Sir Peter Lely, Raphael Mengs, Jos. Vernet, and Geo. Morland.—Open daily, Sundays and Fourth of July excepted, from 10 A.M. to 4 P.M. from Oct. 1 to May 1, and from 9 A.M. to 4 P.M. from May 1 to Oct. 1. On Tuesdays, Thursdays, and Saturdays, admission free ; other days, 25 cents. During winter, weekly Night Exhibitions are held, admission 10 cents. On Mondays, Wednesdays, and Fridays persons are allowed, under certain regulations, to draw from the casts and copy the pictures.—Catalogue, 25 cents. Photographs are also published (136 up to date, of different styles or sizes) of pictures, etc., contained in the Gallery, which are for sale at the door.—Number of visitors from Jan. 1 to Dec. 1, 1883, 65.209.—It is the intention of Mr. Corcoran to establish a *Free Art School* in connection with the Gallery. Students are allowed to draw from the casts in the gallery, and medals are given to the most proficient.

PUBLIC BUILDINGS.—For a description of the works of art in and around the *Capitol*, such as Greenough's statue of Washington ; the groups, reliefs, and figures by Crawford, Greenough, Persico, Capellano, Powers, etc.; the bronze doors by Randolph Rogers and Crawford ; the paintings by John Trumbull, J. Vanderlyn, W. H. Powell, J. G. Chapman, R. W. Weir, in the Rotunda ; the frescos by C. Brumidi ; the paintings on the staircases by W. H. Powell, E. Leutze, Walker ; the statues in the National Statuary Hall, including works by most of the best known American sculptors ; and the numerous statues, busts, and paintings scattered through the various halls and rooms, the reader must be referred to the local guide-books.—A collection of the portraits of the various secretaries of the treasury is to be found in the corridors of the *Treasury Department*. Portraits of all the presidents are hung in the *White House.*

UNITED STATES NATIONAL MUSEUM.—Officers : Director, Spencer F. Baird, Sec. of the Smithsonian Institution ; Asst. Dir. and Curator Dept. of Arts and Industries, G. Brown Goode ; Curator of Archæological Dept., Charles Rau ; Lib., Frederick W. True.—This is the only Museum which receives direct aid from the U. S. government. It was organized in 1846 by the act of Congress transferring to the Smithsonian Institution (the well-known scientific institution founded by a bequest to the U. S. of $500,000 by Jas. Smithson, an English scientist, who died in the year 1829) the custody of the " National Cabinet of Curiosities," at that time deposited in the Patent Office buildings. The collections were given a place in the building of the Smithsonian Institution, but are now being installed in the new structure, lately erected for the special uses of the Museum by the government at a cost of about $250,000.—The Museum has an annual allowance from the U. S. of about $75,000.—Its collections in zoology, geology, and anthropology, which are already of an immense extent, and are continually increasing with great rapidity, consist mainly of specimens brought home by U. S. exploring and surveying parties, supplemented by exchanges, by gifts from foreign governments and from individuals, and but rarely by purchases. They are intended to form an Anthropological Museum, organized upon the broadest and most liberal interpretation of the term "anthropology," and illustrating the characteristics of civilized as well as savage races of mankind, and their attainments in civilization and culture. The central idea will be *man*, and the manner in which he adapts the products of the earth to his needs. It follows from this that in the main the Museum is devoted to natural history and ethnology, in which latter department, so far as it relates to the native races of America, it is already richer than any other museum. It is, however, of great

interest and importance also for the study of primitive art, on account of its rich collections of aboriginal antiquities and the products of Indian and Eskimo art of the present day, confined not only
to the U. S., but taking in the whole extent of North, Central, and South America. The celebrated
Catlin Collection of Indian Paintings has been acquired by the Museum, and placed on exhibition
during the year, and through gift from Mr. Pierre Lorillard it has come into possession of a series of
casts of prehistorical sculptures in the temples of Yucatan and Mexico. It possesses also some specimens of art-archæological interest from other parts of the globe. The Museum has obtained a large
number of historical relics, chiefly of Washington, with a few belonging to other historical characters, which, it is hoped, will form the basis of a collection of American costumes. A beginning has
also been made with the formation of a series of collections illustrative of the reproductive arts.—As
the new fire-proof building, which is of immense dimensions, measuring 327 feet in length, and covering a net area of 102,200 square feet, has only been lately finished, everything, as a matter of
course, is in a transition state for the present, and will be so for some time to come.—A scientific
account of the archæological section of the Museum, still housed in the old Smithsonian building, is
to be found in "Smithsonian Contributions to Knowledge, 287. The Archælogical Collection of the
United Sates National Museum, in charge of the Smithsonian Institution, by Charles Rau" (Washington City : Published by the Smithsonian Institution, 1876.) A thorough system of descriptive
labels and guide-book manuals will be provided for the new Museum. [Messrs. Judd & Detweiler,
of Washington, publish a "Visitors' Guide to the Smithsonian Institution and United States
National Museum," by W. J. Rhees ; 58 pp., 8vo., illustrated, 25 cents.]

WASHINGTON ART CLUB.—Corcoran Building.—Organized, 1876.—Officers : Pres.,
W. W. Corcoran ; V. P., Richd. N. Brooke ; Sec., J. M. March, 1522 16th St., N. W.; Treas. and
Custodian, W. G. Newton.—Objects : Cultivation of the Fine Arts, advancement and diffusion of
art knowledge, and the promotion of good-will and social enjoyment.—Present membership : 21
Active, 5 Associate, 2 Honorary members. Total, 28.—Social reunions every fortnight.—The *Art
School* founded by the Club, in charge of Mr. C. E. Messer, is reported to be in a prosperous condition. The aim of the school is to furnish instruction upon a strictly professional basis. The
course embraces the usual drawing from the antique, with life classes for male and female pupils
distinct. There have been as many as 60 pupils at one time, but the attendance varies. The fees
are graded to the character and amount of instruction given.—Annual meeting, second Monday in
May.

96. Wellesley, Mass.

WELLESLEY COLLEGE.—Officers B'd of Trustees : Pres., Rev. Noah Porter, D.D.,
LL.D., of Yale College ; V. P., Rev. Howard Crosby, D.D., LL.D., New York ; Sec. and Treas.,
Mrs. Henry F. Durant.—Pres. of the Faculty : Alice E. Freeman, Ph.D).—Wellesley College was
established to furnish young women who desire to obtain a liberal education, such advantages and
facilities as are enjoyed in institutions of the highest grade.— *The Department of Art.* Teachers :
S. Emil Carlsen, Still Life and Landscape ; C. W. Sanderson, Landscape in Water Color ; Ida
Bothe, Drawing from Casts and Life, and Painting ; Alice Mills, Drawing and Painting. Drawing
forms part of the regular course of study in the Freshman Year of both the classical and the scientific
course, and all the classes in Botany receive free instruction in flower-painting in water colors.
Drawing and Painting are open to Juniors and Seniors in the regular four years' course. Private
lessons in the various branches of art are given to those who desire them. The medium used may be
pencil, charcoal, crayon, water colors, or oil. A regular course of five years' instruction in art
studies is also given, and students who enter any one of the regular courses may combine with it
the course in art, their regular college studies being distributed through five years instead of four.—
Art Collections. These consist of 650 framed engravings, photographs, and drawings ; 350 stereo-
scopic views, illustrative of the history of art ; 75 paintings, copies of old, and originals by modern
masters, foreign as well as American ; 50 drawings by Hammatt Billings ; 100 statues and busts ;
176 casts, chiefly for use in the Department of Modelling ; metal work, ceramics, coins, and ancient
armor.

97. West Point, N. Y.

UNITED STATES MILITARY ACADEMY.—Supt., Col. Wesley Merritt; Chas. W. Larned, Prof. of Drawing.—The following is the complete official programme of the *Course of Instruction in Drawing*, as furnished by the authorities in charge of the Academy. Its aim does not pretend to be high art ; it is simply art in harness, in the shop, and in the field.—First Year. (3d Class.) 1. Topography and Map Drawing ; 2. Construction of Problems in Descriptive Geometry, Shades and Shadows, and Perspective ; 3. Reconnaissance and Field Work. Course of Instruction: Beginning with the academic year, the 3d class is instructed in the conventional signs of topography, and shortly after the inception of the work a lecture on that subject is delivered by the head of the department, or one of his assistants. After the completion of the conventional signs lectures are delivered embracing the following subjects : Drawing instruments, their use and care ; drawing papers, names, qualities, and uses ; methods of preparing paper for use ; general rules to be observed in rectilinear and map drawing ; construction of borders ; lettering, different styles, and methods of construction ; scales, proportional and Vernier, scales of distance, their varieties and construction. Immediately thereafter a third lecture embracing the following subjects : Definition of topography and its objects ; historical sketch of its progress and methods ; explanation of the different systems and their relative merits ; methods of hill shading ; construction of scales of shade and their application ; principles of contours and sections. Following these lectures the work of drawing scales of shade, inclination, distance, proportion, the drawing of maps from skeleton and plaster models, and the study of hill shading in ink and pencil is carried on. Before the semi-annual examination, a lecture embracing the following subjects is delivered : Methods of projection of meridian and parallels ; methods of plotting from field work ; plotting meridian and compass variations. Between the close of the semi-annual examination and the first of March instruction is given in colored topography, beginning with conventional tints, and including the construction of maps from skeleton data. From March 1 to about April 15, construction of problems in descriptive geometry, shades and shadows, and perspective, the problems being generally variations and combinations of those given in text books. From April 15 until close of academic year, June 1, practical topography in the field and reconnaissance. Before going into the field, lectures are delivered, embracing the following subjects : Preparation and arrangement of note book ; use of prismatic compass ; method of field sketching ; use of odometer, pedometer, pacing ; hill sketching ; methods of running contours ; methods of U. S. Coast Survey ; precautions necessary in reconnaissance and field sketching; improvised methods of work ; practicability of slopes for troops. Before the close of the academic year a lecture embracing the following subjects : General methods of large surveys ; measurement of bases ; general principles of triangulation and plotting ; filling in ; establishment of stations ; methods of Coast Survey and Surveys west of 100th meridian. Cadets are required to take careful notes of all lectures, and retain them for use and reference.—Second Year. (2d Class.) 1. Free-Hand Drawing in Black and White ; 2. Theory of Color and Laying of Tints ; 3. Mechanical, Architectural, and Constructive Drawing. Divided into two periods : 1. Free-Hand drawing, from Sept. 1 to Jan. 1 ; 2. Mechanical, architectural, and constructive drawing and color from close of semi-annual examination until June 1. Course of Instruction : Beginning with the academic year lectures are delivered on the subject of free-hand drawing and perspective ; outline ; light and shade ; proportion ; methods and materials. The class is instructed in free-hand drawing in black and white, pencil, crayon, or charcoal, beginning with simple block models after Harding's system, and increasing in complexity until a fair proficiency in the drawing of outline is attained. Shading is then studied in the simpler forms, and the models are increased in difficulty according to the proficiency of the student. The flat is very sparingly used for purposes of illustration, the models used being the "Cours de Dessin " of Ch. Bargue and J. L. Gérôme. Elementary instruction in landscape drawing follows the above. After the close of the semi-annual examination a lecture is delivered embracing the following subjects : Theory of color ; modern chromatics ; quality and character of pigments. Use of Water-Color : Instruction in this course begins by the laying of flat tints and grades, illustrating the laws of harmonious contrast and the formation of compound and broken colors. Succeeding these, problems in mechanical and constructive drawing are undertaken by the students ; architectural plans and elevations and working drawings in military and ordnance construction from data and mechanical models. At the close of the year lectures are given on the subject of the principal orders of architecture, their origin, characteristics, and general proportion. Cadets are required to take careful notes of lectures.—The *Art Works* in possession of this department are confined to a collection of the best drawings of cadets, selected from the work of the different classes for a period of forty years or more ; a number of engravings of greater or less value, and a few original water-colors by G. J. Knox, Allom (11), John Varley (6), Pyne, Prout, Richardson (2), Davidson (2), Salmon, A. Delacroix, Catherwood, Gignoux, Abert, Abery, Cooper, Bartlett, Bentley, and Copley Fielding. There is also a large collection of plaster copies of the antique, wood-cuts, lithographs, etc.—All of these, except the collection of prints, are open to the public daily during the hours pre-scribed by the Superintendent for visitors.

98. Wilkesbarre, Pa.

WYOMING HISTORICAL AND GEOLOGICAL SOCIETY.—Organized and in-corp. 1858.—Officers : Pres., Chas. F. Ingham, M.D.; Cor. Sec., Hon. E. L. Dana ; Rec. Sec., Harrison Wright, Ph.D.; Treas., Sheldon Reynolds.—Objects : The collection and preservation of all matters tending to elucidate the history and geology of Wyoming Valley.—Members in Dec., 1883, 175.—The Society publishes Proceedings, Memorials, etc.—*Collections :* Mineralogical, geo-logical, and conchological ; archæological ; local historical relics ; over 7,000 coins ; library of several thousand titles. Free to the public.—Annual meeting, in February.

99. Worcester, Mass.

AMERICAN ANTIQUARIAN SOCIETY.—Incorporated Oct. 24, 1812.—Officers : Pres., Hon. Steven Salisbury, LL.D. ; V. Ps.. Hon. Geo. F. Hoar, LL.D., Hon. Geo. Bancroft, LL.D.; For. Cor. Sec., Hon. J. Hammond Trumbull, LL.D.; Dom. Cor Sec., Chas. Deane, LL.D.; Rec. Sec., Hon. John D. Washburn ; Treas., Nathaniel Paine ; Libr , Edmund M. Barton. —Objects : The advancement of the arts and sciences, and to aid in collecting and preserving such materials as might be useful in marking their progress, not only in the U. S., but elsewhere ; to assist historians by the preservation of MSS., books, etc. ; the collection, preservation, and eluci-dation of American antiquities, natural, artificial, and literary.—The American members of the Society are limited to 140 ; foreign members unlimited. Initiation fee of American members, $5 ; members residing in New England pay an annual fee of $5 ; life membership, $50.—The Society was practically founded by Isaiah Thomas, who provided the first building occupied by it, gave to it his library, and bequeathed funds to provide for its operations and maintenance. Since then con-siderable donations have been made by Hon. Stephen Salisbury and others, so that the funds held by the Society are now quite considerable.—Besides a very large library, in which there are several old MSS., richly illuminated, early Bibles, and illustrated books, etc., the Society owns a Cabinet con-taining Indian and other antiquities, and relics, coins, medals, engravings, casts of Michelangelo's statue of Christ in Sta. Maria Sopra Minerva, and of the same sculptor's celebrated Moses, and a number of interesting portraits and busts, principally of men prominent in the history of Massa-chusetts. Among the portraits are several by Chester Harding, one supposed to be by Copley, another by Alexander, etc. Others are principally interesting on account of the subjects represented, in-cluding portraits of Gov. Endicott, Gov. Winthrop, Gov. Leverett, five members of the Mather family, etc. Among the busts are works by Ceracchi, Clevenger, Dexter, Kinney, Powers, and King. A partial list of these portraits and busts may be found in "An Account of the American Antiquarian Society, with a List of its Publications," prepared by Nathaniel Paine for the Inter-national Exhibition of 1876, and published by the Society.—The following is from a late report by the Librarian : " It is not surprising that the small but valuable collection of Fine Arts calls many to the rooms, since we already have, for example, original portraits by Alexander, Billings, Copley, Custer, Greenwood, Gullag, Harding, Huntington, Osgood, Pelham, Sully, and Wright, with copies of Parmegianino and Southland ; busts by Clevenger, Dexter, Kinney, Powers, and Volk, with copies of Ceracchi and Houdon ; casts from the world-renowned statues of the Christ and Moses by Michelangelo ; original engravings by Nanteuil and Hogart, and Talviati's beautiful Venetian Mosaic of Columbus. To these should be added Mr. Salisbury, Jr.'s, cases of Central American re-mains, and his stand of Yucatecan and Grecian photographs."—The Hall of the Society [see illus-tration] is open, week days, free to all, from 9 A.M. to 5 P.M., except Saturday afternoons.

ART STUDENTS' CLUB.—377 Main St., room 6.—Organized Mch. 24, 1880.—Officers: Pres., Geo. E. Gladwin, 16 Harvard St.; V. P., R. Süverkrop, 352 Main St.; Sec., Anna C. Freeland, 13 Pearl St.; Treas., F. C. Higgins, 284 Main St.—Objects: To advance the knowledge of art through the exhibition of works of art, the acquisition of books and papers upon art subjects, and the promotion of social intercourse among its members.—Members: Active, limited to 30 (dues $5 p.a.), who must be earnest students of some branch of art; honorary.—Occasional papers are read by members. Meetings for class work, four evenings a week in winter. The Club aims eventually to establish a school of fine arts. For the present there are classes in wood engraving, R. Süverkrop, teacher; life (draped model) and still life, S. Emil Carlsen, teacher; and brass hammering (supervised by members).—The Club holds a yearly exhibition of the work of its members, only five or six of whom are professional artists. The catalogue of the exhibition for 1883, illustrated, enumerated 155 works, by the full force of members.

WORCESTER COUNTY FREE INSTITUTE OF INDUSTRIAL SCIENCE.

—Incorp. May 10, 1865.—Officers: Pres., Hon. Stephen Saulsbury, LL.D.; Sec., Rev. Daniel Merriman, D.D., ; Treas., Waldo Lincoln. Principal, Homer F. Fuller, A.M., Ph.D., 18 Boynton St.—This Institute offers a good education, based on mathematics, the living languages, physical sciences, and drawing, and sufficient practical familiarity with some branch of applied science to secure its graduates a livelihood. It is specially designed to meet the wants of those who wish to be prepared as mechanics, civil engineers, chemists, or designers, for the duties of active life. For the acquisition of practical familiarity with different branches of applied science, the same facilities are offered as in the best schools of technology elsewhere. In mechanics, shop-practice is added to the course and incorporated in it. Thus the students who select chemistry, work in the laboratory; the civil engineers at field work or problems in construction; those who select drawing, in the drawing room; those who select physics, in the physical laboratory. The mechanical section practice in the workshop through the whole course (which in this department extends over three and a half years, while the other courses are absolved in three years); and as the "Washburn Machine Shop" connected with the Institute is managed as a manufacturing establishment, the products of which are sold, the student always works in the wholesome atmosphere of real business. The ease with which more than 90 per cent. of the graduates have secured employment is evidence of the soundness of the principles upon which the school is organized.—*All* students are taught Free-Hand Drawing. By carefully studied exercises in outline drawing, shading and coloring, from copies, models and casts, discipline of the sense of form and proportion is secured, and an ability to delineate objects is acquired, which is of great value in all departments of applied science. In the Mechanical Drawing room, instruction is given in the use of instruments, shading, and coloring, plane and isometric projections, and the theory of shades, shadows, and perspective. All drawing is done under the eye of the instructor. Students who evince marked power in drawing are admitted to special practice in this department. A course of lessons is devised for each student in practice, preparatory to designing for textile fabrics, lithography, fresco and ornamental painting, or similar arts. Students enjoy access to collections of illustrations and examples. Professor of Drawing: Geo. E. Gladwin, 16 Harvard St.—Students, male only, must have attained the age of sixteen, and must give evidence of proficiency in the common English branches; but from 1884 some knowledge of French will be required.—No charge for tuition to residents of Worcester County; others, $150 per year. There are, however, 20 Free State Scholarships, for residents of the State of Massachusetts, and three Free Scholarships, established by the Hon. Geo. F. Hoar, for residents of certain towns.—The school was founded by Mr. John Boynton of Templeton, who gave for the purpose $100,000. The State contributed $50,000, Hon. Stephen Saulsbury over $200,000, Hon. Ichabod Washburn provided the machine shop and an endowment of $50,000, Mr. David Whitcomb over $20,000, and a number of smaller donations, in money, machines, material, etc., have been received from various sources.—The Institute confers the degree of Bachelor of Science, the diplomas designating the department to which the graduate belonged. It also confers honorary degrees.

ARTISTS' DIRECTORY.

THE following list does not pretend to give the names of all American artists. It merely enumerates those architects, sculptors, painters, designers, engravers, etc., who are members of the societies, or have exhibited in the exhibitions enumerated below, and who, having been favorably passed upon by an Examining Committee or by a Jury of Admission, can claim that they have been recognized by an authority supposed to be competent. The numbers inserted after the name of each artist refer to the societies and exhibitions here specified. *Artists will confer a great favor upon the editor by keeping him advised of changes of address, for use in future editions of this Directory.*

1. National Academy of Design.—Academicians.
2. National Academy of Design.—Associates.
3. Society of American Artists.
4. American Water Color Society.
5. Philadelphia Society of Artists.
6. New York Etching Club.
7. Philadelphia Society of Etchers.
8. Society of Painter-Etchers, London.
9. Salmagundi Sketch Club.
10. Art Club, New York.
11. American Art Union.
12. Ladies' Art Association. (Active members.)
13. American Institute of Architects. (Past and present members.)
14. Society of American Wood Engravers.
15. Artists' Fund Society, New York.
16. National Academy, 58th Annual Exhibition. April 2–May 12, 1883.
17. National Academy, Special Autumn Exhibition. Oct. 22–Nov. 17, 1883.
18. Society of American Artists, 6th Annual Exhibition. March 26–April 28, 1883.
19. American Water Color Society, 16th Annual Exhibition. Jan. 29–Feb. 25, 1883.
20. New York Etching Club Exhibition. Jan. 29–Feb. 25, 1883.
21. Philadelphia Society of Etchers, First Exhibition. Dec. 27, 1882–Feb. 23, 1883.
22. Black and White, 5th Annual Exhibition. Dec. 1–21, 1882.
23. Black and White, 6th Annual Exhibition. Dec. 1–21, 1883.
24. Pennsylvania Academy, 54th Annual Exhibition. Oct. 29–Dec. 8, 1883.
25. Philadelphia Society of Artists, 4th Annual Exhibition. Dec. 30, 1882–Jan. 27, 1883.
26. Philadelphia Society of Artists, 2d Water Color Exhibition. April 9–May 12, 1883.
27. Philadelphia Society of Artists, 2d Sketch Exhibition. Nov., 1883.
28. Museum of Fine Arts, Boston. Contemporaneous American Art. Oct. 16–Nov. 27, 1883.
29. Boston Art Club, 27th Exhibition. Jan. 25–Feb. 17, 1883.
30. Boston Art Club, 28th Exhibition. April 14–May 12, 1883.
31. Chicago Interstate Industrial Exposition, 11th Annual. Sept. 5–Oct. 20, 1883.
32. San Francisco Art Association, 9th Annual Exhibition. April, 1883.
33. Boston Art Club, 29th Exhibition. Jan. 19–Feb. 26, 1884.
34. Philadelphia Society of Artists, 5th Annual Exhibition. Jan. 21–Feb. 23, 1884.
35. American Water Color Society, 17th Annual Exhibition. Feb. 4–March 1, 1884.
36. New York Etching Club Exhibition. Feb. 4–March 1, 1884.

Brown, W. M., 706 President St., Brooklyn, N. Y. 11, 16, 17, 34
Brownell, Franklin, 142½ Union St., New Bedford, Mass. 24, 27, 33
Brownscombe, Miss Jennie, Honesdale, Pa. 12, 17, 24, 27
Bruce, A. C., Atlanta, Ga. 13
Brundage, W. T., 14 John St., New York. 9, 22, 23
Brunner, Arnold W., 24 W. 45th St., New York. 35
Brush, Geo. De F., 146 W. 55th St., New York. 3, 18
Brush, Mrs. Jas. H., Greenwich, Ct. 35
Buckingham, J. R., 1151 Broadway, New York. 16, 19, 24, 27, 35
Bucklin, W. S., Red Bank, N. J. 19, 28, 30, 35
Bulson, Thomas Lee, South, near Morton St., Jamaica Plain, Mass. 30
Bunce, Wm. Gedney, 80 E. Washington Sq., New York. 3, 10, 16, 17, 18, 24, 28, 31, 34
Bunker, Dennis Miller, 788 Broadway, New York. 30
Bunner, A. F., Venice. (Care G. Reichard & Co., 226 Fifth Ave., New York). .2, 4, 15, 16, 25, 31
Bunner, Rudolph F., 9 W. 14th St., New York. 16, 17, 19, 27, 28, 30, 33
Burdick, H. R., 2 Cheshire St., Jamaica Plain, Mass. 19, 29, 33
Burgess, H. G., Passaic, N. J. 35
Burgess, Ida J., 96 State St., Chicago. 16
Burke, J. E. 13
Burleigh, Chas. C. (deceased). 24
Burleigh, S. R., 35 N. Main St., Providence. 19, 23, 24, 26, 27, 28, 30, 35
Burling, E., Chicago. 13
Burnett, John I., Vernon Row, Washington. 35
Burns, C. M., Philadelphia. 13
Burns, Elizabeth M., 212 E. 50th St., New York. 16, 17
Burns, M. J., University Building, Washington Sq., New York. 9, 11, 16, 22
Burr, Louis H., 139 W. 55th St., New York. 16, 17, 24, 27
Burrell, Nellie E., San Francisco, Cal. 32
Burrill, E., Jr. 30
Burt, Charles. 23
Bush, C. G., 166 W. 55th St., New York. 22
Bush, Miss Julia. 16
Bush, Norton, San Francisco, Cal. 32
Butler, C. K. 16
Butler, E. K. 16
Butler, Geo. B., Jr., Isola di Capri, Italy. 1
Buttons, S. D., Philadelphia. 13

CABOT, E. C., 60 Devonshire St., Boston. 4, 13, 28, 35
Cady, G. W., 164 Westminster St., Providence, R. I. 13
Cady, J. C., 111 Broadway, New York. 13
Cady, Miss J. E., 224 W. 38th St., New York. 16, 17
Calahan, Jas. J., New York. 20, 23, 36
Calder, Alex. Milne, Philadelphia. 25
Calverley, Charles, 337 Fourth Ave., New York. 1
Campbell, Georgiana, 152 W. 57th St., New York. 16
Campbell, Mary A., 2016 Green St., Philadelphia. 16, 24, 25
Campion, Howard, 719 Sixth Ave., New York. 19, 31
Campion, Sara M., 14th Ave., Mt. Vernon, N. Y. 19, 24, 31
Canning, Miss A. S., 337 Fourth Ave., New York. 31
Cantwell, Jas., 49 Syracuse St., Syracuse, N. Y. 16, 19, 25, 26, 35
Cariss, H. T., 1328 Chestnut St., Philadelphia. 5, 21, 24, 25, 26
Carlebur, F., 11 E. 14th St., New York. 16
Carlin, J., 212 W. 25th St., New York. 15, 16
Carlsen, S. Emil, 27 Tremont Row, Boston. 24, 28, 29, 33
Carpenter, C. E., 65 Westminster St., Providence, R. I. 13

13

ART TEACHERS' DIRECTORY.

THE following list contains only the names of those teachers and lecturers who are connected with the Art Schools, etc., enumerated in this Directory. Private or Studio addresses, when given, are enclosed in parenthesis. Others, so far as known, may be found in the Artists' Directory. Corrections are earnestly solicited.

ADAMS, Chas. L., Mass. Inst. of Technology, Boylston St., bet. Berkeley and Clarendon Sts., Boston.

Adams, Henry, Maryland Inst. for the Promotion of the Mechanic Arts, Baltimore St., over Centre Market, Baltimore.

Adams, S. Herbert, Maryland Inst. for the Promotion of the Mechanic Arts, Baltimore St., over Centre Market, Baltimore.

Allen, Geo. R., Spring Garden Inst., N. E. cor. Broad and Spring Garden Sts., Philadelphia.

Anderson, Jno. O., St. Louis School of Fine Arts, Washington University, St. Louis, Mo.

Anshutz, Thos., Penns. Acad. of the Fine Arts, Philadelphia.

Anthony, Alfred J., Y. M. C. A., cor. Boylston and Berkeley Sts., Boston.

BABCOCK, Rev. Chas., A.M., Cornell University, Ithaca, N. Y.

Babcock, John C., General Society of Mechanics and Tradesman, 18 E. 16th St., New York (64 College Pl.).

Bacher, Otto H., Cleveland Academy of Art, Rooms 25 and 27 City Hall, Cleveland, O.

Bailey, Miss M. A., State Normal Art School of Mass., 1679 Washington St., Boston.

Baldwin, Bert. L., Ohio Mechanics' Institute, Cincinnati.

Balsam, John G., Decorative Art Society, 51 W. Genesee St., Buffalo, N. Y.

Barth, Carl, Franklin Institute, 15 S. 7th St., Philadelphia.

Bartlett, Geo. H., State Normal Art School of Mass., 1679 Washington St., and South Boston School of Art, E. 4th, near Dorchester St., Boston.

Bartlett, Truman H., N. E. Conservatory of Music, School of Fine Arts, Franklin Sq., and Boston School of Sculpture, 394 Federal St., Boston.

Beadenkopf, Geo., Maryland Inst. for the Promotion of the Mechanic Arts, Baltimore St., over Centre Market, Baltimore.

Bell, John W., Cleveland Academy of Art, Rooms 25 and 27 City Hall, Cleveland, O.

Blauvelt, Assist. Prof. C. F., U. S. Naval Academy, Annapolis, Md.

Bolles, John W., Essex Art Association, 21 W. Park St., Newark, N. J.

Bothe, Ida, Wellesley College, Wellesley, Mass., 13 Franklin St., Boston.

Boyle, Ferd. T. L., A.N.A., Brooklyn Institute, Washington, cor. Concord St., Brooklyn, N. Y.

Brackett, W. F., State Normal Art School of Mass., 1679 Washington St., Boston.

Braman, Benj., Cooper Union, 7th St. and 4th Ave., New York.

Brewster, Miss Amanda, Society of Decorative Art, 28 E. 21st St., New York.

Briggs, Wm., N. E. Conservatory of Music, School of Fine Arts, Franklin Sq., Boston.

Brown, Thos. S., South Boston School of Art, E. 4th St., near Dorchester St., Boston.

Brush, Geo. de Forest, Art Students' League, 38 W. 14th St., New York.

Bryant, J., S. F. Chapter of the Am. Inst. of Arch., 270 Montgomery St., San Francisco, Cal.

Burnap, Geo. S., Carolina Art Association, Washington Sq., Charleston, S. C.

Burrison, Henry K., S.B., Mass. Inst. of Technology, Boylston St., bet. Berkeley and Clarendon Sts., Boston.

Burrows, W. S., Ohio Mechanics' Institute, Cincinnati.

Burton, A. E., S.B., Mass. Inst. of Technology, Boyleston St., bet. Berkeley and Clarendon Sts., Boston.

Buxbaum, C. M., Cleveland Academy of Art, Rooms 25 and 27 City Hall, Cleveland, O.

CANAGA, Passed Assistant Engineer A. B., U. S. Naval Academy, Annapolis, Md.
    Canoll, Carina, College of Archæology and Æsthetics, 120 E. 105th St., New York.
Canoll, Prof. J. W. Henry, Æ.LL.D., College of Archæology and Æsthetics, 120 E. 105th St., New York.
Carlsen, S. Emil, Wellesley College, Wellesley, Mass., and Art Students' Club, Worcester, Mass. (27 Tremont Row, Boston.)
Carpenter, N. H., Art Institute, cor. Michigan Ave. and Van Buren St., Chicago.
Carter, C. M., A.M., State Normal Art School of Mass., 1679 Washington St., Boston.
Carter, Miss Grace, Decorative Art Society, 69 N. Charles St., Baltimore.
Carter, Miss M. A. E., Cooper Union, 7th St., and 4th Ave., New York.
Carter, Mary E., N. E. Conservatory of Music, School of Fine Arts, Franklin Sq., Boston.
Carter, Mrs. Susan N., Cooper Union, 7th St., cor. 4th Ave., New York.
Champney, J. Wells, A.N.A., National Academy, New York ; Norwich Free Academy, Norwich, Conn.; and Society of Decorative Art, 303 Main St., Hartford, Conn. (337 Fourth Ave., New York.)
Chandler, Mrs. G. W., Decorative Art Society, 51 W. Genesee St., Buffalo, N. Y.
Chase, Thos., Spring Garden Inst., N. E. cor. Broad and Spring Garden Sts., Philadelphia.
Chase, Wm. M., Art Students' League, 38 W. 14th St., New York.
Chestnutwood, Miss Sarah, Decorative Art Society, 51 W. Genesee St., Buffalo, N. Y.
Chichester, Edward L., Decorative Art Society, 51 W. Genesee St., Buffalo, N. Y.
Chominski, Theodore, Roxbury Crayon Club, 1 Dudley St., Boston.
Churchill, Alfred D., A.M., M.S., E.M., Ph.B., Columbia College, E. 49th St., cor. Madison Ave., New York.
Clark, Miss A. E., Lasell Seminary for Young Women, Auburndale, Mass.
Clark, Theodore M., A.B., Mass. Inst. of Technology, Boylston St., bet. Berkeley and Clarendon Sts., Boston.
Clarke, Benj. Franklin, A.M., Brown University, Providence, R. I.
Clason, Lieut. W. P., U. S. Naval Academy, Annapolis, Md.
Claussen, E. E., Franklin Institute, 15 S. 7th St., Philadelphia.
Clevenger, Dr. S. V., Art Institute, cor. Michigan Ave. and Van Buren St., Chicago.
Cleves, Edwin Chase, B.S., Cornell University, Ithaca, N. Y.
Comfort, Prof. Geo. F., Syracuse University, Syracuse, N. Y. (583 East Ave.)
Corwin, C. A., Art Institute, cor. Michigan Ave. and Van Buren St., Chicago.
Cramer, Eugene, Decorative Art Society, 51 W. Genesee St., Buffalo, N. Y.
Crampton, Jos., General Society of Mechanics and Tradesmen, 18 E. 16th St., New York.
Crane, Miss A. T., Ladies' Art Association, 24 W. 14th St., New York.
Crawford, Lieut. Robt., U. S. N., Spring Garden Inst., N. E. cor. Broad and Spring Garden Sts., Philadelphia.
Croasdale, Miss Elizabeth, Phil. School of Design for Women, S. W. cor. Broad and Master Sts., Philadelphia.
Crocker, Miss, Portland Art League, Portland, Me.
Cross, A. K., State Normal Art School of Mass., 1679 Washington St., Boston.
Crowninshield, Fred., School of Drawing and Painting, Museum of Fine Arts, Dartmouth St. and St. James Ave., Boston.

DARST, C. Brower, Columbus Art School, 15 E. Long St., Columbus, O.
    Davis, John P., Cooper Union, 7th St., cor. 4th Ave., New York.
Dean, Francis W., S.B., Harvard University, Cambridge, Mass. (40 Matthews Hall.)
De Camp, Joseph R., Cleveland Academy of Art, Rooms 25 and 27 City Hall, Cleveland, O.
De Lisser, R. Lionel, Springfield Art Association, Evangelist Building, Springfield, Mass.
De Luce, Percival, Packer Collegiate Inst., Joralemon St., near Clinton, Brooklyn, N. Y.
Denison, Chas. S., M.S., C.E., University of Michigan, Ann Arbor, Mich. (40 S. Ingalls St.)
Denison, Mrs. H. H., Elgin Art Association, 42 Chicago St., Elgin, Ill.
Dennis, Rev. Jas. H., Rochester Art Club, 80 Arcade Building, and Rochester Art Exchange, 191-195 Powers Building, Rochester, N. Y.
De Steiguer, Miss Ida, University of Denver, 14th and Arapahoe Sts., Denver, Col.

Dewing, T. W., Art Students' League, 38 W. 14th St., New York.
Diehl, Prof. Conrad, Missouri State University, Columbia, Mo.
Dielman, Frederic, N.A., National Academy of Design, and Art Students' League, New York. (51 W. 10th St., New York.)
Dole, Mrs. F. L., Decorative Art Society, 51 W. Genesee St., Buffalo, N. Y.
Donlevy, Miss Alice, Ladies' Art Association, 24 W. 14th St., New York.

E AKINS, Prof. Thos., Penns. Academy of Fine Arts, Philadelphia, and Brooklyn Art Association, Brooklyn, N. Y. (1729 Mt. Vernon St., Philadelphia.)
Earle, L. C., Art Institute, cor. Michigan Ave. and Van Buren St., Chicago.
Eglau, Max, Cooper Union, 7th St. and 4th Ave., New York.
Eifler, F., New York Turnverein, 64–68 E. 4th St., New York.
Ellis, Harvey, Rochester Art Club, 80 Arcade Building, Rochester, N. Y.
Ellis, Mrs. M. C. B., Cooper Union, 7th St. and 4th Ave., New York.
Ely, Edward F., Mass. Inst. of Technology, Boylston St., bet. Berkeley and Clarendon Sts., Boston.
Engler, Edmund A., St. Louis School of Fine Arts, Washington University, St. Louis, Mo.
Eustis, Henry L., A.M., Harvard University, Cambridge, Mass. (29 Kirkland St.)
Evans, De Scott, Cleveland Academy of Art, Rooms 25 and 27 City Hall, and Western Reserve School of Design for Women, City Hall Building, Cleveland, O.

F ABER, Herm., Phil. School of Design for Women, S. W. cor. Broad and Master Sts., Philadelphia.
Fairchild, Mary L., St. Louis School of Fine Arts, Washington University, St. Louis, Mo.
Farrar, Miss Frances, Milwaukee College, Milwaukee, Wis.
Ferris, Stephen J., Phil. School of Design for Women, S. W. cor. Broad and Master Sts., Philadelphia.
Fettweis, C. L., Ohio Mechanics' Institute, Cincinnati.
Feurer, Chas., Spring Garden Inst., N. E. cor. Broad and Spring Garden Sts., Philadelphia.
Ficht, C. Otto, General Society of Mechanics and Tradesmen, 18 E. 16th St., New York.
Field, Miss E. C., Ladies' Art Association, 24 W. 14th St., New York.
Foster, John P. C., M.D., Yale College, New Haven, Conn. (109 College St.)
Franklin, Wm. W., Ohio Mechanics' Institute, Cincinnati.
Frieze, Prof. Henry S., LL.D., University of Michigan, Ann Arbor, Mich. (Cornwell Pl.)
Fuchs, Prof. Otto, Maryland Inst. for the Promotion of the Mechanic Arts, Baltimore St., over Centre Market, Baltimore.
Fuller, Homer F., A.M., Ph.D., Worcester County Free Institute, Worcester, Mass.
Fullerton, Emma W., Phil. School of Design for Women, S. W. cor. Broad and Master Sts., Philadelphia.

G ASH, J., S. F. Chapter of the Am. Inst. of Arch., 240 Montgomery St., San Francisco, Cal.
Gay, Miss Emma J., Maryland Inst. for the Promotion of the Mechanic Arts, Baltimore St., over Centre Market, Baltimore.
Gifford, R. Swain, N.A., Cooper Union, 7th St., cor. 4th Ave., New York.
Gilles, Ernest, Technical Art Schools of the Metrop. Museum, 214 E. 34th St., New York.
Gladwin, Geo. E., Worcester County Free Institute, Worcester, Mass. (16 Harvard St.)
Goodnough, Prof. W. S., Columbus Art School, 15 E. Long St., Columbus, O. (161 Hamilton Ave.)
Goodyear, Wm. H., Cooper Union, 7th St. and 4th Ave. New York.
Gookins, J. F., Chicago Academy of Design, Monroe St., American Express B'ldg., Chicago.
Grafly, Chas., Spring Garden Inst., N. E. cor. Broad and Spring Garden Sts., Philadelphia.
Graham, Mrs., Rochester Art Exchange, 191–195 Powers B'ldg., Rochester, N. Y.
Granbery, Miss Virginia, Packer Collegiate Inst., Joralemon St., near Clinton, Brooklyn, N. Y.
Gray, S. R. Spencer, Western Reserve School of Design for Women, City Hall B'ldg., Cleveland, O.
Greely, M. Elizabeth, Adelphi Academy, Lafayette Ave., cor. St. James Pl., Brooklyn, N. Y. (39 Schermerhorn St.)
Gribbon, J. D., Technical Art Schools of the Metrop. Museum, 214 E. 34th St., New York.
Grimsgaard, Miss Laura, Ladies' Art Association, 24 W. 14th St., New York.
Groll, Geo. C., Cleveland Academy of Art, Rooms 25 and 27 City Hall, Cleveland, O.

Grossman, Geo. L., Cleveland Academy of Art, Rooms 25 and 27 City Hall, Cleveland, O.
Gruenewald, G., New York Turnverein, 64–68 E. 4th St., New York.
Grundmann, Otto, School of Drawing and Painting, Museum of Fine Arts, Dartmouth St. and St.
    James Ave., Boston.
Gutherz, Carl, St. Louis School of Fine Arts, Washington University, St. Louis, Mo.
Gutsell, Hiram S., A.M., B.P., Syracuse University, Syracuse, N. Y.

HALL. John, Spring Garden Inst., N. E. cor. Broad and Spring Garden Sts., Philadelphia.
    Hall, Miss Stella, Columbus Art School, 15 E. Long St , Columbus, O.
Hamilton, E. W., R. I. School of Design, 283 Westminster St., Providence, R. I.
Harney, Paul E., St. Louis School of Fine Arts, Washington University, St. Louis, Mo.
Hartley, J. S., Art Students' League, 38 W. 14th St., New York.
Heich, John B., Ohio Mechanics' Institute, Cincinnati.
Heiss, Chas., Cleveland Academy of Art, Rooms 25 and 27 City Hall, Cleveland, O.
Henderson, Annie W., Pittsburgh School of Design for Women, Y. M. C. A. B'ldg., Pittsburgh, Pa.
Henning, H. D. A., Maryland Inst. for the Promotion of the Mechanic Arts, Baltimore St., over
    Centre Market, Baltimore.
Henshaw, Thos., Spring Garden Inst., N. E. cor. Broad and Spring Garden Sts., Philadelphia.
Hertzberg, C., Collegiate & Polytechnic Institute, Livingston St., betw. Court St. and Boerum Pl.,
    Brooklyn, N. Y. (140 Duffield St.)
Heyl, Miss Fanny, Columbus Art School. 15 E. Long St., Columbus, O.
Hinton, Miss Clio, Ladies' Art Association, 24 W. 14th St., New York.
Hinton, Mrs. L. B., Ladies' Art Association, 24 W. 14th St., New York.
Hochstein, A , Ladies' Art Association, 24 W. 14th St., New York.
Hoffman, Mr., Rochester Art Exchange, 191–195 Power's B'ldg., Rochester, N. Y.
Honey, Fred. R., Yale College, New Haven, Ct. (14 Lincoln St.)
Hoppin, Prof. Jas. M., D.D., Yale College, New Haven, Ct. (47 Hillhouse av.).
Hoyt, Miss R. L., State Normal Art School of Mass., 1679 Washington St., Boston.
Humphreys, William H., University of Cincinnati, Cincinnati.
Huntington, F. M., N. E. Conservatory of Music, School of Fine Arts, Franklin Sq., Boston.

IVES, Prof. Halsey C., St. Louis School of Fine Arts, Washington University, St. Louis, Mo.

JAHN, Albrecht, Phil. School of Design for Women, S. W. cor. Broad and Master Sts., Phila-
    delphia.
Jamison, D. Agnes, Pittsburgh School of Design for Women, Y. M. C. A. B'ldg., Pittsburgh, Pa.
Jamison, Miss Henrietta, Columbus Art School, 15 E. Long St., Columbus, O.
Jeffreys, Miss. Rochester Art Exchange, 191–195 Powers B'ldg., Rochester, N. Y.
Jenkins, Mrs. V. B., Chicago Pottery Club, 795 W. Congress St., Chicago.
Jennings, John S., Cleveland Academy of Art, Rooms 25 and 27 City Hall, Cleveland, O.
Johnson, Frost, Technical Art Schools of the Metrop. Museum, 214 E. 34th St., New York.
Juglaris, Tomasso, Boston Art Club, cor. Newbury and Dartmouth Sts., Boston.

KAISER, Alb. J., Ohio Mechanics' Institute, Cincinnati.
    Kastner, Chas., Mass. Inst. of Technology, Boylston St., bet. Berkeley and Clarendon Sts.,
    Boston.
Kate, M. Bessinger, Spring Garden Inst., N. E. cor. Broad and Spring Garden Sts., Philadelphia.
Keen, W. W., M.D., Penns. Acad. of the Fine Arts, and Penns. School of Industrial Art, 1709
    Chestnut St., Philadelphia.
Keimig, W. G., Maryland Inst. for the Promotion of the Mechanic Arts, Baltimore St., over Centre
    Market, Baltimore.
Keller, Martha Jane, University of Cincinnati, Cincinnati.
Kelly, May E., Pittsburgh School of Design for Women, Y. M. C. A. B'ldg., Pittsburgh, Pa.
Kester, Harriet J., Western Reserve School of Design for Women, City Hall B'ldg., Cleveland, O.
Knight, S. J., Ladies' Art Association, 24 W. 14th St., New York.

Kyle, Miss I. D., Ladies' Art Association. 24 W. 14th St., New York.

LAIRD, Miss Alicia, Richmond Art Association, 819 E. Main St., Richmond, Va.
Lamb, Miss, South Boston School of Art, E. 4th St., near Dorchester St., Boston.
Lamb, F. M., N. E. Conservatory of Music, School of Fine Arts, Franklin Sq., Boston.
Lambdin, Geo. C., Phil. School of Design for Women, S. W. cor. Broad and Master Sts., Philadelphia.
Larned, Prof. Chas. W., U. S. Military Academy, West Point, N. Y.
Lehr, Adam, Cleveland Academy of Art, Rooms 25 and 27 City Hall, Cleveland, O.
Leighton, Alton W., M.D., Yale College, New Haven, Ct. (129 College St.).
Leland, Charles G., Ladies' Decorative Art Club, 1512 Pine St., Philadelphia.
Letang, Eugene, Mass. Inst. of Technology, Boylston St., bet. Berkeley and Clarendon Sts., Boston.
Liddle, Geo. H., D.P., Syracuse University, Syracuse, N. Y.
Lietze, Ernest, Ohio Mechanics' Institute, Cincinnati.
Lindsay, Geo. R., Western Reserve School of Design for Women, City Hall B'ldg., Cleveland, O.
Lindsley, Harrison W., Ph.B , Yale College, New Haven, Ct. (Cutler Building).
Lippincott, W. H., National Academy of Design, E. 23d St., cor. 4th Av., New York.
Locher, A., Technical Art Schools of the Metrop. Museum, 214 E. 34th St., New York.
Lonsdale, Thos. V., Spring Garden Inst., N. E. cor. Broad and Spring Garden Sts., Philadelphia.
Lovell, Mrs. V. S., Elgin Art Association, 42 Chicago St., Elgin, Ill.

MACDONALD, Chas. F., Art Association of Indianapalis, cor. Meridian and Circle Sts., Indianapolis, Ind.
Macmillan, Miss Jessie J., Lasell Seminary for Young Women, Auburndale, Mass.
M'Allister, Mary, Phil. School of Design for Women, S. W. cor. Broad and Master Sts., Philadelphia.
Mather, Prof. Richard M., D.D., Amherst College, Amherst, Mass.
Matthews, Miss Edith G., Carolina Art Association, Washington Sq., Charleston, S. C.
Maurer, Edm., Cooper Union, 7th St. and 4th Ave., New York.
Maurer, Emil, Cooper Union, 7th St. and 4th Ave., New York.
Maynard, Geo. W., Cooper Union, 7th St. and 4th Ave., New York.
McComas, W. R., Ohio Mechanics' Institute, Cincinnati.
McDonald, John, Portland Art League, Portland, Me.
McDowell, Miss, Decorative Art Society, 69 N. Charles St., Baltimore.
McLaughlin, A. B., Maryland Inst. for the Promotion of the Mechanic Arts, Baltimore St., over Centre Market, Baltimore.
Meade, Miss M. V., Society of Decorative Art., 28 E. 21st St., New York.
Merrill, W. F., State Normal Art School of Mass., 1679 Washington St., Boston.
Messer, C. E., Washington Art Club, Corcoran B'ldg., Washington, D. C.
Metzner, H., New York Turnverein, 64-68 E. 4th St., New York (212 E. 83d St.).
Miller, Edw. C., Cooper Union, 7th St. and 4th Ave., New York.
Miller, L. W., Penns. School of Industrial Art, 1709 Chestnut St., Philadelphia.
Miller, W. H , Spring Garden Inst., N. E. cor. Broad and Spring Garden Sts., Philadelphia.
Mills, Alice, Wellesley College, Wellesley, Mass.
Molinary, A., Southern Art Union, 203 Canal St., New Orleans, La.
Monckton, Jas. H., General Society of Mechanics and Tradesmen, 18 E. 16th St., New York.
Moore, Chas. H., Harvard University, Cambridge, Mass. (19 Follen St.).
Moran, Peter, Phil. School of Design for Women, S. W. cor. Broad and Master Sts., Philadelphia.
Morgan, Miss Annie, Ladies' Art Association, 24 W. 14th St., New York, and Ladies' Art Association, 167 Taylor St., Brooklyn, N. Y.
Morgan, Matt , Art Students' League, 54 W. 4th St., Cincinnati, O.
Munsell, A. H., A.M., State Normal Art School of Mass., 1679 Washington St., Boston.

NEWELL, Mrs. Favarger, Ladies' Art Association, 24 W. 14th St., New York.
Newell, Hugh, Johns Hopkins University, Baltimore (68 Lexington St.).
Niemeyer, John·H., M.A., Smith College, Northampton, Mass., and Yale College, New Haven, Ct. (8 Art School, New Haven, Conn.).

Noble, Thomas S., University of Cincinnati, Cincinnati.
Norton, Prof. Chas. Eliot, A.M., Harvard University, Cambridge, Mass. (Kirkland St.).
Norton, Miss Dora M., Columbus Art School, 15 E. Long St., Columbus, O.

OLIVER, Prof. M., U. S. Naval Academy, Annapolis, Md.
Osborne, Chas. F., Cornell University, Ithaca, N. Y.

PAGE, Chas., Phil. School of Design for Women, S. W. cor. Broad and Master Sts., Philadelphia.
Page, Hollis B., St. Louis School of Fine Arts, Washington University, St. Louis, Mo.
Palmer, Miss A., A.P., Ingham University, Le Roy, N. Y.
Parker, Dr. Chas., Western Reserve School of Design for Women, City Hall B'ldg., Cleveland, O.
Paul, Miss B. S., Ladies' Decorative Art Club, 1512 Pine street., Philadelphia.
Paxon, Edw. S., Franklin Institute, 15 S. 7th St., Philadelphia.
Peckham, W. C., Adelphi Academy, Lafayette Ave., cor. St. James Pl., Brooklyn, N. Y.
Pennypacker, Sara C., Phil. School of Design for Women, S. W. cor. Broad and Master Sts., Philadelphia.
Perelli, A., Southern Art Union, 203 Canal St., New Orleans, La.
Pissis, A., S. F. Chapter of the Am. Inst. of Arch., 240 Montgomery St., San Francisco, Cal.
Pittman. Benn, University of Cincinnati, Cincinnati.
Platt, Miss Mary M., Packer Collegiate Institute, Joraleman St. near Clinton, Brooklyn, N.Y.
Plumb, H., Cooper Union, 7th St. and 4th Ave., New York.
Porter, Dwight, Ph.B.. Mass. Inst. of Technology, Boylston St., bet. Berkeley and Clarendon Sts.. Boston.
Porter, Prof. Wm. A., Spring Garden Institute, N. E. cor. Broad and Spring Garden Sts., Philadelphia.
Post, Miss C. S., Ladies' Art Association, 24 W. 14th St., New York.
Potin. Mrs., Ladies' Art Association, 24 W. 14th St., New York.
Pritchett, J. A., Polytechnic Society of Kentucky, Fourth Ave., Louisville, Ky.
Purdy, W. S., General Society of Mechanics and Tradesmen, 18 E. 16th St., New York.

RAFTER, Mrs. S. J., Ladies' Art Association, 167 Taylor St., Brooklyn, N. Y.
Randolph, E. F., General Society of Mechanics and Tradesmen, 18 E. 16th St., N.Y.
Randolph, Miss Louisa F., Western Reserve School of Design for Women, City Hall Bld'g., Cleveland, O.
Ranger, Ward V., Syracuse University, Syracuse, N. Y.
Rayen. Miss Sally, Cleveland Academy of Art, Rooms 25 and 27 City Hall, Cleveland, O.
Rebisso, Louis Thos., University of Cincinnati. Cincinnati.
Reddie, J. F., Spring Garden Inst., N. E. cor. Broad and Spring Garden Sts., Philadelphia.
Reid, Miss M. C., Cooper Union, 7th St. and 4th Ave., New York.
Reinhart, Miss Olivia, Maryland Institute for the Promotion of the Mechanic Arts, Baltimore St., over Centre Market, Baltimore.
Remington, Miss May, Cleveland Academy of Art, Rooms 25 and 27 City Hall, Cleveland, O.
Ricker, Prof. N. Clifford, Illinois Industrial University, Champaign, Ill.
Risler, H. J., Western Reserve School of Design for Women, City Hall Bld'g., Cleveland, O.
Roberts, F. C., College of New Jersey, Princeton, N. J.
Robertson, J. Roy, Ladies' Art Association, 24 W. 14th St., New York.
Robitscher, Mrs. Bianca Bondi, Ladies' Art Association, 24 W. 14th St., New York.
Rollins, W. E., S. F. Art Association, 430 Pine St., San Francisco, Cal.
Roos, Prof. Peter, Illinois Industrial University, Champaign, Ill.
Rose, E., R. I. School of Design, 283 Westminster St., Providence, R. I. (32 Hammond St.).
Rossignoli, Nic., Cooper Union, 7th St. and 4th Ave., New York.
Ructenik, Otto S., Cleveland Academy of Art, Rooms 25 and 27 City Hall, Cleveland. O.
Rupert, A. J., Art Institute, cor. Michigan Ave. and Van Buren St., Chicago.

SAMMONS, Prof., Elgin Art Association. 42 Chicago St., Elgin, Ill.
Sanders, G. H., S. F. Chapter of the Am. Inst. of Arch., 240 Montgomery St., San Francisco, Cal.

Sanderson, C. W., Wellesley College, Wellesley, Mass. (4 Mt. Vernon St., Boston.)
Sartain, Wm., A.N.A., Cooper Union, and Art Students' League, New York. (152 W. 57th St.)
Saxton, J. A., A.M., Cooper Union, 7th St. and 4th Ave., New York.
Schwaab, Peter, S.B., Mass. Inst. of Technology. Boylston St., bet. Berkeley and Clarendon Sts., Boston.
Scott, W. W., Cooper Union, 7th St. and 4th Ave., New York.
Shaughnessy, Stephen J., St. John's College, Fordham, N. Y.
Shave, Miss R. M., A.P., Ingham University, Le Roy, N. Y.
Sheppard, W. L., Richmond Art Association, 819 E. Main St., Richmond, Va.
Shirlaw, Walter, Art Students' League, 38 W. 14th St., New York, and Gotham Art Students, 17 Bond St., New York. (51 W. 10th St.)
Sigsbee, Commander C. D., U. S. Naval Academy, Annapolis, Md.
Singer, R., New York Turnverein, 64–68 E. 4th St., New York.
Smith, Miss E. M., Society of Decorative Art, 300 Stockton St., San Francisco, California.
Smith, Miss Helen, Society of Decorative Art, 8 Park Sq., Boston.
Smith, R. Way, Western Reserve School of Design for Women, City Hall B'ldg, Cleveland, O.
Smith, Miss S., Chicago Society of Decorative Art, Rooms 6, 7 and 8, 170 State St , Chicago.
Somerville, Jas., Rochester Art Club, 80 Arcade Building, Rochester, N. Y.
Sondericker, Jerome, B.S., Illinois Industrial University, Champaign, Ill.
Spiller, H. E., South Boston School of Art, E. 4th St.. near Dorchester St., Boston.
Stanwood, James B., Ohio Mechanics' Institute. Cincinnati.
Stimson, John Ward, Technical Art Schools of Metrop. Museum, 214 E. 34th St., New York.
Stone, Miss Lucy, General Society of Mechanics and Tradesmen, 18 E. 16th St., New York.
Stowell, W. J., Maryland Inst. for the Promotion of the Mechanic Arts, Baltimore St., over Centre Market, Baltimore.
Stratton, H. F., Penns. School of Industrial Art, 1709 Chestnut St., Philadelphia.
Süverkrop, R., Art Students' Club, 377 Main St., Worcester, Mass.

TADD, J. Liberty, Ladies' Decorative Art Club, 1512 Pine St. Philadelphia.
Tate, Miss Frances Lawe, Phil. School of Art Needlework, 1602 Chestnut St., Philadelphia.
Thorne, Wm. H., Franklin Institute, 15 S. 7th St., Philadelphia.
Todd, Chas. A., M.D., St. Louis School of Fine Arts, Washington University, St. Louis, Mo.
Torré, Miss Della, Carolina Art Association, Washington Sq., Charleston, S. C.
Torrey, Prof. H. A. P., University of Vermont, Burlington, Vt.
Turner, C. Y., Art Students' League, 38 W. 14th St., New York.
Turner, Ross, Mass. Inst. of Technology, Boylston St., bet. Berkeley and Clarendon Sts., Boston.
Turney, Olive, Pittsburgh School of Design for Women, Y. M. C. A. Building, Pittsburgh, Pa.

UHLE, H., Ladies' Decorative Art Club, 1512 Pine St., Philadelphia.

VANDERPOEL, J. H., Art Institute, cor. Michigan Ave. and Van Buren St., Chicago.
Van De Warker, E. Ely, M.D., Syracuse University, Syracuse, N. Y. (45 Montgomery St.)
Van Ingen, Henry, Vassar College, Poughkeepsie, N. Y.
Van Kuyck, Henry, General Society of Mechanics and Tradesmen, 18 E. 16th St., New York.
Van Note, H. A., College of Archæology and Æsthetics, 120 E. 105th St., New York.
Vinton, F. P., Zepho Club, 427 Washington St., Boston.
Volck, Miss Annie C., Maryland Inst. for the Promotion of the Mechanic Arts, Baltimore St., over Center Market, Baltimore.
Volkmar, Chas., Society of Decorative Art, 28 E. 21st Street, New York.
Volz, E., Technical Art Schools of the Metrop. Museum, 214 E. 34th St., New York.

WADE, Miss C. D., Art Institute, cor. Michigan Ave. and Van Buren St., Chicago.
Wadman, Geo., Ohio Mechanics' Institute, Cincinnati.
Wagner, Fred. R., Penns. Acad. of the Fine Arts, Philadelphia.
Walker, Horatio, Rochester Art Club, 80 Arcade Building, Rochester, N. Y.

Ward, Edgar M., N.A., National Academy of Design, E. 23d St., cor. 4th Ave., New York.
Ward, Miss Ella, Cooper Union, 7th St. and 4th Ave., New York.
Ward, J. Q. A., N.A., National Academy of Design, E. 23d St., cor. 4th Ave., New York.
Ware, Prof. Wm. R., B.S., Columbia College, E. 49th St., cor. Madison Ave., New York.
Wasserscheid, R., Cooper Union, 7th St. and 4th Ave., New York.
Way, Geo. B., Maryland Institute for the Promotion of the Mechanic Arts, Baltimore St., over Center Market, Baltimore.
Webster, Miss Belle, Lasell Seminary for Young Women, Auburndale, Mass.
Weir, Prof. John F., N.A., M.A., Yale College, New Haven, Ct. (58 Trumbull St.)
Wells, Marion F., S. F. Chapter of the Am. Inst. of Arch., 240 Montgomery St., San Francisco, Cal.
Wells, Prof. Newton A., M.P., Syracuse University, Syracuse. N. Y. (5 Harlow Block.)
Whitaker, G. W., R. I. School of Design, 283 Westminster St., Providence, R. I.
Whittaker. John B., Adelphi Academy, Lafayette Ave., cor. St. James Pl., Brooklyn, N. Y. (745 Lafayette Ave.)
Whittemore-Gregg, Rebecca R., University of Cincinnati, Cincinnati.
Wiles, Prof. L. M., A.M., Ingham University, Le Roy, N. Y.
Willard. A. M., Cleveland Academy of Art, Rooms 25 and 27 City Hall, Cleveland, O.
Willard, Wm., N. E. Conservatory of Music, School of Fine Arts, Franklin Sq., Boston.
Williams, Geo. P., Phil. School of Design for Women, S. W. cor. Broad and Master Sts., Philadelphia.
Williams, Thos., Spring Garden Inst., N. E. cor. Broad and Spring Garden Sts., Philadelphia.
Williams, Virgil, S. F. Art Association, 430 Pine St., San Francisco, Cal.
Willits, Geo. S., Franklin Institute, 15 S. 7th St., Philadelphia.
Wilmarth, L. E., N.A., National Academy of Design, E. 23d St., cor. 4th Ave., New York.
Wilson, Miss Clara, Cooper Union, 7th St., cor. 4th Ave., New York.
Wilson, Frederick N., C.E., College of New Jersey, Princeton, N. J.
Wilson, Nettie, University of Cincinnati, Cincinnati.
Winant, Miss H., Southern Art Union, 203 Canal St., New Orleans, La.
Winter, Peter, Winter Art Association, Brooklyn, N. Y. (107 Fort Green Pl.)
Wood, John Z., Rochester Art Club, 80 Arcade Building, Rochester, N. Y.
Woodward, E., R. I. School of Design, 283 Westminster St., Providence, R. I.
Woodward, W., R. I. School of Design, 283 Westminster St., Providence, R. I.

YARWOOD. L. H., Elgin Art Association, 42 Chicago St., Elgin, Ill.

ADDENDUM.

BOYD, CLARENCE. Add to necrological notice given on p. 30:—He was born in Ironton, O., in 1855. After studying at the schools of the National Academy of Design, in New York, he went to Paris, where he studied under Carolus Duran and Léon Bonnat. In 1877 he returned to Louisville, which had been his home from childhood, and practiced his profession. He exhibited his first picture at the National Academy in 1878. His last finished picture, "For Lack of Gold," was in the Annual Spring Exhibition of the National Academy, in 1883.

14

CLASSIFIED INDEX

OF THE INSTITUTIONS, ASSOCIATIONS, ETC., AND OF THEIR VARIOUS DEPARTMENTS, MENTIONED IN THIS DIRECTORY.

1. EVENING ON THE MARKET PLACE AT SAN ANTONIO, TEXAS. (FRAGMENT.) THOMAS ALLEN.

2.—A SAILOR'S STORY. HENRY BACON.

From the catalogue of the

53d ANNUAL EXHIBITION OF THE PENNSYLVANIA ACADEMY, OCT. 23 TO DEC. 9, 1882.

3. BATTERY EN ROUTE.   T. W. TREGO.

4. - MARKET DAY AT PONT AVEN.   C. P. GRAYSON.

From the catalogue of the

53d ANNUAL EXHIBITION OF THE PENNSYLVANIA ACADEMY. OCT. 23 TO DEC. 0. 1882.

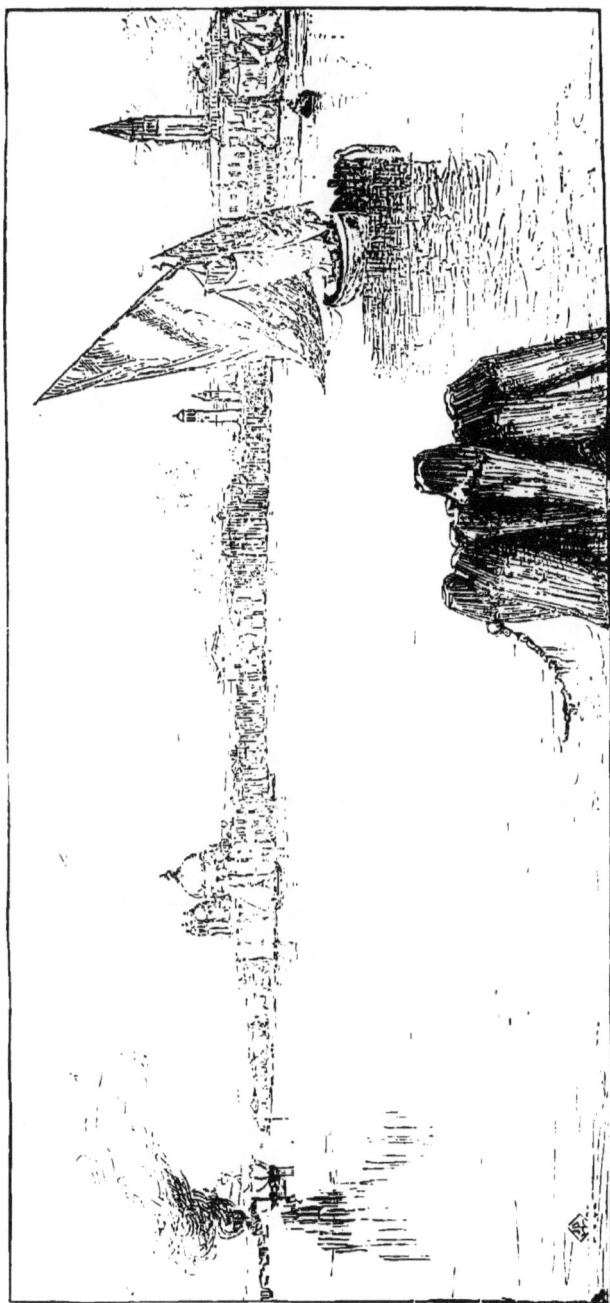

5.—VENICE. WALTER L. PALMER.

From the catalogue of the

53d ANNUAL EXHIBITION OF THE PENNSYLVANIA ACADEMY, OCT. 21 TO DEC. 9, 1882.

G.— MARINES. HARRY CHASE, A. N. A.

From the catalogue of the
SALMAGUNDI SKETCH CLUB'S 5th ANNUAL BLACK-AND-WHITE,
DEC. 1 TO DEC. 21, 1882.

Autumn
Walk

7.—AUTUMN WALK,   F. W. FREER.

From the catalogue of the
SALMAGUNDI SKETCH CLUB'S 5th ANNUAL BLACK-AND-WHITE.
DEC. 1 TO DEC. 21, 1882.

8.—SUMMER TIME O, THE LAND OF WEEDS, CAPISAL LZO-ZE-IL, PROSPECT 5 NNE

From a drawing loaned by the artist

4th ANNUAL EXHIBITION OF THE PHILADELPHIA SOCIETY OF ARTISTS, DEC. 20, 1882, TO JAN. 27, 1883.

9.—LANDSCAPE AND CATTLE. CHARLES F. PIERCE.

From a drawing loaned by the artist.

27th EXHIBITION OF THE BOSTON ART CLUB, JAN. 25 TO FEB. 17, 1883.

10.—WAITING FOR THE TIDE. WALTER F. LANSIL.

From a drawing loaned by the artist.

27th EXHIBITION OF THE BOSTON ART CLUB, JAN. 25 TO FEB. 17, 1883.

11. — A VOICE FROM THE CLIFF. (FRAGMENT.) WINSLOW HOMER N. A.

12. — FISHERMEN IN PORT, COAST OF MAINE. A. T. BELLOWS, N. A.

From the catalogue of the
16th ANNUAL EXHIBITION OF THE AMERICAN WATER COLOR SOCIETY,
JAN. 29 TO FEB. 15, 1883.

13.—CRUMBS.   WALTER SHIRLAW.

From the catalogue of the

16th ANNUAL EXHIBITION OF THE AMERICAN WATER COLOR SOCIETY,
JAN. 29 TO FEB. 25, 1883.

14.—THE CLIFFS OF GREEN RIVER, WYOMING.   THOS. MORAN, A. N. A.

From the catalogue of the
16th ANNUAL EXHIBITION OF THE AMERICAN WATER COLOR SOCIETY,
JAN. 29 TO FEB. 25, 1883.

15.—OLD-TIME FAVORITES. (FRAGMENT.) FREDERICK DIELMAN, N. A.

From the catalogue of the
16th ANNUAL EXHIBITION OF THE AMERICAN WATER COLOR SOCIETY,
JAN. 29 TO FEB. 25, 1883.

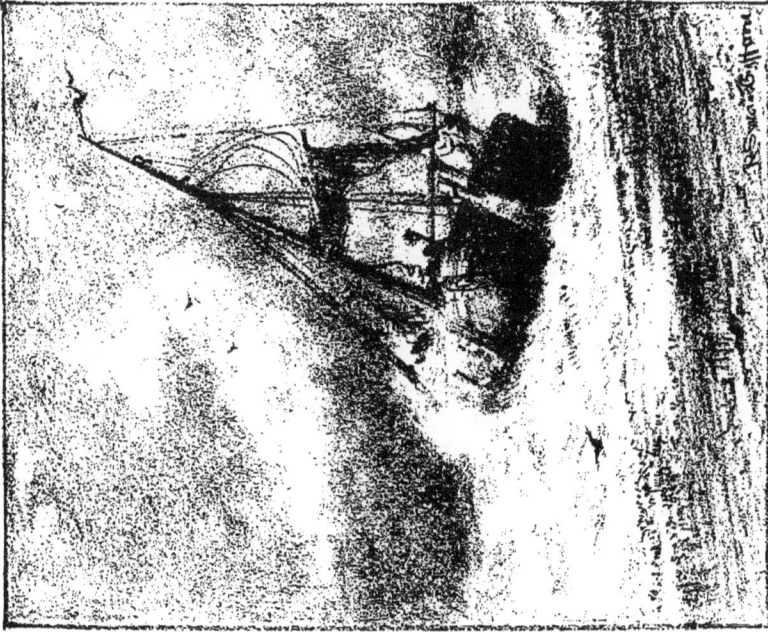

16.—ROUGH WEATHER AT SCHEVENINGEN.   R. SWAIN GIFFORD, N. A.

17.—SWAMP WILLOWS, NEWBURYPORT.   GEORGE H. SMILLIE, N. A.

From the catalogue of the

16th ANNUAL EXHIBITION OF THE AMERICAN WATER COLOR SOCIETY, JAN. 29 TO FEB. 25, 1883.

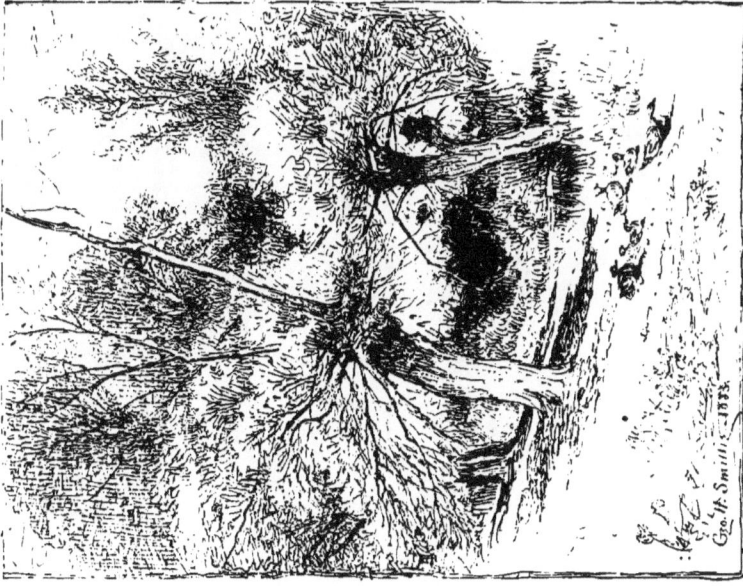

12. THE CLOSING HYMN. ALFRED KAPPES.

From the catalogue of the
16th ANNUAL EXHIBITION OF THE AMERICAN WATER COLOR SOCIETY.
JAN. 27 TO FEB. 23, 1883.

PORTRAIT OF A LADY.   JOHN S. SARGENT.

Drawn by Camille Piton.

Reproduced, by permission, from the Art Amateur.

6th ANNUAL EXHIBITION OF THE SOCIETY OF AMERICAN ARTISTS,
MARCH 29 TO APRIL 29, 1884.

20.—THE GLASS BLOWERS. (FRAGMENT.) CHAS. F. ULRICH, A. N.A.

21.—MY GREAT GRANDMOTHER AND I.   J. G. BROWN, N. A.

From Kurtz's ACADEMY NOTES.

58th ANNUAL EXHIBITION OF THE NATIONAL ACADEMY
OF DESIGN, APR. 2 TO MAY 12, 1883.

A SUMMER MORNING. GEORGE IN. [...]

From Kurtz's Academy Notes

9th ANNUAL EXHIBITION OF THE NATIONAL ACADEMY OF DESIGN, APR. 2 TO MAY 14, 1884.

SILENCE. GILBERT GAUL, N.A.

From Kurtz's Academy Notes.

58th ANNUAL EXHIBITION OF THE NATIONAL ACADEMY OF DESIGN, APR. 2 TO MAY 12.

I.—A MONASTERY LIBRARY.   D. H. KIRKPATRICK.

From Kurtz's Wax and Nudes.

4h ANNUAL EXHIBITION OF THE NATIONAL ACADEMY OF DESIGN. APR   TO MAY   6

26. MOONLIGHT, NEW ENGLAND COAST. M. F. H. DE HAAS, N. A.

From Kurtz's Academy Notes.

58th ANNUAL EXHIBITION OF THE NATIONAL ACADEMY OF DESIGN, APR. 2 TO MAY 12, 1883.

27.—HER ONLY SUPPORT. ROBERT KOEHLER.

90. "THE ZANDAM, HOLLAND. R. SWAIN GIFFORD, N. A.

From Kurtz's Academy Notes.

58th ANNUAL EXHIBITION OF THE NATIONAL ACADEMY OF DESIGN, APR.   TO MAY 1, 1883.

39.—VISITING THE SICK. P. JORIS (DRAWN BY H. R. BURDICK).
From the catalogue of the
FOREIGN EXHIBITION, BOSTON, SEPT. 3, 1883, TO JAN. 12, 1884.

LA PLACE SAINT-GERMAIN-DES-PRÈS. E. M. Jones.

From the catalogue of the

EXHIBITION OF THE N. E. MANUFACTURERS' AND MECHANICS' INSTITUTE. SEPT. 5 TO NOV. 13.

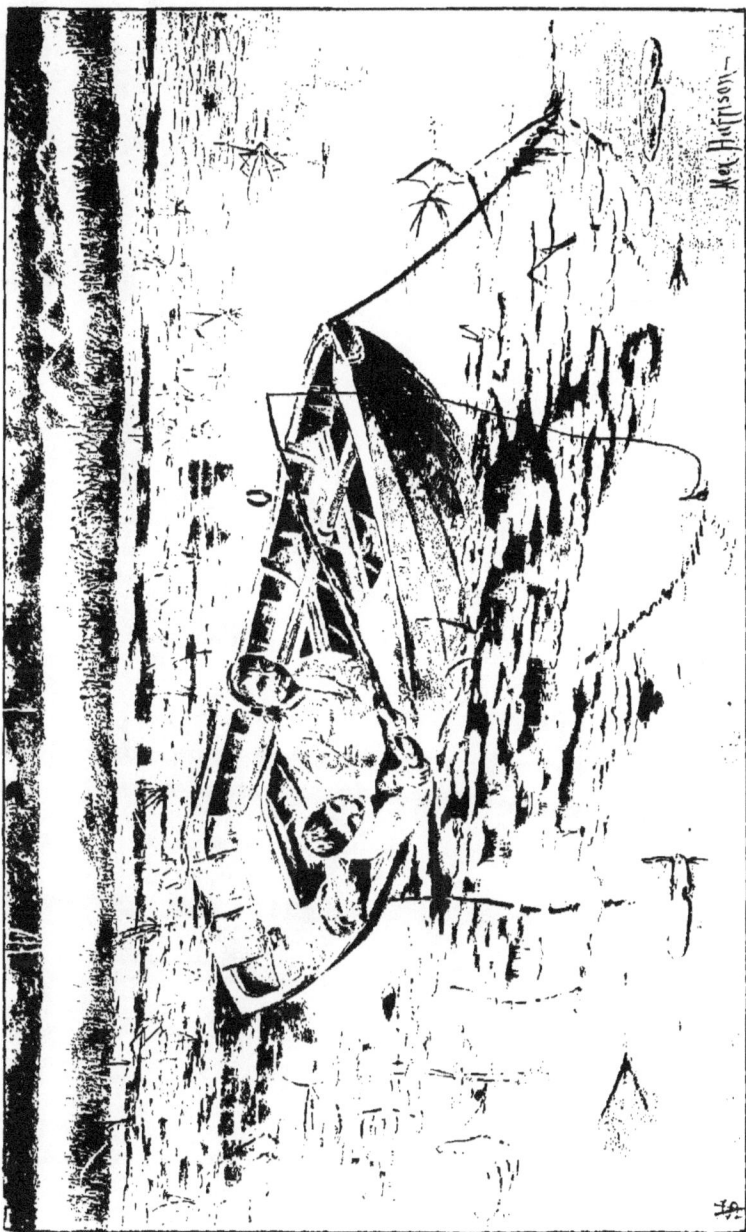

Reo. Huffson—

CANOE MATES, BY C. ALEXANDER PARSONS.

From the catalogue of the Pennsylvania Academy.

10th INDUSTRIAL EXPOSITION, CHICAGO. 54th ANNUAL EXHIBITION OF THE PENNSYLVANIA ACADEMY.

SEPT. 5 TO OCT. 26, 1895.   OCT. 9 TO DEC. 8, 1895.

LONG ISLAND SHIP-YARD. ARTHUR QUARTLEY.

From the catalogue of the

54th ANNUAL EXHIBITION OF THE PENNA. ACADEMY, OCT. TO DEC. 1883.

FIELD FLOWERS — JOHN STUART

From the Magazine of Art.

54th ANNUAL EXHIBITION OF THE PENNSYLVANIA ACADEMY
OCT. 21 TO DEC. 1884

7.—THE MORNING TASK. FRANK M. GREGORY.

From a drawing loaned by the artist.

SALMAGUNDI SKETCH CLUB'S 6th ANNUAL BLACK-AND-WHITE,
DEC. 1 TO DEC. 21, 188.

58.—THE FORD. R. A. MINOR.

59.—BY THE BROOK. CHARLES HARRY EATON.

From the catalogue of the
SALMAGUNDI SKETCH CLUB'S 6th ANNUAL BLACK-AND-WHITE
DEC. 1 TO DEC. 21, 1884.

41.—AMONG THE VINES.

Window, designed by F. S. Church. Executed by L. C. Tiffany & Co.
From the catalogue of the
PEDESTAL FUND ART LOAN EXHIBITION, DEC. 3, 1883, TO JAN. 1, 1884.

42.—J. F. MILLET. WOMAN BATHING. DRAWN BY F. S. CHURCH.
(Erwin Davis Collection.)
From the catalogue of the
PEDESTAL FUND ART LOAN EXHIBITION, DEC. 3, 1883, TO JAN. 1, 1884.

13.—MENDING SACKS. A. NEUHUYS. DRAWN BY GEO. W. EDWARDS.

(Cottier Collection.)

From the catalogue of the

PEDESTAL FUND ART LOAN EXHIBITION, DEC. 3, 1883, TO JAN. 1, 1884.

44.—EL JALEO. JOHN S. SARGENT.

From the MAGAZINE OF ART.

45.—INDIAN GROUP. BRONZE.

J. J. Boyle, sculptor.   Drawn by Joseph Pennell.
Lincoln Park, Chicago.

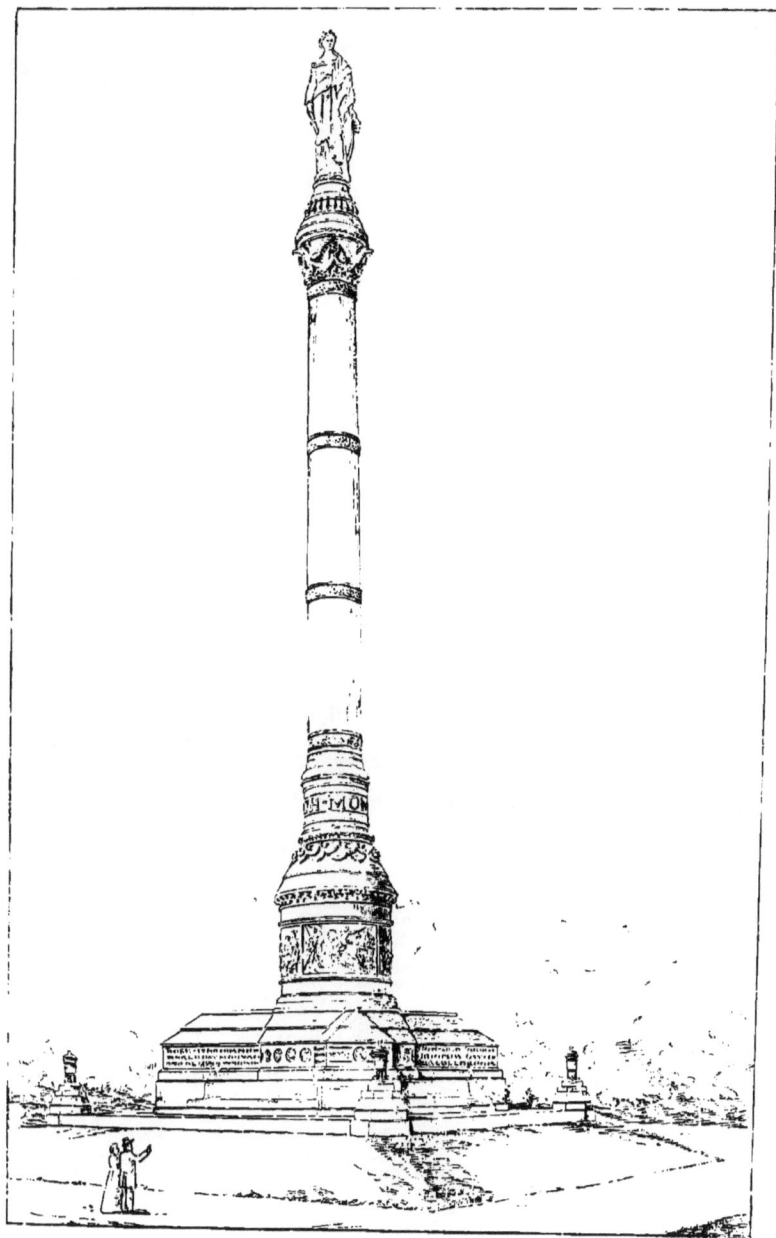

46.—MONMOUTH BATTLE FIELD MONUMENT.

Jas. E. Kelly, Sculptor.   E. T. Littell and D. Smyth, Architects.

From a drawing by the Architects.

47.—LIBERTY ENLIGHTENING THE WORLD.
Bronze Statue by Auguste Bartholdi, to be erected in New York Harbor.
Drawn by Geo. W. Edwards, from the Charcoal by F. Hopkinson Smith.
Reproduced, by permission, from the ART AMATEUR.

48.—WITH THE BIRDS. W. J. HENNESY, N. A
From the MAGAZINE of ART.
SUMMER EXHIBITION, GROSVENOR GALLERY, London, 1883.

49.—AUTUMN. HENRY FARRER.

From a Drawing loaned by the Artist.

EXHIBITION OF AMERICAN WATER COLORS, LONDON, 1

80.—PORTRAIT OF MY MOTHER. J. McNEILL WHISTLER.

From the Magazine of Art.

PARIS SALON, 1

56. — THE PORT OF ISIGNY, CALVADOS, F. M. BOGGS.

From the Magazine of Art.

PARIS SALON, 1882.

52.—WATER CARRIER. CHAS. SPRAGUE PEARCE.
From the illustrated catalogue of the
PARIS SALON, 1883.

53.—ARAGONESE SMUGGLER.   W. T. DANNAT.

From the illustrated catalogue of the
PARIS SALON, 1883.

—

54.—THE MORNING OF THE WEDDING. HENRY MOSLER.

55.—WITHOUT DOWRY. D. RIDGWAY KNIGHT.

From the illustrated catalogue of the
PARIS SALON, 1883.

CROMWELL VISITING MILTON. DAVID NEAL.

BEFORE THE JUDGE. S. H. CRONE.

From the catalogue of the
INTERNATIONAL EXHIBITION, MUNICH.

MUSEUM OF FINE ARTS, BOSTON. As it will be, when finished.

Sturgis & Brigham, Architects.

CLUB HOUSE OF THE BOSTON ART CLUB
Mr Wm R Emerson, Architect

PRINCIPAL EXHIBITION BUILDING OF THE

MASSACHUSETTS CHARITABLE MECHANIC ASSOCIATION, BOSTON.

Wm. G. Preston, Architect

THE BROOKLYN ART ASSOCIATION, BROOKLYN, N. Y.

J. Cleveland Cady, Architect.

Reproduced, by permission, from Harper's Weekly.

65.—CINCINNATI ART MUSEUM. (Now Building.)

J. W. McLaughlin, Architect.

63. —THE WADSWORTH ATHENÆUM, HARTFORD, CONN.

The Oldest Existing Art Building in the United States.

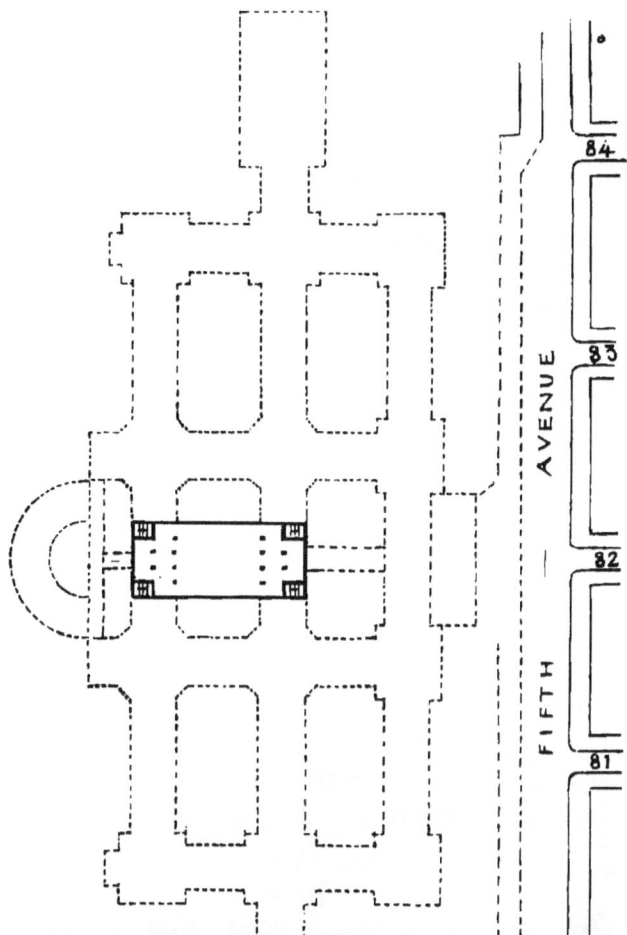

— SCALE — 200 FEET TO AN INCH —

— GENERAL PLAN OF METROPOLITAN MUSEUM OF ART —

THE DOTTED LINES INDICATE THE BUILDING AS PROJECTED

— THE SOLID LINES SHOW THE PORTION AT PRESENT EXECUTED —

— C. VAUX & J. W. MOULD — ARCHITECTS —

FIFTH — AVENUE

75.—NATIONAL ACADEMY OF DESIGN, NEW YORK.
P. B. Wight, Architect.

76.—NEW YORK HISTORICAL SOCIETY.
Mettam & Burke, Architects.

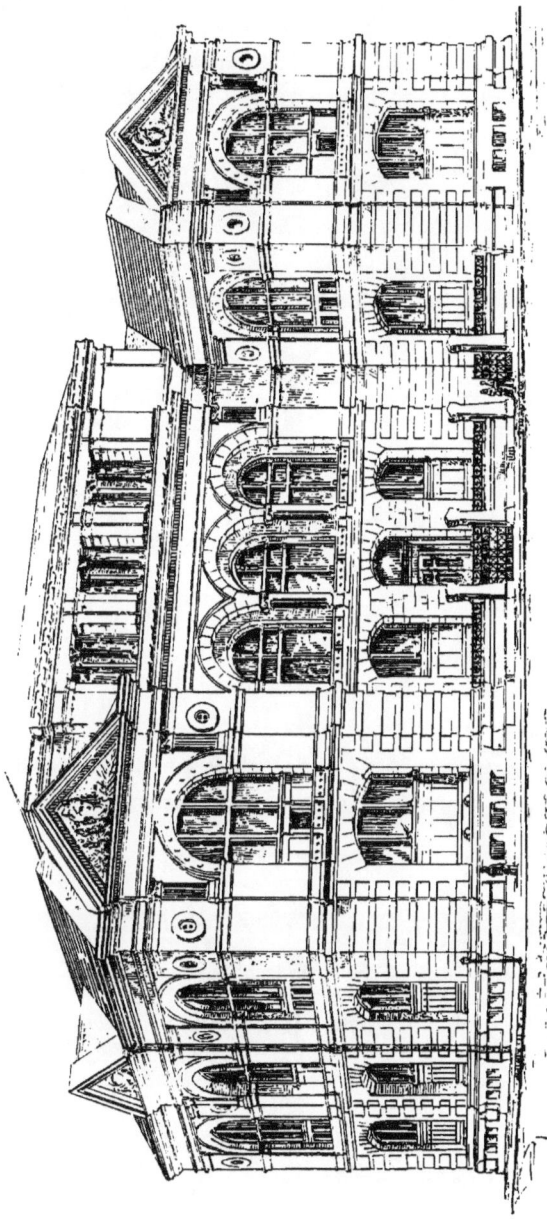

LENOX LIBRARY NEW YORK

Mr R. M. HUNT, ARCHT

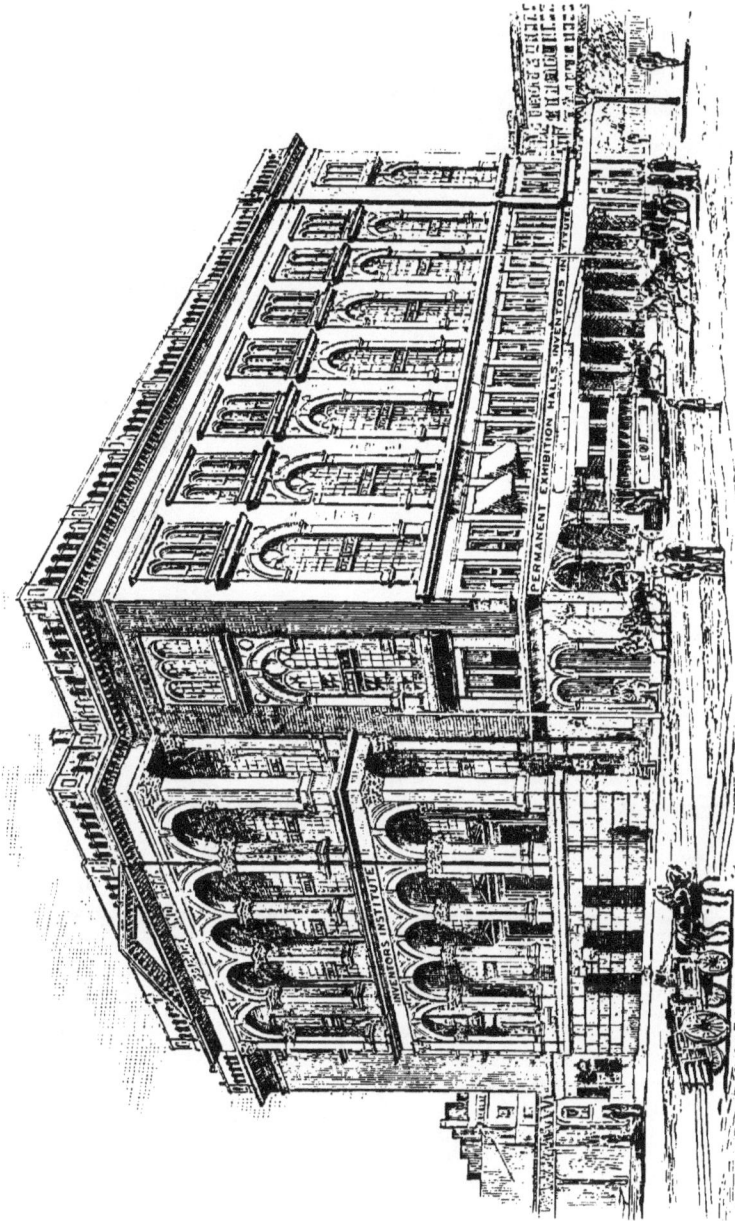

68. THE COOPER UNION, NEW YORK (as originally built).

Frederick A. Petersen, Architect

6. THE PENNSYLVANIA ACADEMY OF THE FINE ARTS, PHILADELPHIA.

Furniss & Hewitt, Architects.

7. PENNSYLVANIA MUSEUM OF INDUSTRIAL ART, PHILADELPHIA.

H. J. Schwarzmann, Architect.

71. PHILADELPHIA SCHOOL OF DESIGN FOR WOMEN.

72.— THE HOUSE OF THE PORTLAND (ME.) ART ASSOCIATION.

Fassett & Stevens, Architects.

73.—ST. LOUIS SCHOOL AND MUSEUM OF FINE ARTS.

Peabody & Stearns, Architects.

SCULPTURE HALL.
95.5½' X 24.6½'

HALL OF BRONZES &c.
61.0 X 13.1

42.4' X 8'0"

CORRIDOR.

CORRIDOR.

AREA
12'

AREA
12'

SCULPTURE ROOMS.
43.3' X 16.1'

TRUSTEES ROOM
33.8' X 24'8

VESTIBULE
27.10 X 24.4¼

JANITOR.

JANITOR.

ENTRANCE

MAIN PICTURE GALLERY.
95.0½' X 44.0'

GALLERY.
43.3¼ X 12'

GALLERY.
43.3¼ X 12'

AREA
12'

AREA
12'

GALLERY.
24.0½'X 32'0½'

OCTAGON.
31.0 X 24.9'

GALLERY
24.0½'X 32'0½'

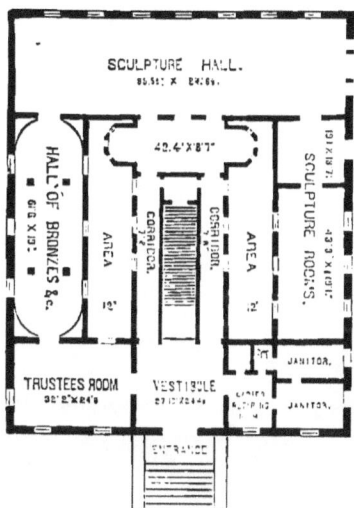

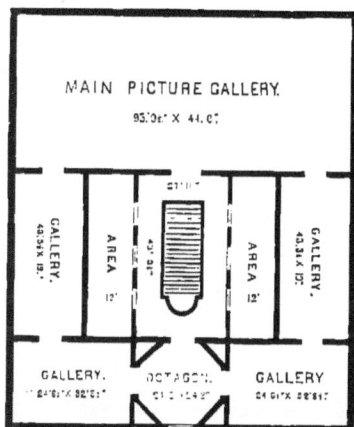

74. —THE CORCORAN GALLERY OF ART, WASHINGTON, D. C.

James Renwick, Architect.

74. UNITED STATES NATIONAL MUSEUM, WASHINGTON, D. C.

Cluss & Schulze, Architects.

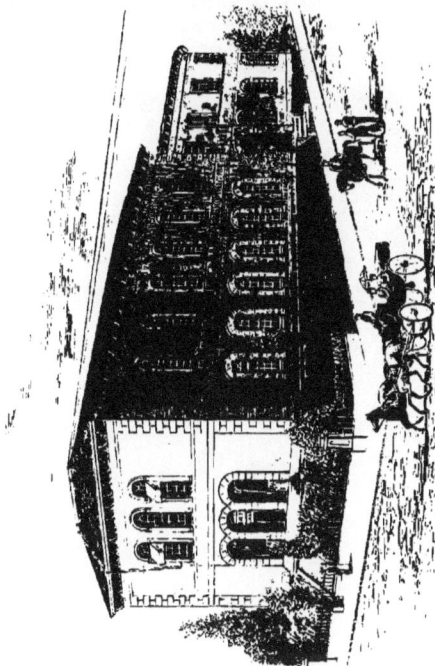

76.—HALL OF THE AMERICAN ANTIQUARIAN SOCIETY.

Worcester, Mass.